Readi...
Learn...

Reading and Learning Power

Dorothy Rubin
Trenton State College

Macmillan Publishing Co., Inc.
New York

Collier Macmillan Publishers
London

Macmillan Publishing Co., Inc.
866 Third Avenue
New York, New York 10022

Collier Macmillan Canada, Ltd.

Library of Congress Cataloging in Publication Data

Rubin, Dorothy.
    Reading and learning power.

    Bibliography: p.
    Includes index.

    1. Reading.   2. Study, Method of.   I. Title.
LB1050.R82   428'.4'3   79-11663
ISBN 0-02-404290-0

Printing: 1 2 3 4 5 6 7 8   Year: 0 1 2 3 4 5 6

With love to my understanding, helpful, and supportive husband Artie, my delightful daughters, Carol and Sharon, and my precious granddaughter, Jennifer. Also, in memory of my dear mother, Clara.

Preface

It may be true that an old dog cannot be taught new tricks, but that does not necessarily mean that the dog cannot learn any. An old and wise dog may refuse to be taught, especially if the subject is something undignified like playing dead or rolling over. But the same dog will gladly learn new skills almost to the end of its life, skills such as opening lock-top plastic garbage containers. The progressive acquisition of such knowledge makes the difference between a dog's life and a dog's luxury, between "getting by" and "getting on."

And the difference between *being taught* and *learning* is the difference between receiving and taking. During our early years, education is mainly a process of being taught, of being presented with things to know. As we mature, education comes to consist more of learning and less of being taught. Our teachers or instructors or professors remain vital to the growth of our understanding, but their roles change. Instead of telling us what to know, they begin to help us find out what we want or need to know. At some point, each of us must realize that entering a classroom to have knowledge poured into an open mind is not enough. We must begin learning how to learn.

Reading and Learning Power is a textbook on learning how to learn. Some of the subjects in it will undoubtedly be familiar. I am certain, for instance, that my readers know something about reading, and there are many lessons on reading in this book. But I hope my lessons will put reading in a new light as a practical, purposeful accomplishment vital to learning. Among the components of effective reading that this book presents are reading for the main ideas of paragraphs and groups of paragraphs, skimming, reading for inference, reading and summarizing, reading critically, and reading to understand analogies. The reading instruction and practice in this book develop *reading beyond the page*, reading beyond the printed word.

Of course, anything to be read is made up of words, and words deserve attention by themselves. *Reading and Learning Power* addresses words under two headings: "Vocabulary" and "Word Analysis." Under "Vocabulary" the reader will encounter words and their meanings. He or she will find instruction and practice in deciphering meaning from context and from combining forms, will experiment with figures of speech and their applications, and will be introduced to the specialized vocabularies of such academic subjects as the social sciences, literature, mathematics, economics, biology, and the physical sciences. The sections headed "Word Analysis" deal with the components of words—with phonics, syllabication, and word parts. Three of the sections discuss the dictionary and its uses. This detailed treatment of words is directly related to the emphasis on reading, for the two topics are inseparable.

The proficiencies in word understanding and reading are essential to the fourth subject presented, learning skills. These are the skills by which we get, keep, and apply information. They include studying, concentrating, listening, following directions, asking questions, taking notes, and preparing for objective and subjective tests. *Reading and Learning Power* treats each of these aspects of learning.

To avoid the monotony of exhausting one subject at a time, I have combined instruction and exercises in each of the four skills—learning, reading, vocabulary, and word analysis—in the separate lessons. Most lessons contain a section on each topic. Each section of each lesson is followed by exercises, for I know that boredom is the enemy of learning and that activity is the antidote to boredom. The answers to each set of exercises are provided at the end of the lesson in which they appear. *Reading and Learning Power* may thus be used as a self-pacing text by the reader who wants immediate news of success. At the end of each unit are three items: a crossword puzzle, homograph riddles, and a true/false test. These offer a change of challenge for variety and a semiformal review of content. Throughout the book I return to topics already introduced to provide overlearning, a chance to practice something to excess and thus fix it in the mind. The book also contains three appendixes for reference and additional information. In them the student will find a list of selected references, instructions for using the library card catalogue, instructions for outlining, and application forms for jobs, credit cards, and so on. In three glossaries I have given lists, with definitions, of special terms presented in the text, of vocabulary words presented in the text, and of combining forms presented in the text.

The organization of the book is flexible. *Reading and Learning Power* can be used with equal success in standard classroom instruction, in a tutorial clinic, or by a student working alone for his or her own improvement. I have done my best to make the book interesting, but I cannot wholly disguise the fact that learning requires hard work. This book will not make studying easy, but it will make studying less frustrating and reduce the possibility of studying to no effect. If the reader adopts the methods I present and perfects them through the exercises I provide, his or her efforts will be rewarded by improved comprehension and assimilation.

I would like to thank Anthony English for being the personification of a perfect editor. His valuable suggestions, creative editing, intelligent insights, and uncanny wit have made working with him an extreme pleasure and privilege.

Very special thanks must go to my daughter Sharon, who not only typed the complete manuscript and gave of her time but also made invaluable and perceptive suggestions and comments.

D. R.

Contents

Unit IV

Unit V

LESSON 15

Appendix I

Appendix II

Appendix III

Glossary A

Glossary B

Glossary C

Index   473

Reading and
Learning Power

Unit I

Learning Skills: Introduction to Studying
Reading: Main Idea of a Paragraph I
Vocabulary: Context Clues I
Word Analysis: Vowels, Consonants, and Syllables
Answers

LEARNING SKILLS: INTRODUCTION TO STUDYING

Jane is having difficulty in her first year at college. She can't seem to "get it together," as the saying goes. At high school she did very well, even though she spent very little time on her studies. At college she's spending more time studying, but she's on the brink of failing three courses. Why?

Perhaps Jane's problem is that she never learned how to study. Jane went to a high school that required hardly any homework, and so she had little opportunity for independent work. She was able to do well in school by attending class every day. Her few out-of-class assignments were not very time consuming, and they were clearly spelled out for her. Many of Jane's college courses, on the other hand, require much out-of-class reading, and independent work is a must. It seems that Jane was just not prepared for college.

Although Jane is putting a lot of time into studying at college, she is not learning, because she has poor study habits. With good study habits, Jane could spend *less* time in studying and learn more.

Although there is no simple formula of study that will apply to all students, educational psychologists have found that some procedures help all students. The key is in building good habits, devising a study system that works for you, and *keeping at it*.

A person cannot relax and study at the same time. Studying requires a certain amount of tension, concentration, and effort in a specific direction. Of course, the amount of tension varies with different individuals. The point is that studying is hard work, and people who are not prepared to make a proper effort are wasting their time.

PEANUTS® By Charles M. Schulz

READING: MAIN IDEA OF A PARAGRAPH I

Recognition of the main idea of a paragraph is important to studying because it not only helps you understand the paragraph on first reading but also helps you remember the content later. (See lessons on studying.)

1. The main idea of a paragraph is what the paragraph develops. It's the central thought of the paragraph. The main idea provides order, progression, and unity to the paragraph by tying together the sentences of the paragraph. Without a main idea, the paragraph would be nothing but a confusion of unrelated, undeveloped parts of different ideas.

Special Note

A paragraph is the smallest developmental unit of a written piece. Development of a paragraph happens when the information in it is demonstrated, explained, applied, defended, described, expanded, or modified in some other way to give it unique meaning, either in its own right or in relation to other bits of information. Not surprisingly, most paragraphs are composed of several sentences, for a single sentence usually cannot deal with all the necessary aspects of development. But the paragraph is a *unit*—that is, something whole in itself. The sentences making up a paragraph must therefore be *unified* in their relation to the information being developed. The sentences in a paragraph are dependent on a core, and we call this core the *main idea*.

2. To find the main idea of a paragraph, you must find what common element the sentences share. Some textbook writers place the main idea at the beginning of a paragraph and may actually put the topic of the paragraph in bold print in order to emphasize it. However, in a literary piece this isn't done. In some paragraphs the main idea is indirectly given, and you have to find it from the clues given by the author.

3. Although there is no foolproof method for finding the main idea, there is a widely used procedure that helps. In order to use this procedure, you should know that a well-written paragraph is always written about *someone* or *something*. The *someone* or *something* is the *topic* of the paragraph. *To find the main idea of a paragraph, you must determine the topic of the paragraph and what the author is trying to say that is special about the topic.* When you put the two together, you should have the main idea of the paragraph.

Special Notes

1. The topic sentence is usually the first sentence in a paragraph, and it states what the paragraph will be about by naming the topic. From the topic sentence you can usually anticipate certain events. You can usually determine that the following sentences will supply supporting details as examples, contrasts, similarities, sequence of events, cause-and-effect situations, and so on to support the main idea.

2. The main idea can be developed in many different ways. Whatever technique is used to develop the main idea, it must support and add meaning to the main idea.

3. A topic sentence may or may not contain the main idea.

4. It is possible for any sentence in the paragraph to be the topic sentence.

5. Some paragraphs may not have a topic sentence.

6. Do not confuse the topic sentence with the main idea. The topic sentence usually anticipates both the main idea and the development of the main idea.

7. Even though the topic sentence is stated explicitly (fully and clearly) in a paragraph, the main idea may not be stated explicitly.

4. Read these two example paragraphs. The first one makes sense because it is well organized. You can tell what the author is trying to say because there is only one main idea and all the sentences in the paragraph expand on the main idea. Notice how disorganized the second paragraph is and how difficult it is to discover what the main idea is because each sentence seems to be about a different topic.

Examples:

Organized Paragraph

In high school and in college, John's one goal was athletic success so that he could be in the Olympics. John's goal to be in the Olympics became such an obsession that he could not do anything that did not directly or indirectly relate to achieving his goal. He practiced for hours every day. He exercised, ate well, and slept at least eight hours every night. Throughout school, John allowed nothing and no one to deter him from his goal.

Disorganized Paragraph

In high school and in college, John's one goal was to be the best so that he could be in the Olympics. He practiced for hours every day. John's family was unhappy about John's obsession to be in the Olympics. John's social life was more like a monk's than that of a star athlete. John's coach was a difficult man to please.

Reread the first paragraph and then choose the word(s) that *best* answers these two questions:

a. What is the topic of the first paragraph?

1. exercise and practice.
2. work.
3. Olympics.
4. John's goal.
5. athletic success.
6. attempts.

Answer: #4

b. What is the author saying about John's goal to be in the Olympics (the topic) that is special and that helps tie the details together? John's goal:

1. meant that John needed time and patience.
2. was a good one.
3. meant that John needed exercise.

4. was not a reasonable one.

5. was the most important thing in John's life.

6. was too much for John.

Answer: #5

If you put the two answers together, you should have the main idea of the first paragraph. Main idea: *The goal, being in the Olympics, was the most important thing in John's life.*

Try one more. After you read this short paragraph, choose the statement that *best* states the main idea.

Frank Yano looked like an old man, but he was only thirty. Born to parents who were alcoholics, Frank himself started drinking when he was only eight. He actually had tasted alcohol earlier, but it wasn't until he was eight or nine that he became a habitual drinker. His whole life since then has been dedicated to seeking the bottle.

1. Frank Yano looks old, but he's not.

2. Frank Yano enjoys being an alcoholic.

3. Frank Yano was a child alcoholic.

4. Frank Yano has been an alcoholic since childhood.

5. Frank Yano would like to change his life of drinking, but he can't.

6. Frank Yano's parents helped him become an alcoholic.

Answer: #4

Numbers 1 and 3 are too specific because they each relate to only one detail in the paragraph. Numbers 2 and 5 are not found in the paragraph; that is, no clues are given about Frank Yano's wanting to change his life or about his enjoying his life as an alcoholic. Number 6 is also too specific to be the main idea because it relates to only one detail. Number 4 is the answer because what is special about Frank Yano is that he has been an alcoholic since early childhood. All the details in the paragraph support this main idea.

Special Note

The main idea of a paragraph is a general statement of the content of the paragraph. You must be careful, however, that your main idea statement is not so general that it suggests information that is not given in the paragraph.

Practice A.

Read these paragraphs. Then choose the statement after each selection that *best* states the main idea of the selection.

1. From "Fathering: It's a Major Role" by Ross D. Parke and Douglas B. Sawin in *Psychology Today,* November 1977.

Vocabulary:

valid—sound, well-founded, having value.

> Fathers are clearly not forgotten. Nor is Mead's famous claim that "fathers are a biological necessity but a social accident" still valid. Fathers are alive, well, and playing an active and important role in infancy—a role that is likely to increase in the future.

a. Fathers are forgotten people.

b. Margaret Mead does not feel that fathers are important in child rearing.

c. Fathers have an important role to play in the life of their infants.

d. Fathers are biologically necessary but are not necessary for fathering.

e. Fathers' role will increase in the future.

2. From "The Intimacy Gap" by Perry London in *Psychology Today*, May 1978.

Vocabulary:

gamut—an entire range from one extreme to the other; *scorn*—an emotion involving both anger and disgust, contempt; *spouse*—a husband or a wife; *ambiguous*—having two or more meanings.

In the old days when a couple announced plans for a divorce or separation, their friends knew the proper social response. It ran the gamut from expressions of surprise and sympathy, to offers of support in a time of crisis, to outbursts of anger and scorn directed at one spouse or the other. Nowadays, as anyone with social skills should know, the reaction is much more ambiguous. It is likely to be a vaguely sympathetic "Oh."

a. People know proper social responses to divorce.

b. Divorce is not greeted with such strong reactions today.

c. Friends make many responses to plans for divorce.

d. Divorce is not as unusual today as it was earlier.

e. Friends' responses to announced plans for divorce have changed.

3. From "Confessions of the First Number" by Cliff Owsley in *The Bedside Phoenix Nest*, Van Rees Press, 1960.

It was inevitable. Sooner or later somebody had to be picked for the rare honor of being the first to give up his name for a digit. The first, that is, outside of regular prisons. My number (or name, as I've come to call it) is now 420 03 2557. My first number is 420, not much different from a three-syllable name such as Adelbert. The middle name or initial is 03, no more difficult than any two-syllable name, say Jasper. And the last or surnumber is 2557, no more unwieldy than a name such as Vanlandingham.

a. Choosing a name.

b. Giving up my name.

c. Choosing a digit.

d. Giving up my name for a digit.

e. We should give up our names for a digit.

4. From *The Art of Creative Writing* by Lajos Egri, Citadel Press, 1965.

Voltaire's *Candide* is a bitter satire on the concept that "all is for the best in this best of all possible worlds." Candide finds a woman who loves him dearly. Right after that, his father-in-law kicks him out of his estate. War breaks out. Candide is forced into the army. His wife is raped, becomes the mistress of the Inquisitor, and is mutilated by pirates. He survives illness, shipwreck, shooting, and all manner of disasters one after the other, until he becomes very old and ill. But this good, simple-minded man never loses his optimism.

a. The story of Candide is a sad one.

b. Candide is optimistic.

c. Candide suffers a lot of hardships.

d. Voltaire's *Candide* is a satire.

e. Candide never loses his optimism despite all of the misfortunes that befall him.

STOP. Check answers at the end of Lesson 1.

Practice B.

In each of these paragraphs the main idea is stated directly. Read the paragraphs. Find the main idea for each, state it, and state where it is found in the paragraph.

1. From "The Element of Success: Competitiveness Isn't That Important" by Jack C. Horn in *Psychology Today*, April 1978.

Vocabulary:

competitiveness—rivalry, the act of seeking to get what someone else is trying to get; *preference*—one's first choice; *to the fore*—to the front, into view.

Research by two University of Texas psychologists suggests that competitiveness may be overrated as a contributor to success. Among the most successful scientists, students, and businessmen they studied, the desire to work hard and a preference for challenging tasks were much more important factors. Only when these traits were absent, did competitiveness come to the fore, supplying the push that made for success.

Main idea:

_____

_____

Where found:

_____

2. From "Youth Is Not a Class" by Amitai Etzioni in *Psychology Today*, February 1978.

Vocabulary:

hyperactive—overactive; *sexually promiscuous*—engaging in sexual intercourse indiscriminantly or with many persons; *abstraction*—something not easy to understand or not concrete, an idea.

    The media have given us a number of different images of youth. For instance, they have been portrayed as sexually hyperactive if not promiscuous; as anxious to find a job but not to work hard; as more liberal than their elders. Yet the only solid generalization that emerges from nationwide studies of voting behavior, attitudes, values, and opinions is that the term "youth" ought to be banned as a meaningless abstraction. Americans under 30 vary immensely and have rather little in common. Moreover, on many issues, they are only slightly different from the other half of the population, or even from the over-65 generation.

Main idea:

_____

_____

Where found:

_____

3. From *You and Your Feelings* by Eda Le Shan, Macmillan Publishing Co., Inc., 1975.

     It is certainly not easy for a teen-ager to try to change the communication between himself and a parent—but it can be done, very gradually. If you were to say, "I know you're worried about me," this can help a parent know that you are really growing up. As you get older and have more self-confidence, you may even be able to say, "As soon as I ask you a question, you start to lecture at me. Couldn't we have a two-way discussion?" Or you might say, "It's hard for me to discuss my feelings with you because somehow you make me feel like a baby again." There is nothing in the world that can make a young person feel more sure that he is really growing up than to discover that there are ways in which he and his parents can move toward better understanding.

Main idea:

_____

_____

Where found:

_____

4. From *The Parent's Handbook on Adolescence* by John L. Schimel, M.D., The World Publishing Co., 1969.

Vocabulary:

indigenous—native; *substantiated*—confirmed, verified.

     What is the background to the marijuana story? The Committee on Mental Health and the Committee on Alcoholism and Drug Dependence of the American Medical Association, August, 1967, has reported that the plant from which it is derived, cannabis, was described as early as 1200 B.C. Its ability to produce changes in consciousness was documented in Chinese writings by 200 A.D. Its derivatives can be smoked, eaten, or drunk, and have become known throughout the world under such names as hashish (hash), ganja, charas, bhang, and dagga. In India its intoxicating properties were known by about the tenth century and it is still used in various forms of indigenous medicine there. In Western countries cannabis was once used for a wide variety of diseases and has even been demonstrated to have antibacterial activities. Today there are no substantiated indications for its medical use and it is no longer an official drug.

Main idea:

_____

_____

Where found:

_____

5. From "Make-Believe World of Teen-Age Maternity" in *The New York Times Magazine*, August 7, 1977.

Vocabulary:

pertinence—relevance.

Many different factors contribute to making a 14- or 15-year-old decide to have a baby, experts say. The question of whether a girl comes from a relatively poor or wealthy background no longer seems to have much pertinence, they point out. The assumption that only the poor and black make up these statistics is unfounded today, they say. Instead, the determining issues range from fundamental psychological considerations true of all adolescent girls—such as idealism and their nascent [growing] sense of femaleness—to sociological conditions. These include the breakdown of the nuclear family and the widespread failure—or absence—of other role models besides a parent to provide guidance through these years of change.

Main idea:

_____

_____

Where found:

_____

STOP. Check answers at the end of Lesson 1.

VOCABULARY: CONTEXT CLUES I (Definition, Explanation, and Description)

1. Many times you can get the meaning of a word from context clues. By *context* we mean the words surrounding a word that can shed light on its meaning.

2. If the writer wants to make sure that you get the meaning of a word, he or she will define, explain, or describe the word in the sentence. For example, the word *context* has been defined because it is a key word in this section. In the following examples the writer actually gives you the definition of a word. (Sentences such as these are generally found in textbooks or technical journals.)

Examples:

a. An *axis* is a straight line, real or imaginary, that passes through the center of rotation in a revolving body at a right angle to the plane of rotation.

b. In geometry, a plane figure of six sides and six angles is called a *hexagon*.

3. Notice how the writer in the next example gives you the meaning of the word by using a synonym. (A synonym is a word that has a similar meaning to another. Notice also how this makes his writing more expressive and clear and avoids repetition. (See Unit II for more on synonyms.)

Example:

Although Senator Smith is *candid* about his drinking problem, he is less *frank* about his investments.

4. In the next examples, notice how the writer *describes* the words that he wants you to know.

Examples:

a. Although my *diligent* friend works from morning to night, he never complains.

b. Interior paints no longer contain *toxic* materials that might endanger the health of infants and small children.

c. The *cryptic* message—which looks as mysterious and secretive as it is—is difficult to decode.

Special Notes

1. The word *or* may be used by the writer when he uses another word or words with a similar meaning. Example: John said that he felt ill after having eaten *rancid* or *spoiled* butter.

2. The words *that is* and its abbreviation *i.e.* usually signal that an explanation will follow. Example: Man is a biped, that is, an animal having only two feet, or Man is a biped, i.e., an animal having only two feet.

Practice A.

Using the context clues, determine the meaning of the underlined word* as it is used in each sentence. Sometimes the clue to help you figure out the word meaning is in the next sentence.

1. I play a <u>dual</u> role in the play. In the first act I'm a teenager, and in the second act I'm middle aged. _____

   _____

2. In the alphabet, the letter "a" <u>precedes</u> the letter "b." _____

   _____

3. Jane is the <u>recipient</u> of three science awards. She received the awards because of her work in controlling air pollution. _____

   _____

4. John is a very <u>conscientious</u> person; i.e., he is very particular, thorough, and careful about everything he does. _____

   _____

*Although many of the words may have more than one meaning, only the meaning used in the sentence is given in the answers section.

5. I resent my <u>sarcastic</u> instructor, who praised me for making a "D" on my last quiz. We both know I can do better._____

_____

6. Ellen has much more <u>stamina</u> than her sister Judy, who has no endurance for exertion._____

_____

7. Some parents <u>revoke</u> privileges when their children misbehave._____

_____

8. It's interesting that the same parents can produce <u>siblings</u> who are so different from one another._____

_____

9. When you <u>pilfer</u> something you steal in small quantities or amounts.____

_____

10. Years ago in England, children worked in coal mines <u>clad</u> only in overalls. One book states that they wore only canvas trousers and that they had an iron chain attached to a leather belt and passing between their legs._____

_____

11. Children years ago probably <u>perceived</u> themselves as being "little adults" because adults looked on them as such._____

_____

12. Before the Massachusetts Act of 1642, the first law making education <u>compulsory</u>, children did not have to attend school._____

_____

13. The Massachusetts Act of 1642 was a <u>significant</u> event in the history of education in the United States because it led the way for other states to pass similar important laws. _____

_____

14. However, those who despise having to go to school until a certain age probably look on the Massachusetts Act of 1642 with scorn._____

    _____

15. What is the extent of my credit? Is it limited or is it unlimited?_____

    _____

STOP. Check answers at the end of Lesson 1.

Practice B.

Match the meaning from column B with the word in column A.

Column A	Column B
_____ 1. dual	a. steal in small quantities
_____ 2. precede	b. brother or sister
_____ 3. recipient	c. dressed
_____ 4. conscientious	d. consisting of two, double
_____ 5. sarcastic	e. see, think of
_____ 6. stamina	f. limit, degree
_____ 7. revoke	g. important
_____ 8. sibling	h. receiver
_____ 9. pilfer	i. required, obligatory
_____ 10. clad	j. withdraw
_____ 11. extent	k. contempt
_____ 12. perceive	l. cutting, sneering, describing by opposite quality
_____ 13. compulsory	m. resistance to fatigue
_____ 14. significant	n. careful, thorough
_____ 15. scorn	o. to go or come before

STOP. Check answers at the end of Lesson 1.

Practice C.

For this set of sentences with missing words choose the word that *best* fits the sentence. Put the word in the blank.

Word List:

dual, precede, recipient, conscientious, sarcastic, stamina, revoke, sibling, pilfer, clad, extent, perceive, compulsory, significant, scorn.

1. After Ralph received his third traffic ticket, he knew that the Motor Vehicle Bureau would soon _____ his driving license.

2. At the graduation ceremony the graduating students_____ the faculty in the processional march.

3. In our state, physical education is_____ for every student.

4. Scientists should be honored for their_____ contributions.

5. I have five brothers and sisters, but there is very little_____ rivalry among us.

6. We hoped that he would have the_____ to finish the race.

7. Although it was freezing outdoors, she was_____ in a summer outfit.

8. People who_____ think that they will get away with it because they don't take a great amount each time.

9. When Jane learned that she was the_____ of a scholarship to the school of her first choice, she was overjoyed.

10. Because we're on a tight budget, we try to buy things that have _____ functions.

11. We looked with_____ on the man who had robbed the old man.

12. To what _____ would you go to achieve your goal?

13. Girls_____ themselves as being given more household responsibilities, whereas boys see themselves as receiving more punishment.

14. The_____ judge could not be bribed.

15. Someone made a(n)_____remark about the aging actress who was trying so hard to look like a teenager.

STOP. Check answers at the end of Lesson 1.

WORD ANALYSIS: VOWELS, CONSONANTS, AND SYLLABLES

1. The letters of the alphabet represent *vowel* and *consonant sounds.* The vowels are represented by the letters *a, e, i, o, u,* and sometimes *y* and *w* in such words as *say, cry, my, buy, how, crow, sew, draw,* and *cow.* The consonants are represented by all the other letters.

2. The vowel sounds vary more than the consonant sounds in different words. Examples: hop, hope, met, mete, cub, cube, bit, bite, fat, fate.

3. There are a number of different vowel sounds for the same letter, but the two that are most often referred to are the *long* and *short* vowel sounds. (See Lesson 3.)

4. A vowel that has a long vowel sounds like its letter name. Examples: $g\bar{o}$, $m\bar{e}$. (Notice that the long vowel mark, the macron [–], is used to indicate the long vowel sound.) (See Lesson 3.)

5. The short vowel sound is found in words such as *măn, fĭt, lĕt.* (Notice that the short vowel mark, the breve [⌣], is used to indicate the short vowel sound.) (See Lesson 3.)

6. A syllable is a vowel or a group of letters with one vowel sound. Examples: a, be, rul, blo, no, boat, king, man, ble, for, bake, run, mon.

ANSWERS: Lesson 1 (pp. 1-19)

Main Idea of a Paragraph I (pp. 2--12)

Practice A

1. c 2. e 3. d 4. e

Practice B

1. Competitiveness may be overrated as a contributor to success. (first sentence) 2. Americans under 30 vary immensely and have rather little in common. (in the next to last sentence of the paragraph) 3. The teenager who improves communication between himself and his parent can feel he is really growing up. (in the last sentence) 4. The marijuana story has a background. (first sentence) 5. Many different factors contribute to making a 14- or 15-year-old decide to have a baby. (first sentence)

Vocabulary: Context Clues I (pp. 12-17)

Practice A

1. dual—double 2. precedes—comes before 3. recipient—receiver 4. conscientious—careful, thorough 5. sarcastic—cutting, sneering, describing by opposite quality, drawing attention to failings by referring to their opposites insincerely 6. stamina—resistance to fatigue 7. revoke—withdraw 8. siblings—brothers or sisters 9. pilfer—steal in small quantities 10. clad—dressed 11. perceived—saw, thought of 12. compulsory—required, obligatory 13. significant—important 14. scorn—contempt 15. extent—limit, degree

Practice B

1. d 2. o 3. h 4. n 5. 1 6. m 7. j 8. b 9. a 10. c 11. f 12. e 13. i 14. g 15. k

18

Practice C

1. revoke 2. precede 3. compulsory 4. significant 5. sibling 6. stamina 7. clad 8. pilfer 9. recipient 10. dual 11. scorn 12. extent 13. perceive 14. conscientious 15. sarcastic

LESSON 2

Learning Skills: Building Good Study Habits
Reading: Main Idea of a Paragraph II
Vocabulary: Context Clues II
Word Analysis: Understanding the Process of Phonics
Answers

Allow Yourself Enough Time to Do Your Work. An Alert, Clear Head Is Necessary for Good Thinking.

LEARNING SKILLS: BUILDING GOOD STUDY HABITS

1. The first step in building good study habits is to determine *when to study*. Some students study only just before an announced test. They stay up all night and cram. All of us have probably done this once or twice. However, if this is your normal way of doing things, you will not do well in school. Cramming does not bring about sustained (permanent) learning. It can be justified only as a *last* resort. To be a good student you must plan your study time and spread it out over a period of time. A regular plan will prevent confusion and help you to retain what you are studying. In your overall time schedule make sure that you allow for social and physical activities. Remember that a rhythm of activities is important. It does not matter whether you study in the evening, before or after dinner, or right after class during free periods. The important thing is that you follow a schedule and that your studying be spread out over the week.

2. The second step in building good study habits is to determine *where* to study. Some students are able to study well in the library, but there are others who cannot. You must choose a place that is comfortable and convenient, has enough light, and is *free from distractions*. Consistency is important. Try to study in the same place each time. By associating a certain place with study, you will need a shorter time to settle down to the task of studying.

3. The third step in building good study habits is to determine your *time in studying*. The amount of time you spend in studying will depend on the subject and how well you know it. Some people claim you must study two or three hours for each class meeting. Such a hard rule is unrealistic. The amount of time will vary. In some subjects you may spend only two or three hours a week studying, whereas in others you may spend ten or more hours. In order to *overlearn* something, you must practice it even after you feel you know it. Therefore, don't feel because you think you know a subject that you don't have to study it. You may not need to study it as much as something else, but you still need to study it.

Special Note

Overlearning is not bad like *overcooking* the roast. Overlearning helps you retain information over a long period of time. Overlearning happens when you continue practice even after you think you have learned the material.

READING: MAIN IDEA OF A PARAGRAPH II

Textbook authors usually see to it that their paragraphs have clear-cut main ideas. The main ideas of paragraphs in other books may be less obvious. The literary author is usually more concerned with writing expressively than with explicitly stating the main ideas. The main idea may be indirectly given. If the main idea is indirectly given, the steps presented in Lesson 1 are especially helpful.

2. Let's look again at the steps involved in finding the main idea.

a. Find the topic of the paragraph.
b. Find what is special about the topic. To do this, gather clues from the paragraph, find out what all the clues have in common, and make a general statement about the clues.

Example:

Read this paragraph. State the topic and what is special about the topic; then state the main idea of the paragraph.

From *Run Softly, Go Fast* by Barbara Wersba, Atheneum, 1971.

> I keep wishing you were alive, so we could start over. I tell myself that I'd do it differently, be patient with you, try to understand . . . when I guess I'd just act the same way. There aren't many chances in life. You grow up and become what you are without realizing it. I plan to be a better person and find myself repeating all the old patterns, being selfish, not seeing people for what they are. And I don't know how to change that. . . . There are times when I feel beautiful, sexless, light, wanting nothing—but then I crash to earth again and want everything. Myself, most of all.

Topic:

What is special about the topic:

Main idea:

Answer:

Topic: Writer's pattern of life

What is special about the topic: It's difficult to change.

Main idea: The writer feels that it's difficult to change one's pattern of life.

Practice A.

Read each of these paragraphs and state its main idea.

1. From *The Dream Watcher* by Barbara Wersba, Atheneum, 1969.

> It was nine o'clock the next morning and I was sitting in English class. In other words, my body was sitting there but my mind was far away. Mr. Finley, the teacher, was discussing *To Kill A Mockingbird* and the whole thing was so boring that I had stopped listening. No matter what book we read in English, it is always a story about youth going through experience and improving it-

self. Southern youth. Northern youth. European youth. To judge from these books you would think that youth did nothing but go through experience and come out great at the end. If Mr. Finley ever gave us a book in which youth went to pieces at the end, I would be more interested.

Main Idea:

2. From *Mrs. Parkinson's Law* by C. Northcote Parkinson, Houghton Mifflin, 1968.

Vocabulary:

obstacles—things that stand in the way; *cosmic*—vast; *archangels*—chief heavenly attendants of God.

A romantic marriage is one between two people who were destined for each other from the beginning of time. All obstacles have been brushed aside because the couple are ideally matched, and neither is capable of a happy marriage with anyone else. Marriages, it used to be said, are made in heaven; in each case the result, no doubt, of what we might fairly describe as a summit conference. Given a cosmic card index, a highly specialized team of archangels may be pictured as deciding that a young man in Seattle could best find happiness with a certain girl in Cardiff. Heavenly guidance might then ensure that each of them booked seats on the same coach tour of Yugoslavia under arrangements made by the Eagerbeaver Travel Agency. Meeting at Trieste, they would dine and dance together at Dubrovnik and announce their engagement at Gatwick.

Main idea:

3. From "Dial Tone" by Irwin Edman in *I Was Just Thinking*. Elinor Parker (ed.) Crowell Pub., 1959.

Vocabulary:

admonishes—advises or warns in a mild manner; *cadence*—rhythmic flow of a sequence of sounds; a rhythmic sequence.

"Wait until you hear the dial tone," the telephone company admonishes, "or you will not be able to make your connection." Sometimes the dial tone is heard at once, and there is a pleasure in the recognition, a sense that all is well. I have long cherished the belief that in reading one has a similar experience. In the first page, sometimes in the first paragraph, of a writer whom one has never read before, one is aware, in the tone and cadence of the sentences themselves, that one has the dial tone, or, perhaps, that the connection has been made. There will doubtless be a good deal about the book that will be a disappointment: perhaps the tone will be lost or the connection broken. But what a thrill it is to come upon it, if for the moment only.

Main idea:

4. From "Confessions of a Blade Wiper" by Lori D'Angelo in *The Bedside Phoenix Nest*, ed. by Martin Levin, Ives Washburn, Inc., 1965.

No one can say I don't try to cooperate. In hallways, I walk, don't run. On the subway, I don't smoke, carry lighted matches, spit, or ride between cars. To make sure I keep my hands off the doors, I keep them in my pockets. Never in my life have I created a nuisance or an insanitary condition.

Main idea:

5. From *The Story of My Life* by Helen Keller, Doubleday & Co., 1954.

As the cool stream gushed over one hand she [Helen Keller's teacher] spelled into the other the word water, first slowly, then rapidly. I stood still, my whole attention fixed upon the motions of her fingers. Suddenly I felt a misty consciousness as of something forgotten—a thrill of returning thought; and somehow the mystery of language was revealed to me. I knew then that "w-a-t-e-r" meant the wonderful cool something that was flowing over my hand. That living word awakened my soul, gave it light, hope, joy, set it free! . . .

Main idea:

6. From *Excuse It Please* by Cornelia Otis Skinner, Dodd, Mead & Co., 1931.

It is my cross in life to be completely unathletic. At college I was a member of the seventh hockey team. Hockey was compulsory; there were only seven teams and the seventh rarely met, because there was no one bad enough to meet them. The instructor who taught me fencing, after the first lesson, advised me to take up folk dancing, and the night after I got over the horse in gym, my class gave me a dinner.

Main idea:

7. From *Charlotte's Web* by E. B. White, Harper & Row, 1952.

[Wilbur, a little pig, has been saved by Charlotte, a beautiful gray spider who lives in the barn with him. He asks her why she did so much for him, and Charlotte replies:] "You have been my friend," replied Charlotte. "That in itself is a tremendous thing. I wove my webs for you because I liked you. After all, what's a life, anyway? We're born, we live a little while, we die. A spider's life can't help being something of a mess, with all this trapping and eating flies. By helping you, perhaps I was trying to lift up my life a trifle. Heaven knows anyone's life can stand a little of that."

Main idea:

STOP. Check answers at the end of Lesson 2.

VOCABULARY: CONTEXT CLUES II (Example and Comparison/Contrast)

1. Many times an author helps you get the meaning of a word by giving you examples illustrating the use of the word. In the following sentence notice how the examples that the writer gives in his sentence help you determine the meaning of the word *illuminated*. Example: The lantern *illuminated* the cave so well that we were able to see the crystal formations and even spiders crawling on the rocks. (From the sentence you can determine that *illuminated* means "lit up.")

2. Another technique writers employ that can help you gain the meaning of a word is *comparison*. Comparison usually shows the similarities between persons, ideas, things, and so on. For example, in the following sentence notice how you can determine the meaning of *passive* through the writer's comparison of Paul to a bear in winter. Example: Paul is as *passive* as a bear sleeping away the winter. (From the sentence you can determine that *passive* means "inactive.")

3. *Contrast* is another method writers use that can help you to figure out word meanings. Contrast is usually used to show the differences between persons, ideas, things, and so on. In the following sentence you can determine the meaning of *optimist* because you know that *optimist* is somehow the opposite of *"one who is gloomy or one who expects the worst."* Example: My sister Marie is an *optimist*, but her boyfriend is one who is always gloomy and expects the worst to happen. (From the sentence you can determine that *optimist* means "one who expects the best" or "one who is cheerful.")

Special Notes

1. The writer may use the words *for example* or the abbreviation *e.g.* to signal that examples are to follow. *Example: Condiments*, e.g., pepper, salt, and mustard, make food taste better. (From the examples of condiments you can determine that condiments are seasonings.)

2. Many times such words as *but, yet, although, however,* and *rather than* signal that a contrast is being used. Example: My father thought he owned an *authentic* antique chest, but he was told recently that it was a fake. (From the sentence you can tell that *authentic* is the opposite of fake; therefore, *authentic* means "not false but genuine or real.")

Practice A.

Using the context clues, determine the meaning of the underlined word(s) in each sentence. Sometimes the clue to help you figure out the word meaning is in the next sentence.

1. The child looked as <u>fragile</u> as delicate chinaware. _____

_____

2. My friend is very <u>diligent</u>, but her brother never finishes anything he starts. _____

_____

3. My English instructor said that we could use short quotations in our papers but not long <u>excerpts</u>. _____

_____

4. The <u>desolate</u> town looked like a ghost town from a Western movie. _____

_____

5. We live in a <u>residential</u> area, and the zoning laws restrict heavy industry from moving into our neighborhood. _____

_____

6. Even as my professor was saying that he would <u>reiterate</u> the assignment only once more, someone interrupted him and asked him to repeat it.

_____

7. I love trustworthy people, and I <u>abhor</u> liars and cheats. _____

_____

8. Peter Pan, Cinderella, and Snow White are all <u>mythical</u> characters. _____

_____

9. I prefer to read novels with <u>intricate</u> rather than simple plots. _____

_____

10. A person with <u>perseverance</u> will stick to what he is doing in spite of difficulties; one without perseverance will give up. _____

_____

11. He <u>feigned</u> friendship with the spy so that he could learn her secrets.

_____

12. She appeared so <u>serene</u> that you would never guess she was a terribly disturbed person. _____

_____

13. When equipment becomes <u>obsolete</u>, you discard it; when a word becomes obsolete, you don't use it anymore. _____

_____

14. Being a cautious person, I am <u>wary</u> of persons who offer everything and expect nothing in return. _____

_____

15-19. When things have something in common which makes us feel happy about their being together, we say they are in <u>harmony</u>, just as we like to see ham and eggs appear on the same plate, both being <u>nutritious</u> protein with <u>complementary</u> taste and <u>texture</u>. By contrast, most of us do not look favorably on oysters with chocolate syrup, because we do not normally expect sweets and seafood to be served together, at least in North American cookery. While several of our senses thus recognize harmony (and its opposite, <u>discord</u>), it is our sense of sight which most often makes us conscious of beauty. (From *A Handbook for Environmental Education* by John W. Brainerd.) _____ ;

_____ ; _____ ;

_____ ; _____ ;

20. I like calm situations, but I always seem to get into <u>chaotic</u> ones.

_____

STOP. Check answers at the end of Lesson 2.

Practice B.

Match the meaning from column B with the word in column A.

	Column A	*Column B*
_____	1. fragile	a. completely confused or disordered
_____	2. diligent	b. uninhabited
_____	3. excerpt	c. detest
_____	4. desolate	d. completing
_____	5. residential	e. complicated
_____	6. reiterate	f. agreement
_____	7. abhor	g. extract
_____	8. mythical	h. persistence
_____	9. intricate	i. nourishing
_____	10. perseverance	j. imaginary

_____	11. feign	k. to say again
_____	12. serene	l. easily broken or damaged
_____	13. obsolete	m. pretend
_____	14. wary	n. the characteristic physical structure of material
_____	15. harmony	o. industrious, hardworking
_____	16. nutritious	p. suitable for homes
_____	17. complementary	q. careful
_____	18. texture	r. disagreement
_____	19. discord	s. out of fashion
_____	20. chaotic	t. calm

STOP. Check answers at the end of Lesson 2.

Practice C.

For this set of sentences with missing words choose the word that *best* fits the sentence. Put the word in the blank.

Word List:

fragile, diligent, excerpt, desolate, residential, reiterate, abhor, mythical, intricate, perseverance, feign, serene, obsolete, wary, harmony, nutritious, complementary, texture, discord, chaotic.

1. I prefer_____ to _____ because I get very confused when there's a lot of conflict.

2. The bus terminal was in a(n)_____ uproar during the train strike.

3. The lawyer said that many killers_____ insanity in order to escape harsh punishment.

4. I prefer to live in a(n)_____ area that is _____ rather than in a heavily industrialized, noisy area.

5. The woman looked_____ next to her big, burly husband.

6. Camelot was a(n)_____ kingdom.

7. Will you_____ that please? I didn't hear you the first time.

8. You should always be_____of strangers who try to sell you things.

9. The_____ of this material is too coarse for a dress.

10. I_____ people who lie and cheat.

11. You never see anyone near Mary's place because it is in such a(n) _____ area.

12. I needed to get permission from the author when I used a(n)_____ from his poem in my article.

13. You need a lot of_____ to go through college and then medical school.

14. Although the horse-drawn buggy is _____ today, it is a pleasant change to go for a ride in one.

15. If you're a(n)_____ person, you're not lazy and you don't shirk your duties.

16. The directions to Mary's house were so_____ that we asked Mary to draw us a map.

17. For some people a cigar is_____ to a good meal.

18. Ice cream, candy, cake, and cookies do not make a(n)_____ diet.

STOP. Check answers at the end of Lesson 2.

WORD ANALYSIS: UNDERSTANDING THE PROCESS OF PHONICS

Phonics is the study of the relationships between the written symbols of a language (graphemes) and the sounds (phonemes) that they represent. Phonics is used in teaching word recognition in reading. It is an aid to decoding words. Students who do well in phonics usually become more independent and self-reliant readers.

Phonics was probably one of the word recognition techniques that helped you learn to read when you first started school. A good way to help you to understand how you learn phonic word attack skills is to experience what takes place using unknown symbols. To simulate this experience you must know the steps involved. First, you usually learn a few sight words. That is, the teacher puts a word such as *go* on the board, points to it, and says "go." You are then asked to say "go." When you learn that some words look alike and/or sound alike, you are beginning the process of word analysis.

Here is an example of how phonics is learned. Follow it step by step.*

In the illustration which follows you will learn a new set of phonic signals. English speech will be represented by symbols other than those of the usual Roman alphabet. Play along with the game. When you finish, you will better understand the task.

Step One

Objective: Learn sight words.

Learn to pronounce the six words below at sight. Test yourself by covering the pictures.

Step Two

Objective: Test yourself on knowledge of sight words.

Match words and pictures. Check yourself by referring back to Step One.

*From Carl J. Wallen, *Word Attack Skills in Reading* (Columbus, O.: Merrill, 1969, pp. 13–18).

Step Three

Objective: Test auditory discrimination readiness.

Answer the following questions with *yes* or *no*.

1. Do the two words represented by the pictures have the same ending sound?

2. Do the two words represented by the pictures have the same ending sound?

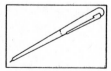 

3. Do the two words represented by the pictures have the same beginning sound?

Step Four

Objective: Test visual discrimination readiness.

Circle the *words* in each column which have the same letters in the same places as those underlined in the word at the top of the column. Column 1 has been completed.

Step Five

Objective: Use phonic word attack to pronounce a new word.

Follow the directions given below.

1. Pronounce these three words.
2. How do the three words look alike?
3. How do the three words sound alike?

4. Pronounce these three words.
5. How do the three words look alike?
6. How do the three words sound alike?

7. Here is a new word.
8. How does it look like the other two groups of words?
9. Can you pronounce the new word?

(If you cannot pronounce the new word, do Steps One, Two, Three, and Four again. Then follow the directions given in Step Five.)

Notice that you pronounced the new word by comparing the look of the new word with the look of familiar words. You assumed that if words have a similar spelling they will have a similar pronunciation.

Thus: 1. *oride*   probably begins like *or* and rhymes with hide.

2. *smeek*   probably begins like smile and rhymes with seek.

3. *virgule*   probably begins like virtue and rhymes with mule.

In phonic word attack the reader compares new words with familiar ones. When he finds words having a similar spelling he assumes that the words will also have a similar pronunciation. Phonic signals are the letters and groups of letters which the reader compares. The reader learned two nonsense phonic signals in the previous exercise and used them in applying phonic word attack to the new word.

Phonic Signals Learned	New Word Attacked
⊗⊥ and ⋎⁊Ⅹ	⊗⊥⋎⁊Ⅹ

ANSWERS: Lesson 2 (pp. 20-36)

Main Idea of a Paragraph II (pp. 21-25)

Practice A

1. A student is sick of books about the improving effect of experience on youth. 2. A romantic marriage is one destined to happen. 3. Making a connection in reading is like making a connection on the telephone. 4. The writer cooperates by obeying public signs. 5. Helen Keller has her first insight into the mystery of language. 6. The writer is completely unathletic. 7. Charlotte feels that helping a friend lifts up your own life.

Vocabulary: Context Clues II (pp. 25-30)

1. fragile—easily broken or damaged, delicate, frail 2. diligent—making constant effort to accomplish something, industrious 3. excerpts—passages taken out of a book, document, film, and so on; extracts 4. desolate—uninhabited, isolated, deserted 5. residential—suitable for homes 6. reiterate—to say again 7. abhor—to detest, loathe, hate extremely 8. mythical—imaginary, fictional, from mythology 9. intricate—complex, complicated 10. perseverance—persistence, steadfastness, the act of continuing in a task once it is undertaken 11. feigned—pretended, made believe 12. serene—calm, peaceful, tranquil, undisturbed 13. obsolete—no longer in general use, no longer in fashion, out of date, archaic 14. wary—cautious, careful 15. harmony—agreement, accord, a consistent, orderly, or pleasing arrangement of parts 16. nutritious—nourishing 17. complementary—completing or making perfect, helping to fill out 18. texture—the characteristic physical structure given to a material by its size, shape, and so on (The term *texture* is usually used in relation to a woven fabric or textile.) 19. discord—disagreement, lack of harmony, difference, conflict 20. chaotic—completely confused or disordered

Practice B

1. l 2. o 3. g 4. b 5. p 6. k 7. c 8. j 9. e 10. h 11. m 12.t 13. s 14. q 15. f 16. i 17. d 18. n 19. r 20. a

Practice C

1. harmony, discord 2. chaotic 3. feign 4. residential, serene 5. fragile
6. mythical 7. reiterate 8. wary 9. texture 10. abhor 11. desolate
12. excerpt 13. perseverance 14. obsolete 15. diligent 16. intricate
17. complementary 18. nutritious

LESSON 3

Learning Skills: How to Study
Reading: Main Idea of a Paragraph III
Vocabulary: Context Clues III
Word Analysis: Vowel Rules
Answers
Crossword Puzzle
Homograph Riddles
True/False Test

LEARNING SKILLS: HOW TO STUDY

1. Although you have a positive attitude toward your learning task and have decided that you will exert the effort and time necessary for studying, you must still know *how to study*. SQ3R* is a widely used study technique developed by a well-known psychologist that has proved helpful to many students. Here are the five steps in this technique:

a. *Survey*—First get an *overall* sense of your learning task before proceeding to details. Skim the whole assignment to obtain some idea(s) about the material and how it is organized.

b. *Question*—Check section headings and change these to questions to set your purposes for reading.

c. *Read*—Read to answer the questions that you have formulated for yourself. While reading notice how the paragraphs are organized, because this will help you to remember the answer. (See lessons on notetaking.)

*Adapted from Francis P. Robinson, *Effective Study*, 4th ed. (New York: Harper & Row, 1970).

d. *Recite—This step is very important*. Without referring to your book, try to answer the questions that you formulated for yourself. (Writing down key ideas will provide necessary notes for future review. See lessons on note-taking.)

e. *Review*—Take a few moments to review the major headings and subheadings of your previous assignment before starting to study the new assignment. (How well you are able to combine or incorporate the new learning with your previous learning will determine how well you will remember the new material.) After you have completed your entire new assignment, take a few moments to go over the major ideas of the entire new assignment before you go on to something else.

Special Notes

1. You read for different purposes. If you are looking for information in an encyclopedia, looking up a word in the dictionary, or finding some item in a newspaper, you can read very rapidly by *skimming*. When you *survey* a reading assignment to determine its organization and to obtain some ideas about it, you can read very rapidly. However, you cannot study material that is unfamiliar to you by skimming or reading rapidly. (See Lesson 7 on skimming.)
2. Many students spend most of their study time reading and rereading their assignment. Studies have shown that the key factor in remembering information is *recall* or *recitation*. The time you spend answering the questions you have formulated is crucial in learning.

2. Let's see if we can adapt the SQ3R technique to suit your personal needs.

Example: Assignment—Reading a chapter in a textbook

Step a. You quickly look over the entire chapter to get an overview of the whole chapter and to see the organization and relationships. In doing this it's a good idea to read quickly the first sentence of each paragraph, because textbook writers generally put the topic sentence at the beginning of the paragraph. (Notice section headings and author's margin notes.)

Step b. You choose a part of the chapter to study. (The amount of material you choose will depend on your concentration ability and your prior knowledge in the area. [See Unit II for information on concentration.])

Step c. You look over the first part of the chapter that you have chosen to study and formulate questions on it. (Most textbooks have section headings that are very helpful for formulating questions.)

Step d. You read the material to answer your questions. While reading, you keep in mind the way that the author has organized his details.

Step e. You attempt to answer questions formulated before reading.

Step f. You go on to the next section of your chapter and follow the same steps. After you have finished your whole assignment, you should review or go over *all* that you have studied. (When you review, you should go back to the beginning of the chapter, look at each section heading, and try to recall the main idea of each paragraph in the section.)

Practice A.

1. Survey this selection from *Understanding Statistics* to determine what it's about. 2. Use the given six questions to set your purposes for reading. 3. Read the selection carefully. 4. Without looking back at the selection, try to answer the questions.

a. (1) Define *average*. (2) What is another term for "average"?

b. (1) How do you obtain the mean? (2) Give the mean of the following scores: 50 50 65 70 70 70 80 80 100.

c. (1) Define *mode*. (2) Give the mode of the scores in question b(2).

d. (1) Define *median*. (2) Give the median of the scores in question b(2).

e. Is the mean or the median less affected by extremes?

f. Why is the mean more used than the median as a measure of central tendency?

(Because this is a more technical selection, you may have to go over parts of it a few times. Remember, just rereading does not help in retaining the information; try to *recall* what you have read by answering your questions.)

From *Understanding Statistics* by Arnold Naimon, Robert Rosenfeld, and Gene Zirkel, McGraw-Hill Book Co., 1972.

Measures of Central Tendency

David Draftbait complained to the chairman of the mathematics department that Professor Noays grades too low. The grades on the first test were as follows:

100
100
100
 63
 62
 60
 12
 12
  6
  2
  0

David indicated that the class average was 47, which he felt was rather low. Professor Noays stated that nevertheless there were more 100s than any other grade. The chairman said that the middle grade was 60.

Each of these three people was looking for one number to represent the general trend of these test grades. Such a number is called an average or a *measure of central tendency*. Mr. Draftbait used the *mean* or arithmetic average, which is obtained by adding the numbers and dividing by the number of numbers. Professor Noays used the *mode*, which is the most frequent number. The chairman used the *median*, which is the middle number when the group of numbers is written in numerical order.

These are three commonly used averages. Which of them is the best? That depends on the particular situation. Consider these nine numbers: 71, 71, 71, 71, 73, 74, 74, 75, and 95. If they represent style numbers of dresses sold today in the Chic Dress Boutique, you can see that the style number 71 was the most popular. It was the mode. This would be important in re-ordering stock. If they represent grades from a psychology final exam, then perhaps you would want the mean, 75, for use in certain statistical testing. If they represent the annual salary for the employees of Smith's Emporium in hundreds of dollars, then you might take the median, $7,300, as the average salary. Note that the mean salary of $7,500 is larger than seven of the nine salaries.

Each average has certain properties. Depending on the context, these properties may or may not be useful. For example, the median is less affected by extreme values, while the mean is affected by every score. In this book we will generally use the mean because it lends itself to statistical testing.

Answers:

STOP. Check answers at the end of Lesson 3.

Practice B.

1. Survey this selection on "Standardized Tests" to determine what it's about. 2. Use the given five questions to set your purposes for reading. 3. Read the selection carefully. 4. Without looking back at the selection, try to answer the questions.

a. What are two major differences between standardized tests and teacher-made tests?

b. What is the greatest value of standardized tests?

c. Define *norms*.

d. What makes a test not appropriate to use?

e. State four factors that can affect students in a testing situation.

Standardized Tests*

Standardized tests are commercial tests which have been constructed by experts in the field and are available from publishers. In developing these tests a large representative sample of students have been used for research and reliability, more than is possible with a teacher-made test. The greatest value of standardized tests is their consistency or sameness.

Standardized tests contain exact instructions on how to administer them. These instructions must be followed by all testers

*From *Teaching Elementary Language Arts* by Dorothy Rubin. Copyright ©1975 by Holt, Rinehart and Winston. Reprinted by permission of Holt, Rinehart and Winston.

so that they can compare scores for different students or groups of individuals. The comparison is easily made, since each standardized test has available a set of norms based on the national sample. Norms are average scores for a given group of students,which help teachers to learn where their own students stand in relation to others in the class, school system, city, state, or nation. Although a child may be doing average work in a particular class, the child may be above average when compared to other norms. Similarly, it is possible for a child to be doing above average in a third-grade class, but to be below average for all third-graders in the nation.

Teachers must be cautious in their analysis of test results. They should not be intimidated by standardized tests and they must recognize the limitations of these tests. Teachers must determine whether a test is appropriate for their students. If the class has not covered the work in the standardized test it obviously would not be valid. Differences in student populations must also be taken into account in interpreting test results.

Other important factors concern the students themselves in the test situation. Students who are overly anxious or upset by a test, who are tired or hungry, or who lack motivation, will not perform as well as others not burdened in this manner. Such factors will adversely affect test performance. Read Dick Gregory's disturbing words:*

> The teacher thought I was stupid. Couldn't spell, couldn't read, couldn't do arithmetic. Just stupid. Teachers were never interested in finding out that you couldn't concentrate because you were so hungry, because you hadn't had any breakfast. All you could think about was noontime, would it ever come? Maybe you could sneak into the cloakroom and steal a bite of some kid's lunch out of a coat pocket. A bite of something. Paste. You can't really make a meal of paste, or put it on bread for a sandwich, but sometimes I'd scoop a few spoonfuls out of the big paste jar in the back of the room. Pregnant people get strange tastes. I was pregnant with poverty.

Answers:

---

*Dick Gregory, *Nigger: An Autobiography* (New York: Dutton, 1964), p. 44.

STOP. Check answers at the end of Lesson 3.

Practice C.

In this excerpt from a consumer and marketing book, formulate (make up) questions that should help you in studying.

From *Consumer Behavior and the Practice of Marketing* by Kenneth E. Runyon, Charles E. Merrill Pub. Co., 1977.

"Economics" may be defined as the way in which a society allocates its goods and services to meet the needs of the members of that society. Different members of society have different needs, and in the aggregate, these needs are infinite. Unfortunately, resources are not infinite. Resources are always limited and insufficient in quantity to meet all of the needs of all of society's members. This became apparent during the energy crisis when production of petroleum and petroleum products was insufficient to meet the consumption needs of the United States and other industrialized nations. Similar shortages, on a worldwide basis, exist in other commodities—food, certain metals, fibers.

Questions:

1.

2.

STOP. Check sample questions at the end of Lesson 3.

Practice D.

1. Survey this selection to determine what it's about. 2. Make up questions for it that would help you in studying. 3. Read the selection carefully. 4. Without rereading the selection, answer the questions that you formulated.

From *Physical Science* 3rd ed., by Verne H. Booth and Mortimer L. Bloom, Macmillan Publishing Co., Inc., 1972.

To most primitive peoples the easiest explanation of natural phenomena seems to have been to invent gods who were assumed to be the creators and the rulers of the universe. These gods were assigned human attributes, particularly those of love and anger. Earthquakes, volcanic eruptions, eclipses, violent storms with their flashing lightning and crashing thunder, floods, droughts, and so on, were interpreted as evidences of the anger of one or more of the gods. Rites to appease the god's anger commonly followed these sometimes catastrophic events by the making of a blood sacrifice of some sort.

Attempts were (and still are) make to control nature or to appease the gods by magic. Some primitive peoples tried to cause rain by performing certain dances; an example is the rain dance of the Hopi Indians of Arizona. Others of us keep the sale of rabbits' feet and other good luck charms a thriving business; some search for four-leafed clovers or visit fortune tellers, astrologers, spiritual mediums, or others who prey upon those who are prone to invoke the supernatural to explain natural phenomena.

Questions:

1.

2.

3.

4.

5.

Answers:

1.

2.

3.

4.

5.

STOP. Check sample questions and answers at the end of Lesson 3..

Practice E.

Study this selection on the transition from child to adult status (position) using the SQ3R technique. Without looking back at the selection, answer the questions given.

From "Puberty Rites in Primitive and Modern Societies" by Rolf E. Muuss in *Adolescence*, Libra Publishers, Inc., 1970.

Vocabulary:

consensus—complete agreement; *aspirations*—hopes or desires; *rites*—formal observances; *status*—position or rank in relation to others.

      The period of adolescence may be long or short, depending on social expectations and on society's definition as to what constitutes maturity and adulthood. In primitive societies adolescence is frequently a relatively short period of time, while in industrial societies with patterns of prolonged education coupled with laws against child labor, the period of adolescence is much longer and may include most of the second decade of one's life. Furthermore, the length of the adolescent period and the definition of adulthood status may change in a given society as social and economic conditions change. Examples of this type of change are the disappearance of the frontier in the latter part of the nineteenth century in the United States, and more universally, the industrialization of an agricultural society.

      In modern society, puberty rites have lost their formal recognition and symbolic significance and there no longer is consensus as to what constitutes an initiation ritual. Social ceremonies have been replaced by a sequence of steps that lead to increased recognition and social status. For example: grade school graduation, high school graduation and college graduation constitute such a sequence, and while each step implies certain behavioral changes and social recognition, the significance of each depends on the socioeconomic status and the educational aspirations of the individual. Puberty rites have also been replaced by legal definitions of status roles, rights, privileges and responsibilities. It is during the nine years from the twelfth birthday to the twenty-first that the protective and restrictive aspects of childhood and minor status are removed and adult privileges and responsibilities are granted. (While there are significant variations in the laws from state to state, the ages discussed here are intended to represent a general pattern.) The twelve-year-old is no longer considered a child and has to pay full fare for train, airplane, theater and movie tickets. Basically, the individual at this age loses childhood privileges without gaining significant adult rights. At the age of sixteen the adolescent is granted certain adult rights which increase his social status by providing him with more freedom and choices. He now can obtain a driver's license; he can leave public schools; and he can work without the restrictions of child labor laws. At the age of eighteen the law provides adult responsibilities as well as rights; the young man can now be drafted, but he also can marry without parental consent. A girl can agree to have sexual intercourse, which prior to the age of eighteen would legally be considered rape. At the age of twenty-one the individual obtains his full legal rights as an adult. He now can vote, he can buy liquor, he can enter into financial contracts, and he is eligible to run for public office. No additional basic rights are acquired as a function of age after majority status has been attained. None of these legal provisions determine at what point adulthood has been reached but they do point to the prolonged period of adolescence in modern society.

Questions:

1. What determines the period of adolescence?

2. Why are there differences in the period of adolescence between primitive and industrial societies?

3. What steps have replaced former social ceremonies that used to mark an adolescent's gaining of status?

4. During what period of years are adult privileges and responsibilities granted?

Answers:

STOP. Check answers at the end of Lesson 3.

READING: MAIN IDEA OF A PARAGRAPH III

Textbook and journal writers usually emphasize the main idea more than other writers because they are concerned that their readers acquire knowledge in a specific area.   Many textbook writers consequently introduce or anticipate the main idea in the first sentence of the paragraph.

Example:

From *Economics* by Campbell R. McConnell, McGraw-Hill Book Co., 1978.

Vocabulary:

assets—anything owned that has value; *contingencies*—uncertainties, possibilities.

Savers. Inflation also casts its evil eye upon savers. As prices rise, the real value, or purchasing power, of a nest egg of liquid savings will deteriorate. Savings accounts, insurance policies, annuities, and other fixed-value paper assets which were once adequate to meet rainy-day contingencies or to provide for a comfortable retirement decline in real value during inflation. Mortgage holders and bond-holders will be similarly affected. A household's accumulated claims upon the economy's output are worth less and less as prices rise.

In the example, the textbook writer states the word "Savers" at the beginning of the paragraph, and then he gives us his main idea in the first sentence—inflation causes problems for savers. From the topic sentence you expect a listing of the problems or effects caused by inflation on savers.

Special Notes

1. Details support, explain, or illustrate the main idea of a paragraph. They are facts that are essential and related to the main idea, and they furnish information about and give meaning to the main idea.

2. Important or supporting details may be arranged in a number of different ways, depending on the writer's purposes. Some of the ways that supporting details may appear are as cause-and-effect situations, examples, sequence-of-events situations, descriptions, definitions, comparisons, or contrasts. Usually, a writer uses a combination of methods in presenting details.

3. In the paragraph on economics, the writer arranges details according to cause and effects. The writer states the cause and then lists the effects.

4. Recognizing the method that the author uses to organize his or her paragraph is helpful in learning information. The better organized the information is, the better able you are to remember it. (See lessons on note-taking.)

Practice A.

State the main idea of each of these paragraphs.

1. From *Biology* by Grover C. Stephens and Barbara B. North, John Wiley & Sons, Inc., 1974.

Human Food Requirements

An individual's food energy requirement is usually expressed as kilocalories* per day. The actual requirement depends on the size and physical activity of the individual. If we can estimate the total number of humans and their average size and activity, then we can also estimate the total amount of food required by the human population. Since size is closely related to age, we can use census information about the number of people in various age categories to get an estimate of size as well as numbers. A normal day's activity is abritrarily defined as eight hours of sleep or bed rest and sixteen hours of light activity with occasional periods of heavier physical work. This pattern of activity can be converted into a requirement for kilocalories of food. These data are then fed into a computer to obtain the total amount of food required each day by the human population. Such a calculation was made by the President's Science Advisory Council in a report on world food. Each person required 2,354 kilocalories per day in 1965 (the date is necessary because the age distribution—and therefore the size—of individuals in the world population is not constant). For that same year, the Food and Agriculture Organization of the United Nations estimated the retail availability of food at 2,420 kilocalories per person per day. However, a tenth of this food is lost between the retail market and actual consumption; hence only 2,178 kilocalories are actually consumed.

Main idea:

2. From *Fundamentals of Physical Science* by Konrad B. Krauskopf and Arthur Beiser, McGraw-Hill Book Co., 1971.

Vocabulary:

kinetic energy—the energy of a body or a system with respect to the motion of the body; *potential energy*—the energy of a body or a system with respect to the position of the body.

---

*The kilocalorie is a metric unit of heat. It represents 1,000 calories, and each calorie is defined as the amount of heat required to raise the temperature of one gram of water by 1° C. In conventional dietary discussions, however, the prefix "kilo-" is usually dropped; the "calories" listed on "calorie counters" are actually kilocalories.

Energy in Other Forms

The two kinds of energy—kinetic and potential—we have spoken of are not the only kinds that occur in nature. Energy in other forms can also perform work. The *chemical energy* of gasoline is used to drive our automobiles; the chemical energy of food enables our bodies and the bodies of domestic animals to perform work. *Heat energy* from burning coal or oil is used to form the steam that drives ships. *Electric energy* and *magnetic energy* turn motors in home and factory. *Radiant energy* from the sun, though man has yet to learn how to harness it efficiently, performs very necessary work in lifting water from the earth's surface into clouds, in producing inequalities in atmospheric temperatures that cause winds, and in making possible chemical reactions in plants that produce foods.

Main idea:

3. From *Criminal Law: An Indictment* by Richard J. Orloski, Nelson-Hall, 1977.

Vocabulary:

custody—possession, charge; *implementing*—carrying out; *judicial magistrate*—a justice of the peace; *preliminary*—introductory; *jurisdictions*—the territories over which the authority of a person, court, etc., is exercised; *arraignment*—the act of bringing a person before a court to answer to a charge; *defendant*—a person against whom a charge is brought; *lodged*—brought before legal authorities; *default*—failure to meet financial obligations; *disposition*—the final settlement of a matter; *proceedings*—the carrying on of a legal action.

After arrest, the most pressing and immediate concern of the accused is getting out of police custody by posting bail. The procedure for implementing this universal desire of all charged with a crime is to take the suspect before a judicial magistrate where the accused is formally advised of the charges being brought against him while a preliminary determination as to the amount of bail is made. This procedure, called in many jurisdictions throughout the nation the preliminary arraignment, is short and simple. The defendant is handed a copy of the charges lodged against him, bail is set, a date for a preliminary hearing is indicated, and the accused is either released after bail is posted or committed to prison in default of bail. As a general rule, no lawyers are present. It is merely a matter of the arresting officer, the accused, and a magistrate. Yet, this step in the proceedings, which usually is completed in less than five minutes, is crucial in determining whether or not the accused will spend the time awaiting disposition of the charges inside of jail.

Main idea:

4. From *The Psychology of Adolescence* by John E. Horrocks, Houghton Mifflin Co., 1976.

Vocabulary:

multiplicity—a great number; *intensification*—the act of becoming stronger or the existence of something to a high degree; *stance*—attitude; *fluctuations* —continual changes from one condition to another; *precede*—go or come before; *languor*—physical weakness, lack of energy; *morbid*—unwholesomely gloomy; *vows*—solemn promises.

Adolescence brings with it a multiplicity of changes in every aspect of a child's life. There is great expansion and intensification of the emotional life as the adolescent reaches out for new experiences and understanding but at the same time adopts a defensive stance against the possible consequences. It is normally a period of hopes and ideals, of longings often divorced from reality, and of passions over matters that older persons often see as being of little consequence. Emotions do tend to show greater fluctuations during adolescence than in the periods that precede and follow it. Periods of great enthusiasm and attempts at high achievement are followed by periods of languor, depression, dissatisfaction, and even of morbid self-analysis. Emotions can lead to violent attachments to members of the opposite sex and intense friendships characterized by pledges and vows.

Main idea:

5. From "Divorce—The First Two Years Are the Worst" by Robert J. Trotter in *Science News*, October 9, 1976.

Poor parenting on the part of divorced parents was apparent in most cases during the two years following divorce. The researchers found that divorced parents made fewer maturity demands of their children, communicate less well with their children, tend to be less affectionate and show marked inconsistency in discipline and a lack of control over their children when compared with parents in intact families. Poor parenting is most apparent when divorced parents, particularly mothers, are interacting with their sons. These parents communicate less, are less consistent with and use more negative sanctions with sons than with daughters. In addition, in the laboratory situation, divorced mothers exhibited fewer positive sanctions and affiliation and more negative behaviors, such as negative commands and opposition to requests, with sons than with daughters. Sons of divorced parents seem to have a harder time of it, says Hetherington, and this may explain why previous studies have shown that the effects of divorce are more severe and enduring for boys than for girls.

Main idea:

STOP. Check answers at the end of Lesson 3.

VOCABULARY: CONTEXT CLUES III

Many words that are spelled the same have different meanings. These words are called *homographs*. The meaning of a homograph is determined by the way the word is used in the sentence. For example, the term *run* has many different meanings. (One dictionary gives 134 meanings for *run*.) In the listed sentences notice how *run's* placement in the sentence and the surrounding words help you to figure out the meaning of each use.

1. Walk, don't <u>run</u>.
2. I have a <u>run</u> in my stocking.
3. Senator Jones said that he would not <u>run</u> for another term.
4. The trucker finished his <u>run</u> to Detroit.
5. She is going to <u>run</u> in a ten-mile race.
6. The play had a <u>run</u> of two years.

In sentence 1 *run* means "go quickly by moving the legs more rapidly than at a walk."
In sentence 2 *run* means "a tear or to cause stitches to unravel."
In sentence 3 *run* means "be or campaign as a candidate for election."
In sentence 4 *run* means "route."
In sentence 5 *run* means "take part in a race."
In sentence 6 *run* means "continuous course of performances."

THE BORN LOSER

Special Notes

1. Some homographs are spelled the same but do not sound the same. For example, *refuse* means "trash"; *refuse* means "to decline to accept." In

sentence "a" in the examples *refuse* (ref'use) meaning "trash" is pronounced differently from the term *refuse* (re fuse') meaning "to decline to accept" in sentence "b." (See Lesson 8 on accents.) In reading, you can determine the meaning of *refuse* from the way it is used in the sentence (context clues).

Examples: a. During the garbage strike there were tons of uncollected *refuse* on the streets of the city.

b. I *refuse* to go along with you in that project because it seems unethical to me.

2. Do not confuse *homonym* or *homophone* (terms to describe words that sound alike but have different spellings and meanings) with *homograph*.

Examples of homonyms or homophones: pear—pare; to—two—too; way—weigh; fare—fair; tow—toe; plain plane.

Practice A.

In each of these ten sentences determine the meaning of *run* from the context. In many instances *run* is part of an idiomatic expression (i.e., custom has assigned a particular meaning to a phrase of two or more words—*run through*, pierce the body with a sword).

1. They seem to run their business very well together._____

_____

2. It was so hot in the car that the ice cream started to melt and run all over the seat._____

_____

3. The bank officers were afraid that there would be a run on the bank because of recent unfavorable publicity._____

_____

4. That coat will run you one hundred dollars._____

_____

5. If the wells in this area <u>run</u> dry, we'll be in trouble._____

   _____

6. If you <u>run</u> across Mary, don't tell her that you saw me here._____

   _____

7. In the long <u>run</u>, everything will probably work out all right._____

   _____

8. It looks as though we will <u>run</u> out of supplies by tomorrow. _____

   _____

9. Let's give them a <u>run</u> for their money. _____

   _____

10. We saw the car <u>run</u> down a helpless pedestrian. _____

    _____

STOP. Check answers at the end of Lesson 3.

Practice B.

In each of these five sets of sentences a particular word is missing. For each set, first determine the missing word that fits into the blanks of all the sentences in the set and then state the different meanings of the word for each sentence. (The words in each set are spelled the same and sound the same.)

Set 1

a. It's dangerous to fool around near a rifle _____.

   _____

b. The sheep_____in a green pasture.

   _____

c. The grades_____from a score of 50 to 100.

   _____

   d. My mother's kitchen_____ is always in use.

_____

   e. The climbers chose a particularly dangerous_____to climb.

_____

Set 2

   a. The_____ of the test scores was 80.

_____

   b. You are a(n)_____man to do that to someone who was not hurting
      you.

_____

   c. What do you _____by that?

_____

   d. He has a(n)_____ appearance.

_____

   e. He is a man of_____ s.

_____

Set 3

   a. He is behaving in such a(n)_____manner.

_____

   b. I can't stand the_____odor in this room.

_____

   c. That is a(n)_____ball.

_____

   d. Barnacles can_____ a ship's propeller.

_____

   e. I don't like people who use_____ language.

_____

STOP. Check answers at the end of Lesson 3.

Practice C.

Fill in the two blanks in each of these sentences with one word that will make sense in both. Write the meanings of the word for each sentence in the blanks at the end of the sentence. (The words are spelled the same, but they do not sound the same.)

1. I will not_____a class that has such poor_____. _____
   _____;
   _____

2. My brother is not_____with the_____of many packaged
   foods._____;
   _____

3. The farmers decided to _____ to buy the_____they needed
   to cut the grain in their fields._____
   _____; _____

4. In the Walt Disney cartoon the largemouth_____spoke in a deep
   _____ voice. _____
   _____; _____

5. We will_____him with a suitcase as a farewell_____at the
   party._____;
   _____

STOP. Check answers at the end of Lesson 3.

Practice D.

Fill in the three blanks in each of these sentences with one word that will make sense in all three. Write the meanings of the word for each sentence in the blanks at the end of the sentence. (The words are spelled the same and sound the same.)

1. My friend_____ paid his_____with a ten-dollar_____.
   _____;_____
   _____;_____

2. The_____ can always_____on others to help him_____
   his riches._____;_____
   _____;_____

3. In a newspaper_____, I read how a(n)_____of soldiers was halted in its march when the street was blocked by the collapse of a(n) _____ from a building._____;_____

_____; _____

4. He drank so much_____to raise his low _____that he will probably be seeing ghostly_____soon. _____

_____; _____

_____; _____

5. The school_____said that the_____reason he is not paying off the_____ on his mortgage is that he doesn't have the funds to do so._____; _____

_____; _____

STOP. Check answers at the end of Lesson 3.

WORD ANALYSIS: VOWEL RULES

1. Many times you may know the meaning of a word when it is said aloud to you but have difficulty recognizing the word when you see it in print. Knowledge of some vowel, consonant, and syllabication rules should help you to decode words better.

2. To be able to pronounce a multisyllabic word, you usually syllabicate the word first and then apply vowel rules to it.

3. Here are three vowel rules:

a. Open syllable rule—An open syllable is a syllable that contains only *one* vowel; the vowel comes at the end of the syllable, and the vowel sound is usually long. Examples: gō, mē, try (trī), nō.

b. Closed syllable rule—A closed syllable is a syllable that contains only *one* vowel; the syllable ends in a consonant, and the vowel sound is usually short. Examples: căn, răt, yĕt, sĭt.

c. Silent *e* rule—In a word or syllable containing two vowels separated by one consonant and having an *e* as the final vowel, the first vowel is usually long and the final *e* is usually silent. Examples: bāké, tūbé, cāné, nōté, tīmé.

Special Notes

1. *Try* is an open syllable because the *y* acts as a vowel. When *y* is the only vowel in a word or syllable, it usually sounds like a long *i* (ī). Examples: my (mī), by (bī).

2. The marks that show how to pronounce words are called *diacritical marks*. The following markings will help you in pronunciation (the way a word sounds). (See lessons on the dictionary.)

    a. The long vowel mark (–) is called a macron. A vowel that has a long vowel mark sounds like its letter name. Examples: gō, mē, nō, bāk¢, fūm¢.

    b. The short vowel mark (⌣) is called a breve. Examples: nŭt, căn, făt, gĕt.

    c. A slash through a letter means that the letter is silent. Examples: bāk¢, tām¢, cūt¢, tāp¢.

3. Letters do not have sounds. They represent or stand for sounds.

4. When we say that a letter is silent, we mean that it does not add a sound to the syllable; however, it is just as important as any other letter in the syllable. It signals information about other letters, and it helps us to determine the sounds represented by other letters.

Practice A.

Underline all the open syllables.

    a   lo   ky   cote   crot   cro   blu

STOP. Check answers at the end of Lesson 3.

Practice B.

Underline all the closed syllables.

    gon   ro   trope   mot   fly   de   dap   sone

STOP. Check answers at the end of Lesson 3.

Practice C.

Underline all the final *e* or silent *e* syllables.

    be   nom   trop   crane   bry   dron   drote

STOP. Check answers at the end of Lesson 3.

Practice D.

Put in the diacritical marks for each of these ten familiar words. Example: nōt¢.

1. can   6. game

2. cake   7. lake

3. go   8. we

4. tale   9. no

5. pen   10. sit

STOP. Check answers at the end of Lesson 3.

ANSWERS: Lesson 3 (pp. 37-70)

Learning Skills: How to Study (pp. 37–47)

Practice A

a. (1) Average is the score that gives the general trend of all scores. (2) A measure of central tendency   b. (1) The mean is obtained by adding all the numbers and then dividing by the number of numbers. (2) 70.6   c. (1) Mode is the most frequent number. (2) 70   d. (1) Median is the middle number when all the numbers are written in numerical order. (2) 70   e. The median is less affected by extremes.   f. The mean lends itself to statistical testing.

Practice B

a. Standardized tests are commercial tests constructed by experts in the field. They are consistent and have norms. Teacher tests are developed by teachers. They do not have the reliability of standardized tests, nor do they have any norms.   b. The greatest value is their consistency or sameness.   c. *Norms* are average scores for a given group of students against which the teacher can make comparisons.   d. It is not appropriate to use a test on content that has not been covered.   e. Four factors that can affect students in taking a test are (1) hunger, (2) overanxiety, (3) tiredness, and (4) lack of motivation.

Practice C (sample questions)

1. Define *economics*.   2. What is the relationship between resources and society's needs?

Practice D (sample questions and answers)

Questions:

1. How did primitive man explain natural phenomena?   2. What were the gods assigned?   3. How were catastrophes interpreted?   4. How do some primitive people try to control nature?   5. Give three examples of how some of us try to control nature.

Answers:

1. Primitive man invented gods who were assumed to be the creators and rulers of the universe. 2. The gods were assigned human traits. 3. Catastrophes were looked upon as evidence of the anger of one or more of the gods. 4. Some primitive people try to control nature by magic. 5. We use rabbits' feet, search for four-leafed clovers, or visit fortune tellers.

Practice E

1. The period of adolescence is determined by society's expectations and by society's definition of it. 2. In primitive societies adolescence occupies a shorter period than in industrial societies because there are no child labor laws or compulsory education. 3. Grade school graduation, high school graduation, and college graduation are the steps that have replaced formal social ceremonies. 4. From the twelfth to the twenty-first birthday adult privileges and responsibilities are gradually granted.

Reading: Main Idea of a Paragraph III (pp. 47-52)

Practice A

1. Human food requirements are able to be estimated. 2. Energy to perform work exists in many forms. 3. The procedure for posting bail to prevent detention is a short and simple one. 4. Adolescence brings a number of changes in a child's life. 5. Divorced parents are often not good parents during the first two years after the divorce.

Vocabulary: Context Clues III (pp. 53-58)

Practice A

1. operate, manage 2. flow, as a liquid 3. series of sudden and urgent demands on it for payment 4. cost approximately 5. exhaust their supply [dry is part of the expression, i.e., run dry] 6. meet or find accidently [across is part of the expression, i.e., run across] 7. end [long run is the whole expression] 8. exhaust the quantity of [run out] 9. close competition 10. strike to the ground [run down]

Practice B

1. range: a. area equipped with targets for shooting weapons b. roam c. pass from one point to another, vary within stated limits d. cooking stove e. chain of mountains 2. mean: a. arithmetic average b. selfish, unaccommodating, offensive c. have in mind, intend d. shabby, poor e. money, riches 3. foul: a. vile, unfair b. stinking, very offensive to the senses, loathsome c. in baseball, batted outside the foul lines of the infield d. clog e. indecent, obscene, profane

Practice C

1. conduct (con·duct′)—direct; conduct (con′duct)—personal behavior or way of acting 2. content (con·tent′)—satisfied; content (con′tent)—all that is contained in something 3. combine (com·bine′)—to unite or join together; combine (com′bine)—a machine for threshing grain 4. bass (băs)—edible (able to be eaten) fish of the perch family; bass (bās)—deep [said of the lowest male singing voice] 5. present (pre·sent′)—give or bestow formally; present (pres′ent)—gift.

Practice D

1. Bill—a name; bill—statement of money owed; bill—piece of paper money 2. count—nobleman in some European countries; count—rely or depend on; count—inventory or check by numbering off 3. column—regular article or feature; column—a long, narrow formation of troops in which the troops are one behind the other; column—a slender, upright support that is generally ornamental 4. spirits—strong alcoholic beverage obtained by distillation; spirits—frame of mind, mood; spirits—supernatural beings 5. principal—head; principal—chief or highest in importance; principal—amount owed or an investment minus the interest or on which interest is computed.

Word Analysis: Vowel Rules (pp. 58-60)

Practice A

a, lo, ky, cro, blu

Practice B

gon, mot, dap

Practice C

crane, drote

Practice D

1. căn 2. cāk¢ 3. gō 4. tāl¢ 5. pĕn 6. gām¢ 7. lāk¢ 8. wē 9. nō
10. sĭt

CROSSWORD PUZZLE

Directions:

The meanings of a number of the words and some of the ideas from Lessons 1–3 follow. Your knowledge of these words and ideas will help you to solve this crossword puzzle.

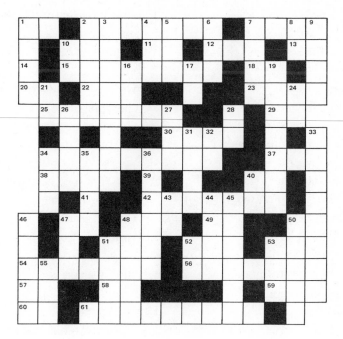

Across

1. A homonym of *sew*
2. Word meaning *delicate*
7. To study for an examination at the last moment
10. Homonym of *sea*
11. Abbreviation of *alternating current*
12. The whole amount or quantity
13. Another word for *mother*
14. A pronoun
15. A word meaning *industrious*
18. ___pretty___a picture

Down

1. To read very quickly
2. Word meaning *pretend*
3. An existing connection; a cousin, brother, or aunt is one
4. A joke; to stop up the mouth of a person
5. Frozen water
6. You do this when you're hungry
7. Word meaning *dressed*
8. Abbreviation for *before noon*
9. The postman brings this
10. Abbreviation for *South Dakota*

20. An address used for married and unmarried women
22. A car needs this to run
23. Word meaning *double*
25. Refers to surrounding words
28. Same as #14 Across
29. What you can get when you finish college
30. Time divisions
34. A word that is spelled the same as another but has a different meaning
37. An adult female sheep
38. A kingdom in SW Asia
39. Fifth letter of the alphabet
40. A suffix (word ending)
41. Same as #14 Across
42. Means *satisfied* and *what something is made up* of
46. An indefinite article
47. Word used to indicate location
48. A counter; anything that obstructs
49. Roman numeral nine
50. Abbreviation of *Rhode Island*
51. Something having the consistency of a jelly
52. To receive or come to have possession
53. At a great distance
54. Refers to all belonging to a group; an officer
56. Word meaning *to come before*
57. Prefix meaning *not*
58. Same as #28 Down
59. Another word for *father*
60. The ending for the past tense of regular verbs
61. Word meaning *complex*

16. A suffix [(word ending) usually spelled *ize*] meaning *make* or *cause to be*
17. Opposite of *yes*
19. The someone or something a paragraph is about
21. Abbreviation for *South Carolina*
24. Abbreviation for *Alcoholics Anonymous*
26. Meaning for *scent*
27. A beverage
28. A form of the verb *to be*
31. The opposite of *close*
32. Abbreviation for *New Hampshire*
33. Word meaning *compulsory*
34. Possessive pronoun
35. All sentences in a paragraph help develop this idea
36. A very important step in studying
40. Opposite of *out*
43. A conjunction
44. One of a series of rows rising one behind the other
45. Word meaning *limit*
46. To present reasons for or against something
47. Belonging to oneself
48. Any animal
50. Police use this to catch speeding motorists
51. To smile broadly
52. Abbreviation for *General Practitioner*
53. Past tense of *feed*
55. Word meaning *terminate*

STOP. Check answers on the next page.

Crossword Puzzle Answers

1 S	O		2 F	3 R	A	4 G	I	5 L	E	6	7 C	R	A	8 A	9 M
K		10 S	E	E		11 A	C		12 A	L	L		13 M	A	
14 I		15 D	I	16 L	I	G	17 E	N	T		18 A	19 S		I	
20 M	21 S		22 G	A	S		.		O		23 D	U	24 A	L	
	25 C	26 O	N	T	E	X	27 T			28 I		29 B	A		33 R
		D	I			30 E	31 O	32 N	S		J				R
34 H	O	35 M	O	G	36 R	A	P	H			37 E	W	E		
38 I	R	A	N		39 E	E		40 I	C			Q			
S		41 I		42 C	43 O	N	44 T	45 E	N	T		U			
46 A		47 O	N	48 B	A	R		49 I	X		50 R	I			
R		W		51 G	E	L		52 G	E	T		53 F	A	R	
54 G	55 E	N	E	R	A	L		56 P	R	E	C	E	D	E	
57 U	N		58 I	S			N			59 D	A	D			
60 E	D		61 I	N	T	R	I	C	A	T	E		R		

HOMOGRAPH RIDDLES

Directions:

Here are several ways to use a single word. Find the right word for each group. Example: I mean to move with sudden speed and to destroy; I am also a punctuation mark. (dash)

1. I can mean in the wrong way or reverse direction, but you can put things on me in the kitchen if you want, and many restaurants have me.

   _____

2. I can mean an obstacle or obstruction, but you can live on me, you can build with me, and I am even how you shape your sweaters after washing them.

   _____

3. In the plural I can mean a place of residence or lodgings, but you can buy things with me, you can use me as a form of measurement, and you can let me help you divide things into parts.

_____

4. I can mean equal, but you can use me as an instrument for adjusting something to a horizontal surface.

_____

5. I can mean to pass time idly, but you can wait in me and if you are tired you can rest on me.

_____

STOP. Check answers at the bottom of the page.

TRUE/FALSE TEST

Directions:

This is a true/false test on Lessons 1–3 in Unit I. Read each sentence carefully. Decide whether it is true or false. Put a T for *true* or an F for *false* in the blank.

_____ 1. The main idea is always a very specific statement.

_____ 2. Rereading is more important than recall in studying.

_____ 3. When you survey an assignment, you read it slowly.

_____ 4. *However* may signal that a contrast is being used.

_____ 5. A diligent person will persevere.

_____ 6. *Try* is an open syllable.

_____ 7. *Read*, the past tense of *to read*, and *red*, the color, are homographs.

_____ 8. Something harmonious is not in discord.

_____ 9. The main idea is always in the topic sentence.

_____ 10. *Tre* is a syllable to which the silent *e* rule applies.

_____ 11. In a well-written paragraph, the sentences develop the main idea.

_____ 12. *Begat* is an obsolete word.

_____ 13. A paragraph usually has more than one main idea.

_____ 14. Often the word *but* signals that a contrast is being used.

_____ 15. All authors directly state their main idea.

_____ 16. Overlearning does not require practice.

_____ 17. A wary person is a cautious or careful person.

_____ 18. *Serene* and *chaotic* are opposites.

_____ 19. Your siblings are your relatives.

_____ 20. It's important that you choose the same particular place in which to study.

STOP. Check answers on the next page.

Answers to True/False Test

1. F 2. F 3. F 4. T 5. T 6. T 7. F 8. T 9. F 10. F 11. T
12. T 13. F 14. T 15. F 16. F 17. T 18. T 19. T 20. T

Unit II

Learning Skills: Concentration—Listening/Reading I
Reading: Central Idea of a Group of Paragraphs
Vocabulary: Context Clues (Synonyms) I
Word Analysis: Vowel and Consonant Combinations
Answers

LEARNING SKILLS: CONCENTRATION—LISTENING/READING I

Although you are acquiring some good study habits, you may still be having difficulty because you can't *concentrate*. Concentration is essential not only for studying but also for listening to lectures. Concentration is sustained (prolonged) attention. If you are not feeling well, if you are hungry or tired, if you are in a room that is too hot or cold, if your chair is uncomfortable, if the lighting is poor or if there is a glare, if there are visual or auditory distractions, you will not be able to concentrate.

1. Concentration demands a mental set or attitude, a determination that you will block everything out except what you are reading or listening to. Skill in concentration can be developed.

2. How many times have you looked up a phone number in the yellow pages of your telephone directory and forgotten the number almost immediately? How many times have you had to look up the *same* number that you have dialed a number of times? Probably very often. The reason for your not remembering is that you did not *concentrate*. In order to remember information, you must concentrate. Concentration demands active involvement.

In this unit you will be presented with a number of concentration exercises that demand more and more of your attention. *Regular practice* of these activities will help you concentrate better. Scoring scales are provided for each practice.

Special Notes

1. Adults spend at least 45 per cent of their time in listening. High school and college students may spend up to 90 per cent of their time in class listening. Obviously listening skills are important and should be developed.

2. All students—unless they have hearing loss—can develop better listening skills.

3. *Paying attention* does not guarantee that you will understand what you are reading or listening to, but it is *an important first step*.

4. The next step involves comprehension skills.

5. Listening comprehension skills are similar to reading comprehension skills except that the message is received aurally (by ear).

6. Each lesson in this unit presents practice for both listening and reading concentration.

7. All listening practice requires *two persons*.

8. Although a number of concentration activities are given for each lesson in this unit, you are not expected to do all of them at one sitting. Remember, a *distribution of practice* is better than a massing of practice.

Practice A.

(Listening)   This practice requires both a speaker and a listener. (Two students can team up and take turns playing the two roles for this activity.) Speaker: "Here are a group of digits [numbers]. Listen carefully. Do not write until you are told to. I will start with just two, but it will become more difficult as we go on. Listen carefully and write the numbers as soon as I stop. For example, if I say '7, 9,' you should write '7, 9.' " (The rate for presentation of digits is one per second.) Listener writes digits. (Two sets of digits are given. The second set is used when the speaker becomes the listener.)

Numbers for Digits Forward:

Span

(2)   9 3
      6 4

(3) 7 1 5
     9 3 7

(4) 8 5 1 4
     1 6 9 3

(5) 7 9 1 5 2
     5 1 3 8 6

(6) 7 4 8 6 2 1
     5 3 9 1 6 2

(7) 8 1 7 5 6 3 9
     4 9 6 5 7 2 1

(8) 3 5 7 9 8 1 2 4
     5 9 6 3 8 4 1 7

(9) 2 5 4 6 9 3 7 1 8
     6 3 5 4 9 1 8 2 7

STOP. Check answers. (Compare your digits with those on this page.)

Scoring Procedure:

To be correct, every digit must be written in the exact order that it was stated.

Points			Maximum Score (Per Set)	
Span (2)	½	point	½	point
Span (3)	1	point	1	point
Span (4)	1½	points	1½	points
Span (5)	2	points	2	points
Span (6)	2½	points	2½	points
Span (7)	3	points	3	points
Span (8)	3½	points	3½	points
Span (9)	4	points	4	points
			18	points

Score for Practice A: _____

Practice B.

(Listening)   This practice requires both a speaker and a listener. (Two students can team up and take turns playing the two roles for this activity.) Speaker: "Here are a group of digits [numbers]. Listen carefully. Do not write until you are told to. I will start with just two, but it will become more difficult as we go on. Listen carefully and write the numbers *backward* as soon as I stop. For example, if I say '7, 9,' you should write '9, 7.' Do not write them first forward and then backward. They must be written in backward form immediately." (The rate for presentation of digits is one per second.) Listener writes digits. (Two sets of digits are given. The second set of digits is used when the speaker becomes the listener.)

Numbers for Digits Backward:

Span

(2)   1 7
      5 2

(3)   3 9 4
      5 1 7

(4)   4 9 5 8
      6 2 9 3

(5)   5 8 1 6 4
      4 9 3 5 2

(6)   9 3 5 2 4 1
      7 1 5 4 6 2

(7)   9 4 2 1 5 7 3
      4 7 1 3 6 2 5

(8)   2 8 1 5 7 9 6 3
      5 9 7 2 4 6 1 8

(9)   3 8 1 7 4 5 9 2 6
      6 1 5 3 9 2 7 4 8

STOP. Check answers. (To check answers, read digits backward.)

Scoring Procedure:

To be correct, every digit must be written in the exact backward order from what was stated.

Points			*Maximum Score (Per Set)*	
Span (2)	½	point	½	point
Span (3)	1	point	1	point
Span (4)	1½	points	1½	points
Span (5)	2½	points	2½	points
Span (6)	3½	points	3½	points
Span (7)	4	points	4	points
Span (8)	4½	points	4½	points
Span (9)	5	points	5	points
			22½	points

Score for Practice B: _____

Practice C.

(Listening) This practice requires both a speaker and a listener. (Two students can team up and take turns playing the two roles for this activity. The speaker should read instructions from his or her own book.) Speaker: "Listen carefully while I give you some directions. Do not start until I have finished reading each set of directions. Remember, do not start until I have finished reading each set of directions." (The Listener's Sheet is printed after the directions.)

Directions:

1. In box 1 circle the 2nd letter of the 2nd word, and in box 2 put a dot in the center figure.

2. In box 2 put a check in the 2nd triangle, and a cross on the 1st letter of the 3rd word in box 1.

3. Put a circle around the last digit in box 3, a cross in the 5th figure in box 2, and a check on the center digit in box 3.

4. Put a circle around the 1st letter of the 1st word in box 1, put a cross on the 3rd letter of the 4th word in box 1, and put a dot in the 2nd circle in box 2.

5. Put a dot in the 1st circle in box 2, a cross in the last figure in box 2, and a circle around the 2nd letter of the last word in box 1.

Listener's Sheet (for Practice C):

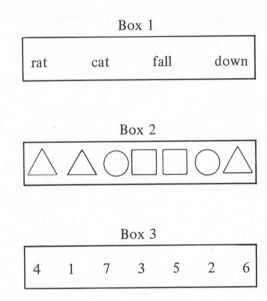

Box 1

| rat | cat | fall | down |

Box 2

Box 3

| 4 | 1 | 7 | 3 | 5 | 2 | 6 |

STOP. Check answers by reading the directions and comparing your Listener's Sheet with the one given at the end of Lesson 4.

Practice D.

(Reading) Here are nine sets of one-syllable words. Read each set of words *once*. Concentrate. Cover the set of words and write it in the blank. Check your results immediately.

1. pen fat _____

2. can hit toy _____

3. pick tall chin me _____

4. boy may so down hit _____

5. wish nice she still give red _____

6. friend go elf make dream bank help _____

7. dress sing man box school fish paint go _____

8. nine five ten six one three eight two four _____

9. new big go prize fall sign play drink thumb buy_____

Practice E.

(Reading) Read each numbered instruction carefully *once*, and then carry out the stated directions on the Following Instructions Sheet.

Instructions:

1. If there is a word that means the opposite of *tall* and a word that rhymes with *boat*, put a line over the two words.

2. If there is a color that signals cars to stop, one that signals them to go, and one that signals them to slow down, put a line over the color that means slow down.

3. If in a sequence of numbers in descending order there are four odd numbers and three even numbers, put a line under the largest odd number.

4. If there are three numbers one after the other that equal 12, and two numbers one after the other that equal less than 12, put a line over the three numbers that equal 12.

5. If there are four numbers one after the other that equal 20 and a word that rhymes with *slice*, put a circle around the rhyming word.

6. If there are two vowels, if there are five letters in order, if there are five odd numbers, and if there are two single-digit numbers that multiplied together equal a two-digit number, circle the two-digit number and the two single-digit numbers.

7. If three consecutive numbers equal 6, if four consecutive numbers equal 18, and if there are two Roman numerals that equal 19, put a line under the Roman numeral for 10.

Following Instructions Sheet:

coat   30   76   54   23   red   A B C D E

green   yellow   7 6 5 4 3 2 1   P Q R T V

in   short   nice   IX   X   XI

STOP. Check answers by rereading the instructions and by comparing your answers with those at the end of Lesson 4.

READING: CENTRAL IDEA OF A GROUP OF PARAGRAPHS

Finding the central idea of a group of paragraphs is important because it helps you to better understand and remember what you have read.

1. Textbook writers are especially interested in your understanding the topic they are discussing. Usually a chapter is divided into a number of sections each made up of paragraphs concerned with the topic. To help you more, some textbook writers put the general topic of the section in bold print or in the margins at the beginning of the section with the more specific topics also presented in the margins of the section further on, indented or printed in smaller type. (See selection in Practice A of this section.) Some textbook writers help you by presenting their material in outline form. (See selection in Practice B of this section.)

2. To find the central idea of a group of paragraphs you must find what common element they all develop. The introductory paragraph usually anticipates the central idea and how it will be developed. Some textbook writers may actually state the central idea in the introductory paragraph or print the general topic in the margin of the introductory paragraph or in bold type at the beginning.

3. The technique presented in Unit I for finding the main idea of a single paragraph also applies to finding the central idea of a group of paragraphs. A section of a textbook, like a single paragraph, is usually written about a particular something or someone. The something or someone is the *topic* of the section. To find the central idea of a section, first find the topic of the section and then determine what particular point or points the section makes about that topic.

Special Note

The central idea of a paragraph or a group of paragraphs can be expressed only as a general statement; the paragraph or group of paragraphs expresses it in detail.

4. Read this group of textbook paragraphs. (Notice that helpful clues are given in the margins to set your purposes for reading.)

From *Educational Psychology: A Realistic Approach* by Thomas L. Good and Jere E. Brophy.*

Vocabulary:

disruptive—disorderly; *peers*—those equal in standing to others, persons belonging to the same group in society; *spontaneously*—without external influence, naturally; *perceived*—viewed; *status*—position or rank in relation to others; *provocative*—annoying, irritating; *punitive*—involving punishment.

Attention-seeking by students

[1] Sometimes seriously disruptive behavior occurs as a deliberate effort to gain approval from peers or even attention from teachers. This appears most typically in students whose general self-concepts (not merely those aspects dealing with school) are poor. Due to a combination of rejection by parents and by peers, they develop the belief that they are looked down upon, disliked, rejected, and so on. A few such students spontaneously find the strength to fight these forces by trying to prove their worth in prosocial ways. However, unless they get some kind of help, most eventually cave in, accepting their perceived status as rejects and attempting to gain attention and at least some acceptance by doing anything that they think might work. Sometimes, students like these will even do something deliberately in order to get negative attention, because this is better than nothing at all.

[2] In any case, it is common for students who are not getting enough of the right kind of attention and respect from parents, teachers, and peers to strive to get it by acting out. Usually this acting out is not extremely antisocial or aggressive, although it may well be extremely disruptive, destructive, immature, and irritating. This can include continual property destruction, "forgetting" and "accidents," provocative remarks or gestures, general clowning around, deliberately playing stupid and making fools of themselves, and the like. One characteristic common to students like these which differentiates them from more seriously antisocial students is that they are rather obviously acting out in order to get attention. Among other things, this means that usually their behavior is quite conspicuous, and they make sure to get caught. Thus, even with behavior like trashing or arson, the trashing is more likely to lead to an uproar than to serious destruction of property, and the arson is more likely to involve a wastebasket fire than a serious attempt to burn down the school.

Suspension-seeking by students

[3] A variation of this occurs frequently with students nearing the age at which they can quit school legally. Many have made up their minds to do so long before the law allows, and thus they will misbehave at school simply because they want to get suspended or otherwise removed from the classroom. For these students, removal from ordinary classrooms is reward rather than punishment, and suspension (or, better yet, expulsion) is the greatest reward of all. Many individuals concerned with schools in our society are re-evaluating the idea of compulsory school attendance, thinking that it might be better to let such students out of the schools if efforts to change their minds fail. Others favor allowing them to transfer to vocational schools or to nonacademic institutions. Why force such students to persist in school when they cause a continuous uproar and rarely achieve a good adjustment? This is a complex issue, and it probably will not be decided for some time. Until it is, however,

teachers are going to have to deal with students like these whether they want to or not. Possible future solutions are not much help to teachers faced with real problems now.

[4]   Students like these require a combination of an accurate diagnosis of what they are doing, a firm refusal to reward their efforts to avoid the classroom, and an attempt to change their attitudes or at least to get them to agree to "go along to get along." In any case, teachers must be especially vigilant and determined in order to make sure that they are not manipulated into "punishing" such students in ways that they actually seek to be "punished." If punishment is required, it should be some action that truly will function as punishment for them, such as in-school detention involving isolation from classmates while they work on school assignments.

[5]   Another common way that students come to be regarded as disruptive at school is for them to indulge in a persistent habit that might be acceptable under some circumstances but forbidden at school. This includes smoking tobacco or marijuana, using pills or other drugs, drinking, using obscene language, overt sexual activity, and the like. Except for involvement with drugs like heroin, such behavior is more typical of students who are relatively bright and well adjusted, compared to the kinds of students described previously.   Nevertheless, it sometimes leads to continuing problems with particular teachers or with the school in general.

[6]   Sometimes the student involved has problems relating to authority figures because of an authoritarian upbringing. Frequently, however, the problem is caused by teachers or other school officials who overreact in initial encounters with the student by making mountains out of molehills.   Students who "test" school rules against such behavior usually will respond well to a firm but low-key reminder that the behavior is against the rules and will not be tolerated. How-

ever, if a school official should overreact by becoming hysterical or abusive or punitive toward the student without justification, the student may respond with resentment and determination to get even. Consequently, teachers who cannot handle problems like these appropriately should either learn to change their behavior immediately or else transfer to grade levels where they will not encounter them.

What is the topic of this group of paragraphs? We could say "students," but this is too general because all of the paragraphs discuss a special kind of student. The better answer would be "disruptive students" or "types of disruptive student behavior." (Notice that the clues given in the margins are topics of individual paragraphs but are too specific to qualify as the topic of the whole group of paragraphs. However, the common element of all the topics in the margins is that they are examples of *disruptive student behavior*.)

What is the writer doing in all the paragraphs? The writer describes various types of behavior problems that appear in school, analyzes the reasons for the behavior, and suggests methods of dealing with disruptive students who exhibit such behavior.

The preceding statement is a succinct summary of what the writer accomplishes in the group of paragraphs, but it is not a statement of the central idea of the paragraphs. (See Lessons 12–15.) To determine the central idea, state what the author is saying that is special and that applies to the various types of disruptive student behavior he describes.

Central Idea:

It is necessary to understand each type of disruptive behavior that happens in school so that the disruptive students can be properly dealt with.

To check that this is the central idea, go over the paragraphs and see whether each develops the central idea as stated.

a. Paragraphs 1 and 2 discuss attention seeking as a type of student behavior. The emphasis is on understanding the reasons for the behavior.

b. Paragraphs 3 and 4 give another type of disruptive behavior and discuss ways of dealing with it.

c. Paragraphs 5 and 6 are concerned with students who "test the rules" and ways to deal with these students.

From looking at the paragraphs you can see that all of them do indeed develop the central theme—that of understanding the different types of disruptive behavior so that students can be properly dealt with.

Practice A.

1. Survey this group of paragraphs. 2. State four questions to set your purposes for reading. 3. Read to answer the questions. 4. Answer the questions. (Try to answer the questions without rereading; that is, try to *recall* the answers from memory. 5. State the central idea of the group of paragraphs.

From *Criminal Justice: Enforcement and Administration* by Alan Kalmanoff, Little, Brown and Co., 1976.

Vocabulary:

credibility—believability; *strategy*—plan; *perception*—giving meaning to sensations, the way one sees things; *bias*—a mental leaning, prejudice; *inconsistencies*—contradictions; *characteristics*—traits; *perpetrator*—one who carries out (a wrong, a crime, etc.); *consciousness*—awareness; *conservative*—one who resists change, reluctant to change.

Typical Defense Strategies

The defense of the most common street crimes often centers on the issue of credibility: who does the judge or jury believe; what actually happened; and who in the case has the most interest in telling the truth. In most situations involving street crimes, defenses based on misidentification or an alibi are not available. Assuming that credibility is the most basic and common issue, the defense, to establish credibility, often depends on issues that make a favorable appeal to public opinion.

Perceptual Bias

Since the early 1960s, the possibility of racism—insofar as it affects people's perceptions—has become an issue that criminal defense lawyers can employ effectively. The public has become sufficiently sophisticated to realize that generalizations made concerning minority groups can so affect a person's ability to perceive that it might affect his or her ability to report truthfully what has occurred. Defense attorneys have begun to use this new consciousness of racism in planning defense strategies.

In some cases, although an attorney may seek to set forth the truth and may specifically point out inconsistencies in testimony or the inability of witnesses to recollect, the essential argument may still center on theoretical issues of racism, conservatism of the police, or the reactionary quality of certain types of individuals. For example, the racist generalization that all Blacks look alike could definitely affect a person's ability to make an identification. If certain characteristics such as height, "darkness," or Afro-style hair are used as identifying points, a good argument could be made by defense lawyers that the victim assumed the defendant to be the perpetrator on the basis of very common characteristics.

Another related point involves the often-accepted belief that police are right-wing, conservative, biased against racial and ethnic minorities and that they occasionally perjure themselves in court. Therefore, in a situation of alleged resistance to a police officer, a common defense argument would be that, if a White person or a wealthy person had said or done the same thing, such a person would not have been arrested for interfering with an officer.

Questions:

Answers:

Central idea:

STOP. Check sample questions and answers at the end of Lesson 4.

Practice B.

1. Survey this group of paragraphs. 2. State three questions to set your purposes for reading. 3. Read the paragraphs to answer your questions. 4. Answer the questions without rereading. 5. State the central idea of the paragraphs.

From *Economics* by Campbell R. McConnell, McGraw-Hill Book Co., 1978.*

Vocabulary:

Proprietorship—ownership; *sole*—being the only one; *enterprise*—a business firm, a project; *rugged*—capable of enduring hardship; *incentive*—stimulus, motive, something that gets a person to do something; *mortality rate*—death rate; *extend*—to grant or offer; *potential*—possible ability; *inaccessible*—impossible to reach; *acquisition*—the act of acquiring; *liability*—a debt, legal obligation to make good any loss or damage that occurs in a business deal; *asset*—anything owned that has value.

Sole Proprietorship

A sole proprietorship is literally an individual in business for himself. It is typically "a one-man show." The proprietor owns or obtains the materials and capital equipment used in the operation of his business and personally supervises its operation. Responsibility for the efficient coordination of the resources he owns or can command rests directly upon the proprietor's shoulders.

Advantages

Obviously, this extremely simple type of business organization has certain distinct advantages:

1. A sole proprietorship is very easy to organize—there is virtually no legal red tape or expense. The businessman merely acquires the needed facilities and is "in business."

2. The proprietor is his own boss and has very substantial freedom of action. Since his own profit income depends upon his enterprise's success, there is a strong and immediate incentive for him to manage the affairs of his business wisely.

Disadvantages

The sole proprietorship looks very rugged and individualistic. And it clearly is. But the disadvantages of this form of business organization are great:

1. With rare exceptions, the financial resources of a sole proprietorship are insufficient to permit the firm to grow into a large-scale enterprise. Specifically, finances are usually limited to what the proprietor has in his bank account and to what he is able to borrow. Since the mortality rate is very great for proprietorships, commercial banks are not overly eager to extend much credit to them.

2. Being in complete control of an enterprise forces the proprietor to carry out all basic management functions. The proprietor must be a jack-of-all-trades and must make all basic decisions concerning, for example, buying, selling, and the acquisition and maintenance of personnel, not to mention the technical aspects which might be involved in producing, advertising, and distributing the product. In short, the potential benefits of specialization in business management are usually inaccessible to the typical small-scale proprietorship.

3. Most important of all, the proprietor is subject to *unlimited liability*. This means that individuals in business for themselves risk not only the assets of the firm but also their personal assets. Should the assets of an unsuccessful proprietorship be insufficient to satisfy the claims of creditors, those creditors can file claims against the proprietor's personal property. The stakes are high insofar as individual proprietorships are concerned.

Questions:

Answers:

Central idea:

STOP. Check sample questions and answers at the end of Lesson 4.

VOCABULARY: CONTEXT CLUES (Synonyms) I

Often a word can be defined by another, more familiar word having basically the same meaning. For example, *void* is defined as *empty* and *corpulent* is defined as *fat*. *Void* and *empty*, and *corpulent* and *fat* are synonyms. Synonyms are different words that have the same or nearly the same meaning. Writers use synonyms to make their writing clearer and more expressive. (See Unit I, Lesson 1.) Although you met the term *synonym* in a preceding lesson, it is being presented again because the principle is often used by authors.

Practice A.

In each sentence determine the meaning of the underlined word from the context clue(s). Try to give a synonym for the underlined word.

1. Many cities are <u>razing</u> old buildings in the belief that demolishing them is the only way to begin to rebuild their communities.

   _____

2. The <u>infamous</u> Al Capone was most notorious for his cruelty.

   _____

3. The <u>exhausted</u> man was so tired he could not move another step.

   _____

4. Although we hold <u>equivalent</u> job titles, our wages are not equal.

   _____

5. We did not have sufficient <u>capital</u> to start a business, nor were we able to borrow enough money from the bank.

   _____

6. When my mother had a very <u>grave</u> illness, the doctor said it was so serious she would probably die.

   _____

7. The Rand Company always gives an <u>annual</u> party, but in some years it is a spring picnic and in others it's a formal dance.

_____

8. Because my friend looks so <u>immature</u>, everyone expects him to act childishly.

_____

9. Although our lives were in <u>jeopardy</u> when the gas line near our house broke, we were not aware of the danger until repairs had begun.

_____

10. It is quite easy to <u>intimidate</u> me, but it is more difficult to frighten my roommate, who is a karate expert.

_____

11. The <u>immense</u> truck was too big to pass under the archway of the old inn.

_____

12. She is a <u>virtuoso</u> in French, and I am an expert in Spanish.

_____

13. None of my friends is <u>egotistical</u>, because I do not like self-centered or vain people.

_____

14. The spy said that the <u>perilous</u> mission was too risky for him.

_____

15. I am always looking for a quick <u>remedy</u>, but I guess fast cures aren't really much good.

_____

STOP. Check answers at the end of Lesson 4.

Practice B.

Match the word from column B with its synonym in column A.

Column A	Column B
_____ 1. raze	a. vain
_____ 2. infamous	b. huge
_____ 3. exhausted	c. cure
_____ 4. equivalent	d. yearly
_____ 5. capital	e. risky
_____ 6. grave	f. money
_____ 7. annual	g. expert
_____ 8. immature	h. equal
_____ 9. jeopardy	i. serious
_____ 10. intimidate	j. danger
_____ 11. immense	k. tired
_____ 12. virtuoso	l. childish
_____ 13. egotistical	m. notorious
_____ 14. perilous	n. frighten
_____ 15. remedy	o. demolish

STOP. Check answers at the end of Lesson 4.

Practice C.

Choose a word from the word list that has the same meaning as the under-lined word in the sentence.

Word List:

egotistical, raze, intimidate, infamous, exhausted, perilous, grave, capital, virtuoso, jeopardy, remedy, annual, immense, equivalent, immature.

1. That is a <u>huge</u> building. _____

2. She is <u>tired</u> from the ten-mile hike. _____

3. We have <u>equal</u> amounts. _____

4. Our school holds its <u>yearly</u> picnic in the spring._____

5. You need <u>money</u> to start a business._____

6. The man on trial is <u>notorious</u> for his crimes._____

7. The <u>self-centered</u> girl didn't stop talking about herself all night._____

8. Her behavior is very <u>childish.</u> _____

9. You cannot <u>frighten</u> me. _____

10. I don't think that there is a <u>cure</u> for the common cold._____

11. The crew will <u>demolish</u> the old building tomorrow._____

12. She had a very <u>serious</u> illness._____

13. They knew that their lives were in <u>danger.</u> _____

14. The mountain path looked too <u>dangerous</u> to me. _____

15. She is an <u>expert</u> in math._____

STOP. Check answers at the end of Lesson 4.

WORD ANALYSIS: VOWEL AND CONSONANT COMBINATIONS

1. *Vowel digraphs* are two vowels adjacent (next) to one another in a word or syllable and standing for a single vowel sound. Examples: *ea* (beat), *oa* (boat), *ai* (sail), *ei* (receive), (neighbor), *ie* (believe), *eo* (yeoman), *ew* (sew), *ou* (rough), *eo* (people).

Special Notes

1. You may have learned a rule in elementary school saying that when two vowels appear together, the first is usually long and the second is silent. This usually does hold true for a number of vowel combinations such as *ai*, *oa*, *ee*, and *ea*. However, there are exceptions to this rule such as *ae*, *uy*, *eo*,

and *ew*. These digraphs are sounded as a single sound but not always with the long sound of the first. Examples: sew, buy, yeoman, Caesar. Also, note that in the word *believe* and in many of the words containing the *ie* combination it's the second vowel that is long and the first that is silent. The rule, therefore, may not be too useful when trying to pronounce an unknown word having vowel digraphs other than *ai, oa, ee,* and *ea.*

2. Some vowel digraphs combine to form one sound that is not the long sound of either vowel. Examples: sew, neighbor, rough.

3. The *ay* in *day* is a vowel digraph because the *y* acts as a vowel, and the *ew* in *sew* is a vowel digraph because the *w* also acts as a vowel.

2. *Diphthongs* are blends of vowel sounds, beginning with the first and gliding to the second. The vowel blends are represented by two adjacent vowels. Examples: *oi* (boil, oil), *oy* (boy, toy), *ow* (cow), *ou* (bough).

Special Notes

1. Notice that *ou* and *ow* can be either a digraph or a diphthong. For example, in the word *how*, *ow* is a diphthong, but in the word *grow, ow* is a digraph. Notice also the words *though* and *bough*. In *though*, the *ou* is a vowel digraph, but in *bough* the *ou* is a diphthong.

2. The vowel combinations *oi* and *oy* are usually diphthongs and sound like *oil* and *boy*.

3. In the *ow* and *oy* combinations the *w* and *y* act as vowels.

3. *Consonant digraphs* usually consist of two consonants which represent one speech sound. Examples: *ch* (chain), *sh* (show), *th* (think), *ph* (phone), *ng* (sing), *gh* (tough).

4. *Consonant blends* are a combination of sounds, not letters. Consonant blends are two or more consonant sounds blended together so that the identity of each sound is retained. Examples: *bl* (blue), *pl* (plum), *cr* (crow), *tr* (train), *sk* (skate), *sw* (swim), *sp* (spy), *sm* (smile), *sn* (snow), *scr* (scream), *str* (stream), *spr* (spread), *spl* (splash).

5. *Silent consonants* refer to two consonants in which one is silent. Examples: *kn* (know), *gn* (gnat), *pn* (pneumonia), *wr* (write).

Practice A.

Underline the words that have vowel digraphs in them.

can   go   beat   cute   cape   coil   goat   lay   live   plane   claim
blouse   cream   saint   swim   shore   bleak

STOP. Check answers at the end of Lesson 4.

Practice B.

Underline the words that have diphthongs in them.

how   glass   plow   cram   soil   cold   stone   out   drought   drown
claim   care   know   bough

STOP. Check answers at the end of Lesson 4.

Practice C.

Underline the words that have consonant digraphs in them.

tough   phone   slain   church   thirst   blame   crawl   travel   birthday
pleasing   strip   ship   steer   slash

STOP. Check answers at the end of Lesson 4.

ANSWERS: Lesson 4 (pp. 71-95)

Learning Skills: Concentration—Listening/Reading I (pp. 71-78)

Practice A

Check answers with digits on p. 72-73.

Practice B

Check answers with digits on p. 74 .

Practice C

Check answer by reading the directions and comparing the following to your responses.

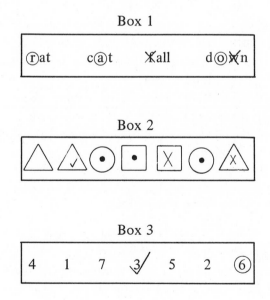

Box 1

ⓡat   c@t   X̶all   d○X̶n

Box 2

△ △✓ ⊙ ▫ ☒ ⊙ △X

Box 3

4   1   7   3̶   5   2   ⑥

Practice D

Check answers immediately after each set.

Practice E

Check answers by rereading the instructions and by comparing the following to your responses.

1. Put a line over *short* and *coat*. 2. Put a line over *yellow*. 3. Put a line under "7." 4. Put a line over "5," "4," and "3." 5. Do nothing. There aren't four numbers one after the other that equal 20. 6. Circle the single-digit numbers "6" and "5" and the double-digit number "30." 7. Put a line under the Roman numeral "X."

Reading: Central Idea of a Group of Paragraphs (pp. 78-86)

Practice A (sample questions and answers)

1. Survey 2. a. What issue is involved in typical defense strategies? b. What is the defense's strategy? c. What does perceptual bias do? What is it? d. What are some issues and examples of perceptual bias used in defense strategies? (Notice how the writer's use of bold print and smaller–type print gives you clues that help to determine the questions and therefore set the purposes for reading.) 3. Read 4. a. Credibility is the issue. b. The defense's strategy is to use issues that make a favorable appeal to public opinion. c. Perceptual bias affects an individual's ability to report truthfully what has occurred. Perceptual bias is the tendency to apply general-izations to individuals. d. Issues: racism, conservatism of police, or the reactionary quality of certain types of individuals. Examples: racist gen-eralizations–all Blacks look alike; police are right-wing, conservative, are biased against racial and ethnic minorities and occasionally perjure them-selves in court. 5. Perceptual bias is an important defense strategy employ-ed by the defense.

Practice B (sample questions and answers)

1. Survey 2. a. What does *sole proprietorship* mean? b. What are two ad-vantages of sole proprietorship? c. What are three disadvantages of sole pro-prietorship? (Notice how the author's outlining of his material helps to determine your questions and set your purposes for reading.) 3. Read 4. a. Sole proprietorship is a one-person business. The person owns all the materials necessary for the business, he operates it himself, and he is respon-sible for everything. b. (1) A sole proprietorship is easy to organize. (2)

The person is his own boss. c. (1) Financial resources may be insufficient. (2) The person must do everything himself. (3) The owner is subject to unlimited liability. This means that the owner risks not only the assets of his firm but also his personal assets. 5. Sole proprietorship has a number of advantages and disadvantages.

Vocabulary: Context Clues (Synonyms) I (pp. 87–90)

Practice A

1. demolishing 2. notorious (known for a bad reputation) 3. tired 4. equal 5. money 6. serious 7. yearly 8. childish 9. danger 10. frighten 11. huge 12. expert 13. self-centered, vain 14. risky 15. cure

Practice B

1. o 2. m 3. k 4. h 5. f 6. i 7. d 8. l 9. j 10. n 11. b 12. g 13. a 14. e 15. c

Practice C

1. immense 2. exhausted 3. equivalent 4. annual 5. capital 6. infamous 7. egotistical 8. immature 9. intimidate 10. remedy 11. raze 12. grave 13. jeopardy 14. perilous 15. virtuoso

Word Analysis: Vowel and Consonant Combinations (pp. 90–92)

Practice A

beat, goat, claim, cream, saint, bleak

Practice B

how, plow, soil, out, drought, drown, bough

Practice C

tough, phone, church, thirst, birthday, ship, slash

LESSON 5

Learning Skills: Concentration—Listening/Reading II
Reading: Central Idea of an Article
Vocabulary: Context Clues (Synonyms) II
Word Analysis: Special Letters and Sounds
Answers

LEARNING SKILLS: CONCENTRATION—LISTENING/READING II

You will be able to concentrate better if you are well rested. To attempt to concentrate after being up almost all night at a party is unrealistic. Concentration is demanding work that requires an alert mind and a healthy body. By all means have fun. A rhythm of activity is very important for everyone. There is a time for recreation and a time for work. Concentration is hard work; therefore you must come to it when you are feeling well and are wide awake.

Practice A.

(Listening) This practice requires both a speaker and a listener. (Two students can team up and take turns playing the two roles for this activity.) Speaker: "Here are a group of digits. Listen carefully. Do not write until you are told to. I will start with just two, but it will become more difficult as we go on. Listen carefully and write the numbers as soon as I stop. For example, if I say " '7, 9,' you should write '7, 9.' " (The rate for presentation of digits is one per second.) Listener writes digits. (Two sets of digits are given. The second set of digits is used when the speaker becomes the listener.)

Numbers for Digits Forward:

Span

(2) 7 9
     5 3

(3) 6 9 1
     4 1 8

(4) 9 1 3 7
     8 4 5 2

(5) 6 1 5 7 9
     1 7 8 5 2

(6) 3 1 7 2 8 5
     6 1 9 7 4 3

(7) 4 6 2 7 1 8 5
     5 1 9 3 7 6 2

(8) 7 5 1 9 6 3 8 2
     8 1 7 6 9 5 2 4

(9) 3 5 6 9 4 8 2 7 1
     4 2 5 9 3 7 6 1 8

STOP. Check answers. (Compare your digits with those on this page.)

Scoring Procedure:

To be correct, every digit must be written in the exact order that it was stated.

Points		*Maximum Score (Per Set)*	
Span (2)	½ point	½ point	
Span (3)	1 point	1 point	
Span (4)	1½ points	1½ points	
Span (5)	2 points	2 points	
Span (6)	2½ points	2½ points	
Span (7)	3 points	3 points	

Span (8)	3½ points	3½ points
Span (9)	4 points	4 points
		18 points

Score for Practice A: ____

Practice B.

(Listening) This practice requires both a speaker and a listener. (Two students can team up and take turns playing the two roles for this activity.) Speaker: "Here are a group of digits. Listen carefully. Do not write until you are told to. I will start with just two, but it will become more difficult as we go on. Listen carefully and write the numbers *backward* as soon as I stop. For example, if I say '7, 9,' you should write '9, 7.' Do not write them first forward and then backward. They must be written in backward form immediately." (The rate for presentation of digits is one per second.) Listener writes digits. (Two sets of digits are given. The second set of digits is used when the speaker becomes the listener.)

Numbers for Digits Backward:

Span

(2) 1 5
     7 2

(3) 9 7 1
     3 5 8

(4) 7 5 1 7
     6 3 2 9

(5) 1 8 4 7 5
     3 5 9 3 1

(6) 6 1 4 7 3 5
     7 9 1 5 1 4

(7) 8 4 1 5 2 6 9
     2 9 5 8 7 3 1

(8) 4 9 7 3 6 2 5 1
     5 8 2 6 4 7 3 9

(9) 8 1 9 7 2 5 3 6 4
      9 4 1 6 3 8 2 7 5

Stop. Check answers. (To check answers, read digits backward.)

Scoring Procedure:

To be correct every digit must be written in the exact backward order from what was stated.

Points	Maximum Score (Per Set)
Span (2) ½ point	½ point
Span (3) 1 point	1 point
Span (4) 1½ points	1½ points
Span (5) 2½ points	2½ points
Span (6) 3½ points	3½ points
Span (7) 4 points	4 points
Span (8) 4½ points	4½ points
Span (9) 5 points	5 points
	22½ points

Score for Practice B: ____

Practice C.

(Listening) This practice requires both a speaker and a listener. (Two students can team up and take turns playing the two roles for this activity.) Speaker: "Listen carefully while I give you some directions. Do not start until I have finished reading each set of directions. Remember, do not start until I have finished reading each set of directions." (The Listener's Sheet is printed after the directions.)

Directions:

1. If the numbers in this group equal 3, put a cross on the higher number.

2. Put a line under all the numbers that have 9 in them; put a cross on the last letter of the word in this group.

3. Put a check on the 1st two stars; put a circle around the 3rd and 5th letters of the opposite of *sad*.

4. Put a circle around the 3rd star, around the two numbers that equal 20, and around the middle letter of the word.

5. Put a cross on the 1st and last letters of the word, put a circle around the smallest number, and put a cross on the largest number.

6. Put a line under the 1st letter of the 1st word, the 2nd letter of the 2nd word, and the 3rd letter of the 3rd word; put a circle around the smallest and the largest numbers.

7. Put a line under the middle star, the 3rd number, the 1st letter of the 2nd word, and under the two numbers that equal 10.

8. Put a cross on M, the letter before R, the letter after A, and the number after 12; put a circle around the letter after M.

9. Put a line above the 2nd number, the 3rd letter, the 1st star, and the 2nd word; put a cross on the 3rd letter of the 1st word.

10. Put a circle around all the odd numbers, the 2nd star, and the middle letter; put a line under the 3rd letter of the 1st word, the 1st letter of the 2nd word, and the 3rd number.

Listener's Sheet (for Practice C):

(1) go 2 1   (2) 90 boy 19 25   (3) * * 4 * happy

(4) * 10 * * 5 15 man   (5) 79 86 45 98 girl   (6)

big cat cow 7 4 1   (7) * * * small dog 3 7 67 5   (8)

L R M G A B C 9 12 15   (9) 17 14 19 pat * * call

C R S U W   (10)   * * sat * 15 20 18 17 A Q L G

M T F fat

STOP. Check answers by reading the directions and comparing your Listener's Sheet with the one given at the end of Lesson 5.

Practice D.

(Reading) Here are nine sets of one-syllable words. Read each set of words *once*. Concentrate. Cover the set of words and write it in the blank. Check your results immediately.

1. blue me _____

2. nine one four _____

3. bell card self charm _____

4. six nine five make one _____

5. six ten eight one den make_____

6. nine part six soap mix five eight_____

7. give all hole for chin top base fit_____

8. four ten one six eight three five nine two_____

9. ask rent plan give nose sign pour feel light plane _____

Practice E.

(Reading) Read each numbered instruction carefully *once*, and then carry out the stated directions on the Following Instructions Sheet.

Instructions:

1. In box 1 circle the number that is equal to (6 × 6) minus 1, and in box 3 circle the 2nd letter of the 3rd word.

2. Circle the middle letter in box 2, the 1st letter of the 4th word in box 3, and the number equal to 5 × 5 in box 1.

3. Put a check on the letter before S, a circle around the number equal to (10 × 10) minus 2, and a circle around the 2nd vowel in the 2nd word in box 3.

4. Put a circle around the last consonant in the last word in box 3, a circle around the 1st letter of the 2nd word in box 3, and a cross on the number in the 50s in box 1.

5. Put a circle around the letter after U and a cross on the letter before Q in box 2, put a circle around the 1st word in box 3 and a cross on the last letter of the 2nd word, and put a cross on the number equal to 8 × 8 in box 1.

Following Instructions Sheet:

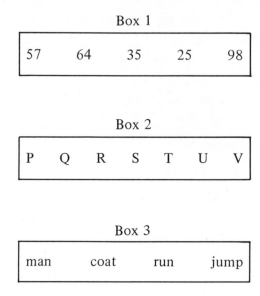

Box 1

| 57 | 64 | 35 | 25 | 98 |

Box 2

| P | Q | R | S | T | U | V |

Box 3

| man | coat | run | jump |

STOP. Check answers by rereading the instructions and by comparing your answers with those at the end of Lesson 5.

READING: CENTRAL IDEA OF AN ARTICLE

The central idea of an article is what gives it unity and order. Without a central idea the article would be no more than a confused jumble of paragraphs.

Writers of articles may not give clues in the margins the way textbook writers do; however, they generally choose titles for their articles that are helpful. Often the title helps you to anticipate the central idea and how it will be developed.

Practice A.

Read this article carefully, and then answer the true/false questions on it. Put a T for *true* or an F for *false* in the blank. (Answer the questions *without rereading* the article.)

From "38 Who Saw Murder Didn't Call Police" by Martin Ginsberg, *The New York Times*, 1964.

Vocabulary:

law-abiding—law-obeying; *chatter*—idle talk, rapid talk to no purpose; *homicide*—any killing of one human being by another; *baffles*—confuses, bewilders; *sheepishly*—embarrassedly as by having done something wrong or foolish; *solemn*—sober, serious, grave.

"38 Who Saw Murder Didn't Call Police"*

For more than half an hour 38 respectable, law-abiding citizens in Queens watched a killer go after and stab a woman in three separate attacks in Kew Gardens.

Twice their chatter and the sudden glow of their bedroom lights interrupted him and frightened him off. Each time he returned, went after her, and stabbed her again. Not one person telephoned the police during the attack; one witness called after the woman was dead.

Still shocked is Assistant Chief Inspector Frederick M. Lussen, in charge of the borough's detectives and a veteran of 25 years of homicide investigations. He can give a matter-of-fact recitation of many murders. But the Kew Gardens slaying baffles him—not because it is a murder, but because the "good people" failed to call the police.

"As we have reconstructed the crime," he said, "the attacker had three chances to kill this woman during a 35-minute period. He returned twice to complete the job. If we had been called when he first attacked, the woman might not be dead now."

At 3:20 A.M. twenty-eight-year-old Catherine Genovese, who was called Kitty by almost everyone in the neighborhood, was returning home from her job. She parked her red Fiat in a lot near the Kew Gardens Long Island Rail Road Station.

She turned off the lights of her car, locked the door, and started to walk the 100 feet to the entrance of her apartment at 82-70 Austin Street, which is in a building with stores on the first floor and apartments on the second.

*©1964 by The New York Times Company. Reprinted by permission.

The entrance to the apartment is in the rear of the building because the front is rented to retail stores.

Miss Genovese noticed a man at the far end of the lot, near a seven-story apartment house at 82-40 Austin Street. She halted. Then, nervously, she headed up Austin Street toward Lefferts Boulevard, where there is a call box to the 102nd Police Precinct in nearby Richmond Hill.

She got as far as a street light in front of a bookstore before the man grabbed her. She screamed. Lights went on in the 10-story apartment house at 82-67 Austin Street, which faces the bookstore. Windows slid open and voices punctuated the early-morning stillness.

Miss Genovese screamed: "Oh, my God, he stabbed me! Please help me! Please help me!"

From one of the upper windows in the apartment house, a man called down: "Let that girl alone!"

The attacker looked up at him, shrugged, and walked down Austin Street toward a white sedan parked a short distance away. Miss Genovese struggled to her feet.

Lights went out. The killer returned to Miss Genovese, now trying to make her way around the side of the building by the parking lot to get to her apartment. The assailant stabbed her again.

"I'm dying!" she shrieked. "I'm dying!"

Windows were opened again, and lights went on in many apartments. The assailant got into his car and drove away. Miss Genovese staggered to her feet. It was 3:35 A.M.

The assailant returned. By then, Miss Genovese had crawled to the back of the building, where the freshly painted brown doors to the apartment house held out hope for safety. At the second door, he saw her slumped on the floor at the foot of the stairs. He stabbed her a third time—killing her.

It was 3:50 by the time the police received their first call, from a man who was a neighbor of Miss Genovese. In two minutes they were at the scene. The neighbor, a 70-year-old woman, and another woman were the only persons on the street. Nobody else came forward.

The man explained that he had called the police after much deliberation. He had phoned a friend in Nassau County for advice and then he had crossed the roof of the building to the apartment of the elderly woman to get her to make the call.

"I didn't want to get involved," he sheepishly told the police.

Six days later, the police arrested Winston Moseley, a 29-year-old business-machine operator, and charged him with the homicide. Moseley had no police record. On Wednesday, a court committed him to Kings County Hospital for psychiatric observation.

The police repeated how simple it would have been to have gotten in touch with them. "A phone call," said one of the detectives, "would have done it."

Today witnesses from the neighborhood, which is made up of one-family homes in the $35,000 to $60,000 range with the exception of the two apartment houses near the railroad station, find it difficult to explain why they didn't call the police.

A housewife, knowingly if quite unexcited, said, "We thought it was a lover's quarrel," A husband and wife both said, "Frankly, we were afraid." They seemed to understand the fact that events might have been different. An upset woman, wiping her hands in her apron, said, "I didn't want my husband to get involved."

One couple, now willing to talk about that night, said they heard the first screams. The husband looked at the bookstore where the killer first grabbed Miss Genovese.

"We went to the window to see what was happening," he said, "but the light from our bedroom made it difficult to see the street." The wife, still worried, added: "I put out the light and we were able to see better."

Asked why they hadn't called the police, she shrugged and replied: "I don't know."

A man peeked out from a slight opening in the doorway to his apartment and rattled off an account of the killer's second attack. Why hadn't he called the police? "I was tired," he said calmly. "I went back to bed."

It was 4:25 A.M. when the ambulance arrived to take the body of Miss Genovese. It drove off. "Then," a solemn police detective said, "the people came out."

True/False Questions:

_____ 1. Kitty was the nickname of Catherine Genovese.

_____ 2. Catherine Genovese held a daytime job.

_____ 3. Catherine Genovese was a teenager.

_____ 4. Catherine Genovese died after the second stabbing.

_____ 5. The police were baffled by the circumstances of the Genovese murder.

_____ 6. The murderer lived in the same building as Catherine Genovese.

_____ 7. The killer drove a red Fiat.

_____ 8. The neighborhood was a poor one.

_____ 9. Most of the houses were apartment buildings.

_____10. The murderer was captured.

_____11. The murderer had prior arrests.

_____12. Witnesses found it difficult to explain why they didn't call the police.

_____13. Catherine Genovese knew her assailant.

_____14. People didn't phone the police because they didn't want to get involved.

_____15. Some people watched the murder.

STOP. Check answers at the end of Lesson 5.

Practice B.

State the central idea of "38 Who Saw Murder Didn't Call Police."

STOP. Check answer at the end of Lesson 5.

Practice C.

Read this article carefully, and then answer the true/false questions on it. Put a T for *true* or an F for *false* in the blank. (Answer the questions *without rereading* the article.)

From "Would You Obey a Hitler?" by Jeanne Reinert, *Science Digest*, (c) Hearst Corp., 1970.

Vocabulary:

inflict—impose (anything unwelcome); *revolt*—turn away with disgust; *qualms*—pangs of conscience; *flaw*—fault; *reinforcement*—technically anything that makes you continue to do something; *activated*—made active or working; *merits*—deserves; *hoaxed*—fooled, deceived; *pilot study*—experimental or trial study before the full-scale study; *predict*—say what is going to happen before it does; *colleagues*—fellow workers in the same profession; *designations*—markings; *virtually*—practically; *blithely*—without thought or regard; *indifferent*—unconcerned; *dumbfounded*—speechless with amazement; *compliance*—act of giving in, conforming, giving in or yielding readily to another; *successive*—following; *dubious*—doubtful; *torment*—bodily or mental suffering; *proceeded*—went on, went forward; *defy*—resist, disobey; *numbing*—without feeling; *callous*—without feeling, unsympathetic, insensitive; *chaos*—disorder; *prevail*—exist; *conform*—act in accord with certain rules; *outrages*—acts of unjustifiable violence; *defiant*—daringly or boldly resistant to authority; *prestige*—power, reputation; *modest*—humble; *reconciliation*—the act of stopping hostility, the act of restoring to friendship.

Would You Obey a Hitler?*

Who looks in the mirror and sees a person ready and willing to inflict pain and suffering on another in his mercy? Even if commanded? All of our senses revolt against the idea.

The drama of a clearcut choice between obeying orders or qualms of conscience seems clearest for a man in uniform. He must *decide* to pull the trigger.

Being behind the trigger is very dramatic, but obeying orders is an everyday event for all of us. Seldom do we have a chance to test our actions when confronted with a clearcut choice between hurting a person and obeying orders.

In the early 1960s, Stanley Milgram, a psychologist at Yale University, devised an experimental setup to give that choice to subjects. He wanted to measure obedience. He had been taken with the historian's thesis that the Germans shared an extreme trait—a willingness to obey orders. This character flaw was, the theory goes, responsible for the German's carrying out Hitler's mad plan against the Jews. Dr. Milgram wanted to test this theory by comparing obedience in America and in Germany. He disguised his obedience tests as experiments in learning.

Imagine yourself as a subject in Dr. Milgram's setup. You walk into a laboratory on the Yale campus after answering an ad that asked for paid volunteers ($4.50 per hour) for an educational experiment.

At your appointment, you and another volunteer, a nervous man in his 50's, are told that the experiment in which you will participate is set up to test the effect of negative reinforcement on the human learning process. Jack Williams, the experimenter conducting the tests, explains that if punishment makes you learn faster, that's negative reinforcement—as opposed to learning faster when rewarded (positive reinforcement). In this experiment the punishment is an electric shock.

Williams also states, "The money is yours for coming to the laboratory. It's yours no matter what happens."

Then Williams takes two pieces of paper, shakes them together in a hat and each of you draw one to see who will be the teacher and who the learner. The nervous volunteer announces he is the learner; your slip of paper says "teacher."

The experimenter seats the learner in a chair and explains the procedure: "We have to strap down your arms to avoid excessive movement during the experiment.

"This electrode," he continues, "is connected to the shock generator in the next room. Do either of you have any questions before we go into the next room?"

"Are these shocks strong, are they dangerous?" asks the learner.

"No," replies Williams, "although they may be extremely painful, they cause no permanent tissue damage."

The experiment involves word pairing (e.g., nice-day, fat-pig, etc.). You, the teacher, read a word to the learner and ask him to match it with one of four other words. The learner pushes one of four switches to indicate which of the four answers he believes is correct. If he is right, you go on to the next set of words. If he is wrong, you push a switch that buzzes and gives him an electric shock. Then you go to the next group of words.

Your position is before the electric shock generator, 30 levers in a row across the instrument panel. Each lever is clearly labelled in 15-volt jumps from 15 to 450 volts. When a lever is pushed down, a pilot light turns bright red, a buzzer sounds, a blue light flashes under the label "voltage energizer," the dial on the meter swings about and mechanical clicks are heard.

To be sure you know what is going on, you are given a sample shock, activated by the third switch, on the wrist. This 45-volt shock lets you know how the shock feels.

You are instructed to call out the voltage level before pressing the lever each time the learner merits a shock. You note that the levers are marked from left to right in broad categories, "slight shock, moderate shock, strong shock, very strong shock, intense shock, extreme intensity shock, danger: severe shock," and the two switches on the far right are simply marked "XXX."

When the lesson begins, the learner makes a lot of mistakes. In fact, he answers about three wrong answers to one right one. As the shocks get stronger, you are, of course, unhappy about their level. It quickly is apparent that the learner is going to give a lot more wrong answers. So you appeal to Williams, who responds, "Please go on." You protest and he says, "The experiment requires that you continue."

The learner is strapped in, he cannot get free. You have already been assured that the money is yours regardless. The experimenter has no actual authority over you. But he is requesting you to obey his commands. Would you do it? Would you injure the learner just because someone told you to do so? You know from your own experience that the shocks are painful. What you do *not* know is that the experiment is rigged. The learner is not being shocked: in fact, he is in cahoots with the experimenter. He is part of a play, and you are the only person hoaxed in the setup.

Before the pilot study, Dr. Milgram took the idea to a class of senior Yale psychology students and asked them to predict the distribution of behavior among 100 subjects. The entire class predicted that only a very small number of people would go to the extreme 450-volt shock. They predicted from none to three percent of any 100 people. Dr. Milgram's colleagues also thought few, if any, subjects would go beyond the shock labeled "very strong shock."

But they did go beyond. In fact, Dr. Milgram got such complete obedience that there was nothing to measure. He was, after all, interested in getting people to *disobey*. His first 40 people went beyond the expected breakoff point. Not one stopped before 300 volts. Only 14 persons stopped shocking the strapped-in learner before going to the very end of the shocks.

In the pilot studies, no noise was heard from the strapped-in learner. Dr. Milgram had thought that the labels and voltage designations would stop the teachers. But instead virtually everyone "went blithely to the end of the board, seemingly indifferent to the verbal designations."

Dr. Milgram never expected such obedience. So he began to vary the props and scripts in his private play to see what changes would encourage the teacher to rebel.

The first change was to add protests from the victim. Mild protests did no good. Then the victim began to put up a vigorous fight. Dr. Milgram was appalled that many subjects, nonetheless, went to the end of the board, giving the harshest punishment. But at least some subjects did break off and give the experimenters something to measure. It also proved that obedience was much, much stronger than suspected. The victim's cries were tape-recorded so all subjects heard the same protests.

Finding in pilot studies that the teacher turned his eyes away from the victim who could be seen dimly behind a silvered glass, various ways were devised to make it more difficult for the teacher to ignore his victim.

Voice protests were heard. The victim was in another room, but the door was left ajar. At 75 volts, the learner grunted when shocked, also at 90 and 105 volts. At 120 volts, he shouted that the shocks were painful. At 135 volts, he groaned and at 150 he screamed, "Get me out of here! I won't be in the experiment anymore! I refuse to go on!" At 180 volts, he screamed, "I can't stand the pain." Still, 37.5 percent of the teachers went to 450 volts.

Each successive scheme brought the teacher and learner into more personal contact until in the final scheme the victim received a shock only when his hand rested on the shockplate. The experimenter then ordered the teacher to push the subject's hand down on the plate. The teacher actually had to physically subdue the victim against his will to give him the shock. No one was more surprised than Milgram that the very first person so commanded reached over and fell upon the victim's arm. Thirty out of every

100 were still willing to go all the way with the shock level when commanded.

Dumbfounded by this high compliance, Dr. Milgram then decided the prestige of Yale was causing his subjects to be especially obedient. So the experiment was moved to Bridgeport, 20 miles away. There a modest suite of offices was rented in a run-down section. The sign on the door said, "Research Associates of Bridgeport," a deliberately vague title. If anyone asked what the work was for, they were told, "for industry."

Yet, even with this dubious authority, the levels of obedience were high, although not as high as on the Yale campus. Forty-eight percent of the people were totally obedient to the commands versus 65 percent under the same conditions at Yale.

What these scores do not show is the torment that accompanied the teacher's task. Subjects would sweat, tremble, stutter, bite their lips and groan as they were caught up in the web of conflict—to obey the calm experimenter's commands or the call of the poor man being shocked. The teachers often broke out in hysterical laughter.

Persons would argue with the experimenter, asking if he would take the responsibility. They wondered aloud if the victim had a heart condition. Some would exclaim, "You keep the money," but many times they kept on pulling the levers, despite all of their words to the contrary. They would complain that the other guy was suffering, that it was a hell of an experiment. Some got angry. Some just stood up and proceeded to leave the laboratory.

No teacher was kept at the controls once they had reached 450 volts. People either stopped before 350 volts, or carried on to the end, proving there was no limit to their obedience. Hateful as they found it to obey, it must have seemed better for them than to break off.

When those who pressed the levers to the end finished their task, the experimenter called a halt. The obedient teachers were relieved. They would mop their brows. Some fumbled for cigarettes.

Then Mr. Williams rushed to assure the teachers that it wasn't as bad as it seemed. Most important, the teachers met their screaming victim and had a reconciliation. The real purposes of the experiment were explained, and the participants were promised that the full results of the experiment would be sent to them when it was complete. They were asked to describe how they felt and how painful they believed the shocks to be. Also they were to rate on a scale how tense they were during the experiment. Dr. Milgram wanted to be sure that the persons understood that they had been hoaxed and that the man was only acting as he screamed in agony.

Dr. Milgram never imagined that it would be so hard to get people to defy the commands. As he explains, "With numbing regularity good people were seen to knuckle under the demands of authority and perform actions that were callous and severe. Men who in everday life are responsible and decent were seduced by the trappings of authority. . . ."

To date, Dr. Milgram has tested 1,000 people with the steady results—very, very obedient. Of course, if people were not willing to conform to the many rules that link us in a broader society, chaos would prevail. But Milgram's results suggest quite the opposite, that perhaps we have forgotten the formula for saying no. It looks as though few outrages are so grand as to force us to be defiant. "I was only following orders" is going to be with us for a long time.

True/False Questions:

_____ 1. From the article we should believe that most people are likely to obey orders.

_____ 2. The learner strapped in the chair felt pain when the teacher pressed the lever.

_____ 3. The teacher in the experiment did not know how the shock felt.

_____ 4. The teacher would get the money only if he completed the lesson.

_____ 5. The teacher pressed the lever when the learner made a wrong response.

_____ 6. The learner was part of the experiment; that is, he made errors on purpose.

_____ 7. In the pilot study the learners did not make any sounds.

_____ 8. When learners cried out, teachers behaved somewhat differently than when learners did not cry out.

_____ 9. Many teachers still continued to press the lever when the learner cried out.

_____ 10. Dr. Milgram felt that the prestige of Yale influenced the subjects.

_____ 11. An entire senior class of psychology students at Yale predicted that a large number of the teachers would go to the highest 450-volt shock.

_____ 12. Dr. Milgram's colleagues made the same prediction; that is, that most persons would go to the 450-volt shock.

_____ 13. When the surroundings were changed, the levels of obedience were exactly as high as they were at Yale.

_____ 14. The teachers were tormented by their task.

_____ 15. The teachers who pressed the lever to the extreme volt shock were relieved when the task was over.

STOP. Check answers at the end of Lesson 5.

Practice D.

State the central idea of "Would You Obey a Hitler?"

STOP. Check answer at the end of Lesson 5.

VOCABULARY: CONTEXT CLUES (Synonyms) II

Writers use synonyms to make their sentences more descriptive, expressive, or vivid. Read the three example sets of sentences. The second sentence in each set is more descriptive than the first.

Examples:

1. (a) The frightened child *looked* at the man.
   (b) The frightened child *peered* at the man.
2. (a) We *walked* through the park.
   (b) We *strolled* through the park.
3. (a) The *noise* brought the police to the scene.
   (b) The *uproar* brought the police to the scene.

Practice A.

In these sentences determine the meaning of the underlined word from the context clues. Try to give a synonym for the underlined word.

1. It was an <u>affront</u> to me when Jack refused to shake my hand.

   _____

2. We told him not to give a <u>verbose</u> speech because nobody wanted to listen to a long talk after dinner. _____

3. If you're <u>affluent</u>, you can afford a number of luxuries.

   _____

4. The drug was so <u>potent</u> that it knocked me out._____

5. I prefer <u>modest</u> people to conceited ones. _____

6. I become nervous when anyone <u>interrogates</u> me because I never know how to answer questions under pressure._____

7. The decision you made was a <u>prudent</u> one, but George made a rather foolish choice._____

8. She reduced the whole argument to a <u>succinct</u> statement that got quickly to the point._____

9. She was <u>adamant</u> about her decision, and no one tried to talk her out of it._____

10. He felt a wave of <u>apprehension</u> even before he opened the telegram.

    _____

11. I could not hear the salesclerk over the <u>tumult</u> in the bargain basement.

    _____

12. My friend is <u>reluctant</u> to resign his position, although he is unhappy; however, I would be unwilling to work in a place where I was unhappy.

    _____

13. After subjecting the patient to three weeks of tests, the doctors still haven't diagnosed his <u>malady</u>._____

14. The <u>valiant</u> woman saved the boy's life by throwing him a rope over the breaking ice._____

15. Her objection was <u>valid</u>, but the audience was not really interested in sound reasons._____

STOP. Check answers at the end of Lesson 5.

Practice B.

Match the word from column B with its synonym in column A.

	Column A	Column B
_____	1. verbose	a. question
_____	2. affluent	b. unyielding
_____	3. potent	c. disturbance
_____	4. affront	d. wealthy
_____	5. modest	e. brief
_____	6. interrogate	f. insult
_____	7. prudent	g. wordy
_____	8. succinct	h. illness
_____	9. adamant	i. fear
_____	10. apprehension	j. powerful
_____	11. tumult	k. sound
_____	12. reluctant	l. courageous
_____	13. malady	m. wise
_____	14. valiant	n. unwilling
_____	15. valid	o. humble

STOP. Check answers at the end of Lesson 5.

Practice C.

Choose a word from the word list that has the same meaning as the underlined word in the sentence.

Word List:

valiant, reluctant, tumult, succinct, verbose, modest, affluent, potent, prudent, adamant, valid, malady, apprehension, interrogate, affront.

1. Maria said that she felt a great amount of anxiety before exams.
   _____

2. We were unwilling to go to the meeting because we felt that it would be a waste of time. _____

3. Although I do not like egotistical people, my friend Marsha is too humble. _____

4. We were all in a terrible state of shock when the police came to question us about the accident._____

5. On the early frontier, the pioneer women had to be as brave as the men.
   _____

6. Your decision to remain in school rather than drop out is a sensible one.
   _____

7. The child's illness was so strange that the doctors were uncertain how to treat it._____

8. Student opinion is a powerful force in the design of new academic programs._____

9. Jane took it as a personal insult when her groom's best man interrupted the ceremony to propose to her maid of honor.
   _____

10. My friend George becomes very wordy after he has some wine.
    _____

11. May was unyielding in her insistence that Milo should wear shoes and socks with his tuxedo. _____

12. Although you have a sound reason for not wanting to go, we would like you to reconsider. _____

13. There was a <u>commotion</u> in our dormitory when we learned that a prowler was in the building. _____

14. Because my parents are not <u>wealthy,</u> I have to put myself through school. _____

15. Our speech professor insists on speeches that are <u>concise</u> and lively.

_____

STOP. Check answers at the end of Lesson 5.

WORD ANALYSIS: SPECIAL LETTERS AND SOUNDS

1. As already mentioned, *y* is used as both a consonant and a vowel. (See Lessons 1 and 4.) When *y* is at the beginning of a word or syllable it is a consonant. Examples: yes, yet, young, yellow, your, canyon, graveyard.

Special Note

In the words *canyon* and *graveyard, y* begins the second syllable; therefore it is a consonant. (See Lessons 6 and 7 on syllabication.)

2. When *y* acts as a vowel, it represents the short *i* sound, the long *i* sound, or the long *e* sound.

a. *Y* usually represents the short *i* sound when *y* is in the middle of a word or syllable that has no vowel letter. Examples: hymn, gym, synonym, cymbal.

b. *Y* usually represents the long *i* sound when it is at the end of a single-syllable word that has no vowel letter. Examples: by, try, why, dry, fly.

c. *Y* usually represents the long *e* sound when it is at the end of a multisyllabic word (a word with many syllables). Examples: baby, ferry, candy, daddy, family.

3. Some words beginning with *c* or *g* can cause you problems because the letters *c* and *g* stand for both a hard and a soft sound.

a. The letter *g* in *gym, George, gentle,* and *generation* stands for a soft *g* sound. A soft *g* sounds like *j* in *Jack, jail, justice.*

b. The initial letter *c* in *cease, center, cent, cite* stands for a soft *c* sound. A soft *c* sounds like *s* in *so, same, sew*.

c. The initial letter *g* in *go, get, game, gone*, and *garden* stands for a hard *g* sound. A hard *g* sound appears in words such as *bug, tag, got, tug*, and *go*.

d. The initial letter *c* in *cat, came, cook, call, course*, and *carry* stands for a hard *c* sound. A hard *c* sounds like *k* in *key, king, kite, kettle*.

Special Note

Notice that the letter *c* represents a sound that is either like an *s* in *see* or like a *k* in *kitten*.

4. The letter *q* is always followed by the letter *u*. It represents either one sound or a blend of two sounds.

a. At the beginning of a word *qu* almost always represents a blend of two sounds (*kw*). Examples: queen, quick, quilt, quiet, queer, quack.

b. When *qu* appears at the end of a word, in a que combination, it represents one sound (*k*). Examples: unique, antique, clique.

5. The *schwa* sound is symbolized by an upside down *e* (ə) in the phonetic (speech) alphabet. The schwa sound frequently appears in the unstressed (unaccented) syllables of words with more than one syllable. The schwa, which usually sounds like the short *u* in *but*, is represented by a number of different vowels. Examples: believe—(bə • lēvȼ) police—(pə • lēs) divide—(də • vīdȼ) robust—(rō • bəst) Roman—(rō • mən). In the examples the italicized vowels represent the schwa sound. Although the spelling of the unstressed syllable in each word is different, the sound remains the same for the different vowels. (See Lessons 7 and 8.)

Special Note

The pronunciations presented in paragraph 5 come from *Webster's New Collegiate Dictionary*, which is not to say that these are the only pronunciations for these words. Pronunciations may vary from dictionary to dictionary and from region to region. However, when the schwa sound appears in a dictionary, it usually sounds like the short *u* in *but*. (See Lesson 11 on the dictionary).

6. A vowel followed by *r* in the same syllable, is controlled by the *r*. As a result, the preceding vowel does not have the usual long or short vowel sound. Examples: car, fir, or, hurt, perch.

Special Note

If a vowel is followed by *r* but the *r* begins another syllable, the vowel is *not* influenced by *r*. Examples: ī · rāt¢, tī · rād¢.

Review of Some Vowel Rules

1. A long vowel is one that sounds like the name of the vowel.

2. A single vowel followed by a consonant in a word or syllable usually has a short vowel sound.

3. A single vowel at the end of a word or syllable usually has a long vowel sound.

4. A vowel digraph consists of two adjacent vowels with one vowel sound. Usually the first vowel is long and the second is silent. There are exceptions, such as *believe*, in which the two vowels form a single sound where the first vowel is not long.

5. In words or syllables containing two vowels separated by a consonant, and one vowel is a final *e*, the first vowel is usually long and the final *e* is silent, as in *bāk¢*.

6. A vowel followed by *r*, is controlled by the consonant *r*.

7. When *y* is at the end of a word containing no other vowels the *y* represents the long sound of *i*, as in *my, sky*.

8. Diphthongs are blends of vowel sounds, beginning with the first and gliding to the second, as *oi* in *boil* and *ou* in *house*.

Practice A.

In the blank before each word write the number of the statement in the Clues to Vowel Sounds that helps you determine the vowel sound in the word.

Clues to Vowel Sounds:

1. A single vowel letter at the beginning or in the middle is a clue to a short vowel sound—as in *hat, let, it, hot*, and *cup*.

2. A single vowel letter at the end of a word is a clue to a long vowel sound —as in *we*, *by*, and *go*.

3. Two vowel letters together are usually a clue to a long vowel sound—as in *rain*, *day*, *dream*, *feel*, and *boat*.

4. Two vowel letters, one of which is a final *e*, are a clue to a long vowel sound—as in *age*, *ice*, *bone*, and *cube*.

5. A vowel letter followed by *r* is a clue to a vowel sound that is neither long nor short—as in *far*, *bird*, *her*, *horn*, *care*, and *hair*.

_____	she	_____	grave	_____	curb
_____	pill	_____	plot	_____	up
_____	oak	_____	drain	_____	pair
_____	lung	_____	harsh	_____	coax
_____	mane	_____	whine	_____	charm
_____	hurl	_____	freak	_____	plead
_____	bean	_____	glare	_____	flag
_____	hi	_____	fry	_____	pride
_____	heel	_____	bray	_____	birch
_____	scar	_____	stem	_____	note
_____	mule	_____	bale	_____	ebb
_____	firm	_____	port	_____	bait
_____	doze	_____	toast	_____	lime
_____	aim	_____	try	_____	spare
_____	flock	_____	fleet	_____	ox
_____	nor	_____	odd	_____	berth
_____	brisk	_____	lope	_____	so
_____	cab	_____	fern	_____	stray
_____	greed	_____	fuse	_____	cork
_____	goal				
_____	perch				

STOP. Check answers at the end of Lesson 5.

ANSWERS: Lesson 5 (pp. 96-124)

Learning Skills: Concentration—Listening/Reading II (pp. 96-102)

Practice A

Check answers with digits on p. 97.

Practice B

Check answers with digits on pp. 98–99.

Practice C

Check answers by reading the directions and comparing the following to your responses.

(1) go ~~2~~ 1   (2) 90 bo~~x~~ 19 25   (3) ~~*~~ ~~*~~ 4 * ha(p)p(y) (4) *
10 * (*) (5) (15) m(a)n   (5) 79 86 (45) ~~98~~ ~~girl~~ (6) big cat cow
(7) 4 (1)   (7) * * * small dog 3 7 67 5   (8) ~~I~~ R ~~M~~ (G) A
~~B~~ C 9 12 ~~15~~   (9) 17 14 19 pa~~x~~ * * call C R S U W
(10) * (*) sat * (15) 20 18 (17) A Q L (G) M T F fat

Practice D

Check answers immediately after each set.

121

Practice E

Check answers by rereading the instructions and by comparing the following to your responses.

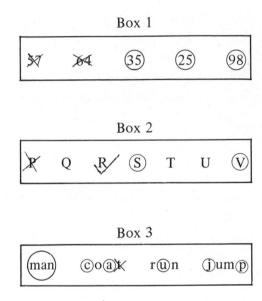

Box 1

Box 2

Box 3

Reading: Central Idea of an Article (pp. 102–113)

Practice A

1. T 2. F 3. F 4. F 5. T 6. F 7. F 8. F 9. F 10. T 11. F 12. T 13. F 14. T 15. T

Practice B

People watched a murder but did not phone the police or otherwise try to save the victim.

Practice C

1. T 2. F 3. F 4. F 5. T 6. T 7. T 8. T 9. T 10. T 11. F 12. F 13. F 14. T 15. T

Practice D

An experiment showed that people are likely to hurt others if commanded to do so by someone in authority.

Vocabulary: Context Clues (Synonyms) II (pp. 113–117)

Practice A

1. insult 2. wordy 3. wealthy 4. powerful 5. humble 6. questions 7. wise, sensible 8. brief, concise 9. stubborn, unyielding 10. anxiety, fear 11. disturbance, commotion 12. unwilling 13. illness, sickness, disease 14. courageous, brave 15. sound

Practice B

1. g 2. d 3. j 4. f 5. o 6. a 7. m 8. e 9. b 10. i 11. c 12. n 13. h 14. l 15. k

Practice C

1. apprehension 2. reluctant 3. modest 4. interrogate 5. valiant 6. prudent 7. malady 8. potent 9. affront 10. verbose 11. adamant 12. valid 13. tumult 14. affluent 15. succinct

Word Analysis: Special Letters and Sounds (pp. 117–120)

Practice A

2	she	1	flock	2	fry
1	pill	5	nor	3	bray
3	oak	1	brisk	1	stem
1	lung	1	cab	4	bale
4	mane	3	greed	5	port
5	hurl	3	goal	3	toast
3	bean	5	perch	2	try
2	hi	4	grave	3	fleet
3	heel	1	plot	1	odd
5	scar	3	drain	4	lope
4	mule	5	harsh	5	fern
5	firm	4	whine	4	fuse
4	doze	3	freak	5	curb
3	aim	5	glare	1	up

5	pair	5	birch	1	ox
3	coax	4	note	5	berth
5	charm	1	ebb	2	so
3	plead	3	bait	3	stray
1	flag	4	lime	5	cork
4	pride	5	spare		

LESSON 6

Learning Skills: Concentration–Listening/Reading III
Reading: Central Idea of a Story
Vocabulary: Context Clues (Antonyms)
Word Analysis: Syllabication Rules
Answers
Crossword Puzzle
Homograph Riddles
True/False Test

LEARNING SKILLS: CONCENTRATION–LISTENING/READING III

Your attitude or mental set toward what you are doing influences greatly how well you do. *Positive* thinking works. Go to lectures prepared to learn, and approach your assignments with interest. If you are not interested in the lecture or your reading assignment, you will not be able to concentrate.

If you have practiced the given concentration exercises at regular times during the week, you should be increasing your attention span. This lesson includes the Detroit Test of Oral Directions, which is an assessment of your listening concentration skill.

Practice A.

(Listening) This practice requires both a speaker and a listener. (Two students can team up and take turns playing the two roles for this activity.) Speaker: "Here are a group of digits. Listen carefully. Do not write until you are told to. I will start with just two, but it will become more difficult as we go on. Listen carefully and write the numbers as soon as I stop. For example, if I say '7, 9,' you should write '7, 9.' " (The rate for presentation of digits is one per second.) Listener writes digits. (Two sets of digits are given. The second set is used when the speaker becomes the listener.)

125

Numbers for Digits Forward:

Span

(2)   7 4
      9 1

(3)   4 1 2
      6 2 9

(4)   3 8 5 4
      9 7 2 6

(5)   5 2 7 1 3
      6 9 8 4 7

(6)   1 6 9 2 5 4
      7 5 8 6 3 1

(7)   9 4 6 3 8 5 2
      2 7 5 6 9 3 8

(8)   1 7 4 9 3 8 2 5
      5 9 3 8 1 6 4 2

(9)   3 8 1 9 2 5 3 7 4
      6 2 5 9 4 8 3 7 1

STOP: Check answers. (Compare your digits with those on this page.)

Scoring Procedure:

To be correct, every digit must be presented in the exact order that it was stated.

Points	Maximum Score (Per Set)
Span (2) ½ point	½ point
Span (3) 1 point	1 point
Span (4) 1½ points	1½ points
Span (5) 2 points	2 points
Span (6) 2½ points	2½ points
Span (7) 3 points	3 points

Span (8)   3½ points   3½ points

Span (9)   4   points   4   points
                            —————————
                            18   points

Score for Practice A: ____

Practice B.

(Listening) This practice requires both a speaker and a listener. (Two students can team up and take turns playing the two roles for this activity.) Speaker: "Here are a group of digits. Listen carefully. Do not write until you are told to. I will start with just two, but it will become more difficult as we go on. Listen carefully and write the numbers *backward* as soon as I stop. For example, if I say '7, 9,' you should write '9, 7.' Do not write them first forward and then backward. They must be written in backward form immediately." (The rate for presentation of numbers is one per second.) Listener writes digits. (Two sets of digits are given. The second set of digits is used when the speaker becomes the listener.)

Numbers for Digits Backward:
 Span

(2)   5 9
      6 2

(3)   7 5 1
      3 4 6

(4)   1 9 7 3
      5 8 2 4

(5)   6 8 3 9 1
      7 5 1 4 3

(6)   9 6 5 7 2 1
      7 4 8 5 3 6

(7)   9 1 5 3 7 2 4
      5 3 1 6 7 8 2

(8)   1 4 5 9 3 6 8 7
      3 9 6 4 7 2 5 1

(9)   4 9 5 8 6 1 3 7 2
      2 5 7 9 3 1 4 8 6

STOP. Check answers. (To check answers, read digits backward.)

Scoring Procedure:

To be correct, every digit must be presented in the exact backward order from what was stated.

Points		Maximum Score (Per Set)
Span (2)	½ point	½ point
Span (3)	1 point	1 point
Span (4)	1½ points	1½ points
Span (5)	2½ points	2½ points
Span (6)	3½ points	3½ points
Span (7)	4 points	4 points
Span (8)	4½ points	4½ points
Span (9)	5 points	5 points
		22½ points

Score for Practice B: ___

Practice C.

(Listening)   The Detroit Test of Oral Directions* is an assessment of a student's listening concentration skill. This test requires both a speaker (tester) and a listener (subject). (Two students can team up and take turns playing the two roles for this test.) The General Instructions, Oral Instructions, Listener's Sheet, and Scoring follow.

General Instructions

Place the sheet before the subject. Give the directions for each set *slowly* and *very* clearly without special emphasis on any word or phrase. Be sure that the subject waits until the directions for a given set are *completed* before he is permitted to start. Say, "You see this page. I am going to tell you some things to do with what you see on this page. Now, listen carefully, and each time after I get through, you do just exactly what I have said to do. Be sure to wait each time until I finish and say, 'Do it now.' Look at No. 1. It has three drawings." (Point to all three on the Listener's Sheet. Pause.)

Give directions for each set as indicated. Say, "Stop," at the end of each time allowance. Any set must be entirely correct for credit.

* From *Detroit Tests of Learning Aptitude* by Harry J. Baker. Reprinted by permission of Bobbs-Merrill Educational Publishing.

It is best to call attention to the next set by saying, "Look at No. 2," "Look at No. 3," etc., throughout the test.

Continue through three successive failures.

Oral Instructions:

Time allowance is 10 seconds each for numbers 1 to 6, inclusive.

1. Put a 1 in the circle and a cross in the square box. Do it now!

2. Draw a line from the thimble to the star that will go down under the comb and up over the hammer. Do it now!

3. Be sure to wait until I get all through. Draw a line from the rabbit to the ball that will go up over the fish, and put a cross on the fish. Do it now!

4. See the three circles. Put a number 2 in the 1st circle, put a cross in the 2nd circle, and draw a line under the 3rd circle. Do it now!

5. Draw a line from the bottom of the 1st circle to the top of the 2nd and put a cross in the 2nd circle. Do it now!

6. Put a 3 in the part that is the large box only and a cross in the part that is in both boxes. Do it now!

Time allowance is 15 seconds each for numbers 7, 8, and 9.

7. This drawing is divided into parts. Put a number 1 in the biggest part, a 2 in the smallest part, and a 3 in the last part. Do it now!

8. Draw a circle around the pig, put a line under the apple, and make a cross on the cow. Do it now!

9. Draw a line under the letter F. Cross out the letter K, and draw a line above O. Do it now!

Time allowance is 20 seconds each for numbers 10, 11, and 12.

10. Cross out the number that is 3 × 5, cross out every number that is in the 30s, and cross out the largest number. Do it now!

11. Put the 1st letter of the 1st word in the 1st circle, the 2nd letter of the 1st word in the 2nd circle, the last letter of the 1st word in the 4th circle, and the last letter of the last word in the last circle. Do it now!

12. Put a cross in the big square, a letter F in the triangle, a number 4 in the little square, and a letter H in the 1st circle. Do it now!

Time allowance is 30 seconds each for numbers 13 to 17, inclusive.

13. Cross out a number that is 8 × 8, the number that is 1 less than 100, the number that is 5 × 5, the number in the 50s, and the 4th number in the line. Do it now!

14. Put the last letter of the 2nd word in the 3rd circle, the 1st letter of the 3rd word in the 5th circle, and the 2nd letter of the 1st word in the last circle. Do it now!

15. Draw a line under the letter after S, cross out J and V, and draw a line over the first letter before O. Do it now!

16. Put the 3rd letter of the alphabet in the 3rd figure, a 6 in the diamond, the letter L in the 1st circle, a number 4 in the triangle, and the 1st letter of the alphabet in the last figure. Do it now!

17. Cross out the even number in a square, the odd number in the 2nd triangle, the number in the 3rd circle, the biggest number that is in a square, and the number in a circle before 12. Do it now!

Listener's Sheet:

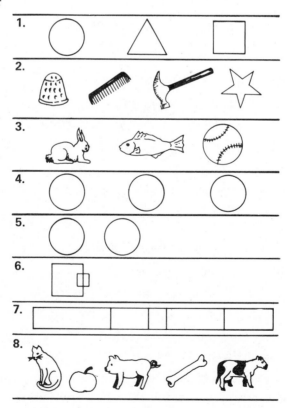

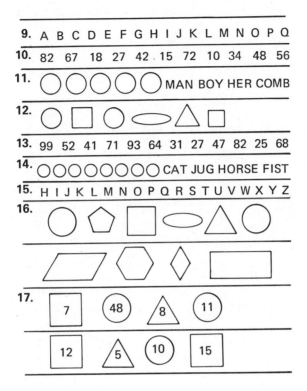

9. A B C D E F G H I J K L M N O P Q

10. 82 67 18 27 42 15 72 10 34 48 56

11. ◯◯◯◯◯ MAN BOY HER COMB

12. ◯ ▢ ◯ ⬭ △ ▢

13. 99 52 41 71 93 64 31 27 47 82 25 68

14. ◯◯◯◯◯◯◯◯ CAT JUG HORSE FIST

15. H I J K L M N O P Q R S T U V W X Y Z

16. ◯ ⬠ ▢ ⬭ △ ◯
    ▱ ⬡ ◇ ▭

17. 7 ⦅48⦆ △8 ⦅11⦆
    12 △5 ⦅10⦆ 15

STOP. Check answers by reading the directions and comparing your Listener's Sheet with the one given at the end of Lesson 6.

Scoring:

Credit as follows:

     Items 1–6, 1 point each   Items 10–13, 3 points each

     Items 7–9, 2 points each   Items 14–17, 4 points each

Maximum Score:

40 points

Practice D.

(Reading) Here are nine sets of one-syllable words. Read each set of words *once*. Concentrate. Cover the set of words and write it in the blank. Check your results immediately.

1. can dog_____
2. milk mail book_____
3. sad none in may_____
4. name said bike pen man_____
5. chair name key same hop note_____
6. witch rob sleep some read check nut_____
7. spoon mate can more all book sad show _____
8. boat lamp paint long dock teach knife win chair _____
9. sew ball two four nine help swim eight one six _____

Practice E.

(Readings) Read each numbered instruction carefully *once*, and then carry out the stated directions on the Following Instructions Sheet.

Instructions:

1. Put a dot in the middle figure in box 1, a cross on the number that is 1 less than 5 X 5 in box 2, and a circle around the 2nd letter of the 1st word in box 3.

2. Put a cross on the 1st square in box 1, a dot in the 2nd circle in box 1, a circle around the 2nd vowel in the 4th word in box 3, and a cross on the number equal to 10 X 10 in box 2.

3. In box 3 put a circle around the 1st letter of the 4th word, a cross on the 3rd letter of the 3rd word, a circle around the 2nd letter of the 3rd word, and a cross on the 3rd letter of the 1st word.

4. In box 2 circle the number equal to 1 less than 4 X 4, in box 4 circle the letter before N and the letter after O, and in box 3 circle the 3rd letter of the 2nd word.

5. Put a cross on the 1st letter of the 3rd word and the 2nd vowel in the 1st word in box 3, put a cross on the 3rd letter in box 4, put a circle around the last square in box 1, and put a circle around the number equal to 4 X 3 in box 2.

Following Instructions Sheet:

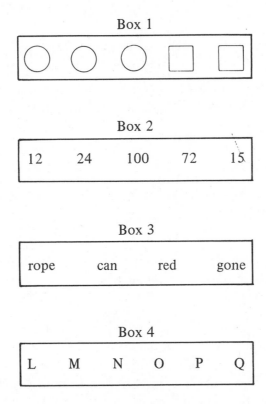

Box 1

Box 2

12   24   100   72   15

Box 3

rope   can   red   gone

Box 4

L   M   N   O   P   Q

STOP. Check answers by rereading the instructions and by comparing your answers with those at the end of Lesson 6.

Practice F.

(Reading)   Read each numbered instruction carefully *once*, and then carry out the stated directions on the Following Instructions Sheet.

Instructions:

1. If there are two numbers that equal 7 and a word that rhymes with *may*, put a line under the rhyming word.

2. If there is a word that means the same as *large*, a word opposite to *go*, and a word that rhymes with *fan*, put a circle around the three words.

3. If there are two numbers that equal 8, two numbers that equal 67, and a word the opposite of *over*, underline the two numbers that equal 8.

4. If there are five consecutive letters, four words that each contain a different vowel, and at least four odd numbers, put a cross on the five consecutive letters.

5. If there are six words, three even numbers, two numbers that equal 45, and three numbers that equal 16, put a line under the letter M.

6. If there are two numbers that equal 25, two numbers that equal 95, and three numbers that equal 79, put a circle around the three numbers that equal 79.

Following Instructions Sheet:

1 7 3 4 play dog man M N O P Q 35 32 63 15 10   stop
under big

STOP. Check answers by rereading the instructions and by comparing your answers with those at the end of Lesson 6.

READING: CENTRAL IDEA OF A STORY

It is usually more difficult to state the central idea of a story than of an article or essay, because the central idea of a story is implied rather than stated directly. The technique presented in Lessons 1 and 3 should prove helpful in finding the central idea of stories. First, find the topic of the story and then determine what the writer is saying that is special about the topic. Remember, all the paragraphs in the story should develop the central idea. The central idea is a general statement of the content of the story.

Practice A.

Read this short story carefully and then answer the true/false questions on it. Put a T for *true* or an F for *false* in the blank. (Answer the questions without rereading the story.)

From "The Flower" by Sharon Anne Rubin Johnson.

Vocabulary:

surpassed—was superior to; *contemptible*—vile, despicable; *hideous*—ugly, dreadful; *demon*—devil; *sequence*—the following of one thing after another, order; *ferocious*—savage, fierce; *irresistible*—too tempting to resist; *agony*—extreme and prolonged pain and suffering; *briskness*—liveliness; *persistently*—

continuously, without giving up; *stealthily*—secretly, with hidden cautious movement; *horticulturist*—gardener, one skilled in the art and science of flowers; *placid*—calm; *grotesque*—ugly, misshapen; *beholders*—onlookers; *frenzy*—wild excitement; *despair*—hopelessness.

"The Flower"

I looked forward eagerly to seeing my sweetheart as I set out early in the morning to walk to her house. I had done this many times, so the experience was not new to me. The houses, the cobblestone street, the tall leafy oaks—everything the same. I walked on with not a care in the world—until I saw the flower. It was the most beautiful thing I have ever seen. Its color was a creamy white that shone like silk. I am not a horticulturist, so I cannot tell you its name. It looked something like a rose but much fuller and softer. It had many, many petals that gave it a look like a ruffled gown. My words do not do it justice, for it was so beautiful that just one look at it made its beholder want it passionately.

The flower was in a garden of many varied flowers, all very beautiful, but this flower surpassed all the rest. The garden was situated approximately half a mile off the main road on a dirt path. I had passed it often when using the path to shorten my journey, but I had not noticed the flower previously. Now that I had seen it, though, I decided it would make a lovely gift for my beloved. So I hastened to pick it. But it was not to be mine. Just as I touched the velvet stem—just as I was to pull it from its place— a dog, a scruffy, contemptible, hideous dog, jumped up from the ground with a snarl such as I had never heard before. I had seen him on other occasions but had taken little notice of him; he had seemed a placid enough fellow. But now this beast that I looked at was surely no dog at all but a demon in disguise. I can remember distinctly the glare in his eyes that froze me in my steps. I thought then that I truly knew what it was to see a dog's lips curl. And, oh, that terrible growl. It was the most remarkable thing about him. His whole body seemed to tremble with it. It started as a low grumble that grew louder and louder till I thought my eardrums would burst. I thought to myself no lion could outroar this small but monstrous dog.

After I recovered my senses, I wasted no time in escaping. I was lucky that there was a fence. I shudder to think of my fate had there been none.

So, I proceeded to my sweetheart's without the flower. This sequence was to recur many times. Whenever I passed the flower and was about to pick it, the dog would leap into the air and become a ferocious beast. And each time I passed it, the flower seemed to become more beautiful, more and more irresistible. You cannot imagine the agony I went through. How often I stealthily crept up to the flower, how many times I held in my hands the graceful stem but each time gave in to the dog. At night he haunted my dreams. During the day I heard his unearthly snarls persistently. Always on my mind was the flower, the beautiful flower. I feared for my sanity.

I had no idea who was the master of the brute. Indeed, I often wondered if anyone could possess him. I saw not one house along the path, and had always thought the land there unoccupied by humans. But, then again, I had never looked for any human signs. Nevertheless, whether the area was occupied by people or not, I knew what I was to do to maintain my sanity. I would have to get rid of the dog.

From my point of view it was quite a simple task. As I have said, the dog was always quiet until I started to pick the flower. The more I thought about it, the easier the deed seemed. I felt better than I had in weeks, but I was anxious to have it done so that I could possess the flower.

It was late in the afternoon when I started once more to the flower. My legs seemed to acquire a briskness of pace I had never known them to have. When I reached the spot, I stopped for a moment unsure. In all my time spent thinking of killing the dog I had never given much thought to details. But then a wild instinct drove me on. My feet clambered over the fence and before I realized it I was standing on the other side. My heart was pounding furiously as I took a step toward the sleeping dog. I was almost upon him when some instinct must have awakened him, for I had approached him with the utmost of caution. I saw the dog make ready for attack, but before he could move, I sprang upon him. It was a thrilling battle, but I never once doubted who would emerge the victor. I was merely a tool for my hate and revenge. They commanded me, and I carried out their commands. When I felt him a corpse in my hands, I buried the dog in the garden and would have picked the flower then, but for the blood and dirt that covered me like a blanket. I found a stream not too far from the flower and I cleansed myself there. By the time all this was accomplished it was quite dark, so I spent the night beside the stream.

Such a gloomy night I have yet to experience again. It was pitch black, without a star in the sky. But I had a great feeling of satisfaction and relief. I was at last free of the hideous beast. My dreams were untormented. My thoughts still centered on the flower, but this time with content, for in the morning I would have it for mine.

I arose at dawn the next morning and rushed to the flower at last. My feelings I cannot describe, so content, so happy, so joyous was I that morning—until I reached the flower. In frenzy I thought at first that I was in the wrong garden. But, no, I remembered the bush and trees; everything there was the same, untouched, except for the flower. Where could it be? I searched every branch of the bush but not a trace of the flower was to be found. Then, as I hung my head low in despair my eyes caught sight of something under the bush. It was a flower; but surely, surely, not the flower! Its stem was broken and coarse; its crumpled and squashed petals were a grotesque brown that seemed a decayed ghost of life. But, yes, it was the flower. At the very tip of one of the brown petals was a minute tinge of white. A white that could not be mistaken. Yet as I touched the spot the pureness of the white disappeared, and in its place spread the dullness and drabness of the brown.

True/False Questions:

_____ 1. We know the name and age of the person in the story.

_____ 2. The person in the story is a man.

_____ 3. The garden was situated on the main road.

_____ 4. The person wanted the flower as a gift.

_____ 5. The dog protected the flower.

_____ 6. The person made a number of attempts to pick the flower.

_____ 7. The person was obsessed with the desire to own the flower.

_____ 8. The dog was always ferocious.

_____ 9. The person killed the dog while the dog was asleep.

_____ 10. The person spent the night sleeping under a sky filled with shining stars.

STOP. Check answers at the end of Lesson 6.

Practice B.

State the central idea of "The Flower."

STOP. Check answers at the end of Lesson 6.

Practice C.

Read this short story carefully and then answer the true/false questions on it. Put a T for *true* or an F for *false* in the blank. (Answer the questions without rereading the story.)

From "The Day We Lost Max" by Lael Littke.

Vocabulary:

robust—healthy; *apt*—suitable; *cowered*—shrank with fear; *wilted*—became limp; *ajar*—partly open; *furrow*—a deep, narrow rut or a track make by a wheel.

The Day We Lost Max*

We probably wouldn't even have noticed that Max had fallen out of the truck if Randolph hadn't seen him go. That's the way Max was. He could sit right next to you for hours, sucking his thumb and sometimes humming a little to himself, and you wouldn't even know he was there, and when you finally noticed he wasn't, you wouldn't be able to remember just when it was he left. He was Aunt Veona's youngest, the last of eleven robust children, and Aunt Veona herself said she sometimes had a hard time remembering he was around since in all his five years he had made hardly any more noise than the soft slurping as he sucked his thumb, and the occasional humming.

*Reprinted by permission of Larry Sternig Literary Agency. First printed in *Ladies' Home Journal*, October, 1969.

Aunt Veona, Mama, three of our kids, and six of Aunt Veona's were on our way to visit Aunt Blanche up Pigeon Creek when Max fell out. It was crowded in the back of the pickup truck, what with nine of us kids trying to cling somewhere so we wouldn't bounce out. Randolph said Max stood up, probably to shift his position, and just then the truck hit a bump in the rutted dirt road. Max went over the side without a sound.

"Max fell out," said Randolph in a hoarse, scared voice.

We didn't hear him over the roar of the old truck's engine, so Randolph began pointing frantically back down the road. There, beside a clump of weeds into which he had fallen, Max stood watching us retreat, a thumb still in his mouth.

"Mama!" screamed Utahna, banging on the driver's cab. "Mama, Max fell out!"

"Stop that banging!" bellowed Aunt Veona.

My brother Orvid pounded on Mama's side. "Max fell out!" he yelled.

Mama called something, but we couldn't hear it above the engine's noise.

We all looked at one another, our eyes enormous. "Mama!" we wailed collectively. "Stop!"

Alas! Too often had we cried "Wolf" in the past. Too often we had played tricks on Mama and Aunt Veona. If they heard us at all they discounted our cries as just another prank.

What could we do? Leonard volunteered to crawl out of the truck bed onto the running board, but Aunt Veona saw him in the mirror and in turning around to tell him to get back in, made the truck zigzag across the road.

Through the window of the cab we could see Mama and Aunt Veona talking together, so engrossed in their conversation that they probably wouldn't have noticed if all of us had fallen out. They always discussed Life when they were driving along like that, and any child lucky enough to ride up front could learn some pretty interesting things since they were apt to forget you were there, especially if you sat still and pretended to be asleep.

I had an idea they were talking about how Opal Calder had run off with a linoleum salesman three months ago, and had just come home; and how everyone told Orville he shouldn't take her back. But he said he was tired of feeding the chickens and getting his own meals, and Opal was a good worker and a fine cook even though she did crave a little excitement now and then.

By the time Aunt Veona stopped the truck in Aunt Blanche's yard we were all in a state of shock and just sat there trying to find our voices.

Aunt Blanche and several of her children came running out to welcome us.

"My stars," she said looking into the back of the truck where we sat, "the kids are all carsick. All pale and bug-eyed."

Aunt Veona climbed down from the cab and looked at us. "What's the matter?" she asked.

"Max fell out," whispered Utahna.

"Max?" said Aunt Veona.

"Fell out," whispered Randolph.

Mama got down from the running board where whe was standing, and she and Aunt Veona stirred through all of us children as if they expected to uncover Max somewhere in our midst.

"Max isn't here," Aunt Veona said.

"He fell out," said Maudie.

"In some weeds," said Arthur. "He ain't hurt bad."

"Unless his head was cracked," suggested Utahna.

Aunt Veona grabbed the nearest child, who happened to be Arthur, and shook him hard. "Why didn't you tell me?" she demanded.

"They banged on the top of the cab," recalled Mama. "I thought they were playing."

"We'd better hurry back and get him," said Aunt Blanche. She, Mama, and Aunt Veona climbed into the cab, and five of her kids got in back with us.

Max was nowhere in sight when we got to the place where he had fallen out.

"He's gone," Aunt Veona said weakly after we had searched all the clumps of bushes nearby.

"Maybe he's dead," whispered Utahna.

"Hush," said Mama. "If he were dead he'd still be here, wouldn't he?"

We stared at each other silently.

"Remember, how he used to not cry when he fell and hurt himself?" said Maudie, sniffing back her tears.

"How he'd just suck his thumb all the harder?"

"Remember how he used to just sit and listen when all of us were talking around the stove at night?" Randolph said. "And how once he fell asleep by the woodbox and we forgot he was there and left him all night?"

Georgie broke into loud wails. Violet, one of Aunt Blanche's kids, joined him. "I can't remember which one was Max," she wept.

Aunt Veona was close to tears herself. "He was the best little boy," she sniffed. "Made me a little birthday card last week all by himself."

"No, Mama," said Leonard. "That was me."

"Well," said Aunt Blanche briskly, "let's not stand here talking about him as if we'd never see him again. Let's all get back in and drive down the road. Maybe somebody picked him up and is looking for us."

"Maybe he's kidnapped," whispered Utahna, creating another crisis. Faced with thirteen blubbering children, Aunt Veona shoved us all in the truck and we drove back down the road, peering all along the way for a small boy who sucked his thumb.

"If Max was here," said Randolph as we bounced along, "I would ask him if he was hurt and I'd tell everybody to shut up long enough to hear what he said."

"Look," cried Utahna, who was standing up so she could see better, "here comes the sheriff."

We cowered down in the truck bed, since we were all a little afraid of the tall law man with his big hat and vast stomach.

As the sheriff's car drew alongside us, we saw Max sitting beside Sheriff Smith.

"Maybe it's against the law to fall out," whispered Utahna.

Sheriff Smith hailed Aunt Veona, who stopped the truck with a jerk. "Max," she shrieked, tumbling from the cab and almost strangling Max as she hugged him through the open window of the sheriff's car. After a short spell of weeping, she lifted him out, and felt his head for possible injuries.

"Feller picked him up and brought him to town," said Sheriff Smith.

Max looked at the ground, sucked his thumb, and said nothing.

"I didn't know whose kid he was," continued the sheriff. "Said his name was Macth, but didn't know if he had another name. Said he fell out of a big truck full of more people than he could count." Sheriff Smith looked us over and nodded, "Had to be you."

"He *said* all that?" exclaimed Aunt Veona.

"Lady, that isn't all he said," Sheriff Smith told her. "About talked my ear off. Told me you said his Uncle Archie wears a girdle. Said your kids smoked a pack of cigarettes out in the willows yesterday."

We wilted under his gaze.

"Let's see now. He said he didn't think you'd notice he was gone because his Uncle Ellis said you're kind of careless and it runs in the family and that's why you've got so many kids."

"That's enough," snapped Mama. She nodded toward all of us kids who were listening with our mouths ajar.

Aunt Veona's mouth was ajar, too. "Max said all that?"

The sheriff nodded. "And more. Talked like he'd never get another chance."

Our gazes shifted to Max, who stood tracing a furrow in the dust with his toe while he sucked his thumb and hummed softly.

"Max," said Aunt Veona. "Are you all right? How do you feel?"

Max looked at her. His eyes shifted to the vast crowd of us children who looked at him quietly and expectantly. It was probably the first time he'd ever seen us all silent.

Suddenly he removed his thumb from his mouth and shoved his hand into his pocket. A grin split his face.

"Thwell," he said.

True/False Questions:

_____ 1. Max had ten brothers and sisters.

_____ 2. Max was a listener.

_____ 3. Max didn't speak because no one listened to him.

_____ 4. Max jumped out of the truck on purpose.

_____ 5. Max's mother and aunt were very careful about what they said in front of the children.

_____ 6. The children often played pranks on their mothers.

_____ 7. People were not usually aware that Max was around.

_____ 8. Max was good in arithmetic.

_____ 9. Max's family was known in the community.

_____ 10. Max spoke with a lisp.

_____ 11. The mothers were careful about their children.

STOP. Check answers at the end of Lesson 6.

Practice D.

State the central idea of "The Day We Lost Max."

STOP. Check answer at the end of Lesson 6.

VOCABULARY: CONTEXT CLUES (Antonyms)

1. Antonyms are words opposite in meaning to each other. Examples: tall—short; fat—thin; least—most; worst—best.

2. In Lesson 2 you learned that when a writer uses contrast in a sentence you can often figure out word meanings from the context. Antonyms help to make sentences clearer and more informative. Examples: My biology professor gives *succinct* lectures, but his assistant is *verbose*. My math professor claims that all the problems she gives us are *simple* ones, but we feel that they are *intricate* and hard to solve.

Practice A.

In these sentences determine the meaning of the underlined word from the context clues.

1. My sister is an optimist and can see a good side to everything, unlike my

   brother, the pessimist. _____

   _____

2. You are so trusting and naive, yet your friends are all so sophisticated.

   _____

3. I prefer studying ancient rather than modern history. _____

   _____

4. Whenever Professor Mollusca tries to give a <u>lucid</u> explanation, he only makes the matter more obscure._____

_____

5. It's a delight to meet a <u>competent</u> person for a change; everyone else in this office is unqualified._____

_____

6. My friend is so <u>vindictive</u> that he will not forgive his brother for a wrong done ten years ago._____

_____

7. Make your flattery and compliments <u>subtle</u> instead of obvious._____

_____

8. How is it possible for the same family to include one brother <u>robust</u> enough to play semiprofessional hockey and another so frail as to collapse in a game of Twenty Questions?_____

_____

9. I always seem to make <u>innumerable</u> mistakes in my themes, but my friend Jack makes very few._____

_____

10. The defense was fortunate to get an <u>eminent</u> lawyer rather than someone unknown._____

_____

11. I prefer the company of an honest and sincere person to that of a <u>deceitful</u> one._____

_____

12. A group of sensitive and refined friends will help you pass a pleasant evening; a group of <u>coarse</u> friends will give you a boisterous but degrading one._____

_____

13. Peggy used to be interested in everything happening around her, but lately she has become <u>indifferent</u>._____

_____

14. Although I am myself a rather <u>thrifty</u> person, I enjoy going to my friend's extravagant parties. _____

_____

15. The lawyer claimed the evidence submitted was <u>pertinent</u> to the case, but the judge said that it was irrelevant and therefore not appropriate.

_____

STOP. Check answers at the end of Lesson 6.

Practice B.

Match the word from column B with its antonym in column A.

	Column A	Column B
_____	1. pessimist	a. interested
_____	2. naive	b. forgiving
_____	3. ancient	c. refined
_____	4. lucid	d. irrelevant
_____	5. competent	e. modern
_____	6. vindictive	f. few
_____	7. subtle	g. optimist
_____	8. indifferent	h. confusing
_____	9. eminent	i. weak
_____	10. robust	j. sophisticated
_____	11. coarse	k. obvious
_____	12. thrifty	l. unknown
_____	13. deceitful	m. extravagant
_____	14. pertinent	n. unqualified
_____	15. innumerable	o. honest

STOP. Check answers at the end of Lesson 6.

Practice C.

Choose a word from the word list that has the same meaning as the under-lined word or phrase in the sentence.

Word List:

pessimist, naive, ancient, lucid, competent, subtle, indifferent, vindictive, deceitful, thrifty, eminent, robust, coarse, innumerable, pertinent.

1. At our campus last week, a <u>noted</u> professor lectured on "Life in the Twentieth Century."_____

2. The point that he made was <u>relevant</u> to what we were discussing.

   _____

3. It's depressing to be in his company because he is a <u>gloomy person</u>.

   _____

4. How can you trust someone who is always <u>lying</u>? _____

5. The museum visitors seemed <u>uninterested</u>._____

6. Although I try to be as <u>economical</u> as possible, I still don't seem to be able to make ends meet._____

7. I wonder why she has to resort to using such <u>vulgar</u> language all the time._____

8. It doesn't seem possible that a grown woman can be so <u>childlike</u>.

   _____

9. Her <u>delicate</u> and mysterious smile has captured many men's hearts.

   _____

10. The archeologists discovered some <u>very old</u> objects that they said were used as tools years ago._____

11. Because you are highly <u>qualified</u> in your field, I'm sure you will have no problem getting a good job._____

12. Mr. Jones is not ordinarily a <u>vengeful</u> man, but when he gets behind the steering wheel he becomes an aggressive monster ready to crowd another motorist off the road for some fancied affront._____

13. The professor's lecture on "man's inhumanity to man" was so <u>clear</u> that I had no trouble understanding it._____

14. The <u>sturdy</u> men carried huge knapsacks up the mountain trail.

_____

15. I have <u>a great many</u> tasks to do before I go away, and I shall never be able to finish them._____

STOP. Check answers at the end of Lesson 6.

WORD ANALYSIS: SYLLABICATION RULES

In previous lessons you learned that a syllable is a vowel or a group of letters containing one vowel sound. Syllabication is the breaking of a multi-syllabic word into single syllables. It is important because to pronounce a multisyllabic word you must syllabicate it before you apply vowel rules to each of its syllables. Knowledge of syllabication is also helpful in spelling and writing.

In attacking a multisyllabic word, first analyze the word to determine its syllabic units, apply vowel rules to the syllables, and then blend them into a whole word.

Syllabication Rules:

Rule 1. Vowel Consonant/Consonant Vowel Rule:

(vc/cv) Vowel followed by two consonants and a vowel. If a vowel in a word is followed by two consonants and a vowel, the word is divided between the two consonants. Examples: bit/ter, bat/ter, but/ter, con/tain, cor/rect, for/ty, writ/ten, can/dy.

Rule 2. Vowel/Consonant Vowel Rule:

(v/cv) Vowel followed by a single consonant and a vowel. If a vowel is followed by one consonant and a vowel, the consonant usually goes with the second syllable. Examples: ba/by, ti/ger, po/lice, la/dy, pu/pil, le/ver, o/pen, bea/con.

Special Note

An exception to the v/cv syllabication rule exists. If the letter *x* is between two vowels, the *x* goes with the first vowel rather than with the second one. Examples: ex/am, ex/alt, ex/it, ex/act, tax/i, ox/en, ox/y/gen, ox/ide.

Rule 3. Special Consonant le Rule:

(v/*cle*) or (vc/*cle*) Vowel or consonant followed by a consonant plus *le*. If a consonant comes just before *le* in a word of more than one syllable, the consonant goes with *le* to form the last syllable. Examples: bub/ble, raf/fle, can/dle, strug/gle, driz/zle, a/ble, ca/ble, rum/ble.

Rule 4. Compound Words:

Compound words are divided between the two words. (See Lesson 9 on word parts.) Examples: cow/boy, grand/child, boy/friend.

Rule 5. Prefixes and Suffixes:

Prefixes and suffixes usually stand as whole units. (See Lesson 9 on word parts.) Examples: re/word, un/do, pre/date, kind/ly, shape/less.

Practice A.

Here are a number of two-syllable words. Draw a line(/) between the first and the second syllable of the word. In the blank put the number of the syllabication rule you used to syllabicate the word. (The "special consonant *le* rule" takes precedence over the "vowel consonant/consonant vowel rule"; e.g., in a word such as *hassle*, the rule would be "consonant special *le*" rather than "vowel consonant/consonant vowel."

garbage _____	tangle _____
handle _____	able _____
pupil _____	collar _____
hobby _____	nimble _____
beacon _____	mirror _____
elbow _____	eager _____
wrinkle _____	pilot _____
tiger _____	smuggle _____
baby _____	person _____
table _____	reason _____
borrow _____	acorn _____
tailor _____	cargo _____
purpose _____	rifle _____

simple _____   lazy _____

notice _____   pepper _____

master _____   corner _____

preplan _____   after _____

return _____   pleasing _____

giggle _____   captain _____

cowgirl _____   amble _____

shuffle _____   iron _____

STOP. Check answers at the end of Lesson 6.

Practice B.

Here are a number of multiple choice questions. Circle the *best* answer. (Circle only one answer.)

1. Which are examples of vowels?

    a. a, i.   c. ch, th.
    b. bl, sl.   d. r, m.

2. Which are examples of blends?

    a. ph, th.   c. t, b.
    b. br, sl.   d. a, e.

3. Consonant digraphs are

    a. two consonants each of which is sounded.
    b. two consonants in which only one consonant is sounded.
    c. two consonants in which there is always a silent letter.
    d. two consonants that represent one speech sound.

4. Examples of consonant digraphs are

    a. bl, st, br, cl.   c. th, ch, sh, ph.
    b. kn, wr, qu.   d. thr, str, phr, shr.

5. Examples of silent consonants are

    a. th, sh.   c. wr, kn.
    b. bl, br.   d. ph, ch.

6. Long vowel sounds exist in

    a. not, get.   c. hid, hat.
    b. we, she.   d. none of the above.

7. Short vowel sounds exist in
   a. hide, cape.
   c. fan, but.
   b. coat, beat.
   d. con, boy.

8. *Y* represents long vowel sounds in
   a. cry, baby.
   c. boy, toy.
   b. yet, yellow.
   d. all of the above.

9. Examples of closed syllables are
   a. pot, hit.
   c. boy, coil.
   b. coat, bee.
   d. be, go.

10. Examples of open syllables are
   a. blank, bloom.
   c. more, bake.
   b. boa, please.
   d. we, no.

11. From these nonsense syllables choose the closed syllable.
   a. noa.
   c. plo.
   b. cron.
   d. crune.

12. From these nonsense syllables choose the open syllable.
   a. sloap.
   c. kra.
   b. moes.
   d. slape.

13. An open syllable is defined as
   a. a syllable that ends in a vowel.
   b. a syllable that ends in a consonant.
   c. a syllable that ends in a vowel and the vowel is always long.
   d. a one-vowel syllable in which the vowel is at the end of the syllable and the vowel is usually long.

14. A closed syllable is defined as
   a. a vowel in the middle of a word or syllable.
   b. a single vowel in a syllable that ends in a consonant and the vowel is usually short.
   c. a double vowel in the middle of a syllable.
   d. a single vowel at the end of a syllable.

15. The silent *e* rule applies when
   a. two vowels are together and have one vowel sound.
   b. two vowels are separated by a consonant.
   c. two vowels are separated by a consonant and the final vowel is an *e*, the first vowel is usually long, and the final *e* is silent.
   d. two vowels are separated by a consonant and the first is long.

16. An example of the silent *e* rule is
    a. pan.   c. cape.
    b. he.   d. goat.

17. From these nonsense syllables choose the one that fits the silent *e* rule.
    a. bolo.   c. bram.
    b. blone.   d. neno.

18. A vowel digraph is
    a. two vowels together and each one sounded.
    b. two vowels together in which the first is long and the second is silent.
    c. two vowels together that stand for one sound.
    d. two vowels adjacent to one another.

19. An example of a vowel digraph is
    a. ei.   c. oi.
    b. oy.   d. none of the above.

20. From these nonsense words choose the one that has a vowel digraph.
    a. blase.   c. blai.
    b. bloi.   d. bloy.

21. A diphthong is
    a. a blend of two vowel sounds.
    b. two vowels together.
    c. two vowels separated by a consonant.
    d. two vowels together making one sound.

22. An example of a diphthong is
    a. oe.   c. ei.
    b. oi.   d. ae.

23. An example of a word with a diphthong is
    a. believe.   c. flow.
    b. cry.   d. coy.

24. An example of a nonsense word with a diphthong is
    a. ploimete.   c. thay.
    b. prat.   d. cheitete.

25. One of these is not a vowel digraph.
    a. ai.   c. oe.
    b. ei.   d. oy.

26. One of these words does not contain a diphthong.
    a. know.   c. how.
    b. boil.   d. boy.

27. One of these words does not contain a vowel digraph.
    a. sew.   c. mouse.
    b. yeoman.   d. though.

28. A syllable is
    a. a vowel with one vowel sound.
    b. a group of letters.
    c. both a and d.
    d. a group of letters with one vowel sound.

29. Syllabication
    a. breaks down single-syllable words.
    b. breaks down multisyllabic words into single syllables.
    c. both a and b.
    d. none of the above.

30. To pronounce a multisyllabic word, you must first
    a. apply vowel rules.
    b. syllabicate the word and then apply phonic analysis.
    c. apply phonic analysis first.
    d. do none of the above.

31. In syllabicating the words *butter, candy, pillow, chatter,* and *seldom,* you
    a. divide the words after the two consonants.
    b. divide the words before the two consonants.
    c. divide the words between the two consonants.
    d. do none of the above.

32. When the words in #31 are divided, the first syllable in each of the words is
    a. an open syllable.   c. both a and b.
    b. a closed syllable.   d. none of the above.

33. All of the vowels in the first syllable of the words in #31 are
    a. long.   c. silent.
    b. short.   d. digraphs.

34. In syllabicating the nonsense words *pronno, plaimmete, craslo,* and *flotmon*, you
    a. divide the words between the two consonants.
    b. divide the words before the two consonants.
    c. divide the words after the two consonants.
    d. do not divide the words.

35. In #34 the syllabication rule is
    a. if a word has two consonants, divide between them.
    b. if a word has two consonants, divide after the second.
    c. if a word has two consonants, divide before them.
    d. if a vowel in a word is followed by two consonants and a vowel, divide the word between the two consonants.

36. When the nonsense word *pronno* is divided into two syllables, the first syllable is
    a. an open syllable. c. a diphthong.
    b. a vowel digraph. d. a closed syllable.

37. When the nonsense word *pronno* is divided into two syllables, the first syllable has
    a. a short vowel and the second has a long vowel.
    b. a long vowel and the second has a short vowel.
    c. a short vowel and the second has a short vowel.
    d. a long vowel and the second has a long vowel.

38. When the nonsense word *plaimmete* is divided into two syllables, the first syllable
    a. is an open syllable. c. has a vowel digraph.
    b. is a closed syllable. d. has a diphthong.

39. When the nonsense word *plaimmete* is divided into two syllables, the second syllable has
    a. a silent *e*. c. a closed syllable.
    b. an open syllable d. none of the above.

40. In syllabicating the words *tiger, begin, fever, pupil,* and *paper*, you
    a. divide the words after the middle consonant.
    b. divide the words after the first consonant.
    c. divide the words after the first vowel and before the middle consonant.
    d. do not divide the words.

41. In #40 the syllabication rule is
    a. divide words after middle consonants.
    b. divide words after a vowel.
    c. divide words after two consonants.
    d. when a vowel is followed by one consonant and a vowel, the consonant usually goes with the second syllable.

42. In #40 the first syllables of all the words are
    a. open syllables.   c. unstressed syllables.
    b. closed syllables.   d. none of the above.

43. In syllabicating the nonsense words *enoi, craneit, planain,* and *phosoy,* you
    a. divide the words after the middle consonant.
    b. divide the words after the first vowel and before the middle consonant.
    c. divide the word after the middle consonant.
    d. divide the word after the second vowel.

44. When the nonsense word *craneit* is divided into syllables, the
    a. first syllable is open and the second contains a diphthong.
    b. first syllable is open and the second is closed.
    c. first syllable is open and the second contains a vowel digraph.
    d. first and second syllables are both open.

45. When the nonsense word *enoi* is divided into syllables, the
    a. first syllable is open and the second is open.
    b. first syllable is closed and the second is open.
    c. first syllable is open and the second contains a vowel digraph.
    d. first syllable is open and the second contains a diphthong.

46. The word *helpful* is divided between *help* and *ful* because
    a. the vc/cv rule applies.
    b. the v/cv rule applies.
    c. it is a compound word.
    d. *ful* is a suffix, and suffixes usually stand as whole units.

47. The words *return* and *redo* are divided between *re* and *turn* and *re* and *do* because
    a. the v/cv syllabication rule applies.
    b. the vc/cv syllabication applies.
    c. *re* is a prefix and prefixes usually stand as whole units.
    d. none of the above.

STOP. Check answers at the end of Lesson 6.

ANSWERS: Lesson 6 (pp. 125-167)

Learning Skills: Concentration—Listening/Reading III (pp. 125–134)

Practice A

Check answers with digits on p. 126.

Practice B

Check answers with digits on p. 127.

Practice C

Check answers by reading the directions and comparing the following to your responses.

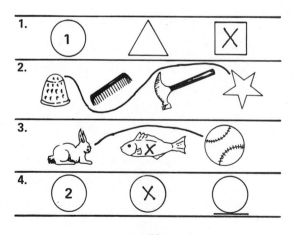

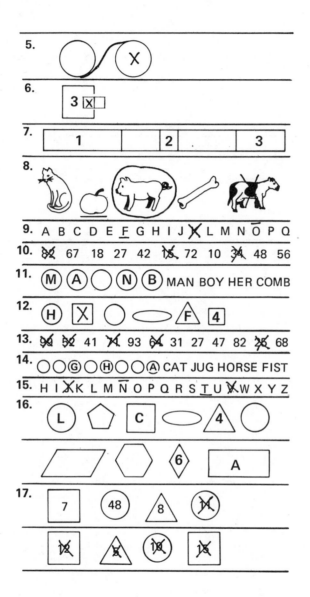

Practice D

Check answers immediately after each set.

Practice E

Check answers by rereading the instructions and by comparing the following to your responses.

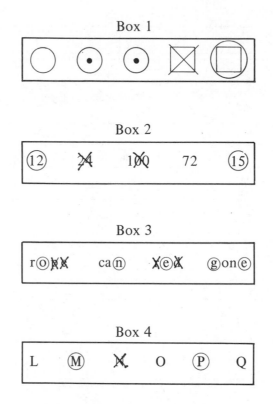

Box 1

Box 2

Box 3

Box 4

Practice F

Check answers by rereading the instructions and by comparing the following to your responses.

1. Put a line under *play*. 2. Put a circle around *big, stop,* and *man*. 3. Underline numbers 1 and 7. 4. Put a cross on the letters M, N, O, P, and Q. 5. Do nothing. There aren't three numbers that equal 16. 6. Put a circle around the numbers 63, 15, and 1.

Reading: Central Idea of a Story (pp. 134-143)

Practice A

1. F 2. T 3. F 4. T 5. T 6. T 7. T 8. F 9. F 10. F

Practice B

Beauty or purity cannot be obtained by immoral means. (This is the implied central idea. Although the author does not directly state the central idea, she gives us enough clues so that we can make this generalization. At the literal—that is, more direct—level, we could say the following: An individual becomes so obsessed with a flower that he resorts to a gruesome act to obtain it. See Lessons 7–9 for more on implied meaning.)

Practice C

1. T 2. T 3. T 4. F 5. F 6. T 7. T 8. F 9. T 10. T 11. F

Practice D

A young child can lose his identity in a large family. (This is the implied central idea. The more literal or direct central idea is the following: Max, the youngest child in a very large family, is quiet because no one listens to him or notices him.)

Vocabulary: Context Clues (Antonyms) (pp. 143-147)

Practice A

1. one who looks on the dark side of things, one who expects the worst to happen 2. childlike, foolishly simple, unsophisticated 3. relating to a remote period, to a time early in history, old 4. clear 5. qualified 6. vengeful, inclined to revenge 7. elusive (hard to identify), indirect, delicate 8. strong 9. very many, countless 10. distinguished, famous, noted 11. given to trickery, cheating 12. vulgar, lacking taste, common 13. without interest, uninterested, apathetic 14. economical, clever at managing money 15. relevant, to the point, relating to or bearing on the matter at hand

Practice B

1. g 2. j 3. e 4. h 5. n 6. b 7. k 8. a 9. l 10. i 11. c 12. m 13. o 14. d 15. f

Practice C

1. eminent 2. pertinent 3. pessimist 4. deceitful 5. indifferent 6. thrifty 7. coarse 8. naive 9. subtle 10. ancient 11. competent 12. vindictive 13. lucid 14. robust 15. innumerable

Word Analysis: Syllabication Rules (pp. 147–155)

Practice A

gar/bage	1	col/lar	1	re/turn	5
han/dle	3	nim/ble	3	gig/gle	3
pu/pil	2	mir/ror	1	cow/girl	4
hob/by	1	ea/ger	2	shuf/fle	3
bea/con	2	pi/lot	2	la/zy	2
el/bow	1	smug/gle	3	pep/per	1
wrin/kle	3	per/son	1	cor/ner	1
ti/ger	2	rea/son	2	af/ter	1
ba/by	2	a/corn	2	pleas/ing	5
ta/ble	3	car/go	1	cap/tain	1
bor/row	1	ri/fle	3	am/ble	3
tai/lor	2	sim/ple	3	i/ron	2
pur/pose	1	no/tice	2		
tan/gle	3	mas/ter	1		
a/ble	3	pre/plan	5		

Practice B

1. a 2. b 3. d 4. c 5. c 6. b 7. c 8. a 9. a 10. d 11. b 12. c
13. d 14. b 15. c 16. c 17. b 18. c 19. a 20. c 21. a 22. b
23. d 24. a 25. d 26. a 27. c 28. c 29. b 30. b 31. c 32. b
33. b 34. a 35. d 36. d 37. a 38. c 39. a 40. c 41. d 42. a
43. b 44. c 45. d 46. d 47. c

CROSSWORD PUZZLE

Directions:

The meanings of a number of the words and some of the ideas from Lessons 4–6 follow. Your knowledge of these words and ideas will help you to solve this crossword puzzle.

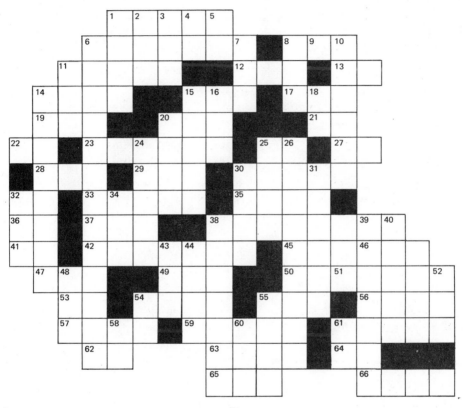

Across

1. Police use this to catch speeders
6. Word meaning *money or wealth, excellent*
8. Word meaning *a knock, a quick, sharp blow, to speak* (slang)
11. Word meaning *slept lightly*
12. Homonym of *won*
13. Strong as a(n)____

Down

1. Word meaning *demolish*
2. A gorilla
3. Past tense of *do*
4. A short word meaning *in, on,* or *near*
5. Abbreviation of *Rear Admiral*
6. Sustained attention
7. Antonym of *high*
8. Homonym of *read*
9. An indefinite article

14. Finished
15. Homonym of *toe*
17. You do this to the letter *i*
19. Abbreviation for *Incorporated*
20. Abbreviation for *Central Intelligence Agency*
21. A prefix meaning *again, back*
22. Abbreviation for *for example*
23. Meaning for *virtuoso*
25. Abbreviation for *cubic centimeter*
27. Opposite of *yes*
28. Word meaning *to go rapidly, to extend in time, a trip*
29. A lyric poem
30. The vowel sound in the word *hit* is___
32. Abbreviation for *bachelor of arts*
33. Tested, proved
35. A cord, rope, wire, or string
36. Abbreviation for *Associated Press*
37. Same as #34 Down
38. Word meaning *brief*
41. A consonant digraph
42. *Honest* is the___of *deceitful*
45. Same as #22 Across
46. A long time period
48. To sit on eggs, fixed or appointed in advance
50. French for *wine*
51. Word meaning *dull*
53. A vowel digraph
54. Crazy
55. Abbreviation of *cents*
56. Same as #35 Across
57. The vowel sound in the word *we* is___
59. To follow

10. Powerful
11. A male's name, to put on
14. Examples of these are *ai, ei,* and *ie*
15. Exhausted
16. A grain
18. A small word used to connect words
20. To give up or surrender
24. A particular place, a definite position in a scale, a sharp end
25. Stylish
26. Vain
30. A very rundown part of the city
31. Rules
32. A flying mammal
34. Past tense of *run*
38. *Content* is a(n)___of *satisfied*
39. The top limit, the overhead interior part of a room
40. The subject of a paragraph
43. Combining form of *egg*
44. Pleasing
47. A number
49. A snakelike fish
52. Last three letters of *included*
54. Abbreviation of *left guard* in football
55. Remedy
58. Same as #27 Across
60. A girl's nickname
61. Word meaning *perform*

61. Cut into small cubes
62. Homonym of *know*
63. Equal to 36 inches
64. Antonym of *off*
65. An example of a "special *le*" syllable
66. An optimist is one who sees ____ in everything

STOP. Check answers on the next page.

Crossword Puzzle Answers

The crossword grid contains the following answers:

- R A D A R (1–5)
- C A P I T A L (6)
- R A P (8–10)
- D O Z E D (11)
- O N E (12)
- O X (13)
- D O N E (14)
- T O W (15–16)
- D O T (17–18)
- I N C (19)
- C I A (20)
- R E (21)
- E G (22)
- E X P E R T (23–24)
- C C (25–26)
- N O (27)
- R U N (28)
- O D E (29)
- S H O R T (30–31)
- B A (32)
- T R I E D (33–34)
- L I N E (35)
- A P (36)
- R A N (37)
- S U C C I N C T (38–40)
- T H (41)
- A N T O N Y M (42–44)
- E G (45)
- E O N (46–47)
- S E T (48–49)
- V I N (50)
- I N S I P I D (51–52)
- E I (53)
- L O C O (54)
- C T S (55)
- L I N E (56)
- L O N G (57–58)
- E N S U E (59–60)
- D I C E D (61)
- N O (62)
- Y A R D (63)
- O N (64)
- M L E (65)
- G O O D (66)

HOMOGRAPH RIDDLES

Directions:

Here are several ways to use a single word. Find the right word for each group. Example: I mean money or wealth; I also mean excellent; I'm the official seat of government, and you can't begin a sentence without me. (capital)

1. I show the way; I begin; I can be ahead; I play the principal role in the show; I'm a heavy, soft, bluish-gray metal. _____

2. I'm an emblem, but I can swim too because I'm a sea mammal. I'm what you can do to your lips, and I can fasten things. _____

3. I'm an accepted custom, rule, or opinion, but I'm also a formal meeting of members for political or professional purposes. _____

4. I'm a tree, and I'm part of your hand. _____

5. I cause you to be hungry; I am firm; I mean loyal and devoted; I describe a clock ahead of time; and I mean quick, speedy, swift._____

6. I mean the only one, but I can be eaten, and I am part of your foot.

_____

STOP. Check answers at the bottom of the page.

Is the word "order" a homograph?

SMIDGENS   by Bob Cordray

Yes, because it has more than one meaning for the same spelling: *order*—a command, a list of things, proper arrangement of things, a group of persons united by common purposes, and so on.

TRUE/FALSE TEST

Directions:

This is a true/false test on Lessons 4–6 in Unit II. Read each sentence carefully. Decide whether it is true or false. Put a T for *true* or an F for *false* in the blank.

_____ 1. *Optimist* and *pessimist* are antonyms.

_____ 2. A thrifty person is economical.

_____ 3. A lucid speech would be confusing.

_____ 4. *Antonym* and *synonym* are antonyms.

_____ 5. The central idea of a group of paragraphs is always directly stated.

1. lead 2. seal 3. convention 4. palm 5. fast 6. sole

_____ 6. Setting purposes for reading is helpful for studying.

_____ 7. Concentration skill can be developed.

_____ 8. A person who behaves in a subtle manner is behaving in a very obvious manner.

_____ 9. A *schwa* looks like an upside down *e*.

_____ 10. The central idea of a group of paragraphs is what unifies them.

_____ 11. Final consonants are found at the beginning of words.

_____ 12. *Economical* and *extravagant* are synonyms.

_____ 13. Synonyms can make writing clearer.

_____ 14. *Eminent* and *unknown* are antonyms.

_____ 15. Vowel sounds are more consistent than consonant sounds.

_____ 16. Knowledge of vowel rules helps one to be a more effective, independent reader.

_____ 17. The syllable *mas* is an example of a closed syllable.

_____ 18. The syllable *maet* is an example of an open syllable.

_____ 19. The syllable *mone* is an example of an open syllable.

_____ 20. The syllable *slope* is an example of the final *e* or silent *e* rule.

_____ 21. A multisyllabic word must be syllabicated before applying phonic analysis.

_____ 22. Not until after a multisyllabic word is broken into parts can you determine how to pronounce the word.

_____ 23. In an open syllable the vowel is usually short.

_____ 24. In a closed syllable the vowel is usually short.

_____ 25. A syllable has one vowel sound.

STOP. Check answers on the next page.

Answers to True/False Test

1. T 2. T 3. F 4. T 5. F 6. T 7. T 8. F 9. T 10. T 11. F
12. F 13. T 14. T 15. F 16. T 17. T 18. F 19. F 20. T 21. T
22. T 23. F 24. T 25. T

Unit III

Reading: Skimming
Reading/Learning Skills: Summaries (Textbooks)
Vocabulary: Context Clues (Social Sciences)
Word Analysis: Applying Vowel Rules to Syllabicated Syllables
Answers

READING: SKIMMING

1. You read for many purposes. If you are reading for pleasure, you may read either quickly or slowly based on the way you feel. If you are reading information that is new to you or studying, you will probably read very slowly. If, however, you are looking up a phone number, a name, or a date, or looking over a paragraph for its topic, you will read much more rapidly. Reading rapidly to find or locate information is called *skimming*. (See Lesson 10 on parts of the textbook.) All skimming involves fast reading; however, there are different kinds of skimming. Skimming for a number, date, or name can usually be done much more quickly than skimming for the topic of a paragraph (see Lesson 3 on SQ3R) or to answer specific questions.) (Some people call the most rapid reading *scanning* and the less rapid reading skimming.)

2. Skimming is an important skill because it is often the only way to get the job done in a reasonable time. Read this list and check the items that apply to you.

_____ 1. Skim newspaper headlines.

_____ 2. Skim the movie ads.

_____ 3. Skim tape or record catalogues.

_____ 4. Skim the yellow pages of the phone book for some help.

_____ 5. Skim the television guide to find a particular show.

_____ 6. Skim the dictionary to find the syllabication, spelling, meaning, or history of a word.

_____ · 7. Skim the want ads.

_____ 8. Skim the clothing ads.

_____ 9. Skim the index of a textbook.

_____ 10. Skim the telephone directory.

How many more can you list?

Special Notes

1. You read rapidly to locate some specific information, but once you find what you want you may read it more slowly.

2. Do not confuse skimming with studying. Although you use the skimming technique as part of the SQ3R method when you survey, skimming material is not the same as studying material. Studying requires much slower and more concentrated reading.

3. You can skim material most rapidly when it is clearly organized according to some logical system: alphabetically in telephone books and dictionaries, topically in catalogues, and chronologically or numerically or geographically in charts, tables, and schedules.

Example:

Very quickly skim this excerpt from a finance table to find the finance charge for $423.00 and the monthly payments.

If Cash Price (Including any sales tax and shipping charge), less Down Payment If Any amounts to	We Shall Add for FINANCE CHARGE	Amount Payable Monthly is
$100.00 to $110.00	$ 15.30	$ 5.00
110.01 to 120.00	19.10	5.00
120.01 to 130.00	23.20	5.00
130.01 to 140.00	27.70	5.00
140.01 to 150.00	32.65	5.00
150.01 to 160.00	38.00	5.00
160.01 to 170.00	38.40	5.50
170.01 to 180.00	41.90	5.75
180.01 to 190.00	43.20	6.25
190.01 to 200.00	45.60	6.50
200.01 to 210.00	49.30	6.75
210.01 to 220.00	50.40	7.25
220.01 to 230.00	52.80	7.50
230.01 to 240.00	55.20	8.00
240.01 to 250.00	57.60	8.25

250.01	to	260.00	60.00	8.50
260.01	to	270.00	62.40	9.00
270.01	to	280.00	64.80	9.25
280.01	to	290.00	67.20	9.75
290.01	to	300.00	69.60	10.00
300.01	to	310.00	72.00	10.25
310.01	to	320.00	76.45	10.50
320.01	to	330.00	81.05	10.50
330.01	to	340.00	85.80	10.75
340.01	to	350.00	90.65	10.75
350.01	to	360.00	95.65	11.00
360.01	to	370.00	100.80	11.00
370.01	to	380.00	106.05	11.00
380.01	to	390.00	111.45	11.25
390.01	to	400.00	114.40	11.50
400.01	to	410.00	120.00	11.50
410.01	to	420.00	125.70	11.75
420.01	to	430.00	128.20	12.00
430.01	to	440.00	134.70	12.00
440.01	to	450.00	140.80	12.00
450.01	to	460.00	144.00	12.50
460.01	to	470.00	150.25	12.50
470.01	to	480.00	156.65	12.50
480.01	to	490.00	160.00	12.75
490.01	to	500.00	169.85	12.75
500.01	to	510.00	176.65	12.75
510.01	to	520.00	183.60	12.75
520.01	to	530.00	187.20	13.00
530.01	to	540.00	197.85	13.00
540.01	to	550.00	201.60	13.25

Answer: $128.20; $12.00

Special Note

Obviously, you must know the alphabet in order to use the many sources of information that are arranged in alphabetical order. (See lessons on the dictionary.)

4. Skim less rapidly when you are looking for more than just a word or group of words. Looking for the topic of a paragraph or for specific details about the topic of a paragraph requires relatively slow skimming.

Example:
Skim this paragraph and state its topic.

From "TV & Sports" by Joan M. Chandler in *Psychology Today*, April 1977.

TV money has transformed professional athletes from some-what scruffy mercenaries playing children's games to respected members of the community. Newspaper and radio coverage has put sport stars in the limelight for generations, but TV has made them richer and more famous than ever. O.J. Simpson, Chris Evert, Jack Nicklaus, and many others make as much or more from advertisements, endorsements, and other outside interests as they do from their games.

Answer: The effect of TV money on professional athletes.

5. When you skim you pass over many words and phrases. In many informative passages the message of each paragraph will reveal itself even if the minor words and phrases are left out. Following is a paragraph that has a number of words and phrases omitted. Quickly skim the skeleton message and then, without looking back, answer the true/false questions on it. Compare your answers with those given.

Example:

_____kids_____sissies_____ nature; I was_____sissy_____ conviction. I_____ _____intelligent, rational child,_____ _____see _____myself_____not___was fighting sinful;_____ _____ _____dangerous.

True/False Questions:

_____ 1. The child was unhappy about being a sissy.

_____ 2. The child had a poor opinion of himself.

_____ 3. The child consciously became a sissy.

_____ 4. The child disapproved of fighting.

_____ 5. The child purposefully avoided fighting.

Answers: 1. F 2. F 3. T 4. T 5. T

Practice A.

Very quickly skim this list of names to supply the requested information.

Sample Telephone Directory:

Smith D.	Old Haven Rd.	372-4401
Smith Davis	Broad St.	420-7713
Smith Donald	John St.	651-7801
Smith Douglas	5 Connor Rd.	491-3270
Smith Dudley	24 Stuart Rd.	659-4590
Smith E.	113 13th St.	862-7321
Smith E.	14 Nassau St.	937-6542
Smith E.	91 Arlington Rd.	420-5143
Smith E.	27 Roger Lane	862-9450
Smith E.P.	Cherry St.	659-7700
Smith Earl lawyer	1012 Terry St.	491-4420
Smith Edgar	987 Delaware Ave.	651-3157
Smith Edw. L.	56 Lover's Lane	372-7011
Smith Edw. M.	Skillman Rd.	428-1276
Smith F. Rev.	9 Morris Ave.	937-5520
Smith Frank	25 Mead St.	651-4376
Smith Fred	457 Province Rd.	659-7701
Smith G.	11 Jackson St.	372-1113
Smith G.R.	101 Bank St.	372-5012
Smith Gerald	Clark Rd.	651-4403
Smith George M.D.	Merry Lane	862-9901
Smith Harry	Laurel St.	491-3598
Smith Henry	Old York Rd.	420-7011

Questions:

1. What is the first name of the Smith living on Delaware Ave.?_____

2. What is the phone number of Dr. Smith?_____

3. What is the address of Rev. Smith?_____

4. What is the first name of the Smith who is a lawyer? _____

5. What is the phone number of Harry Smith?_____

6. Where does Edward L. Smith live? _____ ·

7. What is the phone number of Dudley Smith?_____

8. What is the first name of the Smith with the phone number 651-4403?

   _____

9. What is the address of the Smith with the phone number 862-9450?

   _____

10. What is the first name of the Smith with the phone number 420-7011?

    _____

STOP. Check answers at the end of Lesson 7 and by going over the list more slowly.

Practice B.

Very quickly skim the train schedule to answer the questions.

Train Number →		180	168	170	172	174	150	176	142	178	162	60	66
Train Name →		The Pilgrim	The Benjamin Franklin	The Minute Man	The Patriot	The Colonial	The Flying Yankee	The Senator	The Bankers	The Merchants Limited	The Bostonian	The Montrealer	The Night Owl
Frequency of Operation →		Daily	Daily	Daily	Daily	Daily	Daily	Daily	Daily	Daily	Fr and Su Only	Daily	Daily
Type of Service →		⊠	▷⊠🍴 Amclub	▷⊠🍴 Amclub	▷⊠🍴 Amclub	▷⊠ Amclub	⊠	▷⊠ Amclub	▷⊠🍴 Amclub	▷⊠ Amclub	⊠	✈★ ▷×🍴	▷⊠🛏 Sleeping Car

Kilometers	Miles		180	168	170	172	174	150	176	142	178	162	60	66
0	0	WASHINGTON, DC.............Dp			7 05 a	9 05 a	11 05 a	12 00 n	1 05 p	2 05 p	3 10 p	4 05 p	6 05 p	10 30 p
14	9	Beltway Station (Lanham), MD				R 7 18 a	R 9 18 a	㉑11 18 a		㉑1 18 p	R 2 18 p		R 4 18 p	R 6 18 p	R10 43 p
64	40	BALTIMORE (Penn. Sta.).........				7 49 a	9 45 a	11 46 a	12 38 p	1 49 p	2 49 p	3 50 p	4 45 p	6 49 p	11 15 p
113	70	Aberdeen, MD ⦿☆...........				8 18 a									
174	108	WILMINGTON, DE............				8 49 a	10 45 a	12 49 p	1 18 p	2 49 p	3 49 p	4 51 p	5 45 p	7 49 p	12 25 a
216	134	PHILADELPHIA, PA (30th St. Sta.).........		7 15 a	9 15 a	11 15 a	1 17 p	1 42 p	3 15 p	4 15 p	5 18 p	6 15 p	8 15 p	12 55 a
222	138	North Philadelphia, PA..............		7 24 a				2 15 p		4 25 p				1 10 a
267	166	TRENTON, NJ...........		(7 52 a) Su Only	9 52 a	11 51 a	1 52 p	2 53 p	3 52 p	4 52 p	5 51 p	6 53 p	8 55 p	1 39 a
282	175	Princeton Jct. (Princeton) ⊕...........												
307	191	New Brunswick..............												
320	199	Metropark (Iselin)												
344	214	NEWARK, NJ (Penn. Sta.)...........		8 36 a	10 40 a	12 36 p	2 40 p	3 40 p	4 40 p	5 40 p	6 32 p	7 49 p	9 40 p	2 27 a
360	224	NEW YORK, NY (Penn. Sta.)........Ar		8 50 a	10 55 a	12 51 p	2 55 p	3 55 p	4 55 p	5 55 p	6 47 p	7 55 p	9 55 p	2 45 a
360	224	NEW YORK, NY (Penn. Sta.)........Dp	7 10 a	9 10 a	11 10 a	1 05 p	3 10 p	4 10 p	5 10 p	6 15 p	7 00 p	8 05 p	10 10 p	3 10 a
404	251	Rye, NY..............	①7 48 a	①9 48 a		①1 43 p						①10 48 p	①3 50 a
418	260	Stamford, CT..............	①8 00 a	①10 00 a	①12 00 n	①1 55 p	①4 00 p				①7 03 p	①7 46 p	①8 55 p	①11 00 p	①4 03 a
454	282	Bridgeport................	①8 25 a	①10 25 a	①12 25 p	①2 20 p	①4 25 p				①7 28 p	①8 10 p	①9 20 p	①11 25 p	①4 28 a
481	299	NEW HAVEN.............Ar	8 45 a	10 45 a	12 45 p	2 40 p	4 45 p	5 38 p	6 42 p	7 50 p	8 28 p	9 40 p	11 45 p	4 45 a

		Connecting Train Number →		404	406	408	410							400
		Connecting Train Frequency →		Daily	Mo thru Fr	Daily	Daily							Mo thru Fr from New Haven
481	299	NEW HAVEN............Dp		11 00 a	1 20 p	3 20 p	5 20 p				8 00 p		11 55 p	6 30 a
502	312	Wallingford⊕...........		11 19 a	1 39 p	3 39 p	5 39 p				8 19 p			7 09 a
512	318	Meriden...............		11 31 a	1 51 p	3 51 p	5 51 p				8 29 p		12 20 a	7 20 a
523	325	Berlin (New Britain)		11 42 a	2 02 p	4 02 p	6 02 p				8 39 p		12 30 a	7 31 a
541	336	HARTFORD...............		11 55 a	2 15 p	4 15 p	6 15 p				8 52 p		12 45 a	7 45 a
550	342	Windsor ⦿...........		E12 06 p	E 2 25 p	E 4 25 p	E 6 25 p				D 9 07 p			7 55 a
560	348	Windsor Locks⦿..........		12 14 p	2 34 p	4 34 p	6 35 p							8 04 a
568	353	Thompsonville, CT⦿ (Enfield) ...		12 22 p	2 42 p	4 42 p	6 42 p							8 13 a
581	361	SPRINGFIELD, MA...........		12 40 p	3 00 p	5 00 p	7 00 p				9 30 p		1 20 a	8 30 a
481	299	NEW HAVEN, CT.............Dp	8 55 a	10 55 a	12 55 p	2 50 p	4 55 p	5 53 p	6 52 p		8 38 p	9 50 p	Thru	5 05 a
534	332	Old Saybrook..............	9 29 a	11 29 a	1 28 p	3 23 p	5 28 p		7 25 p		9 11 p	10 23 p	train	E 5 39 a
563	350	New London.............	9 50 a	11 50 a	1 48 p	3 44 p	5 50 p	6 45 p	7 45 p		9 30 p	10 41 p	to	6 02 a
578	359	Mystic, CT⦿ (Mystic Seaport)......	10 02 a	E12 02 p	2 00 p	3 57 p	6 01 p		7 56 p		9 41 p	11 02 p	Montreal	E 6 15 a
592	368	Westerly, RI...........	10 12 a	12 13 p	2 10 p	4 10 p	6 11 p		8 06 p		9 51 p	11 12 p		E 6 27 a
620	385	Kingston..............	10 26 a	12 29 p	2 24 p	4 26 p	6 24 p		8 22 p		10 07 p	11 28 p		E 6 47 a
663	412	PROVIDENCE, RI⊕............	10 54 a	12 57 p	2 50 p	4 54 p	6 50 p	7 41 p	8 50 p		10 32 p	11 55 p		⑤7 25 a
715	444	Route 128, MA...........	11 27 a	1 29 p	3 21 p	5 24 p	7 20 p	D 8 23 p	9 20 p		D11 02 p	12 25 a		D 8 03 a
732	455	BOSTON (Back Bay Sta.).......Ar	D11 45 a	D 2 00 p	D 3 50 p	D 5 56 p	D 7 52 p	D 8 43 p	9 52 p		D11 31 p	D12 41 a		D 8 20 a
734	456	BOSTON, MA (South Sta.)........Ar	11 50 a	2 07 p	3 57 p	6 06 p	8 00 p	8 50 p	10 00 p		11 40 p	12 48 a		8 25 a

Questions:

1. What is the name of the train that leaves Washington, D.C., at 1:05 P.M. daily?_____

2. How many miles is it from Washington to New Haven?_____

3. What is the number of the connecting train that leaves Providence, R.I. at 2:50 P.M. Monday through Friday?_____

4. What time will you get into New York if you leave Washington at 9:05 A.M.?_____

5. What time will you get into New London if you leave New York, N.Y. (Penn. Sta.) at 11:10 A.M.?_____

STOP. Check answers at the end of Lesson 7 and by going over the train schedule more slowly.

Practice C.

Skim this index to answer the questions.

From *Teaching Elementary Language Arts* by Dorothy Rubin, Holt, Rinehart and Winston, 1975, p. 452.

Questions:

1. On what pages would you find skills in written composition?_____

2. On what pages would you find instruction in word usage?_____

3. On what pages would you find activities in voice usage?_____

4. On what pages would you find tongue twisters?_____

5. On what pages would you find sentence writing in written composition?

_____

STOP. Check answers at the end of Lesson 7 and by going over the index more slowly.

Practice D. Quickly skim these want ads to answer the questions.

Help Wanted 2600	Help Wanted 2600	Help Wanted 2600	Help Wanted 2600
Cont'd From Preceding Page **TEACHER** , So. Bx, bilingual person (Spanish) encouraged to apply. Base sal $7000. Call 665-8550 TEACHER-Shorthand(Gregg) & Typing, licensed. Bilingual(English-Spanish), part-time: day or eve, immediate; mid-manhattan school. Phone 391-2416 Telephone-Interconnect Design/Maintenance Mgr Liberal Salary & Fringes Exp nec. Instructor/Trainer desirable. Send resume & sal hist PP334 TIMES **TELETYPE OPERATORS** Min 2 yrs exp to work w/model 28 ASR TTY + Telex Machines. Liberal bnfts opply for advancement. Grand Central area. **949-0888** Equal Opportunity Employer M/F TELETYPE We Move Careers **$230** Agency 41E42st 986-5805 TELETYPE F/PD $210+bonus Commodity Firm. (agency) 18 John St 962-3660 Teletype/Nites Fee Pd To $235 Bank 4-12mdnite or 6:30-2:30am DRUM agency 150 Bway 233-7550 TELETYPE WALL ST $200-235 f/pd top instlt co, excl potl, bnfts Agency 181 Bway BA7-5150 **TELEX OPERATOR** Expd Telex operator for busy & friendly midtwn Manhtn ofc. Knowl of switchbrd also helpful but not nec. Salary $160. 679-8339 TELEX OPR "Days" $155-$200 F/Pd. Dom & int'l machines. Mr Pell 349-5983 Agency 160 Bway **TELEX-APPLY BY PHONE** Agency 475 5 Ave 689-5555 **TELLERS** Major bank needs several people with minimum 6 months commercial teller exp Position available midtown & downtown Salary Open **TELLERS** H.S. Grad,6 months work experience Excel benefits,commercial banking TRAINEES to $235 150 BWAY Agency TEMPORARY NO FEE	Textile,Supv inspectn dept,nrby NJ PIECE GOODS QC $20M+ No fee MU9-5500 Able agency 475 5 Av **TOOL & DIEMAKERS** 1st class, experienced in jewelry or allied work. All benefits including pension. 248 Montgomery St, Bloomfield, NJ 201-743-6666 **TOOL MAKER** Min 5 yrs exp. Maintain tools, dies, jigs, fixtures & machinery. A/C/toolroom, steady, benefits, LIC area, Equal Opply Employer 212-392-3333 TOOL & DIEMAKERS F/pd $6-8/hr Diemakg for progresv dies $7-8/hr Diesetter $5-7/hr agency 51 E 42, 661-2810 **TOOL & DIE MAKER** Expd all around. Queens Plaza area. 212-729-4776 **TOOLMAKERS** Plastic molds, jigs, fixtures and assembly machines. Steady, interesting work. Large company in Queens. Highest rates & benefits in area. TW 9-4422 Equal Opportunity Employer **TRAFFIC $15,000/negot** Domestic trucking/rates, type own docs/corres. Busy small midtown metal trading firm seeks dedicated career oriented person. 541-8614 TRAFFIC ASST MGR F/pd to $17K heavy truck exp, 3-person dept, top Upper Bronx mfg co ALL-AMERICAN agency 505 5 Ave (42) **TRAVEL AGENTS** **COME FLY WITH US!** Major travel firm with locations in Union & Short Hills, N.J, Long Island and Staten Island offers training advancement and full benefits. Please send resume to: **TRAVEL** TRAVEL Agents Fee pd to $300 **COMMERCIAL** Must have at least 3 years strong experience in all phases. Excellent opportunity to get into other areas. 505 FIFTH AVENUE 697-7855 9th Flr Hrs 8AM-6PM agency TRAVEL TRAINEES $175 Mdtn Ad agency seeks person with at least 6 mos exp & ability to type 40 WPM. Some travel to West Coast for Co. Great benefits. FEE PAID Call: 16 E42 St 687-7570 **TRAVEL AGENT** For lrg busy office, mature, expd all phases of travel, gd typing skills, sal open. Call 516/569-5533 TRAVEL AGENCY-Immed opening , expd preferred, must type, varied duties. Call 212 PL 2-3395	Type Setter/Word Processor High School Graduate preferred. Experienced type setter with experience on Compugraphic EditWriter,good command of English language. Paid benefits. Non-profit organization. Midtown location. Call for appointment ...754-9732 Equal Opportunity Employer M/F TYPESETTER-Mag Publg Exp Pfd COMPUGRAPHIC Mgr $19-20M set up new in-hse dept, supv sml group f/p. agency 280 Mad/40st **TYPESETTER** dys/nights. Top salary & benefits. VIP exp only. 687-4740 TYPISTS/TEMP **RECORDS** Fashion, Publishing, Advertising, TV, Airline, Engineering, Recording, Brokerage & Banking. We are overflowing w/assignments in these areas. Min 50+ wpm. Long-term assignments avail. 679-9280 **TYPIST** Prestige E. Side construction firm seeks flexible person in billing dept. Diversified clerical duties, receptionist board relief. Heavy figure typing a must. Call 5-7PM 759-3800 **TYPIST** Interesting,F/T position for expd rapid typist in pleas midtn 5th Ave office. $175. 752-8361 **TYPIST** Min 1 yr exp. Speed 50-60 wpm. Accuracy a must. Billing & to assist Bookkeeper. Diversified duties, Midtown. Salary open. 697-3457 **TYPIST** interesting diverse job. Must be good typist. Billing exp prefrd. Call Personnel Dept betw 10AM & 12 Noon only 212-242-6052 **TYPIST/CLERK** Midtown publisher's sales dept. Diversified duties, pleasant surroundings, all benefits. For appt 661-4500 x461 **TYPISTS-TEMP** Earn top $ working where & when you want. Immediate openings. Friday pay. 889-0300. **TYPIST-IBM Selectric** Medical reports-3 days per wk. M-W-F. Mature, reliable, returnee prefd. 594-3034 **TYPIST-DIVERSIFIED** Flair for figures. Pleas mdtn ofc. Good opply. BENEFITS $64-7875 Typist Clerk-Bank, Fee Paid, $160 FREE LUNCH, fantastic benefits 505 5 Ave (42 St) agency TYPIST F/T 60wpm 23 opnings. Start immed. Top $. Temp 269-3036 **TYPIST** Audio-visual production co needs good typist. 541-5300	WAITRESS M/F, part time, bar-cocktails, in Jackson Heights vicinity. Call , 274-2800 WALL STREET **BRANCH CASHIER** We're a major stock brokerage firm and we're seeking an experienced cashier with minimum 2 years experience. Responsibilities include follow-up of trades, checking original trades for accuracy, receiving and processing checks and securities and other accounting related branch activities. Salary is commensurate with experience. FOR IMMEDIATE INTERVIEW **482-6750** Member, New York Stock Exchange An Equal Opportunity Employer WALL ST FEE PAID **FOR WALL ST** COMPLIANCE, invest bnks $220-235 FOREIGN OPERATIONS $13-14M VAULT, comml bank $10-12M Comdty Operatns or Mgn $20-30M ORDER, top instlt co $250-300 R&D, mgr & supvr $18-26M REORG, well run dept $12-14M MARGIN, qual instlt co $300 P&S, supvr & asst $200-260 STOCK REC, opty run dept $220-260 BRANCH OPERATIONS $14-15,M DIVDND, stk, cash/bond int $180-250 BOND CLKS, govt or muni $200-260 REGISTRATN CLKS, invst bk $10-11M TRANSFER, 4 person dept $170-230 COMDTY, order or oprtns $170-240 STK LOAN/BANK LOAN $200-220 ACCTG CLKS, solid cos $170-220 NEW ACCTS, all bnfts $175-180 SEGRETATION, secure firm $165 181 Bway BA7-5150 WALL **BROKERAGE FIRM CLERK** Some exp in securities industry, relocate to Atlanta. Send resume to: Personnel Dept, 2 Peach Tree St NW, Atlanta, Ga 30303 WALL ST FEE PD P&S BOND MGR $20K ASST ACCTG SUPVSR $16K Trading area. Must hve brkge bkgd. P&S BOND CLERK $16K Call Randall Kadish 964-9100 150 Bway Rm 800 Agency **Wall St-Reg'd Reps** with order rm exp. To work for a growing NYSE discount stock brokerage firm. Good telephone personality req'd Mail resume to PP293 TIMES

From *The New York Times* Classified Section, Wednesday, August 2, 1978. p. B–16.

Questions:

1. What language other than English is required for the teacher positions?

   _____

2. What is an agency on 181 Broadway advertising as the salary for a person to handle new accounts in a Wall St. brokerage firm.? _____

3. How much experience must you have to get a job with travel agents at 505 Fifth Ave.? _____

4. What is the address of the agency that wants travel trainees with at least six months experience?_____

5. What is the minimum speed that typists seem to need? _____

STOP. Check answers at the end of Lesson 7 and by slowly going over the classified advertisements.

Practice E.

Skim this passage that has many words omitted and then, without looking back, answer the true/false questions on it. Put a T for *true* or an F for *false* in the blank.

From *The Last Clock* by James Thurber, The New Yorker Magazine, Inc., 1959.

_____ _____days went _____,_____ ogre ate all_____clocks_____ _____town–mantle_____, grandfather_____, travelling_____, station- ary_____, alarm_____, eight _____-clocks, steeple_____, and tower _____–sprinkling them with watches,_____ _____ _____watches _____salt and pepper, until_____ _____no more watches. People overslept, and failed _____ _____ _____work, _____ _____ church, or anyplace_____ _____ they _____ _____be on time. Factories closed_____, shopkeepers shut _____ _____ _____, school_____not open, trains no_____ran,_____ people stayed_____home.

True/False Questions:

_____ 1. The ogre ate all the clocks.
_____ 2. Watches were used as salt and pepper.
_____ 3. Everything closed except schools.
_____ 4. People were on time without watches.
_____ 5. The trains kept their usual schedule.

STOP. Check answers at the end of Lesson 7 and by skimming more slowly for the answers to each question.

Practice F.

Skim these paragraphs. Without looking back, first state the topic of the paragraphs and then answer the true/false questions on the paragraphs. Put a T for *true* or an F for *false* in the blank.

From "Newsline" in *Psychology Today*, November 1976.

Fat babies are likely to end up as fat adults. Researchers at the University of Rochester School of Medicine compared the weight of 366 adults between 20 and 30 years of age with the weights their doctors recorded for them at six weeks, three months, and six months of age.

The researchers also questioned the young adults about their weight and length at birth, educational level, social class, and the present weight of their parents. Overweight was defined as more than 10 per cent above the median for a person's height and age, and obesity as over 20 per cent.

One-third of the infants who were overweight at birth grew up to be fat adults, whereas only one-fifth of the thin or average newborns did.

1. Topic:

True/False Questions:

_____ 1. It's stated that fat babies are happy babies.

_____ 2. Fat babies usually became fat adults.

_____ 3. No thin or average weight babies became fat as adults.

_____ 4. Overweight was defined as more than 10 per cent above the median for a person's height and age.

_____ 5. Two thirds of the overweight infants grew up to be fat adults.

STOP. Check answers at the end of Lesson 7.

READING/LEARNING SKILLS: SUMMARIES (Textbooks)

In many courses you are required to write summaries of articles or other readings. Summarizing material helps you to retain the most important facts in a long passage. A good summary should be brief and should include only essential information. The central idea of the article and the important facts should be stated but not necessarily in the sequence presented in the article. The sequence in the article must be followed in the summary only if that sequence is essential. In a summary you must include only the information stated in the article, not what you think should have been stated or your opinions. (You may want to review the lessons on main idea.) A short article and a sample summary of it follow. Read the article and write your own summary of it in the space provided. Compare your summary with the one provided.

Example:

From Criminal Justice: Enforcement and Administration by Alan Kalmanoff, Little, Brown and Co., 1976.

Vocabulary:

alleged—asserted without proof; *segments*—parts; *impetus*—force, stimulus; *affront*—insult; *inhospitable*—not friendly or receptive, providing no shelter or sustenance; *harassment*—persistent annoyance; *extraneous*—not essential or vital.

Laws against victimless crime, such as gambling, prostitution, and drug abuse, are controversial. Whereas laws against violence or robbery receive the support of both the victim and the community, vice laws often deal with behavior reflecting private moral standards. Some critics even argue that prostitution and drug addiction are not really crimes at all and should therefore be legalized and regulated rather than punished. The police themselves do not believe in the possibility of eradicating prostitution, gambling, or drug addiction. Rather, they act to "keep the lid on" and to uphold, in a symbolic way, moral standards espoused by the legislature and some segments of the community.

Vice enforcement receives some of its impetus from extraneous phenomena, unrelated to any valid justification for penalizing victimless crime. For instance, the high visibility of victimless crime may seem a public affront to the police and thus motivate police to harassment. Furthermore, significant public opposition to behavior associated with victimless crime further supports vice enforcement.

More substantive rationales for vice enforcement include the alleged but unproven relationship between crimes of vice and victim crimes. Vice officers are convinced that prostitutes, gamblers, addicts, and dealers are involved in more serious crime, and vice enforcement is said to provide a means of getting at those involved in related crimes. Another vice squad objective involves the destabilization and harassment of illicit enterprises to "take the profit out" and make the surrounding environment inhospitable to organized crime.

Your summary:

Sample summary: Laws against victimless crime such as gambling, prostitution, and drug abuse are controversial because they often deal with behavior reflecting private moral standards. As a result of these complications, victimless crime is more difficult to control than other crime. However, vice enforcement does exist because the high visibility of victimless crime offends the police and a significant part of the public and, more significantly, because a relationship is alleged between crimes of vice and victim crimes.

In writing a summary it is sometimes a good idea to begin with the writer's conclusion and work backward to pick out essential points leading to that conclusion. Write a brief summary of this paragraph and compare your summary with the one provided.

From Sociology: Studying the Human System by Jonathan H. Turner, Goodyear Pub. Co. 1978.

Humans are either male or female. This seems obvious, but until recently in sociology, the existence of two sexes has been given scant attention. Sociologists have, of course, studied courtship, marriage, family, divorce, labor force participation, and other social patterns where sexual differences are involved. Yet, they have typically ignored the fact that virtually all facets of the human system are punctuated by sexuality, by the existence of two sexes. Social interaction, patterns of social organization, cultural symbols, socialization practices, and processes of deviance and social control all involve a sexual component. Sex and gender are thus a basic element of the human system. . . .

Your summary:

Sample summary: Sex and gender are a basic element of the human system. However, sociologists until recently have ignored this fact, even in studying all the social patterns where sexual differences are involved.

Practice A.

Write a brief summary of these selections.

1. From *The New Marketing* by Robert M. Fulmer, Macmillan Publishing Co., Inc., 1976, p. 183.

Americans are generally not very honest about their motives. We lie to others and we fool ourselves about many of the real reasons we do things. Frequently, we don't even understand our own motives. To admit some of the real drives that push us forward to grasp some product might put us in social jeopardy. Rather than admit that we are selfish or jealous or greedy, we find it far more socially advisable to provide inaccurate explanations that are more socially acceptable (and perhaps praiseworthy).

John wants a big car because he *feels* more important in a big car. However, John's cultural background keeps him from blatantly announcing, "Well, I bought the Deluxe because I feel more important when I'm driving it." Rather, John goes to great length to explain the car's important safety features, high resale record, superior handling, and long-run economy. These things may all be true . . . but they were just as true when John was gaining status with his first small car. Most individuals feel called upon to defend themselves against social dragons who are often not the least bit interested in our defenses. For a people who put great stock in efficiency, we have evolved a highly inefficient procedure for disguising our real motives. Perhaps as we mature as individuals and as a culture, we will learn how useless is the deep emotional drive never to appear emotional.

Your summary:

2. From *An Introduction to Cultural and Social Anthropology* by Peter B. Hammond, 2nd ed., Macmillan Publishing Co., Inc., 1978, p. 74.

Vocabulary:

indigenous—native.

Clothing

Peoples with the simplest subsistence technologies tend to have the simplest techniques of clothing manufacture; there is greater uniformity of style, and fashions change less rapidly. As technology becomes more complex and social stratification develops, clothing fashions reflect these status differences, and dress types become increasingly adapted to the performance of specific tasks. Hoopskirts are out for telephone line-women and female astronauts. But the correlation between technological level and clothing style is by no means direct and unvarying. Humans dress to protect and adorn themselves and to signal their social position; some stylistic variation is almost always possible.

Nor can clothing ever be directly correlated with the kind of climate in which a people lives. Some Arabian desert dwellers—the Bedouin, for example—customarily protect themselves from solar radiation and blowing sand in several layers of loose, flowing garments that cover them from head to foot. Many of the indigenous inhabitants of the almost equally hot Australian desert wear nothing at all. Some Indians living in the colder parts of North America dressed themselves heavily in warm furs. Other Indians at the chilly tip of South America wore only a loose cloak of skins, and sometimes not even that—protecting their bodies only with a bit of animal grease mixed with clay.

Your summary:

3. From *We the People: A History of the United States* by James I. Clark and Robert B. Remini, Glencoe Publishing Co., 1975, p. 82.

Vocabulary:

anesthetic—something that brings relief; *taint*—spoil, contaminate; *sully*—make soiled or tarnished; *chastity*—modesty, purity.

In colonial times, male physicians were largely bumbling experimenters with medicinal herbs, frequently to the sorrow of their patients' survivors who attached leeches to draw off "disordered" blood from feverish bodies when stumped for anything else to do. Barbers doubled as surgeons, operating with no anesthetic save a jolt of rum or frontier whiskey. Most women preferred that midwives attend them in childbirth. Male doctors were often awkward and brutal and, one newspaper editor complained, took liberties "sufficient to taint the Purity and sully the Chastity of any woman breathing."

Midwife Rachel Bunker of Nantucket may have held the record, assisting at a reputed 2,994 births, 31 of them producing twins. Ms. Bunker was no slouch herself when it came to bearing children, nor were her progeny. Upon her death in 1796 she left 113 grandchildren and 98 great-grandchildren. Lucretia Lester of Southold, New York, between 1745 and 1779, attended the birth of 1,300 children, reportedly losing only two.

Women also practiced medicine or, as it was frequently put, "physick" and "chirurgery." They received no training, but then, neither did most men; it was an age, medically speaking, in which one learned by doing. Many of these female amateurs were, apparently, as good as any men, perhaps better than most. One Virginian reported in 1688

A Gentlewoman, that was a notable female Doctress [who] told me, that a Neighbor being bit by a Rattle-Snake swelled excessively; some days afterwards she was sent for, who found him swelled beyond what she thought it had been possible for the Skin to contain, and very thirsty. She gave him *oriental benzoar* shaved, with a strong Decoction of the aforesaid Ditanny, whereby she recovered the Person.

Your summary:

4. From *Teaching Elementary Language Arts* by Dorothy Rubin, Holt, Rinehart & Winston, 1975, p. 120.

Socialization is a process that prepares an individual to live in society. Human beings are social animals. The better we know one another, the better we are able to get along with one another. It is through social discourse such as conversation that we learn more about our friends and neighbors and, many times, about ourselves as well. The need to converse with one another is seen daily in any classroom, whether it is a university graduate class or a kindergarten. When an instructor is interrupted during a class period and must stop to talk to a visitor or leave the class for a short while, what happens? Practically anyone can predict the students' behavior in this situation. They start talking to one another. No prompting is necessary, sometimes to the dismay of the teacher. Children naturally like to talk, to exchange pleasantries, ideas, comments, and so on. The teacher must understand this need in students and provide not only an environment where students will feel free to engage in spontaneous, informal, and nonstructured talks with one another but also provide time for this to take place.

Your summary:

STOP. Check sample summaries at the end of Lesson 7.

VOCABULARY: CONTEXT CLUES (Social Sciences)

The sentences in this section are taken from social science textbooks in psychology, sociology, anthropology, and so on. Notice how the underlined words are usually key words in the sentences. That is, if you do not know the meanings of the underlined words, you will have difficulty determining the author's message.

Practice A.

Use your knowledge of context clues to determine the meanings of the underlined words.

1. Social punishment by peers in the form of ostracism is a powerful means of control. Children do not like to be excluded by their classmates.

   _____ ; _____

2. During adolescence no young person can remain oblivious to the physical changes that are taking place in his or her body._____

3. Adolescence is a biological phenomenon; i.e., there are so many bodily changes taking place that the stage of adolescence is apparent.

   _____

4. During adolescence the percentage of obese children increases. Studies show that girls react more strongly to being very fat than boys.

   _____ ; _____

5. Like the blind men and the elephant, each specialist views humanity from a different position, as a result certain elements are overemphasized and others ignored or diminished. _____ ;

   _____ ; _____ ;

   _____

6. As women assume a larger number of positions of responsibility, ulcers may be more equitably distributed among males and females.

   _____

7. Had agriculture and industry expanded rapidly, Russia would have been, even today, far from becoming a "saturated area" in which the increase of population is inhibited. _____ ;

   _____ ; _____

8. A scientist stated that he was young enough to have escaped the <u>dog-matic</u> teaching in childhood, which placed in <u>bondage</u> the minds of all those who came <u>prior</u> to Darwin, Huxley, and Galton. _____

   _____ ; _____ ;

   _____

9. Good and evil alike, then, grew out of this <u>disposition</u> toward obedience.

   _____

10. The agricultural problem in Russia presented a <u>paradox</u>. A country of <u>boundless</u> territory, with a <u>sparse</u> population, suffered from a shortage of land. _____ ;

    _____ ; _____

11. The <u>wily</u> foreign minister easily outplayed the other statesmen.

    _____

12. Not all societies require sexual <u>fidelity</u>. In <u>polygamous</u> societies, indi-viduals (more usually men than women) are permitted to have more than one <u>spouse</u>. _____ ;

    _____ ; _____

STOP. Check answers at the end of Lesson 7.

Practice B.

Match the meaning from column B with the word in column A.

	Column A	Column B
_____	1. peers	a. mankind
_____	2. ostracism	b. filled to capacity
_____	3. oblivious	c. respond
_____	4. phenomenon	d. earlier in time
_____	5. obese	e. fairly
_____	6. specialist	f. self-contradiction
_____	7. humanity	g. sly

_____ 8. overemphasized   h. a person devoted to a particular field

_____ 9. diminished

_____ 10. equitably   i. held back

_____ 11. expanded   j. unmindful

_____ 12. saturated   k. thinly scattered

_____ 13. inhibited   l. persons who are equals

_____ 14. dogmatic   m. made less

_____ 15. bondage   n. leaning

_____ 16. prior   o. a circumstance that is apparent and can be described

_____ 17. disposition

_____ 18. paradox   p. unlimited

_____ 19. boundless   q. too greatly stressed

_____ 20. sparse   r. exclusion

_____ 21. wily   s. very fat

_____ 22. fidelity   t. a husband or wife

_____ 23. polygamous   u. enlarged

_____ 24. react   v. stating opinions as if they were facts

_____ 25. spouse

w. faithfulness

x. slavery

y. having more than one husband or wife at the same time

STOP. Check answers at the end of Lesson 7.

Practice C.

Here are a number of sentences with missing words. Choose the word that *best* fits the sentence. Put the word in the blank.

Word List:

peers, react, spouses, ostracism, oblivious, phenomenon, obese, specialist, humanity, overemphasized, diminished, equitably, expanded, saturated, inhibited, dogmatic, bondage, prior, disposition, polygamous, fidelity, wily, sparse, boundless, paradox.

1. When the West was young, land was _____ and the population was_____ .

2. Only a(n)_____ fellow who knew all the tricks of the automobile trade would enter the used-car market.

3. A person in public office should not be so_____ that he will not consider new ways of getting the job done.

4. The lesson_____ to this lesson was Lesson 6.

5. The tornado is a(n)_____ of nature.

6. Our professor_____ the chapter of our textbook on intelligence during her lecture, so we knew she was planning to stress it in the exam.

7. _____ infants usually become fat adults.

8. _____ in marriage is important to both _____ .

9. I do not like to compare myself with my_____ because they all seem to do so well.

10. I have studied so hard that my mind is _____with word meanings.

11. It's a(n)_____ that she admires him and hates him at the same time.

12. The prompt salting of the roads by the Sanitation Department_____ _____ the effect of the heavy overnight snowfall on rush hour traffic the next morning.

13. Carmen's allergies_____ her enjoyment of the trip through New England that summer.

14. Her lazy_____ got her fired in the end.

15. _____ marriages are illegal in the United States.

16. People can fall into_____when they carelessly allow governments to take away their rights.

17. A(n)_____ is interested in a particular area of his profession.

18. I _____unfavorably to people who try to take advantage of others.

19. Certain coldhearted people in our society prefer to remain _____ to injustice.

20. _____is one form of punishment inflicted by a group on one of its members who misbehaves.

21. The income tax was originally set up to insure that the cost of government should be_____ shared.

22. If_____is to continue to exist, we must learn to get along with one another better.

23. He pumped so hard that my bicycle tire_____until I thought it would burst.

STOP. Check answers at the end of Lesson 7.

WORD ANALYSIS: APPLYING VOWEL RULES TO SYLLABLES

After you have divided a word into syllables, you must determine how to pronounce the individual syllables. The pronunciation is determined by whether the syllable is open or closed, whether it is a vowel-consonant-final *e* syllable, whether it contains a vowel digraph or diphthong, and whether it is stressed or not.

1. The closed syllable rule applies to syllables that end in consonants and that have one vowel. In a closed syllable the vowel sound is usually short. (See Lesson 5 on *r* controlled vowels.) Examples: but/ton, cot/ton, fas/ten, of/ten.

Special Note

The "schwa" sound is usually described as a short *u* sound and appears as ə. In the words *button, cotton, fasten*, and *often*, the unstressed syllable has a schwa sound rather than the short sound of the vowel. (See Lesson 5 on special letters and sounds and Lesson 8 on accenting.)

2. The open syllable rule applies to syllables that end in one vowel. In an open syllable the vowel sound is usually long. Examples: tī/ger, bā/by (bā/bē), fā/tal, ō/ver, nō/mad.

3. The vowel digraph rule applies to syllables that contain a vowel digraph combination. The syllable may end in a vowel or a consonant. The vowel digraph has only one vowel sound. Examples: ceil/ing, sea/son, neigh/bor, com/plain, re/ceive, tai/lor.

Special Note

Notice that in *ceiling, season, complain, receive*, and *tailor* the first vowel in the syllable containing the vowel digraph says its name and the second vowel is silent. However, there are many exceptions to this. Examples: believe, steak, Caesar, yeoman.

4. The diphthong rule applies to syllables that contain a diphthong combination. The syllable may end in a vowel or a consonant. A diphthong is a blend of two vowel sounds, beginning with the first and gliding to the second. Examples: boil/ing, oys/ter, foi/ble.

Special Notes

1. The *oi* and *oy* combinations sound like the *oi* and *oy* in *oil* and *boy*.
2. Even though a diphthong is a *blend* of two vowel sounds, for syllabication purposes you should consider it as one vowel sound.

5. The silent *e* rule applies to syllables containing a vowel-consonant-final *e* combination. Examples: team/mate, ne/gate, de/note, note/case.
6. A syllable ending in *le* and preceded by a consonant is usually the final syllable in a word. This syllable contains the schwa sound. (See Lesson 8.) Syllables ending in *le* preceded by a consonant sound like *ull* in *bull*, as in *bubble, candle, saddle, table, uncle, apple, fable, syllable.*

Practice A.

Here are a number of nonsense words. Divide each multisyllabic word into syllables and then put in the diacritical marks. Use the following key. (a) To show that a syllable contains a digraph, put a long mark over the first vowel and a slash through the second vowel to represent a silent letter. Examples: crāi̸m, phēi̸. (b) Do not put any markings over diphthongs.

(c) If a nonsense word contains a vowel-consonant-final *e* combination, as in *bāk¢*, put a long mark over the first vowel and a slash through the final *e*. (d) If a syllable is a closed syllable such as hĭt, put the breve (ᴗ) or short mark over the vowel. (e) If a syllable is an open syllable such as *gō*, put in the macron (⁻) or long mark over the vowel.

Nonsense Words:

1. ploinnem
2. craimo
3. choy
4. bleimmete
5. clake
6. drople
7. cropeam
8. nomnete
9. seimo
10. proatteme

STOP. Check answers at the end of Lesson 7.

ANSWERS: Lesson 7 (pp. 168-194)

Reading: Skimming (pp. 168–178)

Practice A

1. Edgar 2. 862-9901 3. 9 Morris Ave. 4. Earl 5. 491-3598 6. 56 Lover's Lane 7. 659-4590 8. Gerald 9. 27 Roger Lane 10. Henry

Practice B

1. The Senator 2. 299 miles 3. 406 4. 12:51 P.M. 5. 1:48 P.M.

Practice C

1. pp. 224–237 2. pp. 357–366 3. pp. 137–138 4. pp. 143–144, 401–402 5. p. 226

Practice D

1. Spanish 2. $175–180 3. at least 3 years 4. 16 E. 42 St. 5. 50 words per minute

Practice E

1. T 2. T 3. F 4. F 5. F

Practice F

Topic: The relationship of weight at birth to weight as an adult

1. F 2. T 3. F 4. T 5. F

Reading/Learning Skills: Summaries (Textbooks) (pp. 178-184)

Practice A (sample summaries)

1. Americans are generally not very honest about their motives. We generally use defenses to hide our real motives for doing things. 2. Clothing styles
tend to reflect the state of advancement of technology; however, the relationship is not a completely direct one. Clothing styles and climate cannot
be directly correlated, either. 3. Most male physicians and all women prac-
titioners in colonial times had no training. They learned "on the job," often
to the misfortune of their patients. The women amateurs were as good as,
if not better than most of the men. 4. Teachers should provide the time for
students to engage in informal talks because conversation is a good means for
them to get to know one another. The better we know one another, the better able we are to get along with one another. (Notice that this summary
starts with the author's conclusion and works backward to pick up the important points leading to that conclusion.)

Vocabulary: Context Clues (Social Sciences) (pp. 185-189)

Practice A

1. peers—persons who are equal in rank; ostracism—exclusion, banishment
2. oblivious—unmindful 3. phenomenon—a circumstance that is apparent
and can be described 4. obese—very fat; react—respond 5. specialist—a
person who devotes himself or herself to a particular branch of a profession;
humanity—mankind, the human race; overemphasized—too greatly stressed;
diminished—made less 6. equitably—fairly, evenly 7. expanded—spread
out, enlarged; saturated—filled to capacity; inhibited—held back, restrained
8. dogmatic—opinionated, excessively positive in stating opinions, stating
opinions as if they were facts; bondage—slavery; prior—earlier in time, preceding 9. disposition—learning, inclination 10. paradox—self-contradiction;
boundless—unlimited; sparse—thinly scattered 11. wily—cunning, sly 12.
fidelity—faithfulness; polygamous—having more than one husband or wife at
the same time; spouse—husband or wife

Practice B

1. l 2. r 3. j 4. o 5. s 6. h 7. a 8. q 9. m 10. e 11. u 12. b
13. i 14. v 15. x 16. d 17. n 18. f 19. p 20. k 21. g 22. w
23. y 24. c 25. t

Practice C

1. boundless; sparse 2. wily 3. dogmatic 4. prior 5. phenomenon
6. overemphasized 7. obese 8. fidelity; spouses 9. peers 10. saturated
11. ˏparadox 12. diminished 13. inhibited 14. disposition 15. polygamous 16. bondage 17. specialist 18. react 19. oblivious 20. ostracism 21. equitably 22. humanity 23. expanded

Word Analysis: Applying Vowel Rules to Syllables (pp. 189–191)

	Syllabication Rule	Vowel Rule
1. ploin/nĕm	vc/cv	diph.; closed syll.
2. crāi̸/mō	v/cv	v. digr.; open syll.
3. choy	——	diph.
4. blēi̸m/mēt¢	vc/cv	v. digr.; silent *e*
5. clāk¢	—	silent *e*
6. drō/ple	spec. *le*	open syll.; unstressed syll.
7. crō/pēa̸m	v/cv	open syll.; v. digr.
8. nŏm/nēt¢	vc/cv	closed syll.; silent *e*
9. sēi̸/mō	v/cv	v. digr.; open syll.
10. prōa̸t/tēm¢	vc/cv	v. digr.; silent *e*

LESSON 8

Reading: Inference
Reading/Learning Skills: Summaries (Stories)
Vocabulary: Context Clues (Mathematics, Economics, Biological and Physical Sciences)
Word Analysis: Accent and Pronunciation of Words
Answers

READING: INFERENCE

When writers do not directly state what they mean but present ideas in a roundabout way, they are using *inference*. Many people think of inference as the ability to read between the lines, but inference is more properly defined as "understanding derived from an indirect suggestion in what is stated." Readers draw inferences; writers make implications or imply meanings.

The ability to draw inferences is especially important in reading fiction. Mystery writers find inference essential to maintaining suspense in their stories. For example, Sherlock Holmes and Perry Mason mysteries are based on the ability of the characters to uncover evidence in the form of clues that are not obvious to others around them.

Inference is an important process that nonfiction authors rely on, also. Good readers must be alert to the ways that authors encourage inference.

Implied Statements

Writers count on inference to make their writing more interesting and enjoyable. To understand what the writer is saying, the reader must be alert to detect the clues that are given. For example, in the sentence *Jane and her boyfriend always put a damper on things when they are around*, you are given clues to the personalities of Jane and her boyfriend, even though nothing is directly said about their personalities. From the statement you cannot help inferring that Jane and her boyfriend are somehow less lively and less adventurous than their friends.

195

You must be careful, however, that you do not read more into a statement than is intended. For example, read the following statement. *As John looked out of the train window, he spied leafless trees.* What season of the year was it? (a) winter, (b) summer, (c) spring, (d) fall, (e) can't tell.

The answer is "(e) can't tell," although a number of people will choose "(d) fall." You don't have enough information to make the inference. It could be any season of the year. We do not know in which part of the world John was traveling. The trees could be leafless as a result of a forest fire, a disease, or some other cause.

PEANUTS ®   **By Schulz**

Practice A.

After you read each set of sentences, determine whether the statements following each one are true or false. Put a T for *true* or an F for *false* in the blank. Explain why you gave your answer on the line after each statement. If there is not enough evidence to determine whether a statement is true or false, write "not enough evidence."

1. Nagging, nagging, nagging. Do this. Do that. Always something. Then when I do it, it's all wrong. Well, I'm glad I left. It's for the best. I can breathe now.

____ a. The person ran away from home. _____

____ b. The person left his wife. _____

____ c. The person quit a job. _____

____ d. The person is a male. _____

____ e. The person is unhappy about the decision to leave. _____

2. Walking slowly under the blazing sun, which was directly overhead, I felt content and almost joyous. The delicious sun seemed to be penetrating right through me. How good it felt! The warmth of the sun always makes me feel good. I wonder if it's because it somehow makes up for the human warmth I crave.

____ a. The person is a female. _____

____ b. The person is hitchhiking._____

____ c. It's summer._____

____ d. It's noon. _____

____ e. The person needs affection. _____

3. If I say no, they'll think I'm chicken; however, if I go along, I may regret it for the rest of my life. How do I get into these situations? The guys mean well, but they're always just too much for me. I don't want to lose my friends, but I have to live with myself, too. I can just see Dean's face when he finds out. Maybe I'd better crack the books and take my chances with the guys.

____ a. The person is a male. _____

____ b. The person is a college student._____

____ c. The person is apprehensive. _____

____ d. The thing that the person is reluctant to do violates the moral or ethical standards of the person. _____

____ e. The thing the person is talking about has to do with playing a prank on Dean._____

____ f. The person will not go along with the guys._____

____ g. The person has been in conflict with the guys before. _____

_____

4. They walked slowly along for some time. Their shadows meeting and separating, meeting and separating. There was no need to speak because everything had already been said. A voice, as if speaking to itself, said, "Life plays funny tricks on you. One day you're the child, and the next day you are the father of that child, and soon, perhaps, even the grandfather of the child." The other person replied, "Yes, I know what you mean. I feel young. There's a young mind in this body, but I become confused when I look in the mirror. The image doesn't conform to mine."

____ a. The persons have not seen each other for a long time._____

_____

____ b. It's daytime._____

____ c. The persons are contemporaries. _____

____ d. The persons are both grandfathers._____

____ e. The persons both feel old._____

___ f. The persons feel that time goes by quickly._____

___ g. The persons are two males._____

5. The men in their undershirts and shorts were aching from carrying their heavy knapsacks all day. They were tired, hungry, dusty, and sweaty. One fourth of them had already turned back. The remaining six were slowly edging away from the mountain pass to make camp for the night. For a moment they stopped because they were awed by the sight of the setting sun. It looked like a ball of fire slowly descending behind the mountain range. After a last look they went in the opposite direction.

___ a. It was a dry day._____

___ b. The men were heading west to make camp._____

___ c. The men were in a desert._____

___ d. The journey had been a hard one._____

___ e. There had been twelve persons at the beginning of the trip._____

6. From George W. Goethals and Dennis S. Klos, *Experiencing Youth*: First-Person Accounts, Second Edition. Copyright © 1976 by Little, Brown and Company (Inc.). Reprinted by permission.

The summer was a hard one–but I fit back into the mold fairly easily. Sophomore year would be better she said. It wasn't. Sophomore year was the critical cut against my mother, giving away her prize, my virginity. It's a very funny story in a lot of ways. Though it was not as calculating as all this, a coldly logical bit of my mind was at work somewhere. My counterpart turned out to be foreign, not exceptionally intelligent (I had to feel superior), someone whose tastes were very unlike mine (I attributed it to cultural differences), and someone with whom I would eventually break up. Since pregnancy would probably tear our house asunder, I went on the pill before ever having intercourse, a move I found ironically calculating at the time. Since the gynecologist was on the same floor as the psychiatric social worker I'd seen and was a disapproving older woman, I was terrified that she would come to take me away, and a tug of war would follow between the two doctors.

___ a. The girl is concerned about what her family thinks._____

____ b. The girl has had some emotional problems. _____

____ c. The girl has a great deal of difficulty discussing her first affair.

_____

____ d. The girl expected to have sexual relations. _____

____ e. The girl is rebelling against her mother. _____

____ f. The girl loves her mother. _____

____ g. Having sexual relations helps the girl solve her problems.

_____

STOP. Check answers at the end of Lesson 8.

Practice B.

Read this selection and then, without looking back, determine whether each statement presented at the end of the selection is true or false. Give evidence for your answer. If there is not enough evidence to write either T or F, write "not enough evidence."

From *Nigger: An Autobiography* by Dick Gregory.*

It's a sad and beautiful feeling to walk home slow on Christmas Eve after you've been out hustling all day, shining shoes in the white taverns and going to the store for the neighbors and buying and stealing presents from the ten-cent store, and now it's dark and still along the street and your feet feel warm and sweaty inside your tennis sneakers even if the wind finds the holes in your mittens. The electric Santa Clauses wink at you from windows. You stop off at your best friend's house and look at his tree and give him a ball-point pen with his name on it. You reach into your shopping bag and give something to everybody there, even the ones you don't know. It doesn't matter that they don't have anything for you because it feels so good to be in a warm happy place where grownups are laughing. There are Daddies around. Your best friend's so happy and excited, standing there trying on all his new clothes. As you walk down the stairs you hear his mother

*From *Nigger: An Autobiography* by Dick Gregory with Robert Lipsyte. Copyright ©, 1964 by Dick Gregory Enterprises. Reprinted by permission of the publisher, E. P. Dutton.

say: "Boo, you forgot to say good-by to Richard, say good-by to Richard, Boo, and wish him a. . . ."

Then you're out on the street again and some of the lights have gone out. You take the long way home, and Mister Ben, the grocer, says: "Merry Christmas, Richard," and you give him a present out of the shopping bag, and you smile at a wino and give him a nickel, and you even wave at Grimes, the mean cop. It's a good feeling. You don't want to get home too fast.

And then you hit North Taylor, your street, and something catches your eye and you lift your head up and it's there in your window. Can't believe it. You start running and the only thing in the whole world you're mad about is that you can't run fast enough. For the first time in a long while the cracked orange door says: "Come on in, little man, you're home now," and there's a wreath and lights in the window and a tree in the kitchen near the coal closet and you hug your Momma, her face hot from the stove. Oh, Momma, I'm so glad you did it like this because ours is new, just for us, everybody else's tree been up all week long for other people to see, and, Momma, ours is just for us. Momma, oh, Momma, you did it again.

My beautiful Momma smiled at me like Miss America, and my brothers and sisters danced around that little kitchen with the round wooden table and the orange crate chairs.

"Go get the vanilla, Richard," said Momma, "Presley, peel some sweet potatoes. Go get the bread out the oven, Dolores. You get away from that duckling, Garland. Ronald, oh, Ronald, you be good now, stand over there with Pauline. Oh, Richard, my little man, did you see the ham Miz White from the Eat Shop sent by, and the bag of nuts from Mister Myers and the turkey from Miz King, and wouldn't you know, Mister Ben, he. . . ."

"Hey, Momma, I know some rich people don't got this much, a ham, and a turkey, Momma. . . ."

"The Lord, He's always looking out for my boys, Richard, and this ain't all, the white folks'll be by here tomorrow to bring us more things."

Momma was so happy that Christmas, all the food folks brought us and Mister Ben giving us more credit, and Momma even talked the electric man into turning the lights on again.

"Hey, Momma, look here, got a present for Daddy. A cigarette lighter, Momma, there's even a place to scratch a name on it."

"What you scratch on it, Richard, Big Pres or Daddy?"

"Nothing, Momma. Might have to give Daddy's present to old Mister White from the Eat Shop again."

She turned away and when she turned back her eyes were wet. Then she smiled her Miss America smile and grabbed my shoulder. "Richard, my little man, if I show you something, you won't tell nobody, will you?"

"What is it, Momma?"

"I got something for you."

"Oh, Momma, you forgot, everything's under the tree."

"This is something special, just for you, Richard."

"Thanks, Momma, oh, thanks, how'd you know I wanted a wallet, Momma, a real wallet like men have?"

Momma always gave each of us something like that, something personal that wasn't under the tree, something we weren't supposed to tell the other kids about. It always came out, though. Garland and I'd be fighting and one of us would say, "Momma likes me better than you, look what she gave me," and we both found out the other got a secret present, too.

But I loved that wallet. First thing I did was fill out the address card. If I got hit by a car someone would know who I am. Then I put my dollars in it, just like men do. Ran outside that night and got on a streetcar and pulled out my wallet and handed the conductor a dollar.

"Got anything smaller, boy?"

"Sure, Mister," I said and I pulled out my wallet again and took a dime out of the coin purse and snapped it shut and put the dollar back in the long pocket and closed the wallet and slipped it into my back pocket. Did the same thing on the way back home.

Did we eat that night! It seemed like all the days we went without food, no bread for the baloney and no baloney for the bread, all the times in the summer when there was no sugar for the Kool-Aid and no lemon for the lemonade and no ice at all were wiped away. Man, we're all right.

After dinner I went out the back door and looked at the sky and told God how nobody ever ate like we ate that night, macaroni and cheese and ham and turkey and the old duckling's cooking in the oven for tomorrow. There's even whiskey, Momma said, for people who come by. Thanks, God, Momma's so happy and even the rats and roaches didn't come out tonight and the wind isn't blowing through the cracks.

How'd you know I wanted a wallet, God? I wonder if all the rich people who get mink coats and electric trains got that one little thing nobody knew they wanted. You know, God, I'm kinda glad you were born in a manger. I wonder, God, if they had let Mary in the first place she stopped at, would you have remembered tonight? Oh, God, I'm scared. I wish I could die right now with the feeling I have because I know Momma's going to make me mad and I'm going to make her mad, and me and Presley's gonna fight . . . .

"Richard, you get in here and put your coat on. Get in here or I'll whip you."

See what I mean, God, there she goes already and I'm not even cold, I'm all wrapped up in You.

"What's wrong, Richard? Why you look so strange?"

"You wouldn't understand, Momma."

"I would, Richard, you tell me."

"Well, I came out to pray, Momma, way out here so they wouldn't hear me and laugh at me and call me a sissy. God's a good God, ain't He, Momma?"

"Yes, Richard."

"Momma, if I tell you something, would you laugh at me, would you say I'm crazy, would you say I was lying? Momma?"

"What is it, Richard?"

"I heard Him talk to me, Momma."

She put her arm around my shoulders and pulled me against her. "He talks to people, Richard, some people that are real special and good like you. Do me a favor, Richard?"

"Sure, Momma."

"Next time you talk to Him, ask Him to send Daddy home."

"Let me stay up and look out the window with you, Momma."

"Everybody's in bed, Richard."

"All my life, Momma, I wanted to stay up with you on Christmas Eve and look out that window with you, Momma. I won't laugh at you."

"What you mean, Richard?"

"You're waiting on him, ain't you? I know, Momma, every Christmas Eve you take a bath and put on that perfume and those clothes from the rich white folks and get down there on your knees in front of that window looking for Daddy."

"Richard, you better get on to bed."

"I know, Momma, that whiskey ain't for people coming by, that's for Daddy."

"Richard, you go on to bed and when he gets here I'll wake you up."

"No, Momma, I want to sit up with you . . . Momma?"

"Yes, Richard?"

"I shoulda got a present for Mister White, 'cause I know Daddy's coming to get his this year."

There were a lot of things I wanted to tell Momma that night while we sat and waited for Daddy, while we prayed on our knees, and dozed and hugged each other against the cold and jumped up like jacks every time we heard a noise on the street. But I never did. Sometimes I think she knew anyway.

I wanted to say to her, Momma, you remember that day I came home and told you I was at Doctor Jackson's house? And how he liked me, Momma, and tole me I'd be a good doctor? How he's going to help me learn to read, and how he told me when it gets too cold to study in my house I could come by his house? Remember that, Momma? It was a lie. I played all that day in a vacant lot.

I guess she knew. She never pressed me for names when I told her about all the people who liked me, all the people I created in my mind, people to help poor folks. I couldn't believe God had made a world and hadn't put none of those people in it.

I made up a schoolteacher that loved me, that taught me to read. A teacher that didn't put me in the idiot's seat or talk about you and your kind. She didn't yell at me when I came to school with my homework all wrinkled and damp. She understood when I told her it was too cold to study in the kitchen so I did my homework under the covers with a flashlight. Then I fell asleep. And one of the other five kids in bed must have peed on it.

I'd go out and sweat and make five dollars. And I'd come home and say, Momma, Mister Green told me to bring this to you. Told me he liked you. Told me he wished he could raise his kids the way you're raising us. That wasn't true, Momma.

Remember all those birthday parties I went to, Momma? Used to steal things from the ten-cent store and give the best presents. I'd come home and tell you how we played pillow kiss and post office and pin the tail on the donkey and how everybody liked me? That was a lie, Momma. One girl cried and ran away when she threw the pillow and it hit me. She opened her eyes and saw she was supposed to kiss me and she cried and ran away.

And on my birthday, Momma, when I came home with that shopping bag full of presents and told you the kids in my class loved me so much they all got me things? That wasn't true. I stole all those little things from the ten-cent store and wrapped them up and put a different kid's name on each one.

"Oh, Richard, if he don't show up this time. . . ."

"He's comin', Momma, it's like you said. He got held up in traffic, the trains were full."

"You know, Richard, your Daddy's a cook, he has to work on Christmas."

"He'll be. here, Momma, you go put those clothes back on."

_____ 1. Richard works hard._____

_____ 2. Richard's father is missing._____

_____ 3. Richard doesn't expect a good Christmas._____

_____ 4. Richard doesn't expect Christmas decorations at his home.

_____

_____ 5. Big Pres is the boyfriend of Richard's mother._____

_____ 6. Richard does not believe in God. _____

_____ 7. Richard never tells lies._____

_____ 8. Richard's teacher is helpful. _____

_____ 9. Richard's teacher understands "poor" children's needs.

_____

_____10. People were kind to Richard's family during Christmas.

_____

_____11. Richard would like to be an adult. _____

_____12. Richard's father has been gone for years._____

_____13. Richard's mother keeps expecting her husband to return.

_____

_____14. Richard tries to build up his mother's ego._____

_____15. Richard is doing well in school. _____

_____16. Richard has a bed of his own._____

____17. Richard has an imagination. _____

____18. Richard's teacher believes in embarrassing children.

_____

____19. Richard wants a girlfriend._____

____20. Richard wonders about rich people. _____

STOP. Do *not* check answers until after you have finished Practice C.

Practice C.

Without looking back at the selection from *Nigger: An Autobiography,* answer these questions by circling the correct letter.

1. The main topic of the selection is

   a. Christmas. b. Richard's mother. c. Richard's family. d. Richard. e. poverty.

2. The most important idea in this selection is that

   a. Richard is poor. b. Richard is unhappy. c. Richard has the ability to survive despite his poverty. d. Richard cares for his mother. e. Richard wants his father to come home.

3. Choose the sentence in which the word *credit* is used in the same way that it is used in the selection.

   a. I give you a lot of credit for that. b. Unless the bank will give us some more credit, we will have to declare bankruptcy. c. He is a credit to his profession. d. I need twelve more credits to graduate. e. Please credit that to my account.

4. From the selection we should *not* believe that very poor people are able to

   a. be happy. b. have love. c. believe in God. d. do very well in school. e. be hopeful.

5. According to the story, three things that belong together are

   a. home, family, park. b. poverty, want, savings. c. school, failure, cold. d. wreath, oven, food. e. love, happiness, fear.

6. The first sentence out of order is

   a. Richard was walking home slowly. b. He visited his friend's house. c. He started to run. d. Something hit his eye. e. He opened the cracked orange door.

7. The idea *not* found in the selection is that

   a. Richard would like his father to come home.   b. Richard tries to help his mother.   c. Richard is an understanding young man.   d. Richard gets into fights with his brothers.   e. Richard expects to be famous when he grows up.

8. Choose the statement that *best* describes the author's purpose for writing this selection.

   a. To show that all poor people are happy.   b. To get others to help poor people.   c. To show what it means to a young boy to be poor.   d. To show how a child can help his mother.   e. To show why a young boy steals.

STOP.   Check answers for Practice B and Practice C at the end of Lesson 8.

Practice D.

Read these two short selections and then answer the questions at the end of each.

1. Two engineers went out to lunch. The waiter sat them at a table situated by a large window overlooking the street. While they were waiting for lunch, their conversation was abruptly interrupted by a thunderous crash. They both turned and looked out the window. "My God! That's my spouse in the accident." The other immediately asked in surprise, "Your spouse? Why didn't you tell me that you were married?" Then the second engineer stood up and stalked out of the restaurant.

   Can you explain why one of the engineers stalked out of the restaurant?

2. The school master, the minister, the schoolmaster's daughter, and the minister's wife are out walking in the woods. They find a bird's nest with

four eggs in it. Each one of them takes out an egg, and yet one egg is left in the nest.

How can this be?

STOP. Check answers at the end of Lesson 8.

READING/LEARNING SKILLS: SUMMARIES (Stories)

Summarizing a story is similar to summarizing a paragraph. Start with the central idea of the story and then state the essential details only. Alternatively, begin with the author's conclusion and then give the essential points leading to that conclusion.

Practice A.

Summarize this story.

Vocabulary:

capital punishment—death penalty; *a priori*—marked by reasoning; *incessantly*—continuously; *capricious*—changeable; *caprice*—a sudden impulse; *minutest*—smallest; *solitary*—alone; *foes*—enemies; *zealously*—eagerly, passionately; *gaoler*—jailer (British spelling); *erudite*—learned; *senile*—characteristic of old age; *emaciation*—a wasted condition of the body; *ethereal*—heavenly; *summits*—highest points; *suffused*— spread through; *Pan*—the ancient Greek god of forests, flocks, and shepherds; *abysses*—bottomless pits; *bartered*—traded; *waive*—give up; *stipulated*—agreed on.

The Bet

ANTON CHEKOV

I

It was a dark autumn night. The old banker was pacing from corner to corner of his study, recalling to his mind the party he gave in the autumn fifteen years before. There were many clever people at the party and much interesting conversation. They talked among other things of capital punishment. The guests, among them not a few scholars and journalists, for the most part disapproved of capital punishment. They found it obsolete as a means of punishment, unfitted to a Christian State and immoral. Some of them thought that capital punishment should be replaced universally by life-imprisonment.

"I don't agree with you," said the host. "I myself have experienced neither capital punishment nor life-imprisonment, but if one may judge *a priori*, then in my opinion capital punishment is more moral and more humane than imprisonment. Execution kills instantly, life-imprisoment kills by degrees. Who is the more humane executioner; one who kills you in a few seconds or one who draws the life out of you incessantly, for years?"

"They're both equally immoral," remarked one of the guests, "because their purpose is the same, to take away life. The State is not God. It has no right to take away that which it cannot give back, if it should so desire."

Among the company was a lawyer, a young man of about twenty-five. On being asked his opinion, he said:

"Capital punishment and life-imprisonment are equally immoral; but if I were offered the choice between them, I would certainly choose the second. It's better to live somehow than not to live at all."

There ensued a lively discussion. The banker, who was then younger and more nervous, suddenly lost his temper, banged his fist on the table, and turning to the young lawyer cried out:

"It's a lie. I bet you two millions you wouldn't stick in a cell even for five years."

"If you mean it seriously," replied the lawyer, "then I bet I'll stay not five but fifteen."

"Fifteen! Done!" cried the banker. "Gentlemen, I stake two millions."

"Agreed. You stake two millions, I my freedom," said the lawyer.

So this wild, ridiculous bet came to pass. The banker, who at that time had too many millions to count, spoiled and capricious, was beside himself with rapture. During supper he said to the lawyer jokingly:

"Come to your senses, young man, before it's too late. Two millions are nothing to me, but you stand to lose three or four of the best years of your life. I say three or four, because you'll never stick it out any longer. Don't forget either, you unhappy man, that voluntary is much heavier than enforced imprisonment. The idea that you have the right to free yourself at any moment will poison the whole of your life in the cell. I pity you."

And now the banker, pacing from corner to corner, recalled all this and asked himself:

"Why did I make this bet? What's the good? The lawyer loses fifteen years of his life and I throw away two millions. Will it convince people that capital punishment is worse or better than imprisonment for life? No, no! All stuff and rubbish. On my part, it was the caprice of a well-fed man; on the lawyer's pure greed of gold."

He recollected further what happened after the evening party. It was decided that the lawyer must undergo his imprisonment under the strictest observation, in a garden wing of the banker's house. It was agreed that during the period he would be deprived of the right to cross the threshold, to see living people, to hear human voices, and to receive letters and newspapers. He was permitted to have a musical instrument, to read books, to write letters, to drink wine and smoke tobacco. By the agreement he could communicate, but only in silence, with the outside world through a little window specially constructed for this purpose. Everything necessary, books, music, wine, he could receive in any quantity by sending a note through the window. The agreement provided for all the minutest details, which made the confinement strictly solitary, and it obliged the lawyer to remain exactly fifteen years from twelve o'clock of November 14th, 1870, to twelve o'clock of November 14th, 1885. The least attempt on his part to violate the conditions, to escape if only for two minutes before the time, freed the banker from the obligation to pay him the two millions.

During the first year of imprisonment, the lawyer, as far as it was possible to judge from his short notes, suffered terribly from loneliness and boredom. From his wing day and night came the sound of the piano. He rejected wine and tobacco. "Wine," he wrote, "excites desires, and desires are the chief foes of a prisoner; besides, nothing is more boring than to drink good wine alone, and tobacco spoils the air in his room." During the first year the lawyer was sent books of a light character; novels with a complicated love interest, stories of crime and fantasy, comedies, and so on.

In the second year the piano was heard no longer and the lawyer asked only for classics. In the fifth year, music was heard again, and the prisoner asked for wine. Those who watched him said that during the whole of that year he was only eating, drinking, and lying on his bed. He yawned often and talked angrily to himself. Books he did not read. Sometimes at nights he would sit down to write. He would write for a long time and tear it all up in the morning. More than once he was heard to weep.

In the second half of the sixth year, the prisoner began zealously to study languages, philosophy, and history. He fell on these subjects so hungrily that the banker hardly had time to get books enough for him. In the space of four years about six hundred volumes were bought at his request. It was while that passion lasted that the banker received the following letter from the prisoner: "My dear gaoler, I am writing these lines in six languages. Show them to experts. Let them read them. If they do not find one single mistake, I beg you to give orders to have a gun fired off in the garden. By the noise I shall know that my efforts have not been in vain. The genuises of all ages and countries speak in different languages; but in them all burns the same flame. Oh, if you knew my heavenly happiness now that I can understand them!" The prisoner's desire was fulfilled. Two shots were fired in the garden by the banker's order.

Later on, after the tenth year, the lawyer sat immovable before his table and read only the New Testament. The banker found it strange that a man who in four years had mastered six hundred erudite volumes, should have spent nearly a year in reading one book, easy to understand and by no means thick. The New Testament was then replaced by the history of religions and theology.

During the last two years of his confinement the prisoner read an extraordinary amount, quite haphazard. Now he would apply himself to the natural sciences, then he would read Byron or

Shakespeare. Notes used to come from him in which he asked to be sent at the same time a book on chemistry, a textbook of medicine, a novel, and some treatise on philosophy or theology. He read as though he were swimming in the sea among broken pieces of wreckage, and in his desire to save his life was eagerly grasping one piece after another.

II

The banker recalled all this, and thought:

"Tomorrow at twelve o'clock he receives his freedom. Under the agreement, I shall have to pay him two millions. If I pay, it's all over with me. I am ruined forever. . ."

Fifteen years before he had too many millions to count, but now he was afraid to ask himself which he had more of, money or debts. Gambling on the Stock-Exchange, risky speculation, and the recklessness of which he could not rid himself even in old age, had gradually brought his business to decay; and the fearless, self-confident, proud man of business had become an ordinary banker, trembling at every rise and fall in the market.

"That cursed bet," murmured the old man clutching his head in despair. . . . "Why didn't the man die? He's only forty years old. He will take away my last farthing, marry, enjoy life, gamble on the Exchange, and I will look on like an envious beggar and hear the same words from him every day: 'I'm obliged to you for the happiness of my life. Let me help you.' No, it's too much! The only escape from bankruptcy and disgrace—is that the man should die."

The clock had just struck three. The banker was listening. In the house every one was asleep, and one could hear only the frozen trees whining outside the windows. Trying to make no sound, he took out of his safe the key of the door which had not been opened for fifteen years, put on his overcoat, and went out of the house. The garden was dark and cold. It was raining. A damp, penetrating wind howled in the garden and gave the trees no rest. Though he strained his eyes, the banker could see neither the ground, nor the white statues, nor the garden wing, nor the trees. Approaching the garden wing, he called the watch-man twice. There was no answer. Evidently the watchman had taken shelter from the bad weather and was now asleep some-where in the kitchen or the greenhouse.

"If I have the courage to fulfil my intention," thought the old man, "the suspicion will fall on the watchman first of all."

In the darkness he groped for the steps and the door and entered the hall of the garden-wing, then poked his way into a narrow passage and struck a match. Not a soul was there. Some one's bed, with no bedclothes on it, stood there, and an iron stove loomed dark in the corner. The seals on the door that led into the prisoner's room were unbroken.

When the match went out, the old man, trembling from agitation, peeped into the little window.

In the prisoner's room a candle was burning dimly. The pris-oner himself sat by the table. Only his back, the hair on his head and his hands were visible. Open books were strewn about on the table, the two chairs, and on the carpet near the table.

Five minutes passed and the prisoner never once stirred. Fifteen years' confinement had taught him to sit motionless. The banker tapped on the window with his finger, but the prisoner made no movement in reply. Then the banker cautiously tore the seals from the door and put the key into the lock. The rusty lock gave a hoarse groan and the door creaked. The banker expected instantly to hear a cry of surprise and the sound of steps. Three minutes passed and it was as quiet inside as it had been before. He made up his mind to enter.

Before the table sat a man, unlike an ordinary human being. It was a skeleton, with tight-drawn skin, with long curly hair like a woman's, and a shaggy beard. The color of his face was yellow, of an earthy shade; the cheeks were sunken, the back long and narrow, and the hand upon which he leaned his hairy head was so lean and skinny that it was painful to look upon. His hair was already silvering with gray, and no one who glanced at the senile emaciation of the face would have believed that he was only forty years old. On the table, before his bended head, lay a sheet of paper on which something was written in a tiny hand.

"Poor devil," thought the banker, "he's asleep and probably seeing millions in his dreams. I have only to take and throw this half-dead thing on the bed, smother him a moment with the pillow, and the most careful examination will find no trace of unnatural death. But, first, let us read what he has written here."

The banker took the sheet from the table and read:

"Tomorrow at twelve o'clock midnight, I shall obtain my freedom and the right to mix with people. But before I leave this room and see the sun I think it necessary to say a few words to you. On my own clear conscience and before God who sees me I declare to you that I despise freedom, life, health, and all that your books call the blessings of the world.

"For fifteen years I have diligently studied earthly life. True, I saw neither the earth nor the people, but in your books I drank fragrant wine, sang songs, hunted deer and wild boar in the forests, loved women. . . . And beautiful women, like clouds ethereal, created by the magic of your poets' genius, visited me by night and whispered to me wonderful tales, which made my head drunken. In your books I climbed the summits of Elburz and Mont Blanc and saw from there how the sun rose in the morning, and in the evening suffused the sky, the ocean, and the mountain ridges with a purple gold. I saw from there how above me lightnings glimmered cleaving the clouds; I saw green forests, fields, rivers, lakes, cities; I heard sirens singing, and the playing of the pipes of Pan; I touched the wings of beautiful devils who came flying to me to speak of God. . . . In your books I cast myself into bottomless abysses, worked miracles, burned cities to the ground, preached new religions, conquered whole countries. . . .

"Your books gave me wisdom. All that unwearying human thought created in the centuries is compressed to a little lump in my skull. I know that I am cleverer than you all.

"And I despise your books, despise all worldly blessings and wisdom. Everything is void, frail, visionary and delusive as a mirage. Though you be proud and wise and beautiful, yet will death wipe you from the face of the earth like the mice underground; and your posterity, your history, and the immortality of your men of genius will be as frozen slag, burnt down together with the terrestrial globe.

"You are mad, and gone the wrong way. You take falsehood for truth and ugliness for beauty. You would marvel if suddenly apple and orange trees should bear frogs and lizards instead of fruit, and if roses should begin to breathe the odor of a sweating horse. So do I marvel at you, who have bartered heaven for earth. I do not want to understand you.

"That I may show you in deed my contempt for that by which you live, I waive the two millions of which I once dreamed as of paradise, and which I now despise. That I may deprive myself of my right to them, I shall come out from here five minutes before the stipulated term, and thus shall violate the agreement."

When he had read, the banker put the sheet on the table, kissed the head of the strange man, and began to weep. He went out of the wing. Never at any other time, not even after his terrible losses on the Exchange, had he felt such contempt for himself as now. Coming home, he lay down on his bed, but agitation and tears kept him a long time from sleeping. . . .

The next morning the poor watchman came running to him and told him that they had seen the man who lived in the wing climb through the window into the garden. He had gone to the gate and disappeared. The banker went instantly with his servants to the wing and established the escape of his prisoner. To avoid unnecessary rumors he took the paper with the renunciation from the table and, on his return, locked it in his safe.

Your summary:

STOP. Check sample summary at the end of Lesson 8.

Practice B.

Without referring to the text of the story, answer these true/false questions. Put a T for *true* or an F for *false* in the blank.

_____ 1. The people at the banker's party were unanimous in feeling that capital punishment was worse than life imprisonment.

_____ 2. The banker felt that capital punishment was more moral than life imprisonment.

_____ 3. Two millions was not a lot of money to the banker at the time of the party.

_____ 4. The banker was used to getting his way.

_____ 5. The banker felt that the lawyer was greedy.

_____ 6. During the lawyer's first year of imprisonment he consumed quantities of wine.

_____ 7. During the first year of imprisonment the lawyer read mainly for pleasure.

_____ 8. The lawyer never wept during his prison stay. ·

_____ 9. The lawyer during his stay read only in his native language.

_____10. The banker did not understand the complexity of the New Testament.

_____11. The banker was not an honorable man.

_____12. The banker never once felt any contempt for himself.

_____13. The lawyer both gained and lost from his stay in the cell.

_____14. The banker was afraid of rumors.

STOP. Check answers at the end of Lesson 8.

Practice C.

Give evidence from the story "The Bet" for every *true* answer in Practice B.

STOP. Check answers at the end of Lesson 8.

Practice D.

Summarize this story.

Vocabulary:

dank—damp; *palpable*—obvious, readily or plainly seen; *jaguar*—a large, ferocious member of the cat family; *amended*—corrected; *lore*—beliefs; *indolently*—lazily; *brier*—pipe; *sensuous*—producing an agreeable effect; *receding*—going away, withdrawing; *doggedly*—stubbornly, determinedly; *vitality*—strength; *opaqueness*—darkness; *perils*—dangers; *lacerated*—torn roughly; *crimson*—vivid red; *quarry*—game; *discerned*—made out; *bizzare*—strange; *amenities*—agreeable manners or courtesies; *affable*—friendly, pleasant; *cosmopolite*—citizen of the world; *appraising*—evaluating; *capital*—great, excellent; *ardent*—enthusiastic; *debacle*—collapse; *obstacle*—something in the way; *surmounted*—overcame; *attributes*—qualities; *condone*—overlook, pardon, forgive; *lascars*—East Indian sailors; *Providence*—God's guiding of human destiny; *barbarous*—savage, uncivilized; *eludes*—escapes or avoids; *knouter*—whipper or lasher; *grotesque*—fantastically ugly; *solicitously*—anxiously, concernedly; *venerable*—admirable because of age; *diverting*—amusing; *deplorable*—regrettable; *haversack*—a single-strapped bag worn over one shoulder and used for carrying provisions; *rowels*—a revolving disk at the end of a spur with sharp points for goading a horse; *futile*—useless; *zealous*—passionate, eager; *pungent*—hot, peppery; *uncanny*—supernatural, extraordinary; *ranker*—more excessive.

The Most Dangerous Game

RICHARD CONNELL

"Off there to the right—somewhere—is a large island," said Whitney. "It's rather a mystery—"

"What island is it?" Rainsford asked.

"The old charts call it 'Ship-Trap Island,' " Whitney replied. "A suggestive name, isn't it? Sailors have a curious dread of the place. I don't know why. Some superstition—"

"Can't see it," remarked Rainsford, trying to peer through the dank tropical night that was palpable as it pressed its thick warm blackness in upon the yacht.

"You've good eyes," said Whitney, with a laugh, "and I've seen you pick off a moose moving in the brown fall bush at four hundred yards, but even you can't see four miles or so through a moonless Caribbean night."

"Not four yards," admitted Rainsford. "Ugh! It's like moist black velvet."

"It will be light enough in Rio," promised Whitney. "We should make it in a few days. I hope the jaguar guns have come from Purdey's. We should have some good hunting up the Amazon. Great sport, hunting."

"The best sport in the world," agreed Rainsford.

"For the hunter," amended Whitney. "Not for the jaguar."

"Don't talk rot, Whitney," said Rainsford. "You're a big-game hunter, not a philosopher. Who cares how a jaguar feels?"

"Perhaps the jaguar does," observed Whitney.

"Bah! They've no understanding."

"Even so, I rather think they understand one thing—fear. The fear of pain and the fear of death."

"Nonsense," laughed Rainsford. "This hot weather is making you soft, Whitney. Be a realist. The world is made up of two classes—the hunters and the hunted. Luckily, you and I are hunters. Do you think we've passed that island yet?"

"I can't tell in the dark. I hope so."

"Why?" asked Rainsford.

"The place has a reputation—a bad one."

"Cannibals?" suggested Rainsford.

"Hardly. Even cannibals wouldn't live in such a God-forsaken place. But it's gotten into sailor lore, somehow. Didn't you notice that the crew's nerves seemed a bit jumpy today?"

"They were a bit strange, now you mention it. Even Captain Nielsen—"

"Yes, even that tough-minded old Swede, who'd go up to the devil himself and ask him for a light. Those fishy blue eyes held a look I never saw there before. All I could get out of him was: 'This place has an evil name among seafaring men, sir.' Then he said to me, very gravely: 'Don't you feel anything?'—as if the air about us was actually poisonous. Now, you mustn't laugh when I tell you this—I did feel something like a sudden chill.

"There was no breeze. The sea was as flat as a plate-glass window. We were drawing near the island then. What I felt was a—a mental chill; a sort of sudden dread."

"Pure imagination," said Rainsford. "One superstitious sailor can taint the whole ship's company with his fear."

"Maybe. But sometimes I think sailors have an extra sense that tells them when they are in danger. Sometimes I think evil is a tangible thing—with wave lengths, just as sound and light have. An evil place can, so to speak, broadcast vibrations of evil. Anyhow, I'm glad we're getting out of this zone. Well, I think I'll turn in now, Rainsford."

"I'm not sleepy," said Rainsford. "I'm going to smoke another pipe up on the afterdeck."

"Good night, then, Rainsford. See you at breakfast."

"Right. Good night, Whitney."

There was no sound in the night as Rainsford sat there, but the muffled throb of the engine that drove the yacht swiftly through the darkness, and the swish and ripple of the wash of the propeller.

Rainsford, reclining in a steamer chair, indolently puffed on his favorite brier. The sensuous drowsiness of the night was on him. "It's so dark," he thought, "that I could sleep without closing my eyes; the night would be my eyelids—"

An abrupt sound startled him. Off to the right he heard it, and his ears, expert in such matters, could not be mistaken. Again he heard the sound, and again. Somewhere, off in the blackness, someone had fired a gun three times.

Rainsford sprang up and moved quickly to the rail, mystified. He strained his eyes in the direction from which the reports had come, but it was like trying to see through a blanket. He leaped upon the rail and balanced himself there, to get greater elevation; his pipe, striking a rope, was knocked from his mouth. He lunged for it; a short, hoarse cry same from his lips as he realized he had reached too far and had lost his balance. The cry was pinched off short as the blood-warm waters of the Caribbean Sea closed over his head.

He struggled up to the surface and tried to cry out, but the wash from the speeding yacht slapped him in the face and the salt water in his open mouth made him gag and strangle. Desperately he struck out with strong strokes after the receding lights of the yacht, but he stopped before he had swum fifty feet. A certain cool-headedness had come to him; it was not the first time he had been in a tight place. There was a chance that his cries could be heard by someone aboard the yacht, but that chance was slender, and grew more slender as the yacht raced on. He wrestled himself out of his clothes, and shouted with all his power. The lights of the yacht became faint and ever-vanishing fireflies; then they were blotted out entirely by the night.

Rainsford remembered the shots. They had come from the right, and doggedly he swam in that direction, swimming with slow, deliberate strokes, conserving his strength. For a seemingly endless time he fought the sea. He began to count his strokes; he could do possibly a hundred more and then—

Rainsford heard a sound. It came out of the darkness, a high, screaming sound, the sound of an animal in an extremity of anguish and terror.

He did not recognize the animal that made the sound; he did not try to; with fresh vitality he swam toward the sound. He heard it again; then it was cut short by another noise, crisp, staccato.

"Pistol shot," muttered Rainsford, swimming on.

Ten minutes of determined effort brought another sound to his ears—the most welcome he had ever heard—the muttering and growling of the sea breaking on a rocky shore. He was almost on the rocks before he saw them; on a night less calm he would have been shattered against them. With his remaining strength he dragged himself from the swirling waters. Jagged crags appeared to jut up into the opaqueness; he forced himself upward, hand over hand. Grasping, his hands raw, he reached a flat place at the top. Dense jungle came down to the very edge of the cliffs. What perils that tangle of trees and underbrush might hold for him did not concern Rainsford just then. All he knew was that he was safe from his enemy, the sea, and that utter weariness was on him. He flung himself down at the jungle edge and tumbled headlong into the deepest sleep of his life.

When he opened his eyes he knew from the position of the sun that it was late in the afternoon. Sleep had given him new vigor; a sharp hunger was picking at him. He looked about him, almost cheerfully.

"Where there are pistol shots, there are men. Where there are men, there is food," he thought. But what kind of men, he wondered, in so forbidding a place? An unbroken front of snarled and ragged jungle fringed the shore.

He saw no sign of a trail through the closely knit web of weeds and trees; it was easier to go along the shore, and Rainsford floundered along by the water. Not far from where he had landed, he stopped.

Some wounded thing, by the evidence a large animal, had thrashed about in the underbrush; the jungle weeds were crushed down and the moss was lacerated; one patch of weeds was stained crimson. A small, glittering object not far away caught Rainsford's eye and he picked it up. It was an empty cartridge.

"A twenty-two," he remarked. "That's odd. It must have been a fairly large animal too. The hunter had his nerve with him to tackle it with a light gun. It's clear that the brute put up a fight. I suppose the first three shots I heard was when the hunter flushed his quarry and wounded it. The last shot was when he trailed it here and finished it."

He examined the ground closely and found what he had hoped to find—the print of hunting-boots. They pointed along the cliff in the direction he had been going. Eagerly he hurried along, now slipping on a rotten log or a loose stone, but making headway; night was beginning to settle down on the island.

Bleak darkness was blacking out the sea and jungle when Rainsford sighted the lights. He came upon them as he turned a crook in the coast line, and his first thought was that he had come upon a village, for there were many lights. But as he forged along he saw to his great astonishment that all the lights were in one enormous building—a lofty structure with pointed towers plunging upward into the gloom. His eyes made out the shadowy outlines of a palatial chateau; it was set on a high bluff, and on three sides of it cliffs dived down to where the sea licked greedy lips in the shadows.

"Mirage," thought Rainsford. But it was no mirage, he found, when he opened the tall spiked iron gate. The stone steps were real enough; the massive door with a leering gargoyle for a knocker was real enough; yet about it all hung an air of unreality.

He lifted the knocker, and it creaked up stiffly, as if it had never before been used. He let it fall, and it startled him with its booming loudness. He thought he heard steps within; the door remained closed. Again Rainsford lifted the heavy knocker, and let it fall. The door opened then, opened as suddenly as if it were on a spring, and Rainsford stood blinking in the river of glaring gold light that poured out. The first thing Rainsford's eyes discerned was the largest man Rainsford had ever seen—a gigantic creature, solidly made and black-bearded to the waist. In his hand the man held a long-barreled revolver, and he was pointing it straight at Rainsford's heart.

Out of the snarl of beard two small eyes regarded Rainsford.

"Don't be alarmed," said Rainsford, with a smile which he hoped was disarming. "I'm no robber. I fell off a yacht. My name is Sanger Rainsford of New York City."

The menacing look in the eyes did not change. The revolver pointed as rigidly as if the giant were a statue. He gave no sign that he understood Rainsford's words, or that he had even heard them. He was dressed in uniform, a black uniform trimmed with gray astrakhan.

"I'm Sanger Rainsford of New York," Rainsford began again. "I fell off a yacht. I am hungry."

The man's only answer was to raise with his thumb the hammer of his revolver. Then Rainsford saw the man's free hand go to his forehead in a military salute, and he saw him click his heels together and stand at attention. Another man was coming down the broad marble steps, an erect, slender man in evening clothes. He advanced to Rainsford and held out his hand.

In a cultivated voice marked by a slight accent that gave it added precision and deliberateness, he said: "It is a very great pleasure and honor to welcome Mr. Sanger Rainsford, the celebrated hunter, to my home."

Automatically Rainsford shook the man's hand.

"I've read your book about hunting snow leopards in Tibet, you see," explained the man. "I am General Zaroff."

Rainsford's first impression was that the man was singularly handsome; his second was that there was an original, almost bizarre qualtity about the general's face. He was a tall man past middle age, for his hair was a vivid white; but his thick eyebrows and pointed military mustache were as black as the night from which Rainsford had come. His eyes, too, were black and very bright. He had high cheekbones, a sharp-cut nose, a spare, dark face, the face of a man used to giving orders, the face of an aristocrat. Turning to the giant in unifrom, the general made a sign. The giant put away his pistol, saluted, withdrew.

"Ivan is an incredibly strong fellow," remarked the general, "but he has the misfortune to be deaf and dumb. A simple fellow, but, I'm afraid, like all his race, a bit of a savage."

"Is he Russian?"

"He is a Cossack," said the general, and his smile showed red lips and pointed teeth. So am I.

"Come," he said, "we shouldn't be chatting here. We can talk later. Now you want clothes, food, rest. You shall have them. This is a most restful spot."

Ivan had reappeared, and the general spoke to him with lips that moved but gave forth no sound.

"Follow Ivan, if you please, Mr. Rainsford," said the general. "I was about to have my dinner when you came. I'll wait for you. You'll find that my clothes will fit you, I think."

It was to a huge, beam-ceilinged bedroom with a canopied bed big enough for six men that Rainsford followed the silent giant. Ivan laid out an evening suit, and Rainsford, as he put it on, noticed that it came from a London tailor who ordinarily cut and sewed for none below the rank of duke.

The dining room to which Ivan conducted him was in many ways remarkable. There was a medieval magnificence about it; it suggested a baronial hall of feudal times with its oaken panels, its high ceiling, its vast refectory table where twoscore men could sit down to eat. About the hall were the mounted heads of many animals—lions, tigers, elephants, moose, bears; larger or more perfect specimens Rainsford had never seen. At the great table the general was sitting alone.

"You'll have a cocktail, Mr. Rainsford," he suggested. The cocktail was surpassingly good; and, Rainsford noted, the table appointments were of the finest—the linen, the crystal, the silver, the china.

They were eating *borsch*, the rich, red soup with whipped cream so dear to Russian palates. Half apologetically General Zaroff said: "We do our best to preserve the amenities of civilization here. Please forgive any lapses. We are well off the beaten track, you know. Do you think the champagne has suffered from its long ocean trip?"

"Not in the least," declared Rainsford. He was finding the general a most thoughtful and affable host, a true cosmopolite. But there was one small trait of the general's that made Rainsford uncomfortable. Whenever he looked up from his plate he found the general studying him, appraising him narrowly.

"Perhaps," said General Zaroff, "you were surprised that I recognized your name. You see, I read all books on hunting published in English, French, and Russian. I have but one passion in my life, Mr. Rainsford, and it is the hunt."

"You have some wonderful heads here," said Rainsford as he ate a particularly well cooked filet mignon. "That Cape buffalo is the largest I ever saw."

"Oh, that fellow. Yes, he was a monster."

"Did he charge you?"

"Hurled me against a tree," said the general. "Fractured my skull. But I got the brute."

"I've always thought," said Rainsford, "that the Cape buffalo is the most dangerous of all big game."

For a moment the general did not reply; he was smiling his curious red-lipped smile. Then he said slowly: "No. You are wrong, sir. The Cape buffalo is not the most dangerous big game." He sipped his wine. "Here in my preserve on the island," he said in the same slow tone, "I hunt the more dangerous game."

Rainsford expressed his surprise. "Is there big game on this island?"

The general nodded. "The biggest."

"Really?"

"Oh, it isn't here naturally, of course. I have to stock the island."

"What have you imported, general?" Rainsford asked. "Tigers?"

The general smiled. "No," he said. "Hunting tigers ceased to interest me some years ago. I exhausted their possibilities, you see. No thrill left in tigers, no real danger. I live for danger, Mr. Rainsford."

The general took from his pocket a gold cigarette case and offered his guest a long black cigarette with a silver tip; it was perfumed and gave off a smell like incense.

"We will have some capital hunting, you and I," said the general. "I shall be most glad to have your society."

"But what game—" began Rainsford.

"I'll tell you," said the general. "You will be amused, I know. I think I may say, in all modesty, that I have done a rare thing. I have invented a new sensation. May I pour you another glass of port, Mr. Rainsford?"

"Thank you, general."

The general filled both glasses, and said: "God makes some men poets. Some He makes kings, some beggars. Me He made a hunter. My hand was made for the trigger, my father said. He was a very rich man with a quarter of a million acres in the Crimea, and he was an ardent sportsman. When I was only five years old he gave me a little gun, specially made in Moscow for me, to shoot sparrows with. When I shot some of his prize turkeys with it, he did not punish me; he complimented me on my marksmanship. I killed my first bear in the Caucasus when I was ten. My whole life has been one prolonged hunt. I went into the army—it was expected of nobleman's sons—and for a time commanded a division of Cossack cavalry, but my real interest was always the hunt. I have hunted every kind of game in every land. It would be impossible for me to tell you how many animals I have killed."

The general puffed at his cigarette.

"After the debacle in Russia I left the country, for it was imprudent for an officer of the Czar to stay there. Many noble Russians lost everything. I, luckily, had invested heavily in A-merican securities, so I shall never have to open a tearoom in Monte Carlo or drive a taxi in Paris. Naturally, I continued to hunt—grizzlies in your Rockies, crocodiles in the Ganges, rhi-noceroses in East Africa. It was in Africa that the Cape buffalo hit me and laid me up for six months. As soon as I recovered I started for the Amazon to hunt jaguars, for I had heard they were unusually cunning. They weren't." The Cossack sighed. "They were no match at all for a hunter with his wits about him, and a high-powered rifle. I was bitterly disappointed. I was lying in my tent with a splitting headache one night when a terrible thought pushed its way into my mind. Hunting was beginning to bore me! And hunting, remember, had been my life. I have heard that in America businessmen often go to pieces when they give up the business that has been their life."

"Yes, that's so," said Rainsford.

The general smiled. "I had no wish to go to pieces," he said. "I must do something. Now, mine is an analytical mind, Mr. Rainsford. Doubtless that is why I enjoy the problems of the chase."

"No doubt, General Zaroff."

"So," continued the general, "I asked myself why the hunt no longer fascinated me. You are much younger than I am, Mr. Rainsford, and have not hunted as much, but you perhaps can guess the answer."

"What was it?"

"Simply this: hunting had ceased to be what you call 'a sporting proposition.' It had become too easy. I always got my quarry. Always. There is no greater bore than perfection."

The general lit a fresh cigarette.

"No animal had a chance with me any more. That is no boast; it is a mathematical certainty. The animal had nothing but his legs and his instinct. Instinct is no match for reason. When I thought of this it was a tragic moment for me, I can tell you."

Rainsford leaned across the table, absorbed in what his host was saying.

"It came to me as an inspiration what I must do," the general went on.

"And that was?"

The general smiled the quiet smile of one who has faced an obstacle and surmounted it with success. "I had to invent a new animal to hunt," he said.

"A new animal? You're joking."

"Not at all, " said the general. "I never joke about hunting. I needed a new animal. I found one. So I bought this island, built this house, and here I do my hunting. The island is perfect for my purposes—there are jungles with a maze of trails in them, hills, swamps—"

"But the animal, General Zaroff?"

"Oh," said the general, "it supplies me with the most exciting hunting in the world. No other hunting compares with it for an instant. Every day I hunt, and I never grow bored now, for I have a quarry with which I can match my wits."

Rainsford's bewilderment showed in his face.

"I wanted the ideal animal to hunt," explained the general. "So I said: 'what are the attributes of an ideal quarry?' And the answer was, of course: 'It must have courage, cunning, and, above all, it must be able to reason.' "

"But no animal can reason," objected Rainsford.

"My dear fellow," said the general, "there is one that can."

"But you can't mean—" gasped Rainsford.

"And why not?"

"I can't believe you are serious, General Zaroff. This is a grisly joke."

"Why should I not be serious? I am speaking of hunting."

"Hunting? Good God, General Zaroff, what you speak of is murder."

The general laughed with entire good nature. He regarded Raindford quizzically. "I refuse to believe that so modern and civilized a young man as you seem to be harbors romantic ideas about the value of human life. Surely your experiences in the war—"

"Did not make me condone cold-blooded murder," finished Rainsford stiffly.

Laughter shook the general. "How extraordinarily droll you are!" he said. "One does not expect nowadays to find a young man of the educated class, even in America, with such a naive, and, if I may say so, mid-Victorian point of view. It's like finding a snuffbox in a limousine. Ah, well, doubtless you had Puritan ancestors. So many Americans appear to have had. I'll wager you'll forget your notions when you go hunting with me. You've a genuine new thrill in store for you, Mr. Rainsford."

"Thank you, I'm a hunter, not a murderer."

"Dear me," said the general, quite unruffled, "again that unpleasant word. But I think I can show you that your scruples are quite ill founded."

"Yes?"

"Life is for the strong, to be lived by the strong. The weak of the world were put here to give the strong pleasure. I am strong. Why should I not use my gift? If I wish to hunt, why should I not? I hunt the scum of the earth—sailors from tramp ships—lascars, blacks, Chinese whites, mongrels—a thoroughbred horse or hound is worth more than a score of them."

"But they are men," said Rainsford hotly.

"Precisely," said the general. "That is why I use them. It gives me pleasure. They can reason, after a fashion. So they are dangerous."

"But where do you get them?"

The general's left eyelid fluttered down in a wink. "This island is called 'Ship-Trap,' " he answered. "Sometimes an angry god of the high seas sends them to me. Sometimes, when Providence is not so kind, I help Providence a bit. Come to the window with me."

Rainsford went to the window and looked out toward the sea.

"Watch! Out there!" exclaimed the general, pointing into the night. Rainsford's eyes saw only blackness, and then, as the general pressed a button, far out to sea Rainsford saw the flash of lights.

The general chuckled. "They indicate a channel," he said, "where there's none: giant rocks with razor edges crouch like a sea monster with wide-open jaws. They can crush a ship as easily as I crush this nut." He dropped a walnut on the hardwood floor and brought his heel grinding down on it. "Oh, yes," he said, casually, as if in answer to a question, "I have electricity. We try to be civilized here."

"Civilized? And you shoot down men?"

A trace of anger was in the general's black eyes, but it was there for but a second, and he said, in his most pleasant manner: "Dear me, what a righteous young man you are! I assure you I do not do the thing you suggest. That would be barbarous. I treat these visitors with every consideration. They get plenty of good food and exercise. They get into splendid physical condition. You shall see for yourself tomorrow."

"What do you mean?"

"We'll visit my training school," smiled the general. "It's in the cellar. I have about a dozen pupils down there now. They're from the Spanish bark San Lucar that had the bad luck to go on the rocks out there. A very inferior lot, I regret to say. Poor specimens and more accustomed to the deck than to the jungle."

He raised his hand, and Ivan, who served as waiter, brought thick Turkish coffee. Rainsford, with an effort, held his tongue in check.

"It's a game, you see," pursued the general blandly. "I suggest

to one of them that we go hunting. I give him a supply of food
and an excellent hunting knife. I give him three hours' start.
I am to follow, armed only with a pistol of the smallest caliber
and range. If my quarry eludes me for three whole days, he wins
the game. If I find him"—the general smiled—"he loses."

"Suppose he refuses to be hunted?"

"Oh," said the general, "I give him his option, of course.
He need not play that game if he doesn't wish to. If he does
not wish to hunt, I turn him over to Ivan. Ivan once had the
honor of serving as offical knouter to the Great White Czar, and
he has his own ideas of sport. Invariably, Mr. Rainsford, invariably
they choose the hunt."

"And if they win?"

The smile on the general's face widened. "To date I have not
lost," he said.

Then he added, hastily: "I don't wish you to think me a
braggart, Mr. Rainsford. Many of them afford only the most
elementary sort of problem. Occasionally I strike a Tartar. One
almost did win. I eventually had to use the dogs."

"The dogs?"

"This way, please. I'll show you."

The general steered Rainsford to a window. The lights from
the windows sent a flickering illumination that made grotesque
patterns on the courtyard below, and Rainsford could see moving
about there a dozen or so huge black shapes; as they turned toward him, their eyes glittered greenly.

"A rather good lot, I think," observed the general. "They
are let out at seven every night. If anyone should try to get into
my house—or out of it—something extremely regrettable would
occur to him." He hummed a snatch of song from the Folies
Bergère.

"And now," said the general, "I want to show you my new
collection of heads. Will you come with me to the library?"

"I hope," said Rainsford, "that you will excuse me tonight,
General Zaroff. I'm really not feeling at all well."

"Ah, indeed?" the general inquired solicitously. "Well, I
suppose that's only natural, after your long swim. You need a
good, restful night's sleep. Tomorrow you'll feel like a new man,
I'll wager. Then we'll hunt, eh? I've one rather promising pros-
pect—"

Rainsford was hurrying from the room.

"Sorry you can't go with me tonight," called the general. "I expect rather fair sport—a big, strong black. He looks resourceful—Well, good night, Mr. Rainsford; I hope you have a good night's rest."

The bed was good, and the pajamas of the softest silk, and he was tired in every fiber of his being, but nevertheless Rainsford could not quiet his brain with the opiate of sleep. He lay, eyes wide open. Once he thought he heard stealthy steps in the corridor outside his room. He sought to throw open the door; it would not open. He went to the window and looked out. His room was high up in one of the towers. The lights of the château were out now, and it was dark and silent, but there was a fragment of sallow moon, and by its wan light he could see, dimly, the courtyard; there, weaving in and out in the pattern of shadow, were black, noiseless forms; the hounds heard him at the window and looked up, expectantly, with their green eyes. Rainsford went back to the bed and lay down. By many methods he tried to put himself to sleep. He had achieved a doze when, just as morning began to come, he heard, far off in the jungle, the faint report of a pistol.

General Zaroff did not appear until luncheon. He was dressed faultlessly in the tweeds of a country squire. He was solicitous about the state of Rainsford's health.

"As for me," sighed the general, "I do not feel so well. I am worried, Mr. Rainsford. Last night I detected traces of my old complaint."

To Rainsford's questioning glance the general said: "Ennui. Boredom."

Then, taking a second helping of Crêpes Suzette, the general explained: "The hunting was not good last night. The fellow lost his head. He made a straight trail that offered no problems at all. That's the trouble with these sailors; they have dull brains to begin with, and they do not know how to get about in the woods. They do excessively stupid and obvious things. It's most annoying. Will you have another glass of Chablis, Mr. Rainsford?"

"General," said Rainsford firmly, "I wish to leave this island at once."

The general raised his thickets of eyebrows; he seemed hurt. "But, my dear fellow," the general protested, "you've only just come. You've had no hunting—"

"I wish to go today," said Rainsford. He saw the dead black eyes of the general on him, studying him. General Zaroff's face suddenly brightened.

He filled Rainsford's glass with venerable Chablis from a dusty bottle.

"Tonight," said the general, "we will hunt—you and I."

Rainsford shook his head. "No, general," he said. "I will not hunt."

The general shrugged his shoulders and delicately ate a hot-house grape. "As you wish, my friend," he said. "The choice rests entirely with you. But may I not venture to suggest that you will find my idea of sport more diverting than Ivan's?"

He nodded toward the corner to where the giant stood, scowling, his thick arms crossed on his hogshead of chest.

"You don't mean—" cried Rainsford.

"My dear fellow," said the general, "have I not told you I always mean what I say about hunting? This is really an inspiration. I drink to a foeman worthy of my steel—at last."

The general raised his glass, but Rainsford sat staring at him.

"You'll find this game worth playing," the general said enthusiastically. "Your brain against mine. Your woodcraft against mine. Your strength and stamina against mine. Outdoor chess! And the stake is not without value, eh?"

"And if I win—" began Rainsford huskily.

"I'll cheerfully acknowledge myself defeated if I do not find you by midnight of the third day," said General Zaroff. "My sloop will place you on the mainland near a town."

The general read what Rainsford was thinking.

"Oh, you can trust me," said the Cossack. "I will give you my word as a gentleman and a sportsman. Of course you, in turn, must agree to say nothing of your visit here."

"I'll agree to nothing of the kind," said Rainsford.

"Oh," said the general, "in that case—But why discuss that now? Three days hence we can discuss it over a bottle of Veuve Cliquot, unless—"

The general sipped his wine.

Then a businesslike air animated him. "Ivan," he said to Rainsford, "will supply you with hunting clothes, food, a knife. I suggest you wear moccasins; they leave a poorer trail. I suggest too that you avoid the big swamp in the southeast corner of the island. We call it Death Swamp. There's quicksand there. One foolish fellow tried it. The deplorable part of it was that Lazarus followed him. You can imagine my feelings, Mr. Rainsford. I loved Lazarus; he was the finest hound in my pack. Well, I must beg you to excuse me now. I always take a siesta after lunch. You'll hardly have time for a nap, I fear. You'll want to start, no doubt. I shall not follow till dusk. Hunting at night is so much more exciting than by day, don't you think? Au revoir, Mr. Rainsford, au revoir."

General Zaroff, with a deep, courtly bow, strolled from the room.

From another door came Ivan. Under one arm he carried khaki hunting clothes, a haversack of food, a leather sheath containing a long-bladed hunting knife; his right hand rested on a cocked revolver thrust in the crimson sash about his waist. . . .

Rainsford had fought his way through the bush for two hours. "I must keep my nerve. I must keep my nerve," he said through tight teeth.

He had not been entirely clear-headed when the château gates snapped shut behind him. His whole idea at first was to put distance between himself and General Zaroff, and, to this end, he had plunged along, spurred on by the sharp rowels of something very like panic. Now he had got a grip on himself, had stopped, and was taking stock of himself and the situation.

He saw that straight flight was futile; inevitably it would bring him face to face with the sea. He was in a picture with a frame of water, and his operations, clearly, must take place within that frame.

"I'll give him a trail to follow," muttered Rainsford, and he struck off from the rude path he had been following into the trackless wilderness. He executed a series of intricate loops; he doubled on his trail again and again, recalling all the lore of the fox hunt, and all the dodges of the fox. Night found him leg-weary, with hands and face lashed by the branches, on a thickly wooded ridge. He knew it would be insane to blunder on through the dark, even if he had the strength. His need for rest was imperative and he thought: "I have played the fox, now I must play the cat of the fable." A big tree with a thick trunk and outspread branches was near by, and, taking care to leave not the slightest mark, he climbed up into the crotch, and stretching out on one of the broad limbs, after a fashion, rested. Rest brought him new confidence and almost a feeling of security. Even so zealous a hunter as General Zaroff could not trace him there, he told himself; only the devil himself could follow that complicated trail through the jungle after dark. But, perhaps, the general was a devil—

An apprehensive night crawled slowly by like a wounded snake, and sleep did not visit Rainsford, although the silence of a dead world was on the jungle. Toward morning when a dingy gray was varnishing the sky, the cry of some startled bird focused Rainsford's attention in that direction. Something was coming through the bush, coming slowly, carefully, coming by the same winding way Rainsford had come. He flattened himself down on the limb, and through a screen of leaves almost as thick as tapestry, he watched. The thing that was approaching was a man.

It was General Zaroff. He made his way along with his eyes fixed in utmost concentration on the ground before him. He paused, almost beneath the tree, dropped to his knees and studied the ground. Rainsford's impulse was to hurl himself down like a panther, but he saw that the general's right hand held something metallic—a small automatic pistol.

The hunter shook his head several times, as if he were puzzled. Then he straightened up and took from his case one of his black cigarettes; its pungent incenselike smoke floated up to Rainsford's nostrils.

Rainsford held his breath. The general's eyes had left the ground and were traveling inch by inch up the tree. Rainsford froze there, every muscle tensed for a spring. But the sharp eyes of the hunter stopped before they reached the limb where Rainsford lay; a smile spread over his brown face. Very deliberately he blew a smoke ring into the air; then he turned his back on the tree and walked carelessly away, back along the trail he had come. The swish of the underbrush against his hunting-boots grew fainter and fainter.

The pent-up air burst hotly from Rainsford's lungs. His first thought made him feel sick and numb. The general could follow a trail through the woods at night. He could follow an extremely difficult trail; he must have uncanny powers; only by the merest chance had the Cossack failed to see his quarry.

Rainsford's second thought was even more terrible. It sent a shudder of cold horror through his whole being. Why had the general smiled? Why had he turned back?

Rainsford did not want to believe what his reason told him was true, but the truth was as evident as the sun that had by now pushed through the morning mists. The general was playing with him! The general was saving him for another day's sport! The Cossack was the cat; he was the mouse. Then it was that Rainsford knew the full meaning of terror.

"I will not lose my nerve. I will not."

He slid down from the tree, and struck off again into the woods. His face was set and he forced the machinery of his mind to function. Three hundred yards from his hiding-place he stopped where a huge dead tree leaned precarioulsy on a smaller, living one. Throwing off his sack of food, Rainsford took his knife from its sheath and began to work with all his energy.

The job was finished at last, and he threw himself down behind a fallen log a hundred feet away. He did not have to wait long. The cat was coming again to play with the mouse.

Following the trail with the sureness of a bloodhound, came General Zaroff. Nothing escaped those searching black eyes, no crushed blade of grass, no bent twig, no mark, no matter how faint, in the moss. So intent was the Cossack on his stalking that he was upon the thing Rainsford had made before he saw it. His foot touched the protruding bough that was the trigger. Even as he touched it, the general sensed his danger and leaped back with the agility of an ape. But he was not quite quick enough; the dead tree, delicately adjusted to rest on the cut living one, crashed down and struck the general a glancing blow on the shoulder as it fell; but for his alertness, he must have been smashed beneath it. He staggered, but he did not fall; nor did he drop his revolver. He stood there, rubbing his injured shoulder, and Rainsford, with fear again gripping his heart, heard the general's mocking laugh ring through the jungle.

"Rainsford," called the general, "if you are within sound of my voice, as I suppose you are, let me congratulate you. Not many men know how to make a Malay man-catcher. Luckily, for me, I too have hunted in Malacca. You are proving interesting, Mr. Rainsford. I am going now to have my wound dressed; it's only a slight one. But I shall be back. I shall be back."

When the general, nursing his bruised shoulder, had gone, Rainsford took up his flight again. It was flight now, a desperate, hopeless flight, that carried him on for some hours. Dusk came, then darkness, and still he pressed on. The ground grew softer under his moccasins; the vegetation grew ranker, denser; insects bit him savagely. Then, as he stepped forward, his foot sank into the ooze. He tried to wrench it back, but the muck sucked viciously at his foot as if it were a giant leech. With a violent effort he tore his foot loose, He knew where he was now. Death Swamp and its quicksand.

His hands were tight closed as if his nerve were something tangible that someone in the darkness was trying to tear from his grip. The softness of the earth had given him an idea. He stepped back from the quicksand a dozen feet or so and, like some huge prehistoric beaver, he began to dig.

Rainsford had dug himself in in France when a second's delay meant death. That had been a placid pastime compared to his digging now. The pit grew deeper; when it was above his shoulders, he climbed out and from some hard saplings cut stakes and sharpened them to a fine point. These stakes he planted in the bottom of the pit with the points sticking up. With flying fingers he wove a rough carpet of weeds and branches and with it he covered the mouth of the pit. Then, wet with sweat and aching with tiredness, he crouched behind the stump of a lightning-charred tree.

He knew his pursuer was coming; he heard the padding sound of feet on the soft earth, and the night breeze brought him the perfume of the general's cigarette. It seemed to Rainsford that the general was coming with unusual swiftness; he was not feeling his way along, foot by foot. Rainsford, crouching there, could not see the general, nor could he see the pit. He lived a year in a minute. Then he felt an impulse to cry aloud with joy, for he heard the sharp crackle of the breaking branches as the cover of the pit gave way; he heard the sharp scream of pain as the pointed stakes found their mark. He leaped up from his place of concealment. Then he cowered back. Three feet from the pit a man was standing, with an electric torch in his hand.

"You've done well, Rainsford," the voice of the general called. "Your Burmese tiger pit has claimed one of my best dogs. Again you score. I think, Mr. Rainsford, I'll see what you can do against my whole pack. I'm going home for a rest now. Thank you for a most amusing evening."

At daybreak Rainsford, lying near the swamp, was awakened by a sound that made him know that he had new things to learn about fear. It was a distant sound, faint and wavering, but he knew it. It was the baying of a pack of hounds.

Rainsford knew he could do one of two things. He could stay where he was and wait. That was suicide. He could flee. That was postponing the inevitable. For a moment he stood there, thinking. An idea that held a wild chance came to him, and, tightening his belt, he headed away from the swamp. The baying of the hounds drew nearer, then still nearer, nearer, ever nearer. On a ridge Rainsford climbed a tree. Down a watercourse, not a quarter of a mile away, he could see the bush moving. Straining his eyes, he saw the lean figure of General Zaroff; just ahead of him Rainsford made out another figure whose wide shoulders surged through the tall jungle weeds; it was the giant Ivan, and he seemed pulled forward by some unseen force; Rainsford knew that Ivan must be holding the pack in leash.

They would be on him any minute now. His mind worked frantically. He thought of a native trick he had learned in Uganda. He slid down the tree. He caught hold of a springy young sapling and to it he fastened his hunting knife, with the blade pointing down the trail; with a bit of wild grapevine he tied back the sapling. Then he ran for his life. The hounds raised their voices as they hit the fresh scent. Rainsford knew now how an animal at bay feels.

He had to stop to get his breath. The baying of the hounds stopped abruptly, and Rainsford's heart stopped too. They must have reached the knife.

He shinned excitedly up a tree and looked back. His pursuers had stopped. But the hope that was in Rainsford's brain when he climbed died, for he saw in the shallow valley that General Zaroff was still on his feet. But Ivan was not. The knife, driven by the recoil of the springing tree, had not wholly failed.

Rainsford had hardly tumbled to the ground when the pack took up the cry again.

"Nerve, nerve, nerve!" he panted, as he dashed along. A blue gap showed between the trees dead ahead. Ever nearer drew the hounds. Rainsford forced himself on toward that gap. He reached it. It was the shore of the sea. Across a cove he could see the gloomy gray stone of the chateau. Twenty feet below him the sea rumbled and hissed. Rainsford hesitated. He heard the hounds. Then he leaped far out into the sea. . . .

When the general and his pack reached the place by the sea, the Cossack stopped. For some minutes he stood regarding the blue-green expanse of water. He shrugged his shoulders. Then he sat down, took a drink of brandy from a silver flask, lit a perfumed cigarette, and hummed a bit from "Madame Butterfly."

General Zaroff had an exceedingly good dinner in his great paneled dining hall that evening. With it he had a bottle of Pol Roger and half a bottle of Chambertin. Two slight annoyances kept him from perfect enjoyment. One was the thought that it would be difficult to replace Ivan; the other was that his quarry had escaped him; of course the American hadn't played the game— so thought the general as he tasted his after-dinner liqueur. In his library he read, to soothe himself, from the works of Marcus Aurelius. At ten he went up to his bedroom. He was deliciously tired, he said to himself, as he locked himself in. There was a little moonlight, so, before turning on his light, he went to the window and looked down at the courtyard. He could see the great hounds, and he called: "Better luck another time," to them. Then he switched on the light.

A man, who had been hiding in the curtains of the bed, was standing there.

"Rainsford!" screamed the general. "How in God's name did you get here?"

"Swam," said Rainsford. "I found it quicker than walking through the jungle."

The general sucked in his breath and smiled. "I congratulate you," he said. "You have won the game."

Rainsford did not smile. "I am still a beast at bay," he said, in a low, hoarse voice. "Get ready, General Zaroff."

The general made one of his deepest bows. "I see," he said. "Splendid! One of us is to furnish a repast for the hounds. The other will sleep in this very excellent bed. On guard, Rainsford." . . .

He had never slept in a better bed, Rainsford decided.

Your summary:

STOP. Check sample summary at the end of Lesson 8.

Practice E.

Without referring to the text of the story, answer these true/false questions. Put a T for *true* or an F for *false* in the blank.

_____ 1. Rainsford's friend Whitney is sympathetic toward the "hunted."

_____ 2. At the beginning of the story Rainsford is going on a hunting trip.

_____ 3. The island is not feared by seamen.

_____ 4. Rainsford was pushed overboard by a sailor.

_____ 5. Rainsford is a good swimmer.

_____ 6. The shots from the island help direct Rainsford to it.

_____ 7. The sun is directly overhead when Rainsford awakes on the island after swimming frantically to reach it.

_____ 8. Rainsford infers that a fairly large animal had been shot.

_____ 9. General Zaroff is not well-born.

_____ 10. Food for General Zaroff is imported by planes.

_____ 11. General Zaroff is wealthy.

_____ 12. General Zaroff is a vain hunter.

_____ 13. General Zaroff never travels or leaves the island.

_____ 14. General Zaroff feels that instinct is no match for reason.

_____ 15. Rainsford had never killed a man.

_____ 16. Rainsford believes in the survival of the fittest.

_____ 17. General Zaroff's "sporting game" amuses Rainsford.

_____ 18. Only one man before Rainsford has won over General Zaroff.

_____ 19. General Zaroff is confident that he will win over Rainsford.

_____ 20. Rainsford uses the dodges of the tiger to evade General Zaroff.

_____ 21. Rainsford fears that General Zaroff is a devil.

_____ 22. Rainsford realizes that General Zaroff is playing with him after the first day of hunting.

_____ 23. Rainsford loses his nerve when he learns that he is the "mouse" in the hunt.

_____ 24. Rainsford builds a trap for General Zaroff.

_____ 25. Rainsford fails to escape from Death Swamp.

_____ 26. Rainsford builds two more traps.

_____27. Rainsford's knife trap kills only a dog.

_____28. Rainsford escapes the hounds by running back into the jungle.

_____29. After Rainsford escapes, General Zaroff feels that Rainsford hadn't played the game.

_____30. Although Rainsford wins the game, he does not trust General Zaroff.

STOP. Check answers at the end of Lesson 8.

VOCABULARY: CONTEXT CLUES (Mathematics, Economics, Biological and Physical Sciences)

The sentences in this section are taken from mathematics textbooks and from books dealing with the biological and physical sciences.

Practice A.

Use your knowledge of context clues to determine the meanings of the underlined words.

1. Science and technology are <u>cumulative</u>, that is, the work of one scientist is built onto another's. _____

2. As the careful researcher <u>scrutinizes</u> his own instruments, observations, and reasonings, so he must also carefully examine what he reads.

   _____

3. Isaac Newton was a shy man who very much disliked the <u>controversy</u> on which Galileo <u>thrived</u>._____;_____

4. The <u>concept</u> of gases <u>exerting</u> pressure is one of the things most people take for granted in this age of automobile tires, gas stoves, gas furnaces, balloons, and so on. _____;_____

5. When spending <u>sags</u>, causing unsold products and increased unemployment, the pressure on prices <u>abates</u> and <u>inflation</u> slows._____;

   _____;_____

6. In <u>rigorous discourse</u> such as logic and mathematics we take pains to distinguish carefully between undefined words and defined words.

   _____;_____

7. A set in mathematics may be referred to as an <u>aggregate</u>. _____

8. One of the most fruitful concepts in mathematics is the "if-then" idea, or the notion of <u>implication</u>. _____

9. The Federal <u>fiscal</u> year, which used to begin July 1st, has been extended to October 1st so that Congress and the Administration can have more time to consider the <u>succeeding</u> year's budget._____ ;

_____

STOP. Check answers at the end of Lesson 8.

Practice B.

Match the meaning from column B with the word in column A.

Column A	Column B
_____ 1. cumulative	a. things gathered into a mass or total
_____ 2. scrutinizes	b. increase in paper money and rise in prices
_____ 3. controversy	
_____ 4. concept	c. exact
_____ 5. aggregate	d. hint or suggestion
_____ 6. fiscal	e. increasing or growing by successive additions
_____ 7. discourse	
_____ 8. thrived	f. declines
_____ 9. implication	g. putting forth, as power
_____10. succeeding	h. dispute
_____11. inflation	i. financial
_____12. rigorous	j. communication of ideas
_____13. sags	k. lessens
_____14. abates	l. observes very carefully
_____15. exerting	m. prospered
	n. following
	o. idea

STOP. Check answers at the end of Lesson 8.

Practice C.

For these sentences with missing words, choose the word that *best* fits the sentence. Put the word in the blank.

Word List:

cumulative, scrutinizes, controversy, concept, aggregate, fiscal, discourse, thrived, implication, succeeding, inflation, rigorous, sags, abates, exerting.

1. The city officials were_____ a great amount of pressure on union leaders to influence the union members not to strike.

2. In a period of_____, unless you get a salary increase, you will have difficulty making ends meet.

3. Government economists rely on_____policy to control the amount of money in circulation.

4. It looks as though my friend John will be_____ his father as president of the family business.

5. I try to avoid_____because I do not like to get into arguments.

6. I'm not sure I understand the_____of what you say; be more direct.

7. My house is a(n)_____of many different materials.

8. He_____every contract he has to sign.

9. He seems to have_____during his last year at school.

10. The_____of relativity is difficult for me to understand.

11. Astronauts receive very_____training.

12. Unless the storm_____we will not be able to go to the party.

13. Our kitchen floor_____because the foundation under it is not very good.

14. Sick leave is_____where I work; so healthy people who have worked here for a long time have quite a number of days off available.

15. In the philosophy club we are always involved in_____.

STOP. Check answers at the end of Lesson 8.

WORD ANALYSIS: ACCENT AND PRONUNCIATION OF WORDS

1. To pronounce a word of more than one syllable you must syllabicate the word, apply phonic analysis, and then blend the syllables into one word. To blend the syllables into one word, you must know something about accenting and how accents affect vowel sounds. You should know that unaccented syllables are usually softened and that homographs (words that are spelled the same but have different meanings) may have different pronunciations because they differ in the placement of accent marks. (See Lesson 3.) Examples: *con'duct* (noun), behavior; *con·duct'* (verb), to lead; *ref'use* (noun), trash, worthless; *re·fuse'* (verb), to decline to accept, to reject.

2. The accent mark (') is used to show which syllable in a word is stressed, that is, spoken with greatest intensity or loudness. This mark usually comes right after and slightly above the accented syllable.

Special Note

In some dictionaries the accent mark is placed right before the accented syllable. (See Lesson 10 on the dictionary.)

3. Here are three accent rules that are nearly always true.

a. In two-syllable words the first syllable is usually stressed, except when the second syllable contains two vowels. Examples of words stressed in the first syllable: pi'lot, a'ble, ap'ple, pro'gram, help'ful, bot'tle, jour'nal. Examples of words stressed in the second syllable: ap point', pro ceed', as tound', sub due', pa rade', po lite'.

b. In three-syllable words usually the first or second syllable is stressed. Examples: cap'i·tal, ho·ri'zon.

c. In three- or four-syllable words that end in *tion* or *ic* the primary accent is usually on the syllable before *ic* or *tion*. Examples: ded·i·ca'tion, de·duc'tion, ro·man'tic, he·ro'ic.

Special Notes

1. A syllable that ends in *le* preceded by a consonant is always an unstressed syllable, that is, the accent never falls on that syllable. The syllable contains a schwa sound.

2. Any syllable that contains the schwa sound is an unstressed syllable.

Practice A.

State the meaning of the words in each of these five sets of syllabicated words with accent marks.

1. rec'ord   _____

   re·cord'   _____

2. pres'ent   _____

   pre·sent' _____

3. con'tent   _____

   con·tent' _____

4. ob'ject   _____

   ob·ject'   _____

5. pro'duce _____

   pro·duce' _____

STOP. Check answers at the end of Lesson 8.

Practice B.

Syllabicate these words and put in the accent mark.

1. reason _____   9. dentist_____

2. tailor _____   10. mumble_____

3. local _____   11. ancestor_____

4. receive _____   12. reaction_____

5. complain _____   13. attention_____

6. wisdom _____   14. conclusion_____

7. cable _____   15. constitution_____

8. provide _____

STOP. Check answers at the end of Lesson 8.

Practice C.

Here are a number of multiple choice questions. Circle the *best* answer. (Circle only one answer.)

1. In the words *proceed, polite, receive,* and *appoint*, the accent falls on
   a. the first syllable.   c. none of the syllables.
   b. the second syllable.   d. both syllables.

2. In syllabicating the words *able, bubble, dazzle, purple,* and *candle*, you would
   a. divide before double consonants.
   b. divide between double consonants.
   c. divide after the first vowel.
   d. divide before the consonant preceding *le*.

3. In #2, the syllabication rule is
   a. divide words before consonants.
   b. if a consonant comes just before *le* in a word of more than one sylla-
      ble, the consonant goes with *le* to form the last syllable.
   c. divide between double consonants.
   d. divide words before three consonants.

4. In #2 the second syllable in each word contains
   a. a consonant plus *le*.
   b. three consonants.
   c. two vowels and a consonant.
   d. two consonants.

5. In #2 the second syllable is
   a. an accented one.
   b. a syllable with silent *e* vowel rule.
   c. an unstressed syllable.
   d. an open syllable.

6. The unstressed syllables in #2 are pronounced like
   a. all.   c. eel.
   b. *ull* in bull.   d. el.

7. In #2 the first syllables in *bubble, dazzle, purple,* and *candle* all
   a. are open syllables.   c. have diphthongs.
   b. have vowel digraphs.   d. are closed syllables.

8. In #2 the first syllable in *able*

    a. is a closed syllable.
    b. is an open syllable.
    c. has a vowel digraph.
    d. has a diphthong.

9. In syllabicating the nonsense words *crable, roble, meinble,* and *monnle,* you would divide the words

    a. so that the consonant preceding *le* goes with *le.*
    b. before the three consonants.
    c. before the two consonants.
    d. after the vowel.

10. In #9 the second syllables are all

    a. open syllables.
    b. unstressed syllables.
    c. silent *e* syllables.
    d. accented syllables.

11. In #9 the first syllable in *crable* and *roble* is

    a. an open one.
    b. a closed one.
    c. none of the above.
    d. an unstressed one.

12. In #9 *meinble* contains

    a. a diphthong in the first syllable.
    b. a closed syllable.
    c. an open syllable.
    d. a vowel digraph in the first syllable.

13. The schwa sound exists in

    a. boat.
    b. bubble.
    c. bat.
    d. contain.

14. The schwa sound does not exist in

    a. cuddle.
    b. beauty.
    c. foible.
    d. wrestle.

STOP. Check answers at the end of Lesson 8.

ANSWERS: Lesson 8 (pp. 195-251)

Reading: Inference (pp. 195–207)

Practice A

1. a. not enough evidence b. not enough evidence c. not enough evidence d. not enough evidence e. F (The person says, ". . . I'm glad I left. It's for the best. I can breathe now.") 2. a. not enough evidence b. not enough evidence c. not enough evidence d. T (It is stated that the sun is directly overhead. If the sun is directly overhead, it's noon.) e. T (It is stated that the person craves human warmth.) 3. a. not enough evidence (The term *guys* is a slang term that is often used to refer to females as well as males.) b. not enough evidence (*Dean* is used as a person's name, not as the title of a college official. The character is probably a student, but we can't be sure.) c. T (The person is fearful about going along with the guys.) d. not enough evidence (He or she may just be afraid of getting hurt.) e. not enough evidence (It may be something that Dean disapproves of.) f. not enough evidence (The person says, *"Maybe* I'd better crack the books and take my chances with the guys.) g. T (The person says that the guys are *always* just too much for me.") 4. a. not enough evidence b. not enough evidence (You can cast a shadow in the daytime and in the night-time.) c. not enough evidence (One person may be in his or her 30s, 40s, etc., and the other may be in his or her 50s, 60s, etc.) d. not enough evidence e. F (It is stated, "I feel young.") f. T (It is stated that one day you're a child and the next you're the father of that child.) g. not enough evidence 5. a. T (It is stated that the men were dusty.) b. F (The sun was setting behind the mountain range. The men were heading *away* from the mountain range, not toward it.) c. not enough evidence d. T (It is stated that the men were tired, hungry, etc., and that one fourth of them had turned back.) e. F (Six is three fourths of eight.) 6. a. T (The girl went on the pill before having intercourse, so that she wouldn't become pregnant when she did have intercourse. She says, ". . . pregnancy would probably tear our house asunder.") b. T (She had visited a psychiatric social worker.) c. F (She speaks quite readily about it.) d. T (She began taking the pill

before she had intercourse.) e. T (She says, "Sophomore year was the critical cut against my mother, giving away her prize, my virginity.") f. not enough evidence g. not enough evidence

Practice B

1. T (It is stated that he's been hustling all day.) 2. T (It is stated that every Christmas Eve Richard's mother waits for his father, but his father never shows up.) 3. T (It is stated that Richard didn't want to get home too fast.) 4. T (It is stated that Richard can't believe it when he sees a wreath and lights in the window of his apartment.) 5. not enough evidence 6. F (Richard prays to God.) 7. F (Richard tells many lies to his mother.) 8. F (Richard's teacher doesn't help him learn to read; she yells at him and puts him in the idiot's seat.) 9. F (It is stated that Richard's teacher doesn't understand why his homework is crumpled and damp. She talks about him and his kind.) 10. T (Richard's family was given a lot of food.) 11. not enough evidence 12. T (It is stated that Richard's mother dresses up *every* Christmas Eve.) 13. T (Although Richard's father has not come home for years, she still dresses up and waits for him every Christmas Eve.) 14. T (Richard lies to his mother and tells her that Mr. Green told him to give her five dollars because Mr. Green wished that he could raise his children as well as Richard's mother.) 15. F (He can't read, and the teacher puts him in the idiot's seat.) 16. F (He sleeps with five other children.) 17. T (He has made up lots of stories.) 18. T (She puts children in an idiot's seat.) 19. not enough evidence 20. T (Richard wonders whether rich people get the one thing that nobody knew they wanted.)

Practice C

1. d 2. c 3. b 4. d 5. c 6. c 7. e 8. c

Practice D

1. One of the engineers was a woman and the other a man, and they were probably having an affair with each other. However, one of the engineers did not know that the other was married. (Because of sex stereotyping, some readers may wrongly assume that both engineers must be men.) 2. There are only three people. The minister's wife is the schoolmaster's daughter.

Reading/Learning Skills: Summaries (Stories) (pp. 207–240)

Practice A (sample summary)

A bet between a banker and a lawyer that results in voluntary imprisonment by the lawyer has strange consequences. At a party during a discussion
of the merits of capital punishment over life imprisonment, a multimillion-
aire banker bets two millions that a young lawyer, who prefers life imprisonment to capital punishment, cannot remain in a cell for five years. The
young lawyer accepts the bet, offering to prolong his stay in solitary confinement to fifteen years. The conditions of the bet are that the lawyer will
see no one and remain confined but have access to music, books, tobacco,
and wine, and communicate his wants via notes.

The lawyer remains in his self-imposed solitary confinement for fifteen
years, during which time he goes through many stages. He spends most of
his time reading and studying frantically. Toward the end of his stay, he
never stops reading and studying. The banker is hard pressed to get the lawyer all the books requested.

When it is just about time for the lawyer to leave his cell, the banker
finds himself in severe financial difficulties. If the banker gives the lawyer
his well-earned two millions, the banker will go bankrupt. The banker therefore decides to kill the lawyer. The night before the lawyer is to receive his
two millions, the banker sneaks into the lawyer's cell to kill him. The banker
sees before him an emaciated, very old-looking man, who is asleep and, the
banker thinks, dreaming of money. The banker, seeing a note on the table,
reads it. In the note, the lawyer renounces the money. The lawyer philoso-
phizes on the wisdom that he has gained from books and professes contempt
for man and material things. The banker, who is relieved and full of contempt for himself, does not kill the lawyer. The next morning the lawyer
leaves his cell before the noon release deadline. To avoid unnecessary rumors, the banker puts the lawyer's renunciation in a safe.

Practice B

1. F 2. T 3. T 4. T 5. T 6. F 7. T 8. F 9. F 10. T 11. T
12. F 13. T 14. T

Practice C

2. The banker made this statement at the party. 3. It is stated that the
banker had too many millions to count. 4. It is stated that the banker was
spoiled. 5. When the banker had some second thoughts about the bet he

stated that the lawyer made the bet for "pure greed of gold." 7. The books that he asked for were of a light character: novels, stories of crime, fantasy, comedies, and so on. 10. The banker couldn't understand why the lawyer spent all year reading only the New Testament since it's "easy to understand and by no means thick." 11. The banker did not want to give the lawyer what was coming to him. He was not willing to live up to his part of the bargain. 13. The lawyer gained wisdom from reading but he suffered great physical and emotional losses. 14. The banker kept the lawyer's note.

Practice D (sample summary)

According to Rainsford, the world is made up of hunters and the hunted, and luckily he is a hunter. He does not feel that hunted animals feel fear or pain. However, when Rainsford falls overboard from a yacht into the Caribbean and finds himself on a strange island, he learns what it's like to be the hunted animal.

On the island Rainsford seeks refuge in a huge castle. The host of the castle is a strange, hospitable man named General Zaroff. Zaroff enjoys many luxuries and considers himself civilized. He is a hunter who lives only for danger and to hunt. But he now hunts only the most dangerous game—man—because hunting other animals is too easy.

General Zaroff explains his hunting game to Rainsford and how he captures men for his sport. Rainsford is shocked. Zaroff forces Rainsford to play the game. Rainsford and Zaroff match wits with one another for almost three days. To survive, Rainsford must be wily and play both the role of the fox and the cat. Rainsford outwits Zaroff at the general's own game.

Practice E

1. T 2. T 3. F 4. F 5. T 6. T 7. F 8. T 9. F 10. F 11. T 12. T 13. F 14. T 15. F 16. F 17. F 18. F 19. T 20. F 21. T 22. T 23. F 24. T 25. F 26. T 27. F 28. F 29. T 30. T

Vocabulary: Context Clues (Mathematics, Economics, Biological and Physical Sciences) (pp. 240–242)

Practice A

1. cumulative—increasing or growing by successive additions 2. scrutinizes—observes very carefully 3. controversy—discussion of a question in which opposing opinions clash, a dispute, a quarrel; thrived—prospered,

flourished 4. concept–idea; exerting–putting forth, as power 5. sags–declines, sinks; abates–decreases, lessens; inflation–an increase in the amount of paper money in circulation that decreases the value of money and causes a large rise in prices 6. rigorous–exact, precise, severe; discourse–a communication of ideas 7. aggregate–things gathered into a mass or total, a collection of things 8. implication–a logical relationship between two propositions in which if the first is true the second is true, that from which an inference can be drawn, something not directly stated, a hint or suggestion 9. fiscal–financial; succeeding–following, coming after

Practice B

1. e 2. l 3. h 4. o 5. a 6. i 7. j 8. m 9. d 10. n 11. b 12. c 13. f 14. k 15. g

Practice C

1. exerting 2. inflation 3. fiscal 4. succeeding 5. controversy 6. implication 7. aggregate 8. scrutinizes 9. thrived 10. concept 11. rigorous 12. abates 13. sags 14. cumulative 15. discourse

Word Analysis: Accent and Pronunciation of Words (pp. 243-246)

Practice A

1. rec'ord (noun), a disk on which sound is recorded; re·cord' (verb), to set down in writing for the purpose of preserving information 2. pres'ent (noun), a gift; pre · sent' (verb), to offer for acceptance 3. con'tent (noun), all that is contained in something; con·tent' (adj), satisfied 4. ob'ject (noun), goal, aim; ob·ject' (verb), to oppose 5. pro'duce (noun), farm products such as vegetables; growth; pro· duce' (verb), to bring forth

Practice B

1. rea'son 2. tai'lor 3. lo'cal 4. re/ceive' 5. com/plain' 6. wis'dom 7. ca'ble 8. pro/vide' 9. den'tist 10. mum'ble 11. an'ces/tor 12. re/ac'tion 13. at/ten'tion 14. con/clu'sion 15. con/sti/tu'tion

Practice C

1. b 2. d 3. b 4. a 5. c 6. b 7. d 8. b 9. a 10. b 11. a 12. d 13. b 14. b

LESSON 9

Reading: Inference (Understanding Jokes and Proverbs)
Reading/Learning Skills: Summaries (Articles or Excerpts from Articles)
Vocabulary: Context Clues (Literature)
Word Analysis: Word Parts
Answers
Crossword Puzzle
Homograph Riddles
True/False Test

READING: INFERENCE (UNDERSTANDING JOKES AND PROVERBS)

In order to be able to understand and enjoy jokes, you must be able to see double meanings and to read between the lines. Often the most important part of the joke is not what is written, but what has been left to imagination. The writer of jokes deliberately does this. For example, this joke is funny because what you expect to follow doesn't:

Student: "I don't think I deserve an F on this paper."

Instructor: "I agree with you, but an F is the lowest grade that I can give."

What makes the joke funny is that you expect a different response. When the instructor says, "I agree with you," you are fooled into expecting the opposite of what he goes on to say: " . . . but an F is the lowest grade that I can give."

This joke is funny because of what is left out:

Robert: "Mother, I just threw down the large ladder in the front yard."
Mother: That's all right. Tell your father and he'll help you pick it up."
Robert: "I don't think that's necessary."
Mother: "Why not?"
Robert: "He already knows because he was on it."

What makes the joke funny is that Robert does not immediately tell his mother that his father has fallen off the ladder. If Robert had, it would not have been a joke. There would have been no element of surprise. The humor in Robert's story is also in the misplaced emphasis. Robert is much more concerned at having knocked down the ladder than at having laid out his father.

There is a joke tradition of irony in which the listener knows something the characters in the plot do not. These are usually longer *humorous* stories as opposed to jokes, but some jokes rely on the form:

Person (Standing ruefully in front of the open hood of the Volkswagen): "No wonder it won't start. The motor's missing."

Second person (Passing by): "That's all right. I've got exactly the same model, and it has a spare motor in the back that you can borrow."

Practice A.

After reading each of these amusing stories, state what makes each a joke.

1. Teacher: "Billy, why are you late for school?"
   Billy: "Well, a sign down the street said . . ."
   Teacher: "What can a sign have to do with it?"
   Billy: "The sign said: 'School ahead, go slow.' "

2. First Cannibal: "I don't like your friend."
   Second Cannibal: "O.K., just eat the vegetables."

3. Jim: "Did I ever tell you about the time I came face to face with a lion?"
   Mary: "No. What happened?"
   Jim: "There I was without a gun. The lion roared and crept closer and closer and closer . . ."
   Mary: "What did you do?"
   Jim: "I moved to the next cage."

4. Jane: "Does your watch tell time?"
   Mary: "No, you have to look at it."

5. John: "My father shaves every day."
   Jim: "My father shaves fifty times a day."
   John: "Is he crazy?"
   Jim: "No, he's a barber."

6. Diner: "This restaurant must have a very clean kitchen."
   Owner: "Thank you, sir, but how did you know?"
   Diner: "Everything tastes of soap."

7. Psychologist: "Why are you always stamping your feet?"
   Patient: "It keeps the wolves from getting me."
   Psychologist: "But there aren't any wolves in these parts."
   Patient: "My method works, doesn't it?"

STOP. Check answers at the end of Lesson 9.

SMIDGENS   **by Bob Cordray**

Many times authors use well-known proverbs to express their ideas. Proverbs are short sayings in common use that very aptly express some obvious truth or familiar experience.

To understand proverbs, you must be able to read between the lines. You cannot read the proverb in its literal sense. For example, the proverb "A rat that has but one hole is soon caught" is not really concerned with the fate of rats. What it implies is that anyone who relies on just one thing will fail.

Practice B.

See how well you can match the ten well-known proverbs in group A with the other ten proverbs in group B. After you match the proverbs, explain them.

Group A	*Group B*
_____1. There's no use crying over spilt milk.	a. The singer covers up his wrong note with a cough.
_____2. Strike while the iron is hot.	b. Few are the friends of adversity.
_____3. Pound the water and it is still water.	c. One hand washes the other.
_____4. The fire engine arrives after the house has burned down.	d. He jumped into the water to escape the rain.
_____5. Out of the frying pan and into the fire.	e. Make hay while the sun shines.
_____6. When two quarrel the third rejoices.	f. It's too late to lock the barn door after the horse is gone.
_____7. A stitch in time saves nine.	g. You can't unscramble eggs.
	h. The wolf devours the sheep while the dogs fight one another.

_____ 8. Roll my log, and I'll roll yours.

_____ 9. The bad worker blames his tools.

_____10. Rats desert a sinking ship.

i. The leopard can never change its spots.

j. An ounce of prevention is worth a pound of cure.

STOP. Check answers at the end of Lesson 9.

Practice C.

See how well you can explain each of these fifteen well-known proverbs.

1. Don't count your chickens until they hatch.
2. Don't put all your eggs in one basket.
3. Beauty is only skin deep.
4. Misery loves company.
5. It's an ill wind that blows no one any good.
6. A tiny leak will sink a big ship.
7. Necessity is the mother of invention.
8. An ape in silk is still an ape.
9. One man's meat is another's poison.
10. Don't bite the hand that feeds you.
11. Barking dogs seldom bite.
12. A good example is the best sermon.
13. Take the bull by the horns.
14. Birds of a feather flock together.
15. Look before you leap.

STOP. Check answers at the end of Lesson 9.

READING/LEARNING SKILLS: SUMMARIES (Articles or Excerpts from Articles)

This section presents three more selections for you to summarize. Remember, a good summary contains the main idea and the essential details of the article.

Practice A.

Write a brief summary of these two articles.

1. "How Much Should You Weigh?" by Michael and Kathryn Mahoney.*

Vocabulary:

sedentary—doing or requiring much sitting.

Many people try to determine how much they should weigh by reading height-weight tables, but since these tables often indicate average weights rather than optimum weights, the figures tend to be too high. There is, however, a formula for estimating your healthiest weight.

Adult women of average build can compute their ideal weight by multiplying their height in inches by 3.5 and then subtracting 110 from the product. Thus, a woman who is five feet tall should weigh about 100 pounds (60 × 3.5 − 110 = 100). For men of average build the formula is height in inches times four, minus 130. A six-foot man should weigh about 158.

It is reasonable to make allowances for bone structure and muscularity: even if Woody Allen and Rosie Grier were the same height, they should not weigh the same amount. But be careful that in making these allowances, you don't mistake fat for muscle. And remember that if you are 30 pounds overweight, it is unlikely that the difference is all in your bones.

The amount of food you need to maintain your ideal weight depends upon how active you are. Begin by rating yourself on the scale below:

13	very inactive
14	slightly inactive

---

*Reprinted from *Psychology Today* magazine. Copyright © 1976 Ziff-Davis Publishing Company.

15	moderately active
16	relatively active
17	frequently, strenuously active

If you are a sedentary office worker or a housewife you should probably rate yourself a 13. If your physical exercise consists of occasional games of golf or an afternoon walk, you're a 14. A score of 15 means that you frequently engage in moderate exertion—jogging, calisthenics, tennis. A 16 requires that you are almost always on the go, seldom sitting down or standing still for long. Don't give yourself a 17 unless you are a construction worker or engage in other strenuous activity frequently. Most adult Americans should rate themselves 13 or 14.

To calculate the number of calories you need to maintain your ideal weight, multiply your activity rating by your ideal weight. A 200-pound office worker, for example, needs 2,600 calories a day; a 200-pound athlete needs 3,400 calories.

To estimate how many calories you are getting now, multiply your current weight times your activity level. If your weight is constant at 140 pounds and you are inactive, you are consuming about 1,820 calories a day (13 times 140). Subtract the number of calories you need for your ideal weight from the number of calories you are consuming, and you will know the size of your energy imbalance.

To reach your ideal weight, we recommend that you correct your calorie imbalance slowly. It's a good idea to lose no more than one percent of your current weight a week. Cut your daily caloric consumption by two times your current weight and you should achieve that goal. Regardless of your weight, you should not get less than 1,200 calories a day. Reducing by much more than one percent of your body weight a week could mean destruction of muscles and organs as well as fat. The same is true of diets that prohibit all fats and carbohydrates.

Your summary:

2. From "The Self-Inflicted Pain of Jealousy" by Gordon Clanton and Lynn G. Smith.*

The experience of jealousy varies enormously from age to age, from culture to culture, from couple to couple, from person to person, and within the same person from time to time. In the United States, particularly among young adults, there has been a change of attitude toward jealousy in recent years. "Normal" jealousy, which had been seen as an inevitable accompaniment of love and supportive of marriage, has come to be seen by some as evidence of personal insecurity and weakness in the relationship, and therefore as a threat to intimate partnership.

The types of jealousy

To sort out the various types of jealousy, one might ask if a particular experience of jealousy comes from feeling excluded, or from a fear of loss. The distinction is important, for it signifies the difference between a small problem and a big one, between the benign and the malignant.

Most jealous flashes come from feeling left out of an activity involving your partner and another person or other people. When your partner pays attention to another, your first reaction is to note that they are "in" and you are "out." They are not noticing you, or at least not giving you as much attention as they are giving each other. You feel excluded, ignored, unappreciated.

This kind of experience is common in our society, and dealing with it gracefully is part of the etiquette of our time—especially as women become more involved in occupational and social activities

*Reprinted from *Psychology Today* magazine. Copyright © 1977 Ziff-Davis Publishing Company.

outside the home. The boss wants to dance with your wife; a woman spends most of the evening at a party in conversation with your husband; your partner and a friend both discover they adore Bergman's films, which you never particularly enjoyed. Such experiences trigger the jealous flash, but typically they do not fan it into a flame. The jealous feelings usually fade when the precipitating event is over, although one might still say on the way home, "I cannot imagine what you and Pat could have found interesting enough to discuss for so long."

If you find yourself troubled or upset by having to share your partner in ways normally considered appropriate among your circle of friends, your feeling of exclusion may be a symptom of an underlying fear of loss, the more serious type of jealousy. If you literally cannot stand to let your partner out of your sight, your jealousy is probably rooted in a persistent fear rather than a temporary irritation. This is more serious, but it need not be fatal to your self-esteem or to your relationship with your partner.

Your summary:

STOP. Check sample summaries at the end of Lesson 9.

Practice B.

Write a short summary of this autobiographical article.

From *Experiencing Youth* by George W. Goethals and Dennis S. Klos.*

I remember being somewhat afraid when I entered college in the fall of 1971. I wasn't quite sure of what I was afraid. I was

---

*From George W. Goethals and Dennis S. Klos, *Experiencing Youth: First-Person Accounts*, Second Edition. Copyright © 1976 by Little, Brown and Company (Inc.). Reprinted by permission.

afraid of new things, new people, and I suppose a new sense of freedom. Funny thing . . . this fear had not been felt when I came up for pre-freshman weekend. I was glad to be so far away from my father. I really hadn't expected him to let me visit that weekend since my upbringing had been the most sheltered of shelters. The day after he said that I could come, he borrowed $185.00 from me to pay the mortgage on his house. I'd had a job since I entered high school and my savings account contained enough for such emergencies, and for everything else I needed, since I really had to rely on my own devices for money.

I remember helping my father out on prior occasions when we lived in South Carolina. I was born in Aiken, South Carolina (there are nine of us in all). My father was a cashier in one of the local chain stores; my mother never worked because she was sheltered just as much as we were, if not more so. We lived in the white neighborhood and were bussed all the way across town to "our" school. "Our" school contained grades one through twelve while the other school was divided into grammar, junior high, and high schools. My older sister Valerie, after reaching high school, attended the same school as I did even though there was a high school just across the street from our house. When they had football games, we could have sat on the front porch and watched, but my father always warned us that when the white kids were using the football field, we were to stay inside the house. It didn't really matter because he made us stay in the house most of the time anyway. We didn't have very many friends over because somehow my father always thought the house wasn't presentable enough. He always wore white shirts to work. The other folks in town always looked up to him because he was the highest paid black man in town, making $80 per week. We were the brightest children in the school we attended. Having the last name Alexis was enough to make one teacher's pet. My first cousin, born out of wedlock, bore the last name Alexis and used to pretend that he was our brother. My older brother would find great pleasure in telling everyone that Raymond was our cousin and not our brother.

When I was thirteen, my father got into a little trouble, trouble that meant consequences for all of us. He came home one day and got the gun. My mother asked where he was going. She held the baby and he started to play with the baby, saying that he was going to kill a snake. I remember his exact words: "I'm going to kill me a snake buddy." He left the house and did not return. At about midnight a friend of my father's came by and told my mother that my father was in jail under a $1000 bond for drunken driving and illegal possession of a weapon. To make matters worse he had threatened a white man with the gun. We were all afraid because conflict with white people in that little town always proved to be overwhelmingly distressing. Once before, some students at my school had marched through the little town for desegregation of the schools and the parents of the leaders of the march had lost their jobs while other parents were threatened with the same loss. The day following the march the KKK arrived and held a rally in the town square, and that was the end of the marches.

I had gotten my first job that summer, baby-sitting. I only had the job because the woman had talked to my father and told him that all I had to do was to watch her two small school-age children and I wouldn't be cleaning and washing dishes. My father had said that we would starve before he saw any of us working in a white woman's kitchen. When my father got into trouble, I was sure I'd lose my job but my employer never even mentioned it. She or her husband continued to pick me up in the afternoons to watch the kids. My father went to court and was fined $1000 plus eighteen months' probation. My mother said he was probably placed on probation because the town did not want the responsibility of taking care of nine children. My father refused to go back to work because he said that now they had him under their thumb and he wouldn't take it. He would tell me to go to the store and get cigarettes; when I asked him for money he would tell me to use my money. I was really afraid because school was gonna start in a couple of weeks (late August) and we didn't have school clothes—actually we barely had food. Relatives gave us all the food we had. Moreover, I didn't want to face the kids at school, whom I hadn't seen all summer, or my teachers. My father would be labeled a troublemaker and that would make us the center for taunting at school. About a week before school was to start, my father's probation officer gave him permission to leave South Carolina and go to Detroit where we had relatives. (Coincidentally the probation officer's last name was the same as my last name—Alexis. He's white of course.) My father left us in the country with a distant cousin, and he and my mother and the two youngest children went to Detroit. He sent for us about three days before the schools opened there.

At that time we lived with an aunt. The grammar school I was to attend had just been integrated. I remembered the problems in Greensborough, North Carolina when the schools had been integrated. Little children were beaten and parents lost their jobs. I was scared, because although I had lived in a white neighborhood in South Carolina, all the things I remembered were negative. When we went to the store they sent their dogs after us. There was even a man who would chase us all the way home in his car, and yell, "Nigger, you goddamned niggers, get on home."

My fear was not unfounded because the white kids would chase us home everyday. We didn't have transfers so we were all placed in the lowest tracks in the school. In my own class, the students resented my answering questions that they couldn't answer. I had always thought that white kids were infinitely brighter than black kids, so I got a bit of pleasure out of knowing that in fact I knew quite a few things that they didn't know. Overall I hated the school because at recess time there wasn't anyone; I was the only black person in the eighth grade and our recess was at a different time from the other grades.

My father finally had saved enough money to rent an apartment of our own and we moved to the heart of the black ghetto in Detroit. The new school was all black, but I encountered some rather strange things there also. When I transferred from the first school, they had placed me in the next highest track. Academically, my experience was a repeat of my sixth-grade experience in South Carolina. I graduated number two in the class but not before being taunted because I spoke "proper," as they called it. By the time the year was over, however, I had new friends. My all-black high school was just across the parking lot from the elementary school. My high school experience was riddled with demonstrations and protests which I took part in because they were fun (none of them being really worthwhile causes) and they also meant no classes. There was no chance of reprisal against me or any of my family because the numbers were so large, and anyway Detroit was such a big place that such threats couldn't be very effective. My father never knew that I'd taken part in them however, because his comments about the situation were always negative.

I had always wanted to go to college, but my father's attitude had made me want to go more than ever. As a young woman in high school, I had none of the privileges that others my age had. I wasn't allowed to attend school functions unless I was in them and in most cases I wasn't allowed to be in them. I wasn't allowed company as other young ladies were, and judging from my older sister's experience, I'd never be allowed any as long as I resided in his house. I wasn't allowed many female friends either, since they had to meet a certain color standard (fair-skinned) set by my father. He wanted me to be a teacher and attend State University as my sister had done. I told him that there were already too many teachers, and at any rate I didn't want to be a teacher. I wanted to be a lawyer. Actually I wanted to get as far away from home as possible so as to have a legitimate excuse for being there very infrequently. My counselors thought that I should go east to school and I agreed wholeheartedly.

One morning, a monitor came in and informed my English teacher that eight students were wanted in the counseling office, myself included. When we arrived, there was a white man who looked rather frightened and a black guy. They were introduced as William Minser and John Wilson from a small liberal arts college in New England. By the time we arrived, Mr. Minser, after reviewing our transcripts, had informed the counselor that he could only look seriously at two students, myself and Avis Fanning. We were numbers one and two in the class respectively. We all remained, and Mr. Minser and John proceeded to tell us about Berkshire College. Berkshire College was becoming coeducational the year we would enter. There were pictures showing black students lying on the grass in front of Talbot Hall and behind Maywell House. The pictures were very beautiful and the people in them looked very happy. It was small and picturesque and reminded me of the small town in South Carolina. I had really loved the town with its mountains, pecan trees, peach trees, and plum trees, that bore pink, yellow, and white flowers in the spring and summer. The pictures of New England town had the same kinds of flowering trees. John informed us that with some hard work we would make it through Berkshire College with relative ease. He told us of the Afro-American Society which sponsored social and cultural events for black students to make things more bearable since there were so few blacks on campus. We were told that there would be a few adjustment problems but that given the educational quality of the school it would be well worth it.

After they had gone, my counselor pulled out the college catalogue and told us about Berkshire College. It was all-male, in the most competitive category of colleges, and had about 1000 students. I wanted to go to a small college because I didn't feel that I'd be able to perform in a big university setting. I didn't get along well with all the concrete and skyscrapers in Detroit and besides New England town was in New England over nine hundred miles away. I couldn't get much further away from home than that.

When Avis and I came to visit Berkshire College, the weekend didn't start out very promising. It was raining and muddy and the New England town we were seeing was nothing at all like the pictures we had been shown. I looked at Avis and she looked at me and we said almost simultaneously, "I don't think I like this place." The next day the sun came out and things looked better. After meeting most of the black students here at the time I began to enjoy myself. There was a big party in the center (Afro Am) and I really began to enjoy the weekend. Prior to visiting Berkshire College, I had received a telegram from Trinity College advising me of the amount of scholarship they would provide. They were providing a full ride for the first year at least. No one bothered to interview me while I was here (we were just watched. I was told later, to discern any adverse reaction), but I did speak with one of the Deans and "quite by accident" (on purpose) mentioned my telegram from Trinity and showed it to him. I was accepted at Berkshire and scholarship announcements were made concurrently. Despite the fact that the cost of attending Berkshire was approximately 200 dollars less than Trinity, the college offered me 100 dollars more in the total package with only 150 dollars of loan for the entire year. Trinity's loan had been about 400 dollars. Well that was it. Berkshire made the best offer in terms of money. I had visited and liked the place. I had never seen Trinity but I knew it was bigger, plus Berkshire was rated higher in the circle of colleges.

During the summer, prior to coming to Berkshire, the conflicts between my father and me continued to mount. I could offer no protest against his house rules since it was simply unheard of as well as unprecedented. I could talk to my mother about it, and though she sympathized completely she couldn't do anything about it. At the time I had a job as a driver training assistant. I could work for twelve hours per day or not work for any hours and still be paid because I always did whatever paper work had to be done. I usually stayed at work the entire twelve hours because it was the only time I had away from home. My father knew that I didn't always work, however. One Saturday morning, I started out for work and my father asked where I was going. I said I was going to work. He told me that there was plenty of work to do around the house and to stay home. It just so happened that on this particular day I had to schedule classes for the next two weeks. This would be a full day's (12 hours) work since the driver education facility was a trailer outside of the school and the only way to contact people was by telephone. I would also have to relocate people who had failed previous classes and reschedule them for the next session. It had to be done on Saturday because people were either in summer school or held jobs during the week. If I didn't do it, the director would have to do it, since no one else had bothered to learn how to. The director was a Japanese guy whom I had adopted as my second father because he always looked out for me. He had taught me to sign his name and anything that came through I could sign . . . including passes for myself when I had been in school. I had my own key to the trailer, and he trusted me completely. I was responsible for signing and submitting time sheets for the driver education instructors and even making out the time sheet for my boss. Around the trailer the instructors called me "Boss Lady" and still do when I go back to visit.   Sometimes the director didn't come in because I was there and no one would ever know he wasn't there since if asked I said he was out to lunch or out in traffic with students.

My boss called that day to tell me I was needed for scheduling. My father told him that I wasn't coming in. I was so angry I didn't know what to do. This very job had supported me all through high school because my father's priority was not his kids. It's true that we were poor, but some of the things we didn't have we could have had. I often thought that he only cared about us as income tax deductions.

At age sixteen I graduated from the chore of dishwashing. My sisters had inherited the job. Well, I washed dishes for three meals that day, following my father's orders. He told me to go into the basement, roll up the carpeting, and mop the floor. I was furious but knew that I couldn't say anything. When he went to work on Monday I went to work also. That morning he told me to be in the house at five o'clock from now on or find someplace else to live. When I went to work the next day I asked my boss about a place to live. He told me I should ask Tony, the other assistant. Tony said he had two older sisters who shared an apartment and he'd ask them about it. In the meantime I could stay at his place. He lived about four blocks from my parents. He loaned me his car and I went home and packed. My mother told me to keep in touch and let her know how I was doing. "Take care of yourself and go to school in September. I love you, Nicole." I took my things to my friend's apartment and returned to work. I moved to my friend's sisters' apartment two days later. When I am in Detroit I still live with one of the sisters and her two children. Needless to say, my chief motive for attending Berkshire College had disappeared. Tony's sisters were four and six years older than myself; we got along swell, and absolutely nothing was required of me. I couldn't pay them rent, so when I wasn't working I attempted to clean, wash dishes, anything, but they wouldn't hear of it. The older sister got up at five every morning and got the kids off to school, then returned to bed. The younger sister would get up when I did to go to work. They were really nice, and I couldn't believe it. Neither of them had completed high school, and when I mentioned not going to school they would not hear that either. We went shopping for a trunk and clothes, and in September I was off to Berkshire College.

When I got to New England town it was beautiful, but there was something quite different from pre-freshman weekend. Everywhere I looked, there were white people. When I had been here before all I saw were black people. I knew that the school was very much predominantly white but somehow I thought that I would only see black folks. The freshman quad was filled with white students and their parents running back and forth. The only black students I saw were the three who had arrived in the cab with me from the airport. Then a sister ran out of the entry I was to live in and offered to help Avis and myself with our bags. She had a very strange (almost white) accent and kept asking if we had met all of these people I had never heard of before. I responded to her rather coldly, I suppose, so she grabbed the bags and ran upstairs. Avis and I had both asked for singles so as to avoid rooming with any white girls and had asked for each other as roommates if that wasn't possible. They gave us singles adjacent to each other. When we got upstairs and Kathy had gone, we both broke into hysterical laughter.

When we went to dinner that night there were two long tables completely filled with black people. All the black folks on campus had congregated in the freshman quad. I didn't feel comfortable because even though all the folks at the table were black, they were strangers. Avis and I leaned on each other pretty heavily at that time. There were also a lot more fellows than there were women so that the women were more or less forced to talk. I couldn't force myself to be very vocal because I had never been very outgoing. That night four or five of the fellows came by and because I didn't know how to talk to men, my responses were very cold and sharp. It didn't take them long to get the message and they left. That night the freshmen were introduced to the Afro-Am society and what a riotous introduction it was. Without going into detailed exposé we were essentially told that we were either *Black* or we weren't. We were told of the racism on this campus and to stand up for our rights. Most of the whites hadn't really encountered black folks or ghetto blacks anyway and wouldn't know how to respond if you decided that you wanted some of everything that Berkshire College had to offer. We were warned about Chriswell house and the Snowden Hall areas as being "redneck" territory. And for certain of us who were frightened or easily intimidated, there were members of the Afro-Am who would be intimidators for the rest of the year.

Well this was Berkshire College. Fortunately for us, most of the freshmen were from all black inner-city schools, and the general personality of the upperclassmen was like home and quite welcomed in the midst of what was beginning to look like an ocean of salt with a few specks of pepper.

There were only sixteen black women and approximately seventy black men. My impression was that most of the women had come here with that thought in mind. The funny thing was that I had never considered the ratio of men to women and consequently had no intention of trying to capitalize on the situation. And besides, I never seemed to see seventy men since I only counted the ones who were potentially attractive.

The women began to play on the ratio but forgot one important variable—or perhaps not one—Smith, Holyoke, Vassar, and Wellesley. There were numerous parties where women from these schools were imported and the Berkshire women were simply ignored. During the week, the Berkshire women were clamored for but once the weekend began, so did the roadtripping. A particular resentment for Smith began to develop. I found it quite amusing, because I didn't feel that I had lost anything in the shuffle.

Classes were another experience. In most classes I was the only black person, and the experience was rather awkward. I remember Government 101 in particular. There were three black students in the class, Brenda, Barton, and myself. I hated this particular class with a passion. All of the white students ran off at the mouth, saying nothing important, as if the only thing they knew how to do was talk. We had been advised that Strauser just loved niggers and it began to show almost immediately. His questions were always a paragraph long and contained so many fifteen-letter words that one needed a dictionary to decipher the questions. Whenever he said anything about blacks, the eyes of the class would immediately turn in our direction since we sat near each other. He also had the terrible habit of putting us on the spot whenever he brought up anything even remotely related to blacks. I began to stare out of the window for the entire class period everyday, because I just didn't want to hear the nothing that the other students took pages of notes on every day.

The assignment for one particular day was the book, *The Greening of America*. When I began reading the book, it sounded so much like the class discussions that I put it down after five pages. In class the next day, he began to ask questions of various students in an effort to get a description of three levels of consciousness contained in the book. As usual, people began to talk a lot of bullshit. He told us to take out a sheet of paper and define them. Well I obviously couldn't, so I wrote that they didn't mean anything to me since there was no clear-cut definition and as far as I was concerned the book was useless since it was based upon the three levels of consciousness as a premise. He collected the papers and read them. Then he said, "Miss Alexis, I believe your definition is the best one here." I'm not sure what the moral of the story is.

My final paper for his course, however, was an expression of the disgust I was beginning to feel for Berkshire College. I completely ignored the topic and wrote about "a semester of Government 101." I got a C— on the paper, but I got the disgust off my chest. I was becoming more and more frustrated because I didn't know how to study, I had never studied, and I just didn't know how to. I was even more frustrated when I received my grades because somehow I had managed to get three B's and one C and I hadn't done any work. I knew I wasn't performing anywhere near where I thought I should be able to, yet I received the highest average of the freshmen black women.

Well, I was the first person to leave here for Christmas vacation. I spent part of the next semester happily away from Berkshire College at a free school in Boston headed by a black man who was a former Berkshire graduate. The school was beautiful, and the people were beautiful, and coming back to Berkshire wasn't something that I looked forward to. Second semester was horrible. I had been labelled a cold sister . . . well to be more specific, a bitch. I wasn't getting along very well with the other women because we just didn't have the same things to talk about. The majority of the women seemed very much interested in competing with each other in terms of men. At the end of the semester, all I could think about was Detroit, the beach, and the good times I was gonna have. I was the first person to leave at the end of the semester.

At the end of the year six of us had gotten together to room for sophomore year. The quad consisted of Avis, Denise, Pamela, and Nicole and the double had Lisa and Kathy. I think we picked the best possible team. The year was rather uneventful. By now we were quite accustomed to the white girls who came into the bathroom and stared. "Wow, that looks really wonderful, fantastic. How do you do that?"

"Oh, there's nothing to it. My hair behaves like this quite naturally. If it did anything else, I'd start to ask questions."

First semester I got my second D, and since I'd never seen D's before I figured it was about time to do something different. By second semester I was about as adjusted to Berkshire as I would ever be. It was also this semester that I had my first contact with one of the new black professors. The upperclassmen who had taken him the first semester were really impressed but also just a little bit frightened. If *they* were afraid, that meant that *we* surely would be; but a bunch of us mustered enough courage to take his course: The Economics of Being Black. I was already very hesitant, and the first few days of class only enhanced my fear. He called all of the black students by their first names and referred to the three solitary white students out of about forty as "Mr." and "Miss." He demanded clear and precise answers to questions and had no bones about telling a student that he didn't know what he was talking about. The first time he called on me, I was so scared that I bungled the whole thing. I think he realized what had happened because he let me slide. Then came the mid-term, the equivalent of a twenty-page paper with five days in which to complete it. We were encouraged to work together to discuss the issues raised and then write our own exams separately. It took him approximately two weeks to return the papers. When he did he placed the grade distribution on the board and announced the names of persons who had received A's or B+'s. I was shocked to no end when I learned that I had received an A—.

Two of my roommates were making plans to exchange during our junior year to Howard University, and things were beginning to look pretty lonely for me for the upcoming year. We had all developed a really close relationship because the black women in the freshman class were rather ridiculous. At the beginning of that year, the sophomore black women had organized a sort of orientation meeting with them. Unfortunately there had been several upperclassmen at Berkshire during the summer programs for the freshmen before they entered. Therefore, the incoming freshmen had already been oriented in a negative fashion toward our entire class, both men and women. We had thought the meeting to be a good idea because during the latter part of our second semester freshman year, the tension had become so high that we all got together and screamed at each other. It was very beneficial because everyone found out how other people felt about them and their actions. At that time we decided that whenever we saw someone obviously screwing up, we'd pull their coat and tell them what we thought about it. She might not agree but at least somebody else's opinion would be known. The freshmen women did not take our efforts very kindly. Their reply was that just because we had really made a mess of things our freshman year, it did not mean that they would follow suit. They felt that they could adequately deal with the men, the academics, and the social environment at Berkshire without any help. The irony was that they were less well equipped to deal with Berkshire than we had been, and we had made mistakes and felt that we would probably make more mistakes. It's true that they should have been better equipped academically than we were, having come from better schools, but in other areas they were lacking, since most of them came from sheltered homes or middle-income families and knew very little about racism, and there was necessarily a tension because the blacks who were already here were from a different background. Quite frankly, however, their reaction was not a surprise.

By the end of the semester the new black women (the majority) found themselves doing terribly academically, and their social lives were very chaotic. The black men began to approach us and asked us to talk to a few of them about the way they carried themselves. I wasn't willing to approach any of them because I felt that it would be taken negatively. I sensed that any attempt at talking with them would be unappreciated and taken as something else. At this time, I began to hear various rumors about the freshmen women being afraid of me. I supposed this to be due to the fact that while I wouldn't approach anyone concerning their affairs, social or otherwise, I had no qualms about speaking exactly what was on my mind in their presence even if it happened to concern one of them. As second semester opened I began to think about the coming year. Avis and Denise would be exchanging to Howard University in September, and Kathy was trying to go to Amherst for the first semester of our junior year. Increasingly I began to think about living arrangements for the next year. Having white roommates was simply out of the question, and just as much out of the question was living with the freshman black women. I didn't feel particularly comfortable with them because there was a distinct difference in values, expectations, and reactions to many things. Quite frankly, I felt that making it academically would be somewhat hindered by the problems of adjustment to our obvious differences if we were thrown into a very close living situation.

Lisa Allen and I had become rather close toward the end of the semester. We could talk to each other about mutually important things. We didn't agree on everything, but our disagreements were handled with ease. She, too, was looking for living arrangements for the coming year. She came to me one day and asked if

I'd like to live off campus the next year. I said, "Sure." She stated that I was the only woman on campus that she could live with and get along with. The only problem was going to be whether or not I could obtain permission from the Dean's Office. She was number one on the list but since I had never thought seriously of moving off campus, I had never signed up. We talked to one of the deans and he said the circumstances were unusual and therefore arrangements could be made. Lisa was the only black junior woman who would return the next year as a senior; therefore, her roommate would necessarily be an underclassman. He moved my name from the bottom of the waiting list to the top.

Junior year I formed the closest relationship to anyone I've ever had, not only at Berkshire but anywhere. Lisa and I became extremely close. She cared about what I thought, and many times, even though she had reservations about what I was feeling, she never attacked but asked questions, her questions making me question in turn and generally causing me to at least reevaluate those feelings. We talked hours on end about Berkshire and what was happening to us and everyone else here. I didn't like Berkshire because it placed me in a state of, I guess, being nowhere. The academics of Berkshire seemed so unreal, the people seemed unreal, and increasingly it became harder to identify with other black students since it seemed the college was doing some grand experiment in coming up with the perfect black Berkshire student. I didn't identify with any black student who felt comfortable here because it implied being comfortable in other places also. I can't be comfortable because I know where I came from and am going back to, and the black people in the world out there, the real world, are terribly uncomfortable.

In October of my junior year I had my first real contact with the New England town Upward Bound Program. Lisa had attended an Upward Bound board meeting where they were discussing one of the young women in the program. She was living with a family in the town and was doing terribly because she couldn't adjust to living with the family and living in New England town. Lisa suggested that she could live with us since we had an off-campus apartment and there was plenty of room. She wanted to consult me, but she was reasonably sure that it was okay. The Board had to get permission from National Upward Bound since Upward Bound students had never lived with college students. National

Upward Bound said yes on the condition that we were black. Laurie came to live with us on trial two days later.

Problems developed because, while she was only sixteen we didn't feel that we had to be strictly motherly types. We wanted to make it a threesome. At first things were okay. Soon, however, Laurie wanted to be left alone completely to do whatever she felt like doing at any given time. When she first came to live with us she would tell us voluntarily where she was going when she went out. There came a time however when she didn't volunteer it and openly resented our asking. She reiterated that we were not her mother and therefore didn't tell her what to do. To complicate matters, Laurie had a medical problem. She had to wear corrective lenses which she refused to wear. One night after numerous other occasions I was having a talk with her about wearing the lenses. She told me it was none of our business; she knew she was supposed to wear them and she would when she got ready to. At that point I blew my stack because the lenses were for her own good not mine, and quite frankly I didn't appreciate her particular response because she lived in our apartment—free of obligation. The Upward Bound Program gave us $60 a month $20 of which went to Laurie in the form of a five-dollar weekly allowance. She was completely selfish. Everything that belonged to her she kept in the corner of the room which she shared with Lisa. She refused to take part in household chores. We went to the Board with the lens problem. The president sent Laurie a message by us. "Either wear the lenses or she would find her another place to live because part of our responsibility was to see that she wore them."

What angered me most was the more we tried to help the more she threw it in our faces. It reminded me of ultra-liberal whites and the shit they put up with in terms of some blacks, which does more harm than good, because of guilt feelings. I had no guilt feeling about Laurie since I came from a rough background myself. In the spring, because of financial difficulties, it was decided to make the Upward Bound House in which all the male students resided, coeducational. I applied for the position of female counselor. Numerous other black women stated that they wanted to apply for the position but, as things will have it, they foolishly did not apply because they felt that inevitably I would get the position.

Lisa graduated, but our friendship remains intact.

In August of my senior year I arrived at the Upward Bound House, which was a total disaster. The remodeling to be completed over the summer was nowhere near completion. I changed into my jeans and began work. The students began to arrive two days later. The program was in financial trouble and community trouble. The students were not performing, and the viability of the program was being questioned. This year we do or die. The five adults in the house had to tighten things up. We constructed rules and discussed them with the President of the Board and the Chairman of the Personnel Committee. They were satisfactory. There were five students returning who knew what a good time they had had the previous year. There would be two new students. We expected protest and it's exactly what we got. In the beginning they tried everything and got punished for it. I heard things reiterated about our not being their parents. There's a fallacy in that argument, however, since we are their legal guardians while they reside here. There being five adults in the house, two white and three black, gave them another tactic. Why not play the counselors off against the resident couple. Needless to say, part of our responsibility became that of educating the resident family concerning what black children will try to do to them. By mid-semester this became very tiresome and irritating. It was taking too much of our time from our studies and there was hardly time to do anything except baby-sit the Upward Bound students who were really playing games anyway. Important things like reminding them New England town wasn't real were being neglected in lieu of the games they wanted to play. It's hard to explain my disappointment in terms of the things they were forcing me to do instead. It's a difficult task to talk to three young ladies about being a woman and what may or may not be happening to them in New England town when they feel that they already know everything that I could possibly tell them. It makes me think of why relationships with the underclassmen are so difficult. I wonder if I'm superiority oriented. I don't think so because I'm willing to listen, at least, and more to anyone who has something to say. I don't start out with the premise, "She doesn't know anything more than I do," particularly since everyone has different experiences that teach them different things.

Living in the house has had repercussions in other areas. My interaction with other students on campus is very limited since most of my time is spent at the house. I still hear the rumor that the other women on campus are afraid of me. It's getting so that I'm not really terribly concerned because for the most part, all they know about me is my name, and I think it would be awful to be so easily intimidated.

I'll be glad to get out of here in June. There are very few people here that I'll miss and I'm sure the opposite is true. I don't feel that I've gotten very much out of college. The most important things didn't happen in class. I feel as though for the past four years I've been in a state of suspension and now it's time to start doing things again.

Hopefully I'll be going to law school next year and the reason is no longer my father. I want to do something beneficial for myself and for others at the same time.

Your summary:

STOP. Check sample summary at the end of Lesson 9.

Practice C.

Without rereading the autobiographical article, answer these true/false questions. Put a T for *true* and an F for *false* in the blank.

_____ 1. The writer, as a child, thought white kids were smarter than black kids

_____ 2. The writer took pride in her ability to answer questions correctly at the integrated school.

_____ 3. The writer told her father that she took part in demonstrations.

_____ 4. The writer spoke standard English.

_____ 5. The writer's father was in "command" in his house.

_____ 6. The father was not demanding where his daughter was concerned.

_____ 7. The writer resented her father.

_____ 8. There were a large number of black students at Berkshire College.

_____ 9. The writer wanted to room with a white girl.

_____ 10. The writer was outgoing.

_____ 11. There was no racism at Berkshire College.

_____ 12. There were more women than men at Berkshire.

_____ 13. The black students usually did not sit next to each other in class.

_____ 14. Usually there were a number of black people in all the writer's classes.

_____ 15. The writer went out a lot.

_____ 16. The writer was used to receiving D's.

_____ 17. The writer found some friends with whom she was compatible.

_____ 18. The writer, as a sophomore, didn't think much of the freshmen women.

_____ 19. Black students from middle-class homes would do better at Berkshire than inner-city black students.

_____ 20. The writer is candid.

_____ 21. According to the writer, black people are "uncomfortable."

_____ 22. The writer felt like an ultra-liberal white in relation to Laurie, the Upward Bound student.

_____ 23. The writer had difficulty relating to the students in the Upward Bound House.

_____ 24. The Upward Bound students "played the resident couple against the counselors."

_____ 25. The writer felt that college made a significant difference in her life.

STOP. Check answers at the end of Lesson 9.

Practice D.

State the reasons that the writer gives for feeling frustrated in her freshman year.

STOP. Check answers at the end of Lesson 9.

VOCABULARY: CONTEXT CLUES (Literature)

The sentences in this section are taken from fiction.

Practice A.

Use your knowledge of context clues to determine the meaning of the underlined words.

1. Hester sought not to acquire anything beyond a <u>subsistence</u>, of the plainest and most <u>ascetic</u> description, for herself, and a simple <u>abundance</u> for her child. Her own dress was of the <u>coarsest</u> materials and the most <u>somber hue</u>; with only one <u>ornament</u>—the <u>scarlet</u> letter, which it was her doom to wear._____ ;_____ ;

   _____ ;_____ ;

   _____ ;_____ ;

   _____ ;_____

2. It is evident that the respect in which my father is held in this house is tempered by a good deal of mirth. He is impressive, but awkward.

   ₂_____;_____;_____

3. In dealing with Mrs. Lincoln's external life we are on somewhat surer ground, though not much, for still the cloud of intangible gossip is likely to mislead us._____;_____; _____

4. An abyss has opened between us—there is no denying it. But, Nora, would it not be possible to fill it up? _____

STOP. Check answers at the end of Lesson 9.

Practice B.

Match the meaning from column B with the word in column A.

	Column A	Column B
_____	1. somber	a. unsubstantial
_____	2. hue	b. bottomless pit
_____	3. tempered	c. self-denying
_____	4. mirth	d. roughest
_____	5. impressive	e. gloomily dark
_____	6. intangible	f. plentiful quantity
_____	7. gossip	g. outward
_____	8. abyss	h. means of support
_____	9. external	i. moderated
_____	10. scarlet	j. idle talk
_____	11. ascetic	k. decoration
_____	12. subsistence	l. amusement
_____	13. abundance	m. bright red
_____	14. coarsest	n. imposing
_____	15. ornament	o. color

STOP. Check answers at the end of Lesson 9.

Practice C.

For this set of sentences with missing words choose the word that *best* fits
the sentence. Put the word in the blank.

Word List:

somber, hue, tempered, mirth, impressive, intangible, gossip, scarlet, abyss,
external, ascetic, subsistence, abundance, coarsest, ornament.

1. Now that bold makeup is popular again, the sales of _____
   lipstick have skyrocketed.
2. Many monks lead a very_____ existence.
3. Happiness is a(n)_____ commodity, which cannot be bought.
4. Be wary of_____ unless you don't mind contributing to the
   spread of rumors.
5. It's going to be a big house, all right. They dug a regular_____
   for the cellar.
6. The_____part of the instrument looked fine, but internally
   it was all rotted away.
7. Although many wealthy children have a(n)_____of material
   goods, they may not have a(n)_____of love and understanding.
8. My boss commands respect because he looks _____, but the
   effect lasts only as long as he keeps his mouth shut.
9. When you wear such_____colors you look like a mortician.
10. That blouse is made of the_____material I have ever seen,
    and it irritates my skin.
11. My brothers are usually a joy to be around because they are so full of

    _____
12. I choose with care the_____that I wear on my dress.
13. Her rather sharp remarks are usually later_____with some
    flattery.
14. While at school I earned a bare_____as busboy in the local
    restaurant.

15. "Sky blue pink" is a phrase used to describe an outlandish _____ .

STOP. Check answers at the end of Lesson 9.

WORD ANALYSIS: WORD PARTS

Knowledge of word parts is helpful in figuring out word meanings. (See Lessons 13–15.) If you can break down a multisyllabic word into its various parts and isolate the *root* (*base*) of the word, you can apply vowel rules to the root to try to determine its pronunciation. Once you have figured out the pronunciation of the word, you may recognize it as one you already know as part of your hearing vocabulary.

1. A *prefix* is a letter or a group of letters added to the beginning of a root (base) word to form a new, related word. Examples: (*re*—again, back; *in*—not; *un*—not; *non*—not; *pre*—before; *co*—together; *de*—away, from, down.

2. A *suffix* is a letter or a group of letters added to the end of a root (base) word to form a new, related word. Examples: *tion*—act of, state of, result of; *al*—relating to; *y*—having, full of, tending to, like; *ic*—relating to, like; *ous*—full of, having; *ly*—like, manner of; *less*—without; *ance*—act of, state of, degree of; *or, ar, er*—one who.

3. A *root* (*base*) is the smallest unit of a word that can exist and retain its basic meaning. It cannot be broken down. *Reword* is not a root word because it can be subdivided into *re* and *word*. *Word* is a root word because it cannot be divided further and still retain its basic meaning. In the word *reworded, word* is a root, *re* is a prefix, and *ed* is a suffix. In the word *rewarded, ward* is not the root word. The root word is *reward*. You cannot break *reward* down any further and retain its basic meaning. (The word *ward* is not related in meaning to the word *reward*.)

Special Notes

1. Prefixes and suffixes cannot stand alone as words.

2. When a suffix is added to a word it generally changes the word into another part of speech. For example, *prince* (noun) plus *ly* (suffix) becomes *princely* (adjective).

3. Verb and participle endings such as *ed, en,* and *ing* are considered suffixes.

4. Endings such as *s* and *es* that are used to form plurals and verb endings, and endings such as *er* and *est* that are used to form comparatives and superlatives, are also considered suffixes.

4. A compound word is formed by combining two or more words. Examples: cowgirl, postman, grandfather, hayride, gatecrasher, pinch-hit, right-of-way.

5. Combining forms are usually defined as roots borrowed from another language that join together or that join with a prefix, a suffix, or both a prefix and a suffix to form a word. Often the English combining forms are derived from Greek and Latin roots. A combining form cannot stand alone as a word in English, but the combining form often can stand alone as an independent word in the language from which it is derived. (See Lessons 13–15 on combining forms used to build vocabulary.) Examples: *bio*—life; *tele*—from a distance; *cardio*—heart; *geo*—earth.

Practice A.

In this list of twenty words check each word carefully and then write the root word in the blank. (Remember the root word must be a word in *English*, and it must retain its basic meaning.)

1. replayed_____   11. charging _____

2. reasoning_____   12. impossibility_____

3. confession_____   13. reported _____

4. immoral _____   14. importing_____

5. commanded_____   15. revengeful_____

6. heroic_____   16. prejudged _____

7. natural_____   17. preconditioned _____

8. dirty_____   18. grievous _____

9. nativity_____   19. tasty _____

10. previewed_____   20. preserved_____

STOP. Check answers at the end of Lesson 9.

ANSWERS: Lesson 9 (pp. 252-292)

Reading: Inference (Understanding Jokes and Proverbs) (pp. 252–255)

Practice A

1. The sign applies to cars, not pupils. Child made wrong inference. 2. The word *like* has a double meaning. In the first line it seems that the first cannibal doesn't like the second cannibal's friend's personality, but in the second line we find that his dislike is apparently based on the friend's inedibility. 3. Mary is led to infer that Jim had actually come face to face with a lion in the wild rather than separated by bars at a zoo. 4. Mary misunderstands what Jane means by *tell*. 5. John jumps to the wrong conclusion. 6. The owner jumps to the wrong conclusion that the diner is complimenting his restaurant. 7. The patient's crazy logic is the surprise.

Practice B

1. g. What's done is done. 2. e. Take advantage of opportunity. 3. i. What is, will be. 4. f. It's useless to do things too late. 5. d. One move can be as bad as another. 6. h. Others can profit when two people quarrel. 7. j. Never put off for tomorrow what you can do today. 8. c. One good turn deserves another. 9. a. Rather than blaming ourselves, we make excuses. 10. b. In times of trouble only your true friends stand by you.

Practice C

1. It's better to wait and see. 2. You shouldn't limit your options to just one. 3. Don't judge others by their external appearance but rather by what they are within. 4. People who have problems feel better knowing that they are not the only ones who have them. 5. There's usually some good to be found in everything. 6. Large things can come from something small. 7. When someone is in greatest need, he will work the hardest. 8. Coverings don't change what's inside. 9. What's good for one may be bad for another. 10. Don't take advantage of those who help you. 11. Those who make the loudest noises are usually the least dangerous. 12. What you do is more

important than what you say. 13. Take the offensive when your cause seems hopeless. 14. People of like interests seem to choose one another's company. 15. Don't jump into anything without investigating it first.

Reading/Learning Skills: Summaries (Articles or Excerpts from Articles) (pp. 256–277)

Practice A (sample summaries)

1. A formula exists not only for estimating your healthiest weight but also for determining the amount of food you need to maintain your ideal weight. To estimate your ideal weight, multiply your height in inches by 3.5 and then subtract 110 pounds from the product. The amount of calories you need to maintain your ideal weight is based on how active you are. Using the given scale, determine your activity level and multiply this by your ideal weight to get the number of calories you need. To reach your ideal weight, determine the size of your energy imbalance and then slowly correct this imbalance.

2. A change in attitude has taken place, especially among young adults, toward jealousy. Jealousy has come to be looked upon as a weakness in a relationship rather than supportive of marriage. The type of jealousy you feel determines how big your problem is. Feeling left out is the most common jealousy problem, and dealing with it is part of the etiquette of our times. The more serious jealousy problem stems from your inability to share your partner in ways that are generally considered appropriate and is probably rooted in a persistent fear of loss rather than a temporary irritation.

Practice B

The writer, a black female, gives an account of her life through college. She was born in South Carolina, is one of nine children, and has a very domineering father. She has had various school experiences. In South Carolina she was bused to an all black school; in Detroit she went to a newly integrated almost all white school for a short time and then to all black schools in the heart of the Detroit ghetto. Although she experiences difficulties in the black as well as the white schools, she does very well academically and earns a scholarship to Berkshire, a predominantly white school in New England.

Her biggest adjustment comes when she goes to this college, where she has to learn to deal with social class differences, with a much larger ratio of male to female students, with classes in which she is the only black person, with teachers who have difficulty interacting with black students and students from lower social classes, with other black students who want all the black students to think and be alike, and with the responsibilities of being a counselor in an Upward Bound program. As graduation nears, the writer feels that she has gotten very little out of college and that the important things did not happen in class. She is looking forward to hopefully going to law school so that she can eventually benefit others as well as herself.

Practice C

1. T 2. T 3. F 4. T 5. T 6. F 7. T 8. F 9. F 10. F 11. F 12. F 13. F 14. F 15. F 16. F 17. T 18. T 19. F 20. T 21. T 22. T 23. T 24. T 25. F

Practice D

She had never learned how to study. Even though she received the highest average of the freshmen black women, she hadn't done any work. She felt that she wasn't working up to her potential.

Vocabulary: Context Clues (Literature) (pp. 277–280)

Practice A

1. subsistence—means of support, the minimum necessary to exist; ascetic—severe, self-denying; abundance—plentiful quantity or supply; coarsest—roughest, most lacking in delicacy of texture; somber—gloomily dark; hue—color; ornament—decoration; scarlet—bright red 2. tempered—moderated; mirth—amusement, jollity; impressive—imposing, awesome 3. external—outward; intangible—unsubstantial, vague, unable to be touched; gossip—idle talk or rumors 4. abyss—bottomless pit.

Practice B

1. e 2. o 3. i 4. l 5. n 6. a 7. j 8. b 9. g 10. m 11. c 12. h 13. f 14. d 15. k

Practice C

1. scarlet 2. ascetic 3. intangible 4. gossip 5. abyss 6. external 7. abundance 8. impressive 9. somber 10. coarsest 11. mirth 12. ornament 13. tempered 14. subsistence 15. hue

Word Analysis: Word Parts (pp. 280–281)

Practice A

1. play 2. reason 3. confess 4. moral 5. command 6. hero 7. nature 8. dirt 9. native 10. view 11. charge 12. possible 13. report 14. import 15. revenge 16. judge 17. condition 18. grieve 19. taste 20. preserve

CROSSWORD PUZZLE

Directions:

The meanings of a number of the words and some of the ideas from Lessons 7–9 follow. Your knowledge of these words and ideas will help you to solve this crossword puzzle.

Across

1. Word meaning *bend downward*
4. Abbreviation that means *before noon*
6. Word meaning *financial*
12. A broad silk sash with a bow worn by Japanese women

Down

1. You use this to stay clean
2. Lessen
3. Slang abbreviation of *soldier*
4. Suffix meaning *relating to*
5. Another way to say *mother*
7. Something not directly stated but implied

13. Another word for *boy*
15. That part of the day when the sun is directly overhead
16. A vowel digraph
17. Abbreviation of *Alcoholics Anonymous*
18. Abbreviation of *Royal Air Force*
20. Another word for *ideas*
24. A pen for pigs
26. Outside
28. A time period
30. An exclamation
31. Anger
32. Unstressed syllable of *braille*
34. Abbreviation of *alternating current*
35. A short saying that expresses some truth
37. To assert without proof
40. A suffix meaning *relating to*
41. Antonym of *yes*
42. Same as #5 Down
43. This can be something you hunt or something you play
45. Evening
46. Roman numeral 110
47. This helps give clues to what an instructor thinks is important
48. Homonym of *son*
49. To annoy

8. Homonym of *sew*
9. Prefix meaning *together*
10. Suffix meaning *act of*
11. An important part of the SQ3R study method
14. Antonym of *wet*
16. A lodging place for travelers
19. An indefinite article
21. Decoration
22. Feminine pronoun in French
23. Abbreviation of *Science Research Association*
24. Comes from a tree, slang for a *fool*
25. Flourish
27. You do this when you want to copy something
29. This helps you to know how to pronounce a word
31. Roman numeral 4
33. A reproductive cell produced by the female
36. Sea
38. To hold out; a mold or form of a human foot; go on
39. Made free from discomfort
44. To think about, to ponder
45. Abbreviation of *and so on*
47. Very small
50. Abbreviation of *southeast*
51. Friends
52. Decay

51. A half quart

52. You do this when you're tired

53. Roman numeral 100

54. Abbreviation of *northeast*

55. Loud, wild speech

56. Wear away

58. Cunning, sly

59. The smallest unit of a word that can exist and retain its basic meaning

60. A student who___is reading very fast

61. Word refers to tree and to wasting away through mourning

55. The edge of something circular

56. An extremely long period of time

57. The eggs of fishes

58. Abbreviation of *West Indies*

59. Abbreviation of *Rhode Island*

STOP. Check answers on the next page.

Crossword Puzzle Answers

											¹S	²A	³G
⁴A	⁵M		⁶F	⁷I	⁸S	⁹C	¹⁰A	L		¹¹R	¹²O	B	I
¹³L	¹⁴A	D	¹⁵N	O	O	N		¹⁶I	E		¹⁷A	A	
		¹⁸R	¹⁹A	F		²⁰C	²¹O	N	C	²²E	P	T	²³S
²⁴S	²⁵T	Y	²⁶E	²⁷X	T	E	R	N	A	L		²⁸E	R	²⁹A
³⁰A	H		³¹I	R	E		N		³²L	L	³³E		³⁴A	C
³⁵P	R	³⁶O	V	E	R	B	³⁷A	³⁸L	L	E	G	³⁹E		C
	⁴⁰I	C	⁴¹N	O		⁴²M	A			⁴³G	⁴⁴A	M	E
⁴⁵E	V	E	⁴⁶C	X	⁴⁷T	E	S	T		⁴⁸S	U	N
⁴⁹T	E	⁵⁰A	S	E	⁵¹P	I	N	T		⁵²R	E	S	T
⁵³C	⁵⁴N	E		⁵⁵R	A	N	T		⁵⁶E	⁵⁷R	O	D	E
		⁵⁸W	I	L	Y		⁵⁹R	O	O	T
	⁶⁰S	K	I	M	S		⁶¹P	I	N	E

HOMOGRAPH RIDDLES

Directions:

Here are several ways to use a single word. Find the right word for each group. Example: I'm a geographical feature; I'm produced by an orchestra; and I mean fine and logical (sound).

1. If I do this to your ears, I can hurt you; you can put things in me; I do this in an arena; I'm a tree; a baseball player stands in me. _____

2. I'm a bushy tail; I'm a short, quick fight; I can refresh one's memory; I make people presentable; I can be used to paint, clean, polish, smooth, and so on. _____

3. I'm a series of marks on a thermometer; I cover a fish; in music I'm very important; I'm an instrument. _____

4. I can move on wheels; I can do this to my "*r*'s"; I am good to eat; I move by rotating; I'm what the instructor calls at the beginning of class.

   _____

5. I'm not worn, soiled, or faded; I'm strong and brisk; I'm pure and cool; I'm not rotten; however, I'm also inexperienced, and I can be bold, saucy, or insulting._____

6. I'm used for support; I'm a smile or a radiant look; I'm a ray of light; I'm part of a ship._____

STOP. Check answers at the bottom of the page.

SMIDGENS   by Bob Cordray

TRUE/FALSE TEST

Directions:

This is a true/false test on Lessons 7–9 in Unit III. Read each sentence carefully. Decide whether it is true or false. Put a T for *true* or an F for *false* in the blank.

_____ 1. *Prepare* is a root word.

_____ 2. All multisyllabic words ending in *le* and having a consonant before the *le* have an unstressed syllable.

_____ 3. An unstressed syllable is never accented.

_____ 4. In two-syllable words the first syllable is usually stressed.

_____ 5. In two-syllable words in which the second syllable has two vowels, the second syllable is usually stressed.

1. box 2. brush 3. scale 4. roll 5. fresh 6. beam

_____ 6. *Replay* is a root word.

_____ 7. *Turn* is a root word.

_____ 8. The word *action* contains a prefix.

_____ 9. The word *action* contains a suffix.

_____ 10. A prefix is added to the beginning of a root word.

_____ 11. Both a prefix and a suffix can be added to the beginning of a root word.

_____ 12. Inferences are made by readers.

_____ 13. Sometimes it's helpful to summarize an article by beginning with the author's conclusion.

_____ 14. Something inhibited is held back.

_____ 15. Something boundless is tied up.

_____ 16. A sponge can be saturated.

_____ 17. All details should be included in a summary.

_____ 18. Only nonfiction writers rely on inference.

_____ 19. Authors make implications.

_____ 20. An aggregate is a collection of things.

_____ 21. When you engage in discourse, you are always engaging in an argument or debate.

_____ 22. To understand jokes you must be able to make inferences.

_____ 23. Something impressive is awesome.

_____ 24. If you are leading an ascetic life you have an abundance of possessions.

_____ 25. The antonym of *coarse* is *delicate*.

_____ 26. A synonym of *hue* is *color*.

_____ 27. The homonym of *red* is *reed*.

_____ 28. A person filled with mirth would not be somber.

STOP. Check answers on the next page.

Answers to True/False Test

1. T 2. T* 3. T* 4. T 5. T 6. F 7. T 8. F 9. T 10. T 11. F
12. T 13. T 14. T 15. F 16. T 17. F 18. F 19. T 20. T 21. F
22. T 23. T 24. F 25. T 26. T 27. F 28. T

*See Lesson 14 on objective tests for true-false questions dealing with "always" and "never."

Unit IV

Learning Skills: Knowing Your Textbook
Reading: Knowing Your Source and Questioning What You Read
Vocabulary: Connotative Meaning
Word Analysis: The Dictionary I
Answers

LEARNING SKILLS: KNOWING YOUR TEXTBOOK

Knowing about the various parts of your textbook is helpful in studying and can save you valuable time and effort. Here are some things you should do after you acquire your textbook:

1. *Survey the textbook.* This helps you to see how the author presents the material. Notice whether the author presents topic headings in bold print or in the margins. Notice if there are diagrams, charts, cartoons, pictures, and so on.
2. *Read the preface.* The preface or foreword, which is at the beginning of the book, is the author's explanation of the book. It presents the author's purpose and plan in writing the book. Here the author usually describes the organization of the book and explains how the book either is different from others in the field or is a further contribution to the field of knowledge.
3. *Read the chapter headings.* The table of contents will give you a good idea of what to expect from the book. Then when you begin to study you will know how each section you are reading relates to the rest of the book.
4. *Skim the index.* The index indicates in detail what material you will find in the book. It is an invaluable aid because it helps you find specific information that you need by giving you the page on which it appears.
5. *Check for a glossary.* Not all books have a glossary; however, a glossary is helpful because it gives you the meanings of specialized words or phrases used in the book.

6. *Check for an appendix.* An appendix contains extra information that does not quite fit into the book but that the author feels is important enough to be presented separately.

7. *Read the first few paragraphs.* The first few paragraphs will give you cues about the writer's vocabulary and writing. If you find that the book is difficult for you because the concepts being presented are completely unfamiliar, you should plan to allot more time for studying this subject until the material becomes familiar.

Practice A.

Read the preface of this book and then answer these questions.

1. Why did the author write this book?

_____

_____

2. How is the material organized in this book?

_____

_____

3. What are some of the unique features of this book?

_____

_____

STOP. Check answers at the end of Lesson 10.

Practice B.

Using the index of this book, state one page on which you would find each of these topics.

1. SQ3R

_____

_____

2. Main idea of a paragraph

_____

_____

3. Objective tests

_____

_____

4. Skimming

_____

_____

5. Alphabetizing

_____

_____

STOP. Check answers at the end of Lesson 10.

Practice C.

State what is in the appendixes to this book.

I.

_____

_____

II.

_____

_____

III.

_____

_____

STOP. Check answers at the end of Lesson 10.

Practice D.

Answer these questions concerning the glossary of this book.

1. How is the glossary divided?

_____

_____

2. Find the word *dual* in the glossary. Define it and state in what lesson you can find it.

_____

_____

3. Find *simile* in the glossary and define it.

_____

_____

STOP. Check answers at the end of Lesson 10.

READING: KNOWING YOUR SOURCE AND QUESTIONING WHAT YOU READ

To be a good reader, you must learn to question what you read and to determine the author's purpose for writing.

1. It is important that you consider the source in judging something you read. For example, an article concerning a medical problem appearing in a popular magazine would be a different kind of article from one appearing in a medical or scientific journal. Also, an *editorial* in a newspaper has a nature different from a newspaper *article* because an editorial is an expression of opinion. An article concerning, say, marriage appearing in an underground newspaper will probably not be as objective as one published in a public newspaper. The character of each source should affect your approach to reading.

2. The qualifications of the person writing the article are as important as the source in which the article appears. For example, an authority in economics, chemical engineering, or computers is not necessarily qualified to write in the area of psychology or education. An article written by a person with a special interest in an area tends to be less objective than one written by a person with no special interest. For example, an article written by a union leader on employee rights would have a different slant from that of one written by a management leader.

3. You should *not* believe everything you read. If something does not make sense, you should question it, even if it is in a textbook written by an authority in the field. For example, if in your biology book you found these statements, "A female needs 5000 fewer calories a day than a male does," and "Humans drink about 1000 quarts of fluid in a week," would you believe them? Reread them. Aren't they senseless? How could a female require 5000 fewer calories than a male does? Most females—or males, for that

matter—do not consume 5000 calories in a day. Also, how could one drink 1000 quarts of fluid in a week? There are seven days in a week. Even if someone drank four quarts of fluid a day (which is a large amount), that person would still have drunk only twenty-eight quarts in a week. The "5000" and the "1000" are obvious errors. The authors probably meant to say 500 calories and 10 quarts.

Practice A.

Study this list of journals, magazines, and other publications. State whether you would expect a tendency toward objectivity or toward nonobjectivity from the publication on each stated topic. Write "NO" for *nonobjectivity* or "O" for *objectivity* in the blank.

Publication	*Topic*	*Objectivity*
1. Newspaper editorial	Sexual freedom	_____
2. Anthropology textbook	Sexual freedom	_____
3. Psychology textbook	Sexual freedom	_____
4. Church newsletter	Sexual freedom	_____
5. Woman's liberation newsletter	Sexual freedom	_____
6. Research journal	Marijuana	_____
7. Newspaper editorial	Marijuana	_____
8. Sociology textbook	Marijuana	_____
9. Underground newspaper	Marijuana	_____
10. Medical journal	Marijuana	_____
11. Popular magazine	Marijuana	_____
12. Church newsletter	Marijuana	_____

STOP. Check answers at the end of Lesson 10.

Practice B.

Here is a list of persons writing on specific topics. State whether you would expect a tendency toward objectivity or toward nonobjectivity on each stated topic. Write "NO" for *nonobjectivity* or "O" for *objectivity* in the blank.

Person	*Topic*	*Objectivity*
1. Family counselor	Sexual freedom	_____
2. Social psychologist	Sexual freedom	_____
3. Orthodox rabbi	Sexual freedom	_____
4. Catholic priest	Sexual freedom	_____
5. Editor in newspaper editorial	Sexual freedom	_____
6. Anthropologist	Sexual freedom	_____
7. Reporter in public newspaper	Sexual freedom	_____
8. Editor in underground newspaper	Sexual freedom	_____
9. College student	Going to college	_____
10. College dean	Going to college	_____
11. Research journal	Going to college	_____
12. College president	Going to college	_____
13. Editor in college newspaper	Going to college	_____
14. Editor in public newspaper	Going to college	_____
15. Sociology textbook	Going to college	_____
16. Editor in educational journal	Going to college	_____

STOP. Check answers at the end of Lesson 10.

Practice C.

Read these selections. Underline anything that does not make sense. Change it so that it does make sense.

1. My three friends and I decided to go South to college. We had lived in Key West, Florida, all of our lives and we wanted a change. We wanted to feel the cold, to see snow, and to meet different people. We chose Vermont because all five of us were accepted at a college there. We were so excited at our good fortune that we didn't go out to celebrate that night. We ate and drank so much that at 3 A.M. we were famished with food and drink. My coworkers and I decided to go home at dusk so that we could watch the sun rise.

2. A survey at some very well-known schools produced some interesting data. According to the recent survey of over 800 students at two of the unknown universities and one high school, over 40 per cent or about 600 of those responding considered themselves shy. This is a very large proportion because college students have a reputation for being brash, bold, and quiet.

3. Regardless of the merits of claims that Norsemen discovered Europe before Columbus, nothing came of their efforts. They erected many permanent settlements. Whether explorers of North America a few thousand years later had used Viking knowledge of the area no one knows. When Christopher Columbus set out from Spain on his eastward voyage in 1429, he seemed to have had no notion of any land lying to the west between Europe and China and Japan.

STOP. Check answers at the end of Lesson 10.

VOCABULARY: CONNOTATIVE MEANING

When we speak or write we often rely more on the *connotative* meanings of words than on their *denotative* meanings to express our real position. The *connotative* meaning of a word includes its *denotative* meaning, the direct, specific meaning. But the connotative meaning also includes all *emotional senses* associated with the word. The connotative use of a word therefore requires an understanding of more than a simple definition. When you respect a word's connotative meanings, you will use the word precisely and effectively.

1. *Credulous* and *trusting* are two words that have a similar denotative meaning: ready to believe or have faith in. However, if you refer to someone as "trusting," you are saying he or she has the admirable trait of believing the best of someone or something. If you refer to the same person as "credulous," you are saying that he or she lacks judgment, that he or she foolishly believes anything. Although both words have the same denotative meaning, in their very different connotative senses one is complimentary and the other belittling or insulting. Connotative meanings are obviously vital to saying the right thing the right way. Writers rely on connotative meanings all the time, especially when they want to influence their readers. Whether a word has a positive (*trusting*) or a negative (*credulous*) connotation makes a great difference to what is actually said.

Special Notes

1. Words often have different overtones or associations for different people. For example, the term *mother* can bring forth images of apple pie, warmth, love, and kindness to one person, whereas for another it can mean beatings, hurt, shame, fear, and disillusionment.
2. Some words lend themselves more readily to emotional overtones or associations than others. For example, the term *home* can bring forth good or bad associations based on the past experiences of an individual. However, the term *dwelling*, which has the same specific definition as *home*, does not have the emotional overtones that *home* does.

2. A number of words have substitutes that more aptly express a particular meaning. For example, read these three sentences:

a. The *girl* walked down the avenue.

b. The *hussy* walked down the avenue.

c. The *maiden* walked down the avenue.

Sentence (a) is more or less neutral. It probably does not evoke (bring forth) any emotional response.

Sentence (b) uses a derogatory (belittling) substitute for *girl*. The term *hussy* has strongly negative overtones.

Sentence (c) uses a term that is more "refined," that is, has more positive overtones.

Practice A.

For each of these ten sets of words, use the following key to indicate whether the word has a neutral, a positive, or a negative connotation. (1)–neutral; (2)–belittling or negative; (3)–lofty or positive. A set may have more than one word in each category or may have no words in one of the categories. Put the number in the blank.

1. A building people live in: (a) shack_____(b) barn_____(c) castle _____(d) house_____

2. One who upholds the law: (a) officer_____(b) policeman_____ (c) pig_____(d) cop_____

3. One engaged in military service: (a) mercenary_____(b) warrior _____(c) soldier_____

4. A girl: (a) woman_____(b) chick_____(c) lady_____(d) female _____

5. A girlfriend: (a) date_____(b) prostitute_____(c) whore_____ (d) companion_____(e) call girl_____

6. A characteristic of an individual: (a) effeminate_____(b) weak_____ (c) gentle_____(d) cowardly_____

7. A characteristic of an individual: (a) passive_____(b) submissive _____(c) patient_____

8. A characteristic of an individual: (a) miserly_____(b) niggardly _____(c) greedy_____(d) thrifty_____

9. A smell: (a) fragrance_____(b) odor_____(c) stink_____(d) scent_____

10. A piece of furniture: (a) old_____(b) run-down_____(c) antique _____(d) obsolete_____

STOP. Check answers at the end of Lesson 10.

Practice B.

Read these sets of sentences carefully. They represent two reports of the same military action. In each pair determine which was written by the ally and which was written by the enemy. (Put your answer in the blank.)

1. _____ "X" divisions advanced five miles!

   _____ "X" divisions stopped in their tracks after only a five-mile advance.

2. _____ The "Y" armies are in disorderly retreat.

   _____ The "Y" armies are withdrawing to prepare for an offensive.

3. _____ The "Y's" take the town of "Z."

   _____ The town of "Z" cost the "Y's" many lives and supplies.

4. _____ The "Y's," outnumbered ten to one, surrendered.

   _____ The "Y's" were quickly beaten and captured.

5. _____ The "Y's" attempted to cover their retreat by sending in a suicide squad.

   _____ A company of "Y's" heroically sacrificed their lives to permit their comrades to withdraw safely.

STOP. Check answers at the end of Lesson 10.

Practice C.

In each of these sentences choose the one of the two words underlined that gives the statement the more positive meaning. (Look up words you do not know in the dictionary.)

1. During the half time the coach exhorted/harangued the team.

   _____

2. She is very particular/fussy about the arrangement of her desk.

   _____

3. Pablo approached the wolf's den cautiously/timorously.

   _____

4. Soon after she was elected to the borough council, Mrs. Vantuono revealed herself to be a born administrator/bureaucrat.

    _____

5. I know this is a small apartment, but I prefer to call it cramped/snug.

    _____

6. They never tell that story about Grandpa without chuckling/snickering at the thought of his misplaced courtesy.

    _____

7. They are a proud/haughty family and will not accept charity from anyone.

    _____

8. The editor is sorry that he must decline/refuse to accept your manuscript.

    _____

9. She doesn't like the working conditions, but the salary/pay is excellent.

    _____

10. Yes, I know the body has a lot of scrapes/blemishes, but you should try the car out on the road to see how smoothly it runs.

    _____

STOP. Check answers at the end of Lesson 10.

WORD ANALYSIS: THE DICTIONARY I

The dictionary is a very necessary tool that all students should be familiar with. To use the dictionary effectively, you must know how to alphabetize.

Practice A.

In each list put the words in alphabetical order.

1. raze, egotistical, jeopardy, annual, huge, wizard, saturated, grave, capital, infamous

    _____

    _____

2. intimidate, colleague, schwa, remedy, exhausted, perilous, apprehensive, malady, tumult, valiant

_____

_____

STOP. Check answers at the end of Lesson 10.

Practice B.

In each list circle the first word out of alphabetical order.

1. adamant, valiant, interrogate, tumult
2. succinct, valid, tumult, wizard
3. affluent, deceitful, thrifty, sturdy
4. indifferent, jeopardy, naive, modest

STOP. Check answers at the end of Lesson 10.

Practice C.

Put all of these words in one alphabetical list.

fragile, residential, harmony, valiant, mythical, diligent, abhor, serene, intricate, texture, excerpt, wary, perseverance, complementary, obsolete

_____

_____

STOP. Check answers at the end of Lesson 10.

Practice D.

In each list put these words, which all begin with the same letter, in alphabetical order.

1. baby, blue, book, brown, burst, bean, binge

_____

2. cushion, cookie, crank, climb, chicken, candle, cease

_____

3. train, tooth, tie, thread, tame, tease, tumble

_____

STOP. Check answers at the end of Lesson 10.

Practice E.

Put all of these words in one alphabetical list.

recipient, conscientious, siblings, raise, compulsory, stamina, intricate, another, always, extent, issue, discord, candid, scorn, perceived, chaotic, dual, desolate, significant, survey

_____

_____

_____

STOP. Check answers at the end of Lesson 10.

Practice F.

In each list put these words, which all begin with the same two letters, in alphabetical order.

1. bread, broom, brake, brim, bruise

_____

2. snow, snail, sneeze, snug, sniff

_____

3. climb, clam, club, clear, clown

_____

STOP. Check answers at the end of Lesson 10.

Practice G.

Put all of these words in one alphabetical list.

complementary, reiterate, discord, review, demolish, diligent, question, serious, recite, read, recall, capital, residential, chaotic, survey, immature, infamous, egotistical, naive, exhausted, equivalent, abhor, annual, defy

_____

_____

_____

STOP. Check answers at the end of Lesson 10.

Practice H.

Practice opening the dictionary in the middle, at quarters, and at thirds. Write the letters that the words you find begin with.

1. Middle _____

2. Quarters 1st _____

3. Thirds 1st _____

STOP. Check answers at the end of Lesson 10.

Practice I.

Given the key words *burst—business*, which are called *guide words* (words that are usually found at the top of each page), answer the questions. (The first guide word is the first word defined on the dictionary page, and the second guide word is the last word defined on the dictionary page.)

Guide words: burst—business

1. Would *burse* be before or after *burst* or after *business*?

_____

2. Would *bury* be before or after *burst* or after *business*?

_____

3. Would *busy* be before or after *burst* or after *business*?

_____

4. Would *burr* be before or after *burst* or after *business*?

———————————

5. Would *bush* be before or after *burst* or after *business*?

———————————

STOP. Check answers at the end of Lesson 10.

ANSWERS: Lesson 10 (pp. 293-310)

Learning Skills: Knowing Your Textbook (pp. 293-296)

Practice A

1. The author wrote the book to help students acquire necessary reading and learning skills. 2. The book is composed of five units. Each unit contains three lessons, and each lesson is made up of four parts. Each part is concerned with a specific reading or learning skill. 3. This book is unique because it integrates essential reading and learning skills. It presents practices, with answers where applicable, in each lesson. Review tests, crossword puzzles, and homograph riddles are also presented at the end of every unit. Information is not massed but distributed. Enough practice is given to encourage "overlearning."

Practice B

1. p. 37, or 38, and so on 2. p. 2, or 3, and so on 3. p. 398, or 400, and so on 4. p. 38, or 168, and so on. 5. p. 303 or 306

Practice C

I. Selected Reference Sources, Using the Card Catalogue II. Outlining III. Application Forms

Practice D

1. The glossary is divided into three parts. Part A contains the special terms found in this book, Part B contains the vocabulary, and Part C contains the combining forms. 2. *double*—Lesson 1 3. A comparison between two unlike objects using *like* or *as*.

Reading: Knowing Your Source and Questioning What You Read (pp. 296-299)

Practice A

1. NO 2. O 3. O 4. NO 5. NO 6. O 7. NO 8. O 9. NO 10. O 11. NO 12. NO

Practice B

1. O 2. O 3. NO 4. NO 5. NO 6. O 7. O 8. NO 9. NO 10. NO 11. O 12. NO 13. NO 14. NO 15. O 16. NO

Practice C

1. <u>South</u>–North; <u>five</u>–four; <u>didn't</u>–did; <u>famished</u>–saturated; <u>coworkers</u>–friends; <u>dusk</u>–dawn 2. <u>unknown</u>–well-known; <u>600</u>–320; <u>quiet</u>–outspoken 3. <u>Europe</u>–America; <u>many</u>–no; <u>thousand</u>–hundred; <u>eastward</u>–westward; <u>1429</u>–1492

Vocabulary: Connotative Meaning (pp. 299-303)

Practice A

1. a. (2) b. (2) c. (3) d. (1)
2. a. (3) b. (1) c. (2) d. (2)
3. a. (2) b. (3) c. (1)
4. a. (1) b. (2) c. (3) d. (1)
5. a. (1) b. (2) c. (2) d. (1) e. (2)
6. a. (2) b. (2) c. (3) d. (2)
7. a. (2) b. (2) c. (3)
8. a. (2) b. (2) c. (2) d. (3)
9. a. (3) b. (1) c. (2) d. (1)
10. a. (1) b. (2) c. (3) d. (2)

Practice B

1. ally; enemy 2. enemy; ally 3. ally; enemy 4. ally; enemy 5. enemy; ally

Practice C

1. exhorted 2. particular 3. cautiously 4. administrator 5. snug 6. chuckling 7. proud 8. decline 9. salary 10. blemishes

Word Analysis: The Dictionary I (pp. 303–307)

Practice A

1. annual, capital, egotistical, grave, huge, infamous, jeopardy, raze, saturated, wizard 2. apprehensive, colleague, exhausted, intimidate, malady, perilous, remedy, schwa, tumult, valiant

Practice B

1. valiant 2. valid 3. thrifty 4. naive

Practice C

abhor, complementary, diligent, excerpt, fragile, harmony, intricate, mythical, obsolete, perseverance, residential, serene, texture, valiant, wary

Practice D

1. baby, bean, binge, blue, book, brown, burst 2. candle, cease, chicken, climb, cookie, crank, cushion 3. tame, tease, thread, tie, tooth, train, tumble

Practice E

always, another, candid, chaotic, compulsory, conscientious, desolate, discord, dual, extent, intricate, issue, perceived, raise, recipient, scorn, siblings, significant, stamina, survey

Practice F

1. brake, bread, brim, broom, bruise 2. snail, sneeze, sniff, snow, snug 3. clam, clear, climb, clown, club

Practice G

abhor, annual, capital, chaotic, complementary, defy, demolish, diligent, discord, egotistical, equivalent, exhausted, immature, infamous, naive, question, read, recall, recite, reiterate, residential, review, serious, survey

Practice H

Answers will vary according to which dictionary is used. Webster's new Twentieth Century Dictionary: 1. m 2. d 3. g

Practice I

1. before *burst* 2. after *burst* 3. after *business* 4. before *burst* 5. after *burst*

LESSON 11

Learning Skills: Following Directions
Reading: Distinguishing Fact from Opinion
Vocabulary: Figures of Speech I
Word Analysis: The Dictionary II
Answers

LEARNING SKILLS: FOLLOWING DIRECTIONS

The ability to follow directions is an important skill that you use all your life. Scarcely a day goes by without the need to obey directions. Cooking, baking, taking medication, driving, traveling, repairing, building, planning, taking exams, doing assignments, filling out applications, and a hundred other common activities require the ability to follow directions.

People who can follow directions well find it easier than those who cannot to take tests and exams. They see more quickly what is asked of them and therefore waste less time sorting what they know to provide the proper answer to the question. Most people learn to follow directions through practice, and you have already had a good deal of that practice in doing the exercises in this book. Now you can refine what you have learned in practice by checking these pointers on following directions:

1. Read the directions *carefully*. Do *not* skim directions. Do not take anything for granted and therefore skip reading a part of the directions.

2. If you do not understand a direction, do not hesitate to ask the instructor to help you to clarify it.

3. Concentrate!

4. Follow the directions that *are* given, not the ones you think ought to be.

5. Reread directions if you need to, and refer to them as you follow them.

6. Follow directions step by step if you are told to.

7. Practice following directions.

Practice A.

This exercise is a *four-minute* test. See how well you do in taking it. Remember to follow directions. Read everything carefully before doing anything.

1. Add 9 and 7 and then divide the sum by 2.

2. Write all the odd numbers from 13 to 25 backward.

3. Write all the even numbers from 2 to 16 and omit all those that have the digit 4 in them.

4. Write five words that rhyme with *get.*

5. Define *thrived.*

6. Write your name at the top of the paper to the extreme right.

7. Starting with letter *A* write every *other* letter of the alphabet.

8. Add 20 and 30, divide by 5, and then multiply by 10.

9. Write your address at the top of the paper to the extreme left.

10. Write the 20th letter of the alphabet and the 14th letter of the alphabet.

11. Write five words that rhyme with *at.*

12. Write a synonym for *intimidate.*

13. Write an antonym for *abate.*

14. Count up to 100 by 10s.

15. Count from 50 backward by 5.

16. Write *I am a good direction follower* at the top of the page.

17. Do only questions 6 and 9.

STOP. Check answers at the end of Lesson 11.

Practice B.

Carry out the instructions, referring to the figures in the box.

Box 1

1. If the number of circles is equivalent to the number of squares and triangles, put a dot in the last circle.

2. If the number of triangles preceding the four letters is equal to the number of circles in the box, put a cross on the 3rd letter in the box.

3. If there are three consecutive figures each one different from the others in the box, circle the 3rd of these consecutive figures.

4. If the number of letters is equal to the number of digits in the box and if both letters and digits appear one after the other, put a dot in the 1st square.

5. If two consecutive digits equal the 3rd digit, put a dot in the 2nd square.

STOP. Check answers at the end of Lesson 11.

Practice C.

In this exercise there are circles with arrows pointing different ways. See how well you can follow directions.

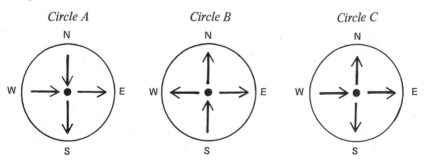

1. If not all three circles have an arrow pointing N, put a circle around W in the 1st circle.

2. If the arrows in either circle B or circle C are not pointing S, put a circle around E in circle C.

3. If the arrows in circles A and B together are pointing in every direction put a circle around N in circle B.

4. If the arrows in circle B and the arrows in circle C are pointing in every direction in each circle, put a circle around S in circle C.

5. If the arrows in circles A, B, and C are pointing W and N in each circle, put a circle around W in circle C.

STOP. Check answers at the end of Lesson 11.

Practice D.

In this exercise there are circles with arrows pointing different ways. See how well you can follow directions.

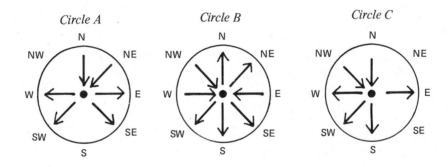

1. If the arrows in each of the three circles are pointing N, NE, S, and SE, put a circle around S in circle B.

2. If in circles B and C together there are arrows pointing W, S, and SW, put a circle around SW in circle A.

3. If the arrows in circle C are pointing in the same directions as all the arrows in circle A, put a circle around S in circle A.

4. If at least one arrow in each of circles A, B, and C is pointing in the same direction, put a circle around N in circle C.

5. If the arrows in circles A, B, and C are missing at least one direction in each circle, put a circle around NW in circle B.

STOP. Check answers at the end of Lesson 11.

READING: DISTINGUISHING FACT FROM OPINION

It's important to determine whether information you read is factual or not. Often opinions are presented as though they are facts. *Opinions are not facts.* Opinions are expressions of attitudes or feelings. Opinions can vary from person to person; they are what has not been or cannot be proved right or wrong. Facts, on the other hand, are what has been proved true. Examples of facts: Trenton is the capital of New Jersey. Mt. Everest is the highest mountain in the world. A meter equals approximately 39.37 inches. Examples of opinions: Trenton is a charming city. Mt. Everest cannot be climbed. The metric system is the better system.

Practice A.

For the following sentences put an O in the blank if the statement is opinion or an F if the statement is fact.

_____ 1. Staying up late if not good for you.

_____ 2. It's not safe to walk alone.

_____ 3. A tomato is a fruit.

_____ 4. You learn more from books than from television.

_____ 5. Eggs are high in cholesterol.

_____ 6. Sibling rivalry is found in all families.

_____ 7. Blood letting was considered a good method to cure many ills years ago.

_____ 8. A karate expert can use his hands as a lethal weapon.

_____ 9. People catch colds from sitting in a draft.

_____ 10. Fat people are usually jolly people.

_____ 11. Ms. Smith is an excellent instructor.

_____ 12. Water skiing is dangerous.

_____ 13. Believers in astrology are usually outgoing persons.

_____ 14. Mr. Mills is an excellent administrator.

_____ 15. Life exists on other planets.

_____ 16. The divorce rate is increasing.

_____ 17. Marriage is outmoded.

_____ 18. Taxes are too high.

_____ 19. The quality of life is deteriorating.

_____ 20. There is usually less air pollution in nonindustrial areas.

STOP. Check answers at the end of Lesson 11.

Practice B.

In front of each statement put the letter T if it's *true* or the letter F if it's *false*.

_____ 1. A seal is a cold-blooded animal.

_____ 2. Man is an animal.

_____ 3. A weed is a plant.

_____ 4. A turtle is a reptile.

_____ 5. A fish is warm-blooded.

_____ 6. *Sire* refers to the male parent of domestic quadrupeds.

_____ 7. Computers can think.

_____ 8. A whale is a mammal.

_____ 9. All animals are bipeds.

_____ 10. Snakes are not apodal animals.

STOP. Check answers at the end of Lesson 11.

Practice C.

Read this selection and then determine whether statements made about the selection are fact or opinion. Write F in the blank if it's fact or O if it's opinion.

From *The Call of the Wild* by Jack London.

Vocabulary:

importuned—annoyed or troubled

Mercedes nursed a special grievance—the grievance of sex. She was pretty and soft, and had been chivalrously treated all her days. But the present treatment by her husband and brother was everything save chivalrous. It was her custom to be helpless. They complained. Upon which impeachment of what to her was her most essential sex prerogative, she made their lives unendurable. She no longer considered the dogs, and because she was sore and tired, she persisted in riding on the sled. She was pretty and soft, but she weighed one hundred and twenty pounds—a lusty last straw to the load dragged by the weak and starving animals. She rode for days, till they fell in the traces and the sled stood still. Charles and Hal begged her to get off and walk, pleaded with her, entreated, the while she wept and importuned Heaven with a recital of their brutality.

_____ 1. The episode happens in cold territory.

_____ 2. The woman is used to getting her way.

_____ 3. There is snow on the ground.

_____ 4. The dogs are huskies.

_____ 5. The dogs are beautiful animals.

_____ 6. There is not enough food for the animals.

_____ 7. The men are courageous.

_____ 8. The woman is considered pretty.

_____ 9. The men are cruel.

_____ 10. The woman is very feminine.

_____ 11. The woman enjoys riding the sled.

_____ 12. The woman is sexy.

_____ 13. The dogs will probably die from exhaustion.

_____ 14. The dogs are carrying a load.

_____ 15. The load is more important than the woman.

STOP. Check answers at the end of Lesson 11.

VOCABULARY: FIGURES OF SPEECH I

Figures of speech are important because they give color, decoration, and life to language. We often use figures of speech without realizing it because they have become part of everyday language. Examples: the body of a letter, the foot of the class, the hands of the clock, the heart of the matter, take it on the chin.

Figurative Language

Figures of speech are important because they give color, decoration, and life to language. We often use figures of speech without realizing it because they have become part of everyday language. Examples: the body of a letter, the foot of the class, the hands of the clock, the heart of the matter, take it on the chin.

1. A *simile* is a comparison between two unlike objects made by using the word *like* or *as*. A metaphor is also a comparison between two unlike objects, but *like* or *as* is not used. Because a simile is signaled by the word *like* or *as*, it is easy to distinguish a simile from a metaphor.

Examples:

a. The clouds were *like masses of whipped cream.*
b. The lion was *as friendly as a kitten.*
c. Her disposition is *like glass*; it breaks easily, and when it breaks it cuts.
d. His mind works *like a computer programmed in the wrong language.*

2. A *metaphor* may be more difficult to recognize because it is not signaled by an identifying word. The comparison is complete: one thing *is* another thing.

*Often the term *metaphor* is used in a generic (general) sense to cover all forms of figures of speech. Therefore, simile, personification, and so on might be referred to as metaphor.

Examples:

a. The clouds were *downy pillows* floating in the sky.
b. The lion was a *friendly kitten.*
c. Her *razor-edge* disposition is always sharpest in the morning.
d. His mind is a *computer.*

3. *Personification* is the giving of human characteristics and capabilities to nonhuman things such as inanimate (nonliving) objects, abstract ideas, or animals. An excellent example of personification is this quote from Joseph Conrad: "The sun looked upon the ship all day, and, every morning rose with a burning, round stare of undying curiosity."

Examples:

a. The *clouds cried* a torrent of tears.
b. *Winter's icy breath and cold fingers* chilled our bodies.
c. *Vengence commanded* me and I was its tool.

Special Note

In writing you should be careful not to overdo or mismatch personifications. Expository writing (writing that explains or conveys information) probably should not include personification—unless personification is the best way to get your point across.

Practice A.

Choose a phrase from the list that most vividly completes these sentences with an expression of personification.

Phrase List:

crept softly, straining, impatiently, opened, devour, wept huge tears, refused, felt naked, smiled, angry, spat fire, thirsty, begged, panting.

1. The rain clouds _____ .
2. The _____ locomotives slowly climbed the hill.
3. The stalled car _____ to move.

4. The fog _____ along the ground.

5. The tunnel _____ its mouth to _____ the cars.

6. The _____ cars waited _____ for the light to change.

7. The _____ land _____ for water.

8. The trees _____ without their leaves.

9. The warm spring sun _____ at us.

10. The _____ volcano _____ .

STOP. Check answers at the end of Lesson 11.

Practice B.

Choose a phrase from the list that most vividly completes a simile in these sentences.

Phrase List:

a glowing orange ball; a frayed brown cord; a gorged buzzard; a rocky road; a light in the night; a seal; a waterfall; a swift bird; a telegraph; a tall bride.

1. The huge 747 lumbered toward its takeoff like _____ _____ .

2. Her tears flowed like _____ .

3. The woodpecker's pecking sounded like _____ tapping out a message.

4. From the airplane, the dirt road looked like _____ _____ .

5. My math course is like _____ .

6. The doe is like _____ in flight.

7. The answer illuminated the subject like _____ _____ .

8. He looked like _____ with his whiskers drooping from his upper lip.

9. The sun rose like _____ in the east.

10. The white poplar tree looked like _____ .

STOP. Check answers at the end of Lesson 11.

Practice C.

Choose a phrase from the list that most vividly completes a metaphor in these sentences.

Phrase List:

a crewcut; a ghost, confetti; a lamb; hot potatoes; razor-sharp; living pin-cushions; a wolf; a smoking volcano; twisted pretzels.

1. My father's whiskers are _____ .

2. The cars in the accident became _____ .

3. He is _____ when it comes to girls.

4. He has lost so much weight that he is merely _____ of his former self.

5. Jane is_____ to allow you to get away with so much.

6. Our overheated car became _____ .

7. Controversial issues are_____ that most politicians try to avoid.

8. Her_____ tongue lashed out at all who defied her.

9. The farmer gave his grain field_____ .

10. The snow was _____ falling from the sky.

STOP. Check answers at the end of Lesson 11.

Practice D.

For these ten lines, taken from famous poems, underline the figure of speech and then state what kind it is.

1. Her face is a garden of delight. (Thomas Campion)

   _____

2. Her brows like bended bows do stand. (Thomas Campion)

   _____

3. The Moon doth with delight look round her when the heavens are bare. (William Wordsworth)

   _____

4. I wandered lonely as a cloud. (William Wordsworth)

   _____

5. The daffodils are tossing their heads in sprightly dance. (William Wordsworth)

   _____

6. The sea bares her bosom to the moon. (William Wordsworth)

   _____

7. The wrinkled sea beneath him crawls. (Lord Tennyson)

   _____

8. There's no frigate like a book to take us lands away. (Emily Dickinson)

   _____

9. The sun is laid to sleep. (Ben Jonson)

   _____

10. The stars threw down their spears and watered heaven with their tears. (William Blake)

   _____

STOP. Check answers at the end of Lesson 11.

Practice E.

Skim p. 267 of the autobiographical article from *Experiencing Youth* in Lesson 9 to find a simile that the writer uses.

1. State the simile. 2. Explain it.

STOP. Check answers at the end of Lesson 11.

Practice F.

These sentences and phrases with missing words are from Clement C. Moore's well-known poem, "The Night Before Christmas." Each missing word is a simile. See how many you can remember. Put your answer in the blank.

1. Away to the window I flew like a _____,

2. As _____ that before
    the wild hurricane fly,
   When they meet with an obstacle,
    mount to the sky;
   So up to the house-top
    the coursers they flew,
   With the sleigh full of toys,
    and St. Nicholas too.

3. And he looked like a _____ just opening his pack,

4. His cheeks were like _____ ,

5. His nose like a _____ !

6. His droll little mouth was drawn up like a _____ ,

7. And the beard on his chin was as white as the _____ ;

8. The stump of a pipe he held tight in his teeth,

    And the smoke it encircled his head like a _____ ;

9. He had a broad face and a little round belly,
   That shook when he laughed,

   like a _____.

10. And away they all flew

    like the _____ .

STOP. Check answers at the end of Lesson 11.

Practice G.

Try to come up with some of your own phrases for Practices A, B, and C.

WORD ANALYSIS: THE DICTIONARY II

1. Even though a dictionary is a necessary tool, you should not use it as a crutch. That is, every time you meet a word whose meaning is unknown to you, first try to use your knowledge of word parts (see Lessons 13–15) and context clues to unlock the meaning. If these techniques do not help, and knowing the word is essential to understanding the passage, then you should look up the meaning.

2. To use the dictionary effectively, you should know that the purpose of dictionaries is not to prescribe or make rules about word meanings and pronunciations, but only to describe. Lexicographers use various methods to compile the words in the dictionary. One important method is based on citations of usage and research consulting older dictionaries. Another method involves choosing a group of people and recording the ways they pronounce and use words. These then are recorded as the accepted standard spellings, definitions, and word usage.

Difficulties exist concerning pronunciation because people in different parts of the country often pronounce words differently. Pronunciation in the East is often different from that in the South or Midwest. As a result, the pronunciation of a word given in the dictionary may not be in accord with your region's pronunciation of it.

To compound this problem, different dictionaries may use different pronunciation keys. The pronunciation key is composed of words with diacritical marks. To know how to pronounce a word in a particular dictionary, you must familiarize yourself with the pronunciation key in that dictionary. For example, look at the way that five different dictionaries present a few similar words.

Word	Webster's New Twentieth Century Dictionary	Webster's Third New International Dictionary	Random House Dictionary of the English Language	The American Heritage Dictionary of the English Language	Funk & Wagnalls Standard College Dictionary
1. coupon	cou'pon	'k(y)ü,pän	k o͞o 'pon	k o͞o 'pŏn	k o͞o 'pon
2. courage	cour'age	'kər • ij	kûr'ij	kur'ĭj	kûr'ij
3. covet	cov'et	'kəvət	kuv'it	kŭv'ĭt	kuv'it

If you had no knowledge of the pronunciation key of the specific dictionary, you would have difficulty pronouncing the words. (See p. 328 for the Guide to Pronunciation in *Webster's New Twentieth Century Dictionary*.) Pronunciation guides are generally found at the beginning of dictionaries. Many dictionaries also have a simplified pronunciation key at the bottom of every page. (See pp. 329–330 for two pages from *Webster's New Twentieth Century Dictionary*.)

Special Note

Although most dictionaries incorporate the schwa sound in their pronunciation keys, *Webster's New Twentieth Century Dictionary* does not.

Practice A.

Using the Guide to Pronunciation in *Webster's New Twentieth Century Dictionary* (p. 328), answer these true/false questions. Put a T for *true* or an F for *false* in the blank.

_____ 1. *-cian, -tian, -sian* are pronounced as *-shun.*

_____ 2. The last syllable of the word *partition* is pronounced *shun.*

_____ 3. *Ph-* sounds like *h* in *home.*

_____ 4. *Oi, oy, ou,* and *ow* can all represent the same sound.

_____ 5. The words *use* and *tune* have the same *u* sound.

_____ 6. The words *pine, ice,* and *clique* all have the same *i* sound.

_____ 7. *Moon, foot,* and *look* all have the same *oo* sound.

_____ 8. *Qu-* sounds like *kw* in *quick.*

_____ 9. *C* stands for either a hard *c* sound as in *case* or an *s* sound as in *cease*.

_____ 10. *Wh-* sounds like *hw* in whale.

STOP. Check answers at the end of Lesson 11.

Practice B.

Using the given dictionary pages (pp. 329–330), answer these questions.

1. Who was Robin Hood?

_____

2. Is the word *rocky* found on p. 329?

_____

3. Between what two words would you find *roc*?

_____

4. How many general definitions are given for *rock*?

_____

5. What parts of speech can *rock* be?

_____

6. What does the slang expression *a pocket full of rocks* mean?

_____

7. What does the expression *on the rocks* mean?

_____

8. Can you get Rock fever? If so, where?

_____

9. Is there a rockfish?

_____

10. Can you eat rock candy?

_____

11. What is rock salt?

_____

12. What part of speech is *robust*?

_____

13. Can a person be robust?

___

14. Is there such a thing as a living rock?

___

15. What is a rock wren?

___

16. How many syllables does *rodent* have?

___

17. How many syllables does *rodeo* have?

___

18. How many syllables does *rocket* have?

___

19. Which syllable is accented in *rodent*?

___

20. Which syllable is accented in *rodeo*?

___

21. According to the pronunciation key at the bottom of p. 329, *ā* sounds like *a* in what word?

___

22. According to the pronunciation key at the bottom of p. 330, *ū* sounds like the *u* in what word?

___

23. The *c* in the word *roc* sounds like _____ in the word _____ in the pronunciation key at the bottom of p. 330.

24. *Roe* can be a deer or _____ .
25. Who wrote *Robinson Crusoe*?

___

STOP. Check answers at the end of Lesson 11.

GUIDE TO PRONUNCIATION

PRONUNCIATION in this dictionary is indicated directly on the entry word by a system of symbols, or diacritical marks. Thus, the symbol c̣ is used to indicate the sound of the hard c in cat, and the word is entered in the vocabulary as c̣at. The Key to Pronunciation printed below gives a complete description of the symbols used and the sounds they represent. The modified sounds are unmarked, as the e in cent, the a in apply, the i in pin, the u in tub, the o in on, and the y in myth.

When two vowels stand together, only the one which indicates the sound of the word is marked, as in strēak, brāin, mōat. The clusters ae and oe ending a syllable are pronounced as ē; when followed by a consonant in the same syllable they are pronounced as e in met.

In a few instances it is impossible to indicate the pronunciation on the word itself; in such cases the word, or part of it, is respelled

in parentheses immediately following the entry. The word is respelled phonetically, that is, according to its sound, regardless of the letters that compose it. Examples of respelling are eight (āt); guide (gīd); heir (âr); and här'le-quin (-kin or -kwin).

The accents are indicated thus: primary ′, secondary ″. The secondary accent or subordinate stress is normally indicated only when it falls at an irregular interval from the primary or main stress, that is, at an interval other than two syllables.

Although full vowel quality is indicated in all syllables, it should be understood that in totally unstressed syllables the vowel quality is variously reduced, or weakened, in colloquial speech to a more or less neutral sound. To avoid the confusion of excessive diacritical marks, sounds in non-English words are indicated by the English sounds most nearly approximating these.

KEY TO PRONUNCIATION

ā	as in	fāte, āle, ā'corn, be-rāte', nat″u-ral-i-zā'tion.
ă	" "	fär, fä'ther, ärch, mär'shal, cär-toon'; also as in whät, wänt.
a	" "	fást, glåss, a-lás'; also as in so'då, å-dapt'å-ble.
a̧	" "	fa̧ll, pa̧w, a̧w'ful, ap-pla̧ud'.
a	" "	fi'năl, sea'măn, tol'er-ănt, men'ăce.
ã	" "	cãre, ãir, mil'i-tãr-y, de-clãre'.
a	" "	at, ac-cord', com-par'i-son, car'ry.
ē	" "	ēve, mēte, hē, Ē'den, in-ter-vēne'; also as in hēre, drēar'y.
e	" "	pre̱y, ei̱ght, o-be̱y'.
ẽ	" "	hẽr, vẽrse, sẽr'vice, in-tẽr'.
e	" "	met, ebb, en-dorse', mon'e-tar-y, dis-tend'.
ee	" "	feed, pro-ceed', lee'way.
ī	" "	pīne, ī-de'a, īce'berg, de-cīde', al-lī'ance.
i	" "	clïque, ma-rïne'; also as in Mar-tï'ni.
i̱	" "	bi̱rd, sti̱r, ex'ti̱r-pate, fi̱rm'a-ment.
i	" "	it, hit, re-mit', cit'y; also as in pos'si-ble, grav'i-ty, pu'pil.
ō	" "	nōte, ōat, sō, ō'pen, hel-lō'; also as in ren'ō-vate, prō-pel'.
ŏ	" "	mŏve, prŏve, tŏmb.
o̧	" "	lo̧ng, cro̧ss, o̧ff, o̧rb, fo̧r-bid', do̧r'mer.
ô	" "	at'ôm, plôv'er; also as in ac'tôr, wôrd, wôrk.
o	" "	not, for'est, non'sense; also as in dog, broth, cost; also as in con-fess', con-cur'.
o̱o̱	" "	mo̱o̱n, co̱o̱, fo̱o̱d, bro̱o̱d'er.
oo	" "	book, hood, foot, look, cook'y.
ū	" "	ūse, fūse, ū-til'i-ty, fū'tile, im-mūne'.
u̱	" "	bu̱ll, pu̱t, fu̱l-fil', bou̱n'ti-fu̱l.
u̇	" "	brüte, jü'ry; also used for the German ü.
û	" "	tûrn, fûr, bûr-lesque', de-mûr'.
u	" "	up, rub, sun'set, in-sult'.
ȳ	" "	crȳ, eȳe.
y	" "	myth, cit'y.
c̣	" "	c̣at, to-bac̣'c̣o.
ç	" "	ma-çhine'.
c	" "	ace, ce'dar.
ch	" "	church.
çh	" "	çhord.

ġ	as in	ġem.
ñ	" "	añ'ger, sphiñx.
ṅ	" "	French boṅ.
ng	" "	ring.
ṣ	" "	mi'ṣer, aṣ.
th	" "	this.
th	" "	thin.
ẕ	" "	aẕure.
au	" "	umlaut.
aw	" "	straw.
ou	" "	out.
oi	" "	oil.
oy	" "	boy.
ew	" "	new, few.
ow	" "	now.

-tûre   as -chêr (in picture).

-tion
-sion   }as -shun (in nation, tension).

-ciăn
-tiăn
-siăn   }as -shun (in Martian, Melanesian, mortician).

-șiăn
-șion   }as -zhun (in Persian, fusion).

-liŏn   as -lyun or -yun (in million).

-ceous
-(s)cious   }as -shus (in cretaceous, delicious, conscious).

qu   as kw (in queen).
-ous   as -us (in porous).

ph-   as f- (in phone, etc.).

-le   as -l (at end of syllable, as in able, cycle, etc.).

-iå   as -yà (in pharmacopoeia).

wh-   as hw- in whale, etc.

kh   as in German doch (dokh).

Robin Hood

Rob'in Hood, in English legend, a traditional outlaw of the 12th century who lived with his followers in Sherwood Forest and robbed the rich to help the poor: he is the hero of many ballads and tales, celebrated for his courage, gaiety, courtesy, skill as an archer, etc.

Rō·bin'i·à, *n.* [from Jean *Robin*, a Fr. botanist, who introduced the trees to Europe in 1635.] a small genus of the *Leguminosæ*, the locusts, comprising North American trees or shrubs, often with prickly spines for stipules, and odd-pinnate leaves. The best-known species is the *Robinia pseudacacia*, the false acacia, or black locust tree.

rob'in snipe, the knot, or red-breasted sandpiper.

Rob'in·sŏn Çrú'sōe, the hero of Daniel Defoe's novel (1719) of the same name, an English sailor who, when shipwrecked on a tropical island, manages to live for years by various ingenious contrivances until he is rescued.

rō'ble, *n.* 1. the *Quercus lobata*, or white oak of California.
2. any of several other trees of the oak family, beech family, etc.

rō'bomb (-bom), *n.* a robot bomb.

rob'o·rȧnt, *a.* strengthening.

rob'o·rȧnt, *n.* a medicine that strengthens; a tonic.

rob'o·rāte, *v.t.* to furnish strength to. [Obs.]

rob·o·rā'tion, *n.* a strengthening. [Obs.]

rō'bŏt, *n.* 1. any of the manlike mechanical beings manufactured by Rossum in Karel Čapek's play R. U. R. (Rossum's Universal Robots), to do manual work for human beings.
2. (a) an automaton; (b) a person who acts or works mechanically and without thinking for himself.

rō'bŏt bomb (bom), a small, jet-propelled airplane steered by a gyropilot and loaded with high explosives: it falls as a bomb when its fuel is used up.

rō'bŏt pī'lŏt, a device that serves as an automatic pilot, as in an airplane.

rō'būr·ite, *n.* [L. *robur*, strength; and *-ite*.] a very powerful, flameless explosive containing chlorinated dinitrobenzene and ammonium nitrate: it is used especially in mining.

rō'bust', *a.* [Fr., from L. *robustus*, from *robus*, an old form of *robur*, an oak, or strength.]
1. having or exhibiting sound health or great strength; strong; vigorous; also, strongly built; sturdy; muscular.
2. coarse; boisterous; rough; rude.
3. suited to or requiring physical strength or stamina; as, *robust* work.

Syn.—sound, lusty, vigorous, hale, hearty.

rō·bus'tious, *a.* 1. strong; sturdy; stout. [Archaic or Humorous.]
2. rough; rude; coarse; boisterous. [Archaic or Humorous.]

rō·bus'tious·ly, *adv.* in a robustious manner.

rō·bus'tious·ness, *n.* the state or quality of being robustious.

rō·bust'ly, *adv.* in a robust manner.

rō·bust'ness, *n.* the state or quality of being robust.

roç, *n.* [Fr., from the Per.] in Arabian and Persian legend, a fabulous bird of prey, so huge and strong that it could carry off the largest of animals.

rō·çaille' (-kä'y'), *n.* [Fr., from *roche*, rock.] a conventional artistic representation of rockwork, in vogue in France as a decoration in the time of Louis XV; also, a kind of rococo or scroll ornament.

roç'ȧm·bōle, *n.* [Fr., from G. *rockenbollen*; *rocken*, rye, and *bolle*, a bulb; so called because it grows among rye.] a European leek, the *Allium scorodoprasum*, a plant used like garlic for seasoning.

Roç·cel'lȧ, *n.* [LL. form of Fr. *orseille*, archil.] a genus of lichens, from a species of which, *Roccella tinctoria*, the dye archil is obtained.

roç·cel'liç, *a.* related to or derived from lichens of the genus *Roccella*.

roccellic acid; an acid obtained from the *Roccella tinctoria*, or archil weed.

roç·cel'lin, *n.* a coal-tar derivative used as a substitute for archil and cochineal in dyeing red.

roç·cel'line, *a.* of or pertaining to the genus *Roccella*.

Roch'dāle prin'çi·ples, principles for the operation of a consumers' co-operative store, as formulated by the Rochdale Pioneers, one of the first co-operative groups in England: they include selling for cash at current market prices, distribution of profits among members, and democratic control.

rŏche, *n.* [Fr.] a rock. [Obs.]

Rō'çhē·à, *n.* [from Francis *Laroche*, a French naturalist.] a genus of South African plants belonging to the order *Crassulaceæ*, characterized by its showy varicolored flowers.

roche al'um, a pure form of alum occurring in natural crystalline fragments.

rŏçhe'lîme, *n.* [Fr. *roche*, rock.] quicklime, especially when in lumps.

Rō·çhelle' pow'dẽr, Seidlitz powder.

Rō·çhelle' sȧlt, [after *Rochelle*, France: so named because discovered by Seignette, an apothecary in Rochelle.] a colorless, crystalline compound, potassium sodium tartrate, $KNaC_4H_4O_6·4H_2O$, used as a laxative.

roche mou·ton·née' (rōsh mō-tŏ̄n-nā'), [Fr., sheepback rock.] a rock worn into a smooth, rounded form by glacial action.

roch'et, *n.* [ME. *rochet*, from O.H.G. *roch*; Ice. *rokkr*, frock or coat; Ir. *rocan*, cloak; Gael. *rochall*, coverlet.] a sort of short linen surplice, with tight sleeves, and open at the sides, worn by bishops and some other church dignitaries.

roch'et, *n.* a kind of gurnard.

rŏch'ing çȧsk, [Fr. *roche*; LL. *roca*, rock.] a tank lined with lead, used in crystallizing alum.

rock, *n.* a roc. [Obs.]

rock, *n.* [ME. *rokke*, from Ice. *rokkr*, a distaff.] a distaff used in spinning; the staff or frame about which flax is arranged and from which the thread is drawn in spinning.

rock, *v.t.*; rocked (rokt), *pt.*, *pp.*; rocking, *ppr.* [ME. *rokken*; AS. *roccian*; prob. akin to G. *rücken*, to pull, push.]
1. to move or sway back and forth or from side to side, especially in a gentle, quieting manner, as a cradle, or a child in the arms.
2. to bring into a specified condition by moving or swaying in this way; as, she *rocked* the baby asleep: also used figuratively, as *rocked* into a false sense of security.
3. to move or sway strongly; to shake; to cause to tremble or vibrate; as, the explosion *rocked* the house.
4. in mezzotint engraving, to prepare the surface of (a plate) by roughening with a rocker (sense 5).
5. in mining, to wash (sand or gravel) in a rocker (sense 4).

rock, *v.i.* 1. to move or sway back and forth or from side to side in or as in a cradle.
2. to move or sway strongly; to shake; to vibrate.
3. to be rocked, as ore.

rock, *n.* 1. the act of rocking.
2. a rocking motion.

rock, *n.* [OFr. *roche*; cf. AS. *-rocc*, ML. *rocca*.]
1. a large mass of stone forming a peak or cliff.
2. (a) stone in the mass; (b) broken pieces of such stone.
3. (a) mineral matter variously composed, formed in masses or large quantities in the earth's crust by the action of heat, water, etc.; (b) a particular kind or mass of this.
4. anything like or suggesting a rock, as in strength or stability; especially, a firm support, basis, refuge, etc.
5. any cause of wreck or destruction; as, the *rock* upon which one breaks: in allusion to a ship.
6. a kind of hard, insoluble, soapy compound formed by the action of lime on fats.
7. the rockfish.
8. the rock dove.
9. a type of hard candy. [Chiefly Brit.]
10. a stone, whether large or small. [Colloq. or Dial.]
11. (a) [*usually in pl.*] a piece of money; as, a pocket full of *rocks*; (b) a diamond or other gem. [Slang.]

on the rocks; (a) out of money; (b) in or into a condition of ruin or catastrophe. [Colloq.]

rock al'um, the purest kind of alum.

rock'-ȧnd-rōll', *n.* a form of popular music, characterized by a strong and regular rhythm, which evolved from jazz and the blues.

rock'ȧ·wāy, *n.* a light horse-drawn carriage with four wheels, open sides, and a standing top.

rock bär'nȧ·çle, a barnacle adhering to rocks along a shore, as *Balanus balanoides*.

rock bā'sin (-sn), a cavity or basin in solid rock.

rock bass, a fresh-water food fish of the sunfish family, found in eastern North America.

rock beau'ty (bū'), a cruciferous alpine plant,

---

rocket

Draba pyrenaica, noted for the beauty and fragrance of its flowers.

rock black'bĩrd, the ring ouzel. [Brit.]

rock'-bot'tŏm, *a.* at rock bottom; lowest possible.

rock bot'tŏm, the very bottom; the lowest limit; as, prices have gone down to *rock bottom*.

rock'-bound, *a.* hemmed in by rocks.

rock brāke, any fern belonging to the genus *Pellæa*; especially, the parsley fern.

rock but'tẽr, a butterlike exudation from rocks, containing aluminum and iron.

rock can'dy, large, hard, clear crystals of sugar.

rock'çist, *n.* any plant of the genus *Helianthemum*; frostweed.

rock çŏd, 1. any one of several species of food fishes of the genus *Scorpæna*, native to Australian waters.
2. a small cod found around rocks; a kind of rockfish.

rock çŏrk, a variety of asbestos resembling cork in its texture.

rock crab, a crab living in rocky places, as the *Cancer borealis* of the New England coast.

rock cress, a plant of the genus *Arabis*.

rock crys'tȧl, a transparent quartz, especially when colorless.

rock dŏve, the common wild pigeon of Europe, living and nesting along rocky coasts.

rock drill, a drill for driving holes into rock, operated either by hand or by artificial power.

rock duck, same as *harlequin duck*.

rock eel, a smooth-bodied elongated fish, *Murænoides gunnellus*, inhabiting the North Atlantic and other northern waters.

rock'ē·lāy, **rock'lāy,** *n.* same as *roquelaure*.

rock'ẽr, *n.* 1. a person who rocks, as a cradle.
2. either of the curved pieces on the bottom of a cradle, rocking chair, etc.
3. a rocking chair.
4. a cradle for washing sand or gravel in gold mining.
5. a device consisting of a small steel plate with a toothed and curved edge, for roughening and thus preparing the surface of a plate to be engraved.
6. a skate with a curved blade.

rock'ẽr, *n.* same as *rock dove*.

rock'ẽr ärm, any one of the arms attached to a rock shaft.

rock'ẽred, *a.* having the shape of a rocker; as, a *rockered* keel of a ship.

rock'ẽr·y, *n.*; *pl.* **rock'ẽr·ies,** a formation of fragments of rocks, soil, etc., about and among which plants are grown; a rock garden.

rock'et, *n.* [It. *rocchetta*, spool or bobbin, a rocket; dim. of *rocca*, a distaff; O.H.G. *roccho*, a distaff.]
1. a projectile consisting of a cylinder filled with a combustible substance which when ignited produces gases that escape through a vent in the rear and drive their container forward by the principle of reaction. Rockets are used as fireworks, signals, and weapons; in World War II rocket bombs proved to be effective military weapons.

FUEL CHAMBER FILLED
WITH ALCOHOL AND
WAR HEAD   LIQUID OXYGEN
MOTOR
STABILIZING
GYROSCOPES   STEERING FINS
V-2 ROCKET BOMB AND DIAGRAM

2. a tilting spear having its point covered so as to prevent injury.

Congreve rocket; a destructive rocket, now no longer used, invented by Sir William Congreve. It was filled with highly inflammable materials, or with an explosive charge.

rock'et, *v.i.* 1. to go like a rocket; to dart ahead swiftly.
2. to fly swiftly and almost straight up when flushed: said of game birds.

rock'et, *n.* [Fr. *roquette*; It. *ruchetta*, dim. of *ruca*, a garden rocket, from L. *eruca*, a colewort.]
1. any of various plants of the genus *Hesperis* with white, pink, yellow, or purple flowers, as *Hesperis matronalis*, the dame's violet.

---

fāte, fär, fȧst, fạll, final, cãre, at; mēte, prey, hẽr, met; pīne, marine, bĩrd, pin; nōte, mŏve, fọr, atŏm, not; mọon, book;

rocketer   **roe**

2. a European plant, *Eruca sativa*, grown like spinach and used in salads.
3. a weed found in some parts of the United States.
   bastard rocket; *Brassica erucastrum*, a European weed.
   dyer's rocket; dyer's-weed, *Reseda luteola*.
   yellow rocket; the *Barbarea vulgaris*.
rock'et·ēr, *n.* a bird that rockets.
rock'et gun, any weapon that launches a rocket projectile; especially, a bazooka.
rock'et lärk'spŭr, a showy annual larkspur, *Delphinium ajacis*.
rock'et launch'ẽr, a device for launching rockets; specifically, in military usage, a bazooka.
rock fal'çòn, same as *merlin*.
Rock fē'vẽr, [from *Rock* of Gibraltar, where the disease is prevalent.] undulant fever.
rock'fish, *n.* any one of several fishes living in rocky places, as (a) the priestfish; (b) any of various food fishes of the North Pacific, as the rock cod; (c) any of several groupers of the waters around Bermuda, Florida, etc. (d) the striped bass; (e) a killifish; (f) the log perch.
rock flour, the pulverized rock formed by the grinding action of a glacier in its bed.
rock gär'den, a garden with flowers and plants growing on rocky ground or among rocks variously arranged.
rock gas, natural gas.
rock goat, the ibex.
rock grouse, same as *rock ptarmigan*.
rock gŭr'net, any Australian food fish of the genus *Centropogon*, particularly *Centropogon australis*.
rock'hāir, *n.* a delicate lichen, *Alectoria jubata*, which grows upon rocks in tufts.
rock'i·ness, *n.* the state or quality of being rocky.
rock'ing, *n.* the act of swinging or swaying backward and forward.
rock'ing chāir, a chair mounted on rockers or springs, so as to allow a rocking movement.
rock'ing horse, a child's toy horse fitted with rockers or springs.
rock'ing shaft, same as *rock shaft*.
rock'ing stōne, a stone, often of great size and weight, so exactly poised on its foundation that it can be rocked, or slightly moved, with but little force.
rock kañ·ga·rōō', a kangaroo living in rocky places.
rock kelp, a kind of seaweed; rockweed.
rock lärk, a kind of European pipit, *Anthus obscurus*.
rock'less, *a.* being without rocks.
rock lil'y, a fernlike plant of tropical America, *Selaginella convoluta*, growing in crowded bunches or tufts.
rock'ling, *n.* any small marine fish of either of the genera *Rhinonemus* or *Onos*, characterized by three or four barbels.
rock lob'stēr, any of several large sea lobsters, distinguished by a spiny covering and the absence of the large claw.
rock man'à·kin, same as *cock of the rock* under *cock*.
rock milk, a light, chalky variety of carbonate of lime deposited from water: also called *agaric mineral*.
rock moss, a lichen, *Lecanora tartarea*, abounding on rocks in the alpine districts of Europe.
rock oil, petroleum. [Chiefly Brit.]
rock par'à·keet, a grass parakeet of Australia, *Euphema petrophila*, which builds its nest in a hole or crevice of a cliff.
rock pig'eôn, a species of pigeon, *Columba livia*, found in Europe, Asia, and Africa: also called *rock dove*.
rock pip'ĭt, the sea lark of Europe, *Anthus obscurus*.
rock plant, a plant distinguished by growing on or among rocks.
   rock plant of St. Helena; same as *petrobium*.
rock plŏv'ẽr, any of the whistling plovers, *Squatarola helvetica*; also, the American sandpiper.
rock ptär'mĭ·găn (tär'), an arctic bird, *Lagopus rupestris*, which, in winter, changes its summer plumage, of a grayish-brown color, to white.
rock rab'bit, a small animal of the genus *Hyrax*; a hyrax.
rock'-ribbed, *a.* 1. having rocky ridges or elevations; as, *rock-ribbed* coasts.
2. firm; rigid; unyielding; as, a *rock-ribbed* policy.
rock'rōṣe, *n.* a plant of either of the genera *Helianthemum* or *Cistus*, bearing large rose-

like flowers of white, purple, or red; also, the flower of this plant.
   Australian rockrose; a shrubby Australian plant bearing roselike flowers with thick and richly colored petals.
   Cretan rockrose; a shrub, *Cistus creticus*, related to the rockrose and yielding labdanum.
rock rū'by, a fine reddish variety of garnet.
rock salm'ŏn (sam'), 1. any fish of the genus *Seriola* of the southern United States, as *Seriola carolinensis*.
2. in England, any fish of the genus *Pollock*, as *Pollock carbonarius*: also called *coalfish*.
rock salt, common salt (sodium chloride) occurring in solid form, especially in rocklike masses.
rock seal, same as *harbor seal*.
rock sēr'pent, a rock snake.
rock shaft, a shaft that rocks or oscillates on its journals rather than revolving, carrying arms or levers for reciprocating motion, as in a locomotive.
rock snāke, any one of many large snakes of the genus *Python*, especially *Python molurus*, of India.
rock snīpe, same as *rock plover*.
rock sōap, a kind of clay having the characteristics of soap: it is a hydrated silicate of aluminum.
rock spar'rōw, a sparrow of the genus *Petronia*, as *Petronia stulta*; also, a sparrow of the North American genus *Peucæa*, as *Peucæa ruficeps*.
rock staff, in machinery, a staff or lever that oscillates or has a rocking motion on a pivotal point.
rock suck'ẽr, a lamprey.
rock tär, petroleum.
rock thrush, any thrush belonging to the genus *Monticola* or *Petrocossyphus*.
rock trout, any species of marine trout belonging to the genus *Hexagrammus*.
rock wär'blēr, a singing bird of Australia, *Origma rubricata*, frequenting rocky ravines.
rock'weed, *n.* any of a number of seaweeds growing upon rocks.
rock'wood, *n.* ligniform asbestos; also, fossilized wood.
rock wool, mineral wool; a fibrous insulating material made by blowing steam through molten siliceous rock: it has the appearance of spun glass.
rock'work, *n.* 1. a wall formed of stones fixed in mortar and having a rough surface.
2. a rock garden.
rock wren (ren), 1. a South American songbird, *Hylactes tarni*.
2. a wren of the genus *Salpinctes*, inhabiting the dry regions of Mexico and the western parts of the United States.
rock'y, *a.; comp.* rockier; *superl.* rockiest, 1. inclined to rock, or sway; unsteady; shaky.
2. weak and dizzy, as from dissipation. [Slang.]
rock'y, *a.* 1. full of or containing rocks; as, a *rocky* mountain; a *rocky* shore.
2. consisting of rock.
3. like or suggesting a rock; specifically, (a) firm; stable; (b) hard; unfeeling; as, a *rocky* heart.
   Rocky Mountain goat; a white, goatlike antelope of the mountains of northwestern North America, with a thick, shaggy coat and a pair of black horns.
   Rocky Mountain grape; the Oregon grape.
   Rocky Mountain locust; a predatory locust or grasshopper, *Caloptenus spretus*, abounding in the western part of the United States.
   Rocky Mountain sheep; same as *bighorn*.
   Rocky Mountain spotted fever; an acute, infectious disease caused by Rickettsia transmitted by ticks, prevalent in the territory in and around the Rocky Mountains; characterized by muscular and articular pain, fever, and spotty, red skin eruptions: it is also epidemic in other parts of the United States.
rŏ·çò'çò, *n.* [Fr., from *rocaille*, rockwork.]
1. a style of architecture and decoration developed in France from the baroque and characterized primarily by elaborate and profuse ornamentation imitating foliage, rockwork, shellwork, scrolls, etc., often done with much delicacy and refinement: it was popular especially in the first half of the 18th century.
2. a style of literature, etc. regarded, often disparagingly, as like this.
rŏ·çò'çò, *a.* 1. of or in rococo.
2. too profuse and elaborate in ornamentation; florid and tasteless.
roç'tà, *n.* [LL., from the Celtic *crot* or *cruit*, a

fiddle.] a medieval musical instrument much like a violin.
rod, *n.* [ME. *rod*, from *rood*; AS. *rod*, a cross, beam, or rod; akin to L. *rudis*, a rod, staff.]
1. a shoot or slender stem of any woody plant, especially when cut off and stripped of leaves or twigs.
2. in Biblical use, an offshoot or branch of a family or tribe; stock or race; as, the *rod* of Isaiah.
3. any straight, or almost straight, stick, shaft, bar, staff, etc., of wood, metal, or other material.
4. (a) a stick or switch, or a bundle of sticks or switches, for whipping or beating as punishment; (b) punishment; chastisement.
5. a kind of scepter or badge of office; as, the usher's *rod*; hence, authority; power.
6. a long, slender pole for fishing or angling; a fishing rod.
7. a measure of length equal to 5½ yards, or 16½ feet: also called a *pole* or *perch*. A square rod is equal to 30¼ square yards.
8. a scale of wood or metal employed in measuring something.
9. a pistol or revolver. [Slang.]
10. in anatomy, any of the rod-shaped cells in the retina of the eye that are sensitive to dim light.
11. in bacteriology, any microorganism shaped like a rod.
   rods of Corti; two sets of stiff rods, the inner and outer rods of Corti, within the epithelium of the organ of Corti covering the basilar membrane of the ear.
   to spare the rod; to refrain from punishing.
rod'den, *n.* rowan. [Scot.]
rōde, *v.* past tense and archaic past participle of *ride*.
rō'dent, *a.* [L. *rodens* (*-entis*), gnawing.] gnawing; also, belonging or pertaining to the order *Rodentia*.
   rodent ulcer; a carcinomatous ulcer, generally on the face, which gradually eats away the soft tissues and bones.
rō'dent, *n.* any mammal of the order *Rodentia*, especially, in popular usage, a rat or mouse.
Rō·den'tĭ·à (-shi-), *n.pl.* [L. *rodens* (*-entis*), from *rodere*, to gnaw.] an order of mammals having two (rarely four) large incisor teeth in each jaw, adapted for gnawing or nibbling: they have no canine teeth, and the incisors grow continually from persistent pulps. The rat, mouse, squirrel, marmot, muskrat, beaver, etc. belong to this order. Also called *Glires*.
rō·den'tĭàl, *a.* of or pertaining to the Rodentia. [Rare.]
rō'dē·ō (or rō-dā'ō), *n.; pl.* **rō'dē·ōṣ,** [Sp., a place for cattle at a market or fair.]
1. the driving together of cattle for branding, etc.; a roundup.
2. an enclosure for cattle that have been rounded up.
3. an exhibition or competition of the skills of cowboys, as horsemanship, lassoing, etc., for public entertainment.
rodge, *n.* the gadwall. [Brit.]
rod'man, *n.; pl.* **rod'men,** one who carries or works with a rod; specifically, one who carries a leveling rod for surveyors.
rod'ō'mont, *n.* a vain boaster; a braggart.
rod'ō'mont, *a.* bragging; vainly boasting.
rod'ō·mon·tāde', *n.* [Fr., from It. *rodomonte*, a bully, from *Rodomonte*, the boastful leader of the Saracens against Charlemagne, in Ariosto's *Orlando Furioso*.] vain boasting or bragging; arrogant boasting, or blusterous, ranting talk.
rod'ō·mon·tāde', *v.i.;* rodomontaded, *pt., pp.*; rodomontading, *ppr.* to boast; to brag; to bluster; to rant.
rod'ō·mon·tā'dist, *n.* a blustering boaster; one who brags.
rod'ō·mon·tā'dō, *n.* rodomontade. [Obs.]
rod'ō·mon·tā'dōr, *n.* same as *rodomontadist*.
rod'man, *n.* same as *rodman*.
rod'stēr, *n.* an angler. [Rare.]
rod'wood, *n.* any one of several shrubs or trees of the West Indies, as white rodwood, red rodwood, black rodwood.
rōe, *n.; pl.* **rōe** or **rōeṣ,** [AS. *ra, raha*.]
1. a small, agile, graceful European and Asiatic deer: also *roe deer*.
2. the female of the red deer.
rōe, *n.* [ME. *rowne*; Ice. *hrogn*; Dan. *rogn*, roe. The *n* was taken for a pl. termination and dropped in the sing. through error.]
1. the eggs or spawn of fishes: the roe of the male is called *soft roe* or *milt*; that of the female *hard roe* or *spawn*.

ANSWERS: Lesson 11 (pp. 311-333)

Learning Skills: Following Directions (pp. 311–315)

Practice A

You should have answered only questions 6 and 9. Students usually make the mistake of not following directions. The directions at the beginning of the exercise stated that you should read everything carefully before doing anything. Because the test is timed, students usually ignore this advice and begin answering questions.

Practice B

Check answers by rereading the instructions and by comparing the following to your responses.

Practice C

Check answers by rereading the instructions and by comparing the following to your responses.

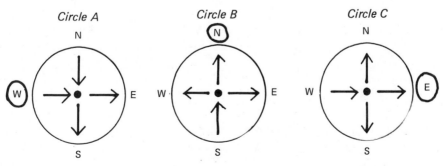

Circle A   Circle B   Circle C

Practice D

Check answers by rereading the instructions and by comparing the following to your responses.

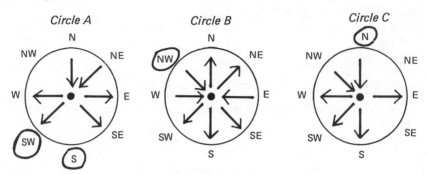

Reading: Distinguishing Fact from Opinion (pp. 315–318)

Practice A

1. O 2. O 3. F 4. O 5. F 6. O 7. F 8. F 9. O 10. O 11. O
12. O 13. O 14. O 15. O 16. F 17. O 18. O 19. O 20. F

Practice B

1. F 2. T 3. T 4. T 5. F 6. T 7. F 8. T 9. F 10. F

Practice C

1. F 2. F 3. F 4. F 5. O 6. F 7. O 8. F 9. O 10. O 11. O
12. O 13. O 14. F 15. O

Vocabulary: Figures of Speech I (pp. 318–324)

Practice A

1. wept huge tears 2. panting 3. refused 4. crept softly 5. opened; devour 6. straining; impatiently 7. thirsty; begged 8. felt naked 9. smiled 10. angry; apat fire

Practice B

1. a gorged buzzard 2. a waterfall 3. a telegraph 4. a frayed brown cord 5. a rocky road 6. a swift bird 7. a light in the night 8. a seal 9. a glowing orange ball 10. a tall bride

Practice C

1. living pincushions 2. twisted pretzels 3. a wolf 4. a ghost 5. a lamb 6. a smoking volcano 7. hot potatoes 8. razor-sharp 9. a crewcut 10. confetti

Practice D

1. garden of delight (metaphor) 2. like bended bows (simile) 3. with delight look round her (personification) 4. as a cloud (simile) 5. tossing their heads in sprightly dance (personification) 6. bares her bosom (personification) 7. wrinkled; crawls (personification) 8. like a book (simile) 9. laid to sleep (personification) 10. threw down their spears and watered heaven with their tears (personification)

Practice E

1. . . . what was beginning to look like an ocean of salt with a few specks of pepper 2. She is describing the ratio of white students to black students.

Practice F

1. flash 2. dry leaves 3. peddler 4. roses 5. cherry 6. bow 7. snow 8. wreath 9. bowlfull of jelly 10. down of a thistle

Word Analysis: The Dictionary II (pp. 324-330)

Practice A

1. T 2. T 3. F 4. F 5. T 6. F 7. F 8. T 9. T 10. T

Practice B

1. traditional outlaw of the 12th century who lived with his followers in Sherwood Forest and robbed the rich to help the poor 2. no 3. robustness and rocaille 4. about 23 5. both a transitive and an intransitive verb and a noun 6. a pocket full of money 7. out of money or in a condition of ruin 8. yes; Rock of Gibralter 9. yes 10. yes 11. common salt 12. adjective 13. yes 14. yes—*rock* can mean rock dove or rockfish 15. a South American songbird 16. two 17. three 18. two 19. the first 20. the first or the second 21. fate 22. use 23. *c*; cat 24. the eggs or spawn of fishes 25. Daniel Defoe

LESSON 12

Learning Skills: Questions
Reading: Detecting Propaganda Techniques
Vocabulary: Figures of Speech II
Word Analysis: The Dictionary III
Answers
Crossword Puzzle
Homograph Riddles
True/False Test

LEARNING SKILLS: QUESTIONS

1. Knowing how and when to ask questions helps students to gain a better insight into a subject, gives the instructor feedback, and slows the instructor down if he or she is going too fast. (See Lesson 14 on notetaking.) Unfortunately, many students are afraid to ask questions. Sometimes their fear may be due to an instructor's attitude. However, often it's because a student doesn't know how to formulate the questions or is "afraid of looking like a fool."

2. Asking questions is an important part of learning! Don't allow any instructor to intimidate you so that you are reluctant to ask questions.

Special Note

If you have missed a class and have copied someone else's notes, you should go to the instructor *outside* class to ask for clarifications.

334

3. Questions about examinations are the most often asked ones. Here are some suggestions on the kind to ask:

a. What kind of examination will it be? If you can get your instructor to tell you whether the test will be essay or objective, you can study for the type to be given. Your preparation for an essay test will be different from your preparation for an objective one. (See Lessons 13–15 on test-taking.)

b. How long will the examination be? This will tell you whether it's a quiz (a minor examination) or a test (one that usually counts more than a quiz). The length of the exam determines the depth or breadth of the exam. If it's a short quiz, you know that less material will be covered than on a full-scale exam.

c. Will dates, names, formulas, and other such specifics be stressed? This is important to know because it will determine whether you emphasize these or not when you study. (See Lesson 14 on notetaking for other clues from instructors.)

d. Will it be an open-book or a closed-book test? This answer will also affect your studying. An open-book examination usually requires you to answer questions in detail and to handle complex issues. Do not be fooled into thinking that open-book tests are easy.

e. What chapters will be covered? You should make sure that you will be reviewing the material to be covered on the test. For example, some instructors make their final examinations cumulative—that is, everything is covered—whereas others cover material on the final examination only from the midterm exam onward.

Do you agree with Charlie's simile?

f. Is it permissible to write essay answers in outline form? Some instructors will not allow you to do this because they are interested in seeing how well you can express yourself as well as how well you recall and organize material.

4. In going over an examination, ask general questions or those that relate to everyone's papers. If you have a specific question on your paper, ask the instructor this question in private at the end of the class.

5. Do not hesitate to question your instructor concerning the marking of your paper. You learn from taking examinations only if you have knowledge of results and understand your mistakes. (See Lessons 13–15 on test-taking.) If you do not understand a comment or a grade, ask for an explanation. (Of course, this should not be done in a belligerent manner.) Usually instructors are very willing to go over such questions with you in private.

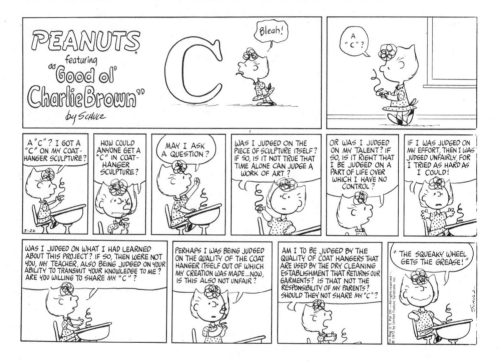

6. A child returned home from school with his report card for his mother's inspection. "But, dear," she said, "What's the trouble?" "There's no trouble, Mom," was the quick reply. "You know yourself things are always marked down after the holidays."

Subjectivity does exist in grading, making it quite unreliable. Different instructors may use different criteria as a basis for their grading. As a student you have not only a right to question your instructor concerning how you will be evaluated but also an obligation to yourself to question if your teacher has not stated grading criteria. These questions should be asked at the beginning of the semester.

7. Father: "Well son, how are your marks?"
    Son: "They're under water."
    Father: "What do you mean 'under water'?"
    Son: "Below 'C' Level."

Although we may joke about our grades, grades do affect us and help to determine how well we will do on future tests. If you do not do well on a test, ask your instructor how you can get help. Do not wait until the final examination to do this. (See lessons on test-taking.)

8. Many instructors at the beginning of the period ask if any students have questions on their readings or on the past lecture(s). This is a good time to ask about any point that is confusing to you. Here are some pointers on asking your questions:

a. Be as specific as possible.

b. State your question clearly.

c. Do not say "I have a question" and then go into a long discourse before asking your question. (The question may be forgotten.)

d. Make sure your question is related to the material.

Special Notes

1. People who ask the best questions are usually those who know the material the best.
2. Asking questions is not a substitute for studying the material.
3. Questions help to clarify material for you.
4. Professors usually want and encourage questions.
5. The questions you ask probably help a number of other students.
6. Don't ask questions merely to look smart.

Practice A.

Check the question(s) that are *good* ones to ask for each topic. (There can be more than one checked.)

1. Test-taking

_____ a. What should we study?

_____ b. Will dates and names be on the test?

_____ c. How long will the examination be?

_____ d. What kind of test is it going to be?

_____ e. How much do we need to know?

_____ f. What chapters should we study?

_____ g. Do you ever give unannounced quizzes?

_____ h. Will this examination count toward our final grade?

2. Word analysis

_____ a. Would you go over the syllabication lecture?

_____ b. Why do you divide *bugle* between the *u* and the *g*?

_____ c. What do you need to know in order to divide words into syllables?

_____ d. Is syllabication something we really need to know?

_____ e. When is *ow* a digraph?

_____ f. Could you give some other examples of digraphs?

_____ g. How does accenting help us to pronounce words?

3. Notetaking

_____ a. What should we know about notetaking?

_____ b. Is it necessary to take notes?

_____ c. Could you repeat the lecture on notetaking?

_____ d. What are "buzz" words?

STOP. Check answers at the end of Lesson 12.

READING: DETECTING PROPAGANDA TECHNIQUES

Propaganda is defined as *any systematic, widespread, deliberate indoctrination* (the act of causing one to be impressed and eventually filled with some view) *or plan for indoctrination.* The term *propaganda* connotes deception or distortion. In other words, people who use propaganda are trying to influence others by using deceptive methods.

Bias refers to *a mental leaning, a partiality, a prejudice, or a slanting of something.*

From the two definitions, you can see that people interested in propagandizing have a certain bias. They use propaganda techniques to distort information and to indoctrinate people to their views or bias.

Some Propaganda Techniques

1. Name Calling—accusing or denouncing an individual by using labels widely disapproved of such as "Red," "fascist," "miser," "reactionary," "radical," "stooge," "pig-headed."

2. Glittering Generalities—seeking acceptance of ideas by using widely admired labels such as "freedom," "American," "Christian," "red-blooded," "democratic," "businesslike."

3. Bandwagon—seeking acceptance through appealing to pluralities. For example, an advertisement states: *"Most* people prefer DAZZLES. They know what's good! Do you?" In the Bandwagon approach you "go along" because everyone else is.

4. Card Stacking—seeking acceptance by presenting or building on half-truths. Only favorable facts are presented, whereas anything unfavorable is deliberately omitted, and vice versa.

5. Transfer—seeking acceptance by citing respected sources of authority, prestige, or reverence such as the home, the Constitution, the flag, the Church, and so on, in such a way as to make it appear that they approve the proposal. For example, in an advertisement, it is stated, "Our forefathers ate hearty breakfasts. Our country is built on strength. Our forefathers would want you to be strong. Eat Product X for strength. Product X will give you a hearty breakfast."

6. Plain Folks—seeking acceptance through establishing someone as "just one of the boys." Example: A presidential candidate is photographed milking cows, kissing babies, wearing workclothes, and so on.

7. Testimonial—seeking acceptance by using testimonials from famous people to build confidence in a product. For example, in TV commercials actors, athletes, and other famous personalities are used to endorse a product.

Practice A.

Name the propaganda technique used in each statement.

1. Don't be the last one to get this fabulous product.

   _____

2. A famous former judge says, "I think that you'll like this car. I drive one, too."

   _____

3. Would you trust someone who is such a spendthrift?

   _____

4. This lovely set of furniture can be installed in your home as soon as you agree to the purchase. For a very small deposit and a monthly payment of twenty dollars, it's a steal.

   _____

5. "Mommy, you have to let me go, all the mothers are letting their children go."

   _____

6. In the name of justice, do what every good American should: vote for John S.

   _____

7. A famous football player says, "This airline is my kind of airline."

   _____

8. Howdy, everyone. I'm delighted to be able to spend this terrific summer day with you in your lovely town. I grew up in a town just like this. Why we even had the same general store in my town. I knew I was doing the right thing coming here to meet you folks. Don't forget to vote for me in two weeks. You're my kind of people.

   _____

9. This nutritious, delicious candy bar is more than a candy bar, it's a meal in itself. Together with a glass of milk you'll get all the calcium, iron, and calories you need for almost a day.

   _____

10. The Church is against violence. Vote for this bill to do away with violence.

   _____

11. Why that's as American as apple pie. You have to vote for it.

_____

12. Would you really back something that was proposed by a reactionary?

_____

13. As a poor country boy, I know what it's like to be without. You can trust me with your money. I won't squander it.

_____

14. The Constitution guarantees our rights. Vote for this bill to continue what the Constitution guarantees.

_____

15. We have to vote for her because she is so businesslike and American.

_____

STOP. Check answers at the end of Lesson 12.

VOCABULARY: FIGURES OF SPEECH II

1. *Hyperbole* is another common figure of speech. It is the use of *excessive exaggeration* for effect. Whenever we say, "I'm so hungry I could eat a horse," or "I'm so tired I could sleep for a year," we are using *hyperbole*. Writers use hyperbole to stretch the truth because they want to make a point emphatically.

Examples:

1. For the *five millionth time,* "No!"
2. She *cried forever*!
3. They have *tons of* expensive things.
4. She's *smaller than my thumb.*
5. His morals are *as upright as wet spaghetti.*

Writers also use hyperbole to portray their feelings. For example, when a writer says, "The Joneses prattled on for an eternity," he is not only telling us that the Joneses talked for a very long time, he is also giving us his feelings about it. If the writer had enjoyed the company of the Joneses, he would not say that they prattled on for an eternity.

Special Note

Hype is used often, especially by the advertising industry in connection with television and movie advertisements. Exaggerated words such as *blockbuster, deathdefying, shocker, stupendous, stupefying, sensational, amazing,* and *unbelievable* are used to promote productions.

2. *Oxymoron* is the combining of contraries (opposites) to portray a particular image or to produce a striking effect. Word contradictions attract our attention and present the author's feelings or ideas expressively. An oxymoron with which you may be familiar is "poor little rich girl." Most often this word contradiction is used sarcastically, that is, the speaker means to ridicule the girl while seeming to be sympathetic. However, it is possible for the phrase "poor little rich girl" to be meant sympathetically—that the girl has a lot of material possessions but does not have other things she needs such as love and understanding.

Examples:

a. Parting is such *sweet sorrow*.

b. A *loud silence* followed the improper remark.

c. This is one of those occasions for *making haste slowly*.

d. She lives in *happy ignorance*.

e. He is suffering from *benign neglect*.

f. They are the *best of enemies*.

g. She was *conspicuous* by her *absence*.

The word contradiction "the dawn of night" could be used in connection with the adventures of Dracula. Example: Dracula awoke at the *dawn of night*. You can probably come up with some other interesting oxymorons in relation to Dracula.

An oxymoron can serve more than one purpose. For example, Arthur Koestler's title *Darkness at Noon* is a word contradiction. Noon is usually the brightest time of the day because the sun is at its zenith. Obviously, Koestler intended his title to attract our attention, but he also had other reasons for using it. Koestler was giving us some clue to what his novel is about. Even if you haven't read his book yet, you get the feeling of something dark, ominous, or evil happening while it's light—the feeling of something evil but unnoticed, a dark cloud gradually covering the light while people are unaware of the gathering gloom.

Practice A.

For each of these sentences state whether hyperbole or oxymoron is being used. Then state what each figure of speech means.

1. The victory was defeating.

   _____

2. This tale is as old as time.

   _____

3. The silence was deafening.

   _____

4. Less is more.

   _____

5. I've been waiting for an eternity.

   _____

6. Life is deadly.

   _____

7. The porch he wanted us to paint was as wide as the Mississippi and almost as long.

   _____

8. In courage, there is cowardice.

   _____

9. Its cold touch burns the skin.

   _____

10. The calm was upsetting.

   _____

STOP. Check answers at the end of Lesson 12.

WORD ANALYSIS: THE DICTIONARY III

A dictionary is a very important reference book. It supplies a great amount of useful information besides word meanings and pronunciation. In the space provided list all the uses that you can think of for the dictionary.

Now compare your list with this one:

I. Uses of the Dictionary

A. Information Concerning a Word
   1. Spelling
   2. Definitions
   3. Correct usage
   4. Pronunciation
   5. Syllabication
   6. Antonyms
   7. Synonyms
   8. Parts of speech
   9. Idiomatic phrases
   10. Etymology—history of the word
   11. Semantics—analysis of the word's meanings

B. Other Useful Information
   1. Biographical entries
   2. Lists of foreign countries, provinces, and cities with population estimates
   3. Charts of other geographical data
   4. Air distances between principal cities
   5. Listing of foreign words and phrases
   6. Complete listing of abbreviations in common use
   7. Tables of weights and measures
   8. Signs and symbols
   9. Forms of address

Special Notes

1. The kind of information presented varies according to the dictionary.
2. An abridged (shortened) dictionary such as *Webster's Collegiate Dictionary* does not contain as many words or as much information as an unabridged dictionary like *Webster's Third New International Dictionary* or *The Oxford English Dictionary*. But an abridged desk dictionary nonetheless contains enough information to serve most needs. Buy a desk dictionary for your regular use, and use the unabridged dictionary in the library for special research and obscure knowledge. Remember, a dictionary is not necessarily the last word on a word. It's a good idea to check two or more dictionaries for comparison.

Practice A.

Look up the meanings given for *rock* in an abridged and an unabridged dictionary. Count general meanings only, that is, count only those that are numbered 1, 2, 3, and so on. Do not count the meanings in which *rock* is used with another word such as *rock candy, rock salt*, and so on.

STOP. Check answers at the end of Lesson 12.

Practice B.

Using your dictionary, answer the following questions.

1. In what countries do cyclopes live?

   _____

2. Where are the Himalayas?

   _____

3. Was Mars the god of fire?

   _____

4. Is *Ill.* an abbreviation for illness?

   _____

5. Is a biped an extinct animal?

   _____

6. Is a millipede part of the metric system?

   _____

7. Is a statute a work of art?

_____

8. Is haiku a Hawaiian mountain?

_____

9. Does jack-in-the-pulpit refer to religion?

_____

10. Is a poetess a man who writes poems?

_____

STOP. Check answers at the end of Lesson 12.

Practice C.

Using the given pages from *Webster's New Twentieth Century Dictionary* (see pp. 350–353), answer the following questions.

1. What is the formal salutation you use in a letter to the mayor?

_____

2. What is the less formal salutation you use in a letter to the governor?

_____

3. How do you [in speaking] address the President of the United States?

_____

4. How do you [in speaking] address the Chief Justice of the Supreme Court?

_____

5. How do you write the envelope address to a King or Queen?

_____

6. What do the following abbreviations stand for? (a) A.C.S._____

_____; (b) A.D. _____; (c) A.B._____

_____; (d)   B.B.C._____; (e)   A.M.A.

_____; (f)   A.M._____; (g)

A.S.S.R._____ ; (h) B.L. _____;

(i) Ca _____

7. Where was Andrew Jackson born?

_____

8. What were the years when Harry S. Truman was in office?

_____

9. Who succeeded Abraham Lincoln to the Presidency?

_____

10. James Monroe was the _____ President of the United States.

_____

11. How old was Grant when he died?

_____

12. How old was Thomas Jefferson when he became President?

_____

13. Quickly skim p. 352 and state which President was born in Iowa.

_____

14. Quickly skim p. 352 and state to which political party Abraham Lincoln belonged.

_____

15. Quickly skim p. 352 and state to which political party John Adams belonged.

_____

16. How old was George Washington when he became President?

_____

17. How many centimeters are there in an inch?

_____

18. How many meters are in a mile?

_____

19. How many feet are in a mile?

_____

20. How many quarts are in a peck?

_____

21. How many pecks are in a bushel?

_____

22. Three miles equals how many kilometers?

_____

23. How many cubic inches equal a cubic foot?

_____

24. A square foot equals how many square centimeters?

_____

25. How many acres are in a square mile?

_____

STOP. Check answers at the end of Lesson 12.

TABLES OF WEIGHTS AND MEASURES

Linear Measure

1 inch		=	2.54 centimeters
12 inches	= 1 foot	=	0.3048 meter
3 feet	= 1 yard	=	0.9144 meter
5½ yards or 16½ feet	= 1 rod (or pole or perch)	=	5.029 meters
40 rods	= 1 furlong	=	201.17 meters
8 furlongs or 1,760 yards or 5,280 feet	= 1 (statute) mile	=	1,609.3 meters
3 miles	= 1 (land) league	=	4.83 kilometers

Square Measure

1 square inch		=	6.452 square centimeters
144 square inches	= 1 square foot	=	929 square centimeters
9 square feet	= 1 square yard	=	0.8361 square meter
30¼ square yards	= 1 square rod (or square pole or square perch)	=	25.29 square meters
160 square rods or 4,840 square yards or 43,560 square feet	= 1 acre	=	0.4047 hectare
640 acres	= 1 square mile	=	259 hectares or 2.59 square kilometers

Cubic Measure

1 cubic inch		= 16.387 cubic centimeters
1,728 cubic inches	= 1 cubic foot	= 0.0283 cubic meter
27 cubic feet	= 1 cubic yard	= 0.7646 cubic meter
	(in units for cordwood, etc.)	
16 cubic feet	= 1 cord foot	
8 cord feet	= 1 cord	= 3.625 cubic meters

Chain Measure

(for Gunter's, or surveryor's, chain)

7.92 inches	= 1 link	=	20.12 centimeters
100 links or 66 feet	= 1 chain	=	20.12 meters
10 chains	= 1 furlong	=	201.17 meters
80 chains	= 1 mile	=	1,609.3 meters

(for engineer's chain)

1 foot	= 1 link	=	0.3048 meter
100 feet	= 1 chain	=	30.48 meters
52.8 chains	= 1 mile	=	1,609.3 meters

Surveyor's (Square) Measure

625 square links	= 1 square pole	=	25.29 square meters
16 square poles	= 1 square chain	=	404.7 square meters
10 square chains	= 1 acre	=	0.4047 hectare
640 acres	= 1 square mile or 1 section	=	259 hectares or 2.59 square kilometers
36 square miles	= 1 township	=	9,324.0 hectares or 93.24 square kilometers

Nautical Measure

6 feet	= 1 fathom	= 1.829 meters
100 fathoms	= 1 cable's length (ordinary)	

(In the U.S. Navy 120 fathoms or 720 feet = 1 cable's length; in the British Navy, 608 feet = 1 cable's length.)

10 cables' lengths	= 1 nautical mile (6,076.10333 feet,	
1 nautical mile	= 1.1508 statute miles (the length of a minute of longitude at the equator)	= 1.852 kilometers by international agreement, 1954)

(Also called geographical, sea, or air mile, and, in Great Britain, Admiralty mile.)

3 nautical miles	= 1 marine league (3.45 statute miles)	= 5.56 kilometers
60 nautical miles	= 1 degree of a great circle of the earth	

Dry Measure

1 pint		= 33.60 cubic inches	= 0.5505 liter
2 pints	= 1 quart	= 67.20 cubic inches	= 1.1012 liters
8 quarts	= 1 peck	= 537.61 cubic inches	= 8.8096 liters
4 pecks	= 1 bushel	= 2,150.42 cubic inches	= 35.2383 liters
	1 British dry quart	= 1.032 U.S. dry quarts.	

According to United States government standards, the following are the weights avoirdupois for single bushels of the specified grains: for wheat, 60 pounds; for barley, 48 pounds; for oats, 32 pounds; for rye, 56 pounds; for corn, 56 pounds. Some states have specifications varying from these.

Liquid Measure

1 gill	= 4 fluid ounces	= 7.219 cubic inches	= 0.1183 liter
	(see next table)		
4 gills	= 1 pint	= 28.875 cubic inches	= 0.4732 liter
2 pints	= 1 quart	= 57.75 cubic inches	= 0.9463 liter
4 quarts	= 1 gallon	= 231 cubic inches	= 3.7853 liters

The British imperial gallon (4 imperial quarts) = 277.42 cubic inches = 4.546 liters. The barrel in Great Britain equals 36 imperial gallons, in the United States, usually 31½ gallons.

Forms of Address

Person Being Addressed	Envelope Address	Salutation		In Speaking
		Formal	Less Formal	
Earl	The Right Honorable The Earl of (name)	My Lord:		Lord (name)
Earl's Wife	The Right Honorable The Countess of (name)	My Lady:		Lady (name)
Governor (of a State)	The Honorable (full name), Governor of (State), (capital city and State)	Sir:	My dear Governor (surname):	Governor (surname)
Judge (see also Supreme Court)	The Honorable (full name), (name of court), (city and State)	Sir (or Madam):	My dear Judge (surname):	Judge (surname)
King (or Queen)	His (Her) Most Gracious Majesty, King, (Queen) (name)	May it please Your Majesty:		*Initially*, Your Majesty; *thereafter*, Sir (or Ma'am)
Knight	Sir (full name), (initials of his order, if any)	Sir:		Sir (given name)
Mayor	The Honorable (full name), Mayor of (city), (city and State)	Sir (or Madam):	My dear Mr. (or Madam) Mayor: *or* My dear Mayor (surname):	Mr. (or Madam) Mayor
Minister (Protestant)	The Reverend (full name), (address, city, and State)	My dear Mr. (or Dr., *if a D.D.*) (surname):		Mr. (or Dr. or, *if a Lutheran,* Pastor) (surname)
Monsignor (Roman Catholic)	The Right Reverend Monsignor (full name), (city and State)	Right Reverend Monsignor (surname):		Monsignor (surname)
Nun	Sister (religious name), (initials of her order)	My dear Sister:	Dear Sister (religious name):	Sister (religious name)
President (of the United States)	The President, The White House, Washington 25, D. C.	Sir:	My dear Mr. President:	Mr. President
Priest (Roman Catholic)	The Reverend (full name), (address, city, and State)	Reverend and dear Sir:	My dear Father (surname):	Father (surname)
Prince (or Princess)	His (Her) Royal Highness, Prince(ss) (given name)	Your Royal Highness:	Sir (or Madam):	Your Royal Highness
Rabbi	Rabbi (full name), (address, city, and State)	My dear Rabbi (or Dr., *if the holder of a doctor's degree*) (surname):		Rabbi (or Dr.) (surname)
Representative (of a State legislature)	The Honorable (full name), Member of Assembly (or other name of the legislature), (capital city and State)	Sir (or Madam):	My dear Mr. (or Mrs. or Miss) (surname):	Mr. (or Mrs. or Miss) (surname)
Senator (of the United States)	The Honorable (full name), United States Senate, Washington 25, D. C.	Sir (or Madam):	My dear Senator (surname):	Senator (surname) or Mr. (or Madam) Senator
Senator (of a State)	The Honorable (full name), (State) Senate, (capital city and State)	Sir (or Madam):	My dear Senator (surname):	Senator (surname)
Supreme Court (Associate Justice)	The Honorable (full name), Associate Justice of the United States Supreme Court, Washington 25, D. C.	Sir:	My dear Mr. Justice:	Mr. Justice
Supreme Court (Chief Justice)	The Honorable (full name), Chief Justice of the United States, Washington 25, D.C.	Sir:	My dear Mr. Chief Justice:	Mr. Chief Justice
Vice President (of the United States)	The Vice President, Washington 25, D. C.	Sir:	My dear Mr. Vice President:	Mr. Vice President

PRESIDENTS OF THE UNITED STATES

No.	Name	Life Dates	Politics	Place of Birth	Dates of Term
1	GEORGE WASHINGTON	1732-1799	Federalist	Virginia	1789-1797
2	JOHN ADAMS	1735-1826	Federalist	Massachusetts	1797-1801
3	THOMAS JEFFERSON	1743-1826	Dem.-Rep.	Virginia	1801-1809
4	JAMES MADISON	1751-1836	Dem.-Rep.	Virginia	1809-1817
5	JAMES MONROE	1758-1831	Dem.-Rep.	Virginia	1817-1825
6	JOHN QUINCY ADAMS	1767-1848	Dem.-Rep.	Massachusetts	1825-1829
7	ANDREW JACKSON	1767-1845	Democrat	South Carolina	1829-1837
8	MARTIN VAN BUREN	1782-1862	Democrat	New York	1837-1841
9	WILLIAM HENRY HARRISON	1773-1841	Whig	Virginia	1841
10	JOHN TYLER	1790-1862	Democrat	Virginia	1841-1845
11	JAMES KNOX POLK	1795-1849	Democrat	North Carolina	1845-1849
12	ZACHARY TAYLOR	1784-1850	Whig	Virginia	1849-1850
13	MILLARD FILLMORE	1800-1874	Whig	New York	1850-1853
14	FRANKLIN PIERCE	1804-1869	Democrat	New Hampshire	1853-1857
15	JAMES BUCHANAN	1791-1868	Democrat	Pennsylvania	1857-1861
16	ABRAHAM LINCOLN	1809-1865	Republican	Kentucky	1861-1865
17	ANDREW JOHNSON	1808-1875	Republican	North Carolina	1865-1869
18	ULYSSES SIMPSON GRANT	1822-1885	Republican	Ohio	1869-1877
19	RUTHERFORD BIRCHARD HAYES	1822-1893	Republican	Ohio	1877-1881
20	JAMES ABRAM GARFIELD	1831-1881	Republican	Ohio	1881
21	CHESTER ALAN ARTHUR	1830-1886	Republican	Vermont	1881-1885
22	GROVER CLEVELAND	1837-1908	Democrat	New Jersey	1885-1889
23	BENJAMIN HARRISON	1833-1901	Republican	Ohio	1889-1893
24	GROVER CLEVELAND	1837-1908	Democrat	New Jersey	1893-1897
25	WILLIAM McKINLEY	1843-1901	Republican	Ohio	1897-1901
26	THEODORE ROOSEVELT	1858-1919	Republican	New York	1901-1909
27	WILLIAM HOWARD TAFT	1857-1930	Republican	Ohio	1909-1913
28	WOODROW WILSON	1856-1924	Democrat	Virginia	1913-1921
29	WARREN GAMALIEL HARDING	1865-1923	Republican	Ohio	1921-1923
30	CALVIN COOLIDGE	1872-1933	Republican	Vermont	1923-1929
31	HERBERT CLARK HOOVER	1874-1964	Republican	Iowa	1929-1933
32	FRANKLIN DELANO ROOSEVELT	1882-1945	Democrat	New York	1933-1945
33	HARRY S. TRUMAN	1884-1972	Democrat	Missouri	1945-1953
34	DWIGHT DAVID EISENHOWER	1890-1969	Republican	Texas	1953-1961
35	JOHN FITZGERALD KENNEDY	1917-1963	Democrat	Massachusetts	1961-1963
36	LYNDON BAINES JOHNSON	1908-1973	Democrat	Texas	1963-1969
37	RICHARD MILHOUS NIXON	1913-	Republican	California	1969-1974
38	GERALD RUDOLPH FORD	1913-	Republican	Nebraska	1974-1977
39	JAMES EARL CARTER, JR.	1924-	Democrat	Georgia	1977

ABBREVIATIONS COMMONLY USED IN WRITING AND PRINTING

A

A, argon.
a, in algebra, known quantity, constant.
A., Absolute; Academy; acre; America; American; angstrom unit; April; Artillery.
A., a., (L. *anno*) in the year; (L. *ante*) before.
a., about; acre(s); active; adjective; alto; ampere; anonymous; answer; are (in metric system).
A. A., Associate of Arts; antiaircraft; antiaircraft artillery.
A. A. A., Amateur Athletic Association; Automobile Association of America.
A.A.A.S., American Academy of Arts and Sciences; American Association for the Advancement of Science.
A. A. G., Assistant Adjutant General.
A.A.P.S.S., American Academy of Political and Social Sciences.
A.A.S., (L. *Academiæ Americanæ Socius*) Fellow of the American Academy.
A.A.S.S., (L. *Americanæ Antiquarianæ Societatis Socius*) Member of the American Antiquarian Society.
A.B., (L. *Artium Baccalaureus*) Bachelor of Arts: see *B.A.*
A.B., able-bodied seaman.
abbr., abbrev., abbreviated; abbreviation.
A.B.C.F.M., American Board of Commissioners for Foreign Missions.
A. B. F. M., American Board of Foreign Missions.
abl., ablative.
ABM, anti-ballistic missile.
abp., archbishop.
abr., abridged; abridgment.
abs., absol., absolute.
A. B. S., American Bible Society.
abt., about.
A. C., (L. *Ante Christum*) before Christ.
A. C., a.c., alternating current.
acc., accusative.
acc., acct., account; accountant.
A.C.S., American Chemical Society; American Colonization Society.
ACW, alternating continuous waves.
a. d., after date.
ad., advertisement.
A.D., (L. *Anno Domini*) in the year of our Lord.
A. D. C., Aide-de-camp.
ad inf., (L. *ad infinitum*) to infinity.
ad int., (L. *ad interim*) in the meantime.
adj., adjective.
Adj., Adjt., Adjutant.
ad lib., ad libit., (L. *ad libitum*) at pleasure.
ad loc., (L. *ad locum*) at the place.
adm., administrator.
Adm., Admiral; Admiralty.
Adm. Co., Admiralty Court.
adv., adverb.
Adv., Advent; Advocate.
ad val., (L. *ætatis*) according to the value.
æ., æt., (L. *ætatis*) of age; aged.
A. E. F., American Expeditionary Forces.
A. F., a. f., audio frequency.
Af., Africa; African.
A.F., Air Force; Anglo-French.
A.F.A.M., A.F. & A.M., Ancient Free and Accepted Masons.
A. F. B. S., American and Foreign Bible Society.
A. F. L., American Federation of Labor: also *A.F. of L.*
A.G., Adjutant General; Attorney General.
Ag., August.

ag., agriculture.
Ag, (L. *argentum*) silver.
A. G. O., Adjutant General's Office.
agr., agric., agriculture.
agt., agent.
A.H., (L. *Anno Hegiræ*) in the year of the Hegira.
a. h., ampere-hour.
A. H. C., Army Hospital Corps.
A. H. M. S., American Home Missionary Society.
A. H. S., (L. *Anno Humanæ Salutis*) in the year of human salvation.
A. I. A., Associate of the Institute of Actuaries.
A.I.C., American Institute of Chemists.
A.I.C.E., American Institute of Civil Engineers.
A.I.E.E., American Institute of Electrical Engineers.
A. I. M. E., American Institute of Mining Engineers; Associate of the Institute of Mechanical Engineers; Associate of the Institute of Mining Engineers.
AK, Alaska.
AL, Alabama.
A.L., American Legion.
al., (L. *alii*) other persons; (L. *alia*) other things.
Al, aluminum.
Ala., Alabama.
A. L. A., American Library Association.
Alas., Alaska.
Ald., Alderman.
Alex., Alexander.
Alf., Alfred.
alg., algebra.
alt., alternate; altitude; alto.
A. M., (L. *Anno Mundi*) in the year of the world; (L. *Artium Magister*) Master of Arts: also *M.A.*; Ave Maria.
A. M., a. m., (L. *ante meridiem*) before noon.
Am., America; American.
A.M.A., American Medical Association.
Amb., Ambassador.
Amb. Co., Ambulance Company.
A. M. D., Army Medical Department.
A.M.E., African Methodist Episcopal.
Amer., America; American.
A. M. I. C. E., Associate Member of the Institution of Civil Engineers (British).
amm., amalgama.
amp., amperage; ampere(s).
A. M. S., Army Medical Staff.
amt., amount.
A. N., Anglo-Norman.
An., (L. *anno*) in the year; anonymous.
anal., analysis.
anat., anatomical; anatomy.
A. N. C., Army Nurse Corps.
anc., ancient.
Angl., Anglican.
Ang.-Sax., Anglo-Saxon.
anon., anonymous.
ans., answer.
A. N. S. S., Associate of the Normal School of Science.
Ant., Antiq., antiquarian; antiquities.
anthrop., anthropological; anthropology.
A. O. C., Army Ordnance Corps.
A. O. D., Army Ordnance Department.
A. O. F., Ancient Order of Foresters.
A. O. H., Ancient Order of Hibernians.
aor., aorist.
A. O. U., American Ornithologists' Union.
A. O. U. W., Ancient Order of United Workmen.
Ap., Apostle; April.
A. P. A., American Protective Association.

A. P. C., Army Pay Corps.
A. P. D., Army Pay Department.
Apl., April.
A.P.O., APO, Army Post Office.
apo., apogee.
Apoc., Apocalypse; Apocrypha.
apog., apogee.
app., appendix.
approx., approximate; approximately.
Apr., April.
aq., aqua.
AR, Arkansas.
a. r., (L. *anno regni*) in the year of the reign.
A. R., Army Regulations; Autonomous Republic.
Ar., Arab., Arabic.
ar., arrival; arrive(s).
A. R. A., Associate of the Royal Academy.
Aram., Aramaic.
arch., architecture.
Archd., Archdeacon.
Archaeol., Archaeology.
Arg., Argentina.
A. R. H. A., Associate of the Royal Hibernian Academy.
A. R. I. B. A., Associate of the Royal Institute of British Architects.
arith., arithmetic; arithmetical.
Ariz., Arizona.
Ark., Arkansas.
Arm., Armenian; Armoric.
Armor., Armoric.
arr., arrival; arrive.
A. R. R., (L. *Anno Regni Regis* or *Reginæ*) in the year of the king's (or queen's) reign.
A. R. S. A., Associate of the Royal Scottish Academy.
A. R. S. L., Associate of the Royal Society of Literature.
art., article.
A.S., A.-S., Anglo-Saxon.
As, arsenic.
A.S.A., American Statistical Association.
A. S. C., Army Service Corps.
A. S. M. E., American Society of Mechanical Engineers.
ass., assistant; association; assorted.
A.S.S.R., Autonomous Soviet Socialist Republic.
asst., assistant.
A.S.S.U., American Sunday-School Union.
Assyr., Assyrian.
astrol., astrology.
astron., astronomical; astronomy.
at., atmosphere; atomic.
a.t., arch treasurer.
ats., at suit of.
A.T.S., American Tract Society; American Temperance Society.
A. T. S. Q. M. C., Army Transport Service Quartermaster Corps.
Att., Atty., Attorney.
Att. Gen., Atty. Gen., Attorney General.
at. wt., atomic weight.
A. U., angstrom unit; astronomical unit.
Au, (L. *aurum*) gold.
A. U. A., American Unitarian Association.
A. U. C., (L. *Anno Urbis Conditæ* or *Ab Urbe Condita*) in the year from the building of the city (Rome).
aug., augment; augmentative.
Aug., August.
Aust., Austria; Austria-Hungary; Austrian.
Austral., Australia; Australasia.
aux., auxil., auxiliary.
A. V., Artillery Volunteers; Authorized Version (of the Bible).
av., average; avoirdupois.
Av., Ave., Avenue.

A. V. C., American Veterans Committee.
A. V. D., Army Veterinary Department.
avdp., avoirdupois.
Av. Sec., Aviation Section.
Av. Sec. S. R. C., Aviation Section, Signal Reserve Corps.
avoir., avoirdupois.
a. w. l., absent with leave.
a. w. o. l., absent without official leave.
ax., axiom; axis.
AZ, Arizona.

B

B., Bible; British; Brotherhood; in chess, bishop; in medicine, bacillus.
B., b., bachelor; battery; bay; bicuspid; book; born; breadth; brother; in baseball, base; also, base hit; in music, bass; basso.
Ba, barium.
B. A., Bachelor of Arts; British Academy; British America.
B. A. F., British Air Force.
B. Ag., B. Agr., Bachelor of Agriculture.
bal., balance.
bank., banking.
Bap., Bapt., Baptist.
bar., barometer; barrel; barrister.
B. Ar., Bachelor of Architecture.
Barb., Barbados.
barr., barrister.
Bart., Baronet.
B. A. S., Bachelor of Agricultural Science; Bachelor of Applied Science.
bat., batt., battalion; battery.
B. B. A., Bachelor of Business Administration.
B. B. C., British Broadcasting Corporation.
bbl., barrel.—bbls., barrels.
B. B. S., Bachelor of Business Science.
B. C., Bachelor of Chemistry; Bachelor of Commerce; before Christ; British Columbia.
B. C., b. c., battery commander; bass clarinet.
bch., bunch.
B. Ch., (L. *Baccalaureus Chirurgiæ*) Bachelor of Surgery.
B. C. L., Bachelor of Civil Law.
B. D., Bachelor of Divinity.
bd., board; bond; bound; bundle.
bd. ft., board foot; board feet.
bdl., bundle.—bdls., bundles.
bds., boards; (bound in) boards; bundles.
Be, beryllium.
B. E., Bachelor of Education; Bachelor of Engineering; Bank of England; Board of Education.
B. E., B/E, b. e., bill of exchange.
B. E. F., British Expeditionary Forces.
Belg., Belgian; Belgic; Belgium.
bf., in printing, boldface.
B/F, in bookkeeping, brought forward.
B. F., Bachelor of Finance; Bachelor of Forestry.
B. F. A., Bachelor of Fine Arts.
bg., bag.—bgs., bags.
B. G., Brigadier General.
B. I., British India.
Bi, bismuth.
Bib., Bible; Biblical.
bibliog., bibliography.
biog., biographical; biography.
biol., biological; biology.
bk., bank; book.
bkts., baskets.
bl., bale; bales; barrel; barrels; black.
B/L, bill of lading.
B. L., Bachelor of Laws; Bachelor of Letters.

B. L. E., Brotherhood of Locomotive Engineers.
B. LL., (L. *Baccalaureus Legum*) Bachelor of Laws: see *LL.B.*
B. L. R., breech-loading rifle.
bls., bales; barrels.
B. M., (L. *Baccalaureus Medicinæ*) Bachelor of Medicine.
B. Mus., (L. *Baccalaureus Musicæ*) Bachelor of Music.
B/O, in bookkeeping, brought over.
b. o., back order; box office; branch office; broker's order; buyer's option.
Boh., Bohemia; Bohemian.
B. O. T., Board of Trade.
bot., botanical; botanist; botany; bottle.
B. O. U., British Ornithologists' Union.
bp., birthplace; bishop.
B. P., bills payable.
B. P. O. E., Benevolent and Protective Order of Elks.
Br, bromine.
Br., Breton; Britain; British.
br., branch; brig; bronze; brother.
Br. Am., British America.
B. R., bills receivable.
brev., brevet.
Brig., brigade; brigadier.
Brig.-Gen., Brigadier-General.
Brit., Britain; Britannia; British; Briton.
Brit. Mus., British Museum.
B. S., Bachelor of Science; Bachelor of Surgery.
b.s., bill of sale.
B.Sc., (L. *Baccalaureus Scientiæ*) Bachelor of Science.
B. S. L., Botanical Society, London.
Bt., Baronet.
B. T. U., British thermal unit.
bu., bushel.
bu., bur., bureau.
B. V., (L. *Beata Virgo*) Blessed Virgin.
B.V.M., (L. *Beata Virgo Maria*) Blessed Virgin Mary.
bvt., brevet; brevetted.
B. W. I., British West Indies.
bx., box(es).
Bz., benzene.

C

C, carbon.
C., c., capacity; carbon; case; cent(s); centigrade; centime; centimeter; century; chapter; chief; church; circa; copper; copy; copyright; corps; cost; cubic; hundredweight.
CA, California.
c., catcher; city; cloudy; center.
Ca, calcium.
ca., cathode; centiare(s); circa.
C. A., Central America; Coast Artillery; Confederate Army.
C. A., c. a., chief accountant; commercial agent; consular agent.
C/A, credit account; current account.
CAA, Civil Aeronautics Authority.
C. A. C., Coast Artillery Corps.
Cal., California; large calorie(s).
cal., calendar; caliber; small calorie(s).
Calif., California.
Can., Canada; Canadian.
Cant., Canticles (Song of Solomon).
cap., capital; (L. *capitulum*) chapter; captain.
Capt., Captain.
Car., carat(s).
C. A. R. C., Coast Artillery Reserve Corps.
Card., Cardinal.
carp., carpentry.
cat., catalogue; catechism.
Cath., cathedral; Catholic.
caus., causative.
cav., cavalry.

ANSWERS: Lesson 12 (pp. 334-361)

Learning Skills: Questions (pp. 334–338)

Practice A

1. b, c, d, f, g   2. b, e, f, g   3. d

Reading: Detecting Propaganda Techniques (pp. 338-341)

Practice A

1. Bandwagon   2. Testimonial   3. Name Calling   4. Card Stacking   5. Bandwagon   6. Glittering Generalities   7. Testimonial   8. Plain Folks   9. Card Stacking   10. Transfer   11. Glittering Generalities   12. Name Calling   13. Plain Folks   14. Transfer   15. Glittering Generalities

Vocabulary: Figures of Speech II (pp. 341–343)

Practice A

1. Oxymoron–Although it was a victory, it brought losses or other problems.   2. Hyperbole–The story is very old.   3. Oxymoron–It was so quiet that it very vividly came to everyone's attention.   4. Oxymoron–This refers to value. Something could be less in quantity but be worth more than something greater in quantity.   5. Hyperbole–Someone has been waiting for a very long time.   6. Oxymoron–Life can have many problems and difficulties.   7. Hyperbole–The person has a very large porch.   8. Oxymoron–It may be that persons do something not because they are very brave but because they are afraid of the consequences if they don't do it.   9. Oxymoron–Something can be so cold that it actually does burn the skin, e.g., dry ice.   10. Oxymoron–If it's quiet when there normally should be noise, the quietness can be frightening.

Word Analysis: The Dictionary III (pp. 344–353)

Practice A

The answer depends on the dictionary used: *Webster's New Twentieth Century Dictionary* (unabridged), about 23 general definitions; *Webster's Third New International Dictionary* (unabridged), about 20 general definitions, along with a great amount of information and detail for each specific meaning under the general definition (there are at least 50 more specific definitions given); *Webster's New Collegiate Dictionary* (abridged), about 16 general definitions; *The Random House Dictionary of the English Language* (college edition), about 22 general definitions but not very much detail about each.

Practice B

1. None. Cyclopes were a race of giants in Greek mythology. 2. The Himalayas are between India and Tibet. 3. No. He was the god of war. 4. No. It's the abbreviation for *Illinois*. 5. No. A biped is a two-footed animal. 6. No. A millipede is a wormlike arthropod with two pairs of legs on each of its segments. 7. No. Statute is an established rule or law. 8. No. Haiku is a Japanese poetic form. 9. No. A jack-in-the-pulpit is a flower. 10. No. It's a woman who writes poems.

Practice C

1. Sir: *or* Madam: 2. My dear Governor (surname): 3. Mr. President 4. Mr. Chief Justice 5. His (Her) Most Gracious Majesty, King (Queen) (name) 6. (a) American Chemical Society; American Colonization Society (b) (*Anno Domini*) in the year of our Lord (c) (*Artium Baccalaureus*) Bachelor of Arts; able-bodied seaman (d) British Broadcasting Corporation (e) American Medical Association (f) (*Anno Mundi*) in the year of the world; (*Artium Magister*) Master of Arts; Ave Maria; (*ante meridiem*) before noon (g) Autonomous Soviet Socialist Republic (h) Bachelor of Laws; Bachelor of Letters; (i) Calcium 7. South Carolina 8. 1945–1953 9. Andrew Johnson 10. 5th 11. 62 or 63 years old* 12. 57 or 58 years old* 13. Herbert Hoover 14. Republican 15. Federalist 16. 56 or 57 years old* 17. 2.54 centimeters 18. 1,609.3 meters 19. 5,280 feet 20. 8 quarts 21. 4 pecks 22. 4.83 kilometers 23. 1,728 cubic inches 24. 929 square centimeters 25. 640 acres

*Can't tell exactly because months aren't given.

CROSSWORD PUZZLE

Directions:

The meanings of a number of the words and some of the ideas from Lessons 10–12 follow. Your knowledge of these words and ideas will help you to solve this crossword puzzle.

Across

1. At the present time
4. Gives off water vapor
9. Same as #2 Down
10. A conjunction
12. A mental leaning
15. Systematic indoctrination
17. Abbreviation for *before noon*
19. To decorate or add beauty to
20. Homonym of *two*
21. What comes out of a volcano
23. One who throws things
25. Long snakelike fishes

Down

1. Antonym of *yes*
2. An exclamation
3. A speech sound or sounds plus meaning
5. "The Bill of Rights guarantees free speech. Join the Free Speakers Organization" is an example of what propaganda technique?
6. Lessen
7. Antonym of *major*
8. Antonym of *happy*
11. *Turn* and *play* are word ___

26. A bugle call
28. Abbreviation of *Falkland Islands*
30. Decay
31. Said at wedding ceremonies
32. Relating to the direct, specific meaning of a word
35. Abbreviation of *Receiving Officer*
36. Thick, sweet liquid
37. Abbreviation of *Central Intelligence Agency*
38. You do this to someone you ostracize
40. Fine sand carried by water
42. A very strong alkaline solution
44. Used to hold sails
45. Abbreviation of *Northern Ireland*
46. Ending for the past tense of regular verbs
47. Abbreviation of *audiovisual*
48. "As sharp as a nail" and "like a beautiful swan" are examples of ___
53. A precious stone
55. Author of "The Raven"
56. Anger
57. Very fat
58. What you need to know on a test

13. Homonym of *sail*
14. Famous Russian scientist who experimented with dogs and classical conditioning
15. An oxymoron is this
16. In favor of
18. Overcame something
22. Occurring in the air
24. A hollow cavity in your skull
26. Exhausted
27. Abbreviation of *Post Office*
29. "Plants and animals are living things" is a(n) ___
32. These are used to change colors
33. "Nature is beautiful" is an example of a(n) ___
34. Musical syllable
36. Persons in bondage are usually ___
39. A figure of speech helps give you a(n) ___ of something
41. Citrus fruits
43. Plural of *yes*
48. A resort
49. Homonym of *eye*
50. When you deceive someone you ___
51. To make an error
52. Perform
54. Pronoun

STOP. Check answers on the next page.

Crossword Puzzle Answers

¹N	²O	³W	■	⁴S	⁵T	E	⁶A	⁷M	⁸S				
⁹O	■	¹⁰O	¹¹R	■	R	■	¹²B	I	A	¹³S	■	¹⁴P	
■	¹⁵P	R	O	¹⁶P	A	G	A	N	D	A	■	¹⁷A	¹⁸M
¹⁹A	D	O	R	N	■	²⁰T	O	■	²¹L	²²A	V	A	
R	■	²³T	O	²⁴S	S	E	R	■	²⁵E	E	L	S	
²⁶T	²⁷A	P	S	²⁸F	I	■	²⁹F	³⁰R	O	T			
³¹I	D	O	■	³²D	E	³³N	O	³⁴T	A	T	I	V	E
³⁵R	O	■	³⁶S	Y	R	U	P	³⁷C	I	A	■	R	
³⁸E	X	³⁹I	L	E	■	⁴⁰S	⁴¹I	L	T	■	⁴²L	⁴³Y	E
D	■	⁴⁴M	A	S	T	⁴⁵N	I	■			⁴⁶E	D	
■	⁴⁷A	V	■	⁴⁸S	I	M	⁴⁹I	⁵⁰L	⁵¹E	S			
⁵²D	⁵³G	E	⁵⁴M	⁵⁵P	O	E	■	⁵⁶I	R	E			
⁵⁷O	B	E	S	E	■	⁵⁸A	N	S	W	E	R	S	

HOMOGRAPH RIDDLES

Directions:

Here are several ways to use a single word. Find the right word for each group. Example: I mean equal in standing to another; I also mean gaze, and I'm a nobleman. (peer)

1. I'm a person employed in manual labor; I'm the cards held by a player; I'm a round of applause; and I'm part of your body.

2. I'm packed firmly; I'm a formal agreement or contract; I'm designed to be small in size; and I'm a small case containing a mirror and face powder or rouge.

3. I keep you safe from harm or danger; I'm a device that prevents injury; I play positions in football and basketball.

4. I'm your usual way of doing things; I'm the duty you pay; and I'm specially made.

5. I mean to hold back or to hinder and to interfere with or curtail; and I'm also a large basket that holds things.

6. I'm a plant; I'm a tail of a deer; I'm used to signal or warn; I'm used to communicate by signaling; and I'm used as a symbol of a nation.

STOP. Check answers at the bottom of the page.

1. hand 2. compact 3. guard 4. custom 5. hamper 6. flag

TRUE/FALSE TEST

Directions:

This is a true/false test on Lessons 10–12 in Unit IV. Read each sentence carefully. Decide whether it is true or false. Put a T for *true* or an F for *false* in the blank.

_____ 1. The preface usually appears in the back of a book.

_____ 2. The glossary is a listing of many of the important terms in the book.

_____ 3. Connotative meanings influence us only negatively.

_____ 4. An appendix in a book is material that the author wants to separate for emphasis.

_____ 5. You should not question statements in a textbook made by authorities.

_____ 6. Editorials are more biased than newspaper articles.

_____ 7. A liberal magazine for men or women would be more biased on the topic of "open marriage" than a newspaper article.

_____ 8. People are influenced by different things.

_____ 9. A laboratory researcher is likely to be more objective than a textbook writer.

_____ 10. "Man is mortal" is a fact.

_____ 11. "Man is inhumane" is a fact.

_____ 12. "Man is an animal" is an opinion.

_____ 13. "Man is capable of reasoning" is a fact.

_____ 14. "Love is important" is an opinion.

_____ 15. Some terms can have both negative and positive connotations based on how they are used in a sentence.

_____ 16. *Brush* comes before *brute* in the dictionary.

_____ 17. If *never* and *night* are the guide words at the top of the dictionary page, *nine* appears on the page.

_____ 18. "You need to lose your mind to experience sanity" is an example of an oxymoron.

_____ 19. The term *like* or *as* is used in a simile.

_____ 20. Simile, metaphor, and personification are all comparisons.

_____ 21. "Her eyes are sparkling gems" is a metaphor.

_____ 22. "The fire laughed at our futile attempts" is an example of the use of personification.

_____ 23. In figures of speech the comparisons are always explicit.

_____ 24. Good question askers usually do better in school than non-question askers.

_____ 25. Asking questions is helpful to others as well as to yourself.

_____ 26. Bias is a mental leaning.

_____ 27. The bias an individual has will not influence him.

_____ 28. "Don't feel left out" is an example of "Testimonial."

_____ 29. In "Plain Folks" a famous person endorses a product.

_____ 30. "I'm so happy I could jump to the sky" is an example of hyperbole.

STOP. Check answers on the next page.

Answers to True/False Test

1. F 2. T 3. F 4. F 5. F 6. T 7. T 8. T 9. T 10. T 11. F
12. F 13. T 14. T 15. T 16. T 17. F 18. T 19. T 20. T 21. T
22. T 23. F 24. T 25. T 26. T 27. F 28. F 29. F 30. T

Unit V

LESSON **13**

Learning Skills*: Notetaking for Studying
Learning Skills: Test-taking
Vocabulary*: Combining Forms I
Reading: Analogies I
Answers

LEARNING SKILLS: NOTETAKING FOR STUDYING

1. Notetaking is a very helpful tool. It is useful not only in writing long papers but also in studying.

2. Notes consist of words and phrases that help you remember important material. They do not have to be complete sentences. However, unless your notes are clear and organized, you will have difficulty using them for study purposes. Examine this set of notes on an article entitled "Why Home Accidents Occur":

Student's Notes:

1. slippery floors
2. bathroom light switch
3. cellar stairs dark
4. ladder broken
5. medicines on shelf
6. light cord bare
7. pots on stove with handles out
8. throw rugs
9. using tools carelessly
10. toys on floor
11. box on stairs
12. putting penny in fuse box
13. thin curtains over stove

*In Unit V there are two sections on Learning Skills, and the Vocabulary section precedes the Reading section because the analogies use words from the Vocabulary section.

Student's List of Main Topics of Article:

I. Failure to see danger
II. Failure to use things correctly
III. Failure to make repairs

It is difficult to make sense of these notes because the main topics are vaguely stated. The items in the list of notes can fit under more than one main topic; they are not precise enough, i.e., they do not contain enough information to unmistakably identify or distinguish them.

3. Notetaking for study purposes can be incorporated in the SQ3R study technique. Here is a suggested procedure combining SQ3R and note-taking:

a. Read the whole selection to get an overview of what you have to study. A preliminary reading helps you to see the organization of the material.

b. Choose a part of the selection to study, basing your choice on your concentration ability. (See Unit II.)

c. Survey the part chosen and note the topic of the individual paragraph or group of paragraphs. Write the topic(s) in your notebook instead of the questions you would write in a normal SQ3R procedure.

d. Read the part.

e. After you finish reading each paragraph, state its main idea. Put down *only* important supporting details under the main idea.

(1) Although you do not have to use a formal outline for your notes, you should *indent* your listing so that the relation of supporting material to main ideas is clear. (See Appendix for types of outlines.)

(2) Try not to take any notes until after you have finished reading the whole paragraph. Remember, *recall* is the essential step in the SQ3R technique. By not taking notes until you have finished reading, you are more actively involved in thinking about the material as you try to construct notes.

4. Good notes are very helpful for review purposes, and they can save you a great amount of time. (See lessons on test-taking.)

Special Notes

1. For study purposes, if the material is new to you, it's usually a good idea to write the topic for each paragraph unless the paragraph is a transitional one (one that merely bridges a shift in content or point of view between two informative paragraphs).

2. Textbook writers sometimes list the topics of their paragraphs in the margins. Be on the lookout for these very helpful guides.

Here is an example of notetaking using the preceding section as the source:

I. Notetaking

    A. A helpful tool

        1. Writing
        2. Studying

    B. Notes must be clear and organized

        1. Whole sentences not needed
        2. Topics should be clearly distinguished

    C. Correlated with SQ3R

        1. Follow steps in SQ3R
        2. Note topics—not questions
        3. After reading, recall main idea
        4. Insert details under main idea

    D. Useful for review

From this example, you can readily see the four important ideas, namely, *notetaking is a helpful tool, notes should be clear and organized, notetaking is correlated with SQ3R,* and *notetaking is useful for review.*

5. Some students, instead of writing notes out, underline or mark important passages in their textbook. There are a number of problems associated with the habit of underlining:

    a. Some students automatically mark passages as they are reading and do not combine studying with notetaking.

    b. Some students tend to *overmark* the text. As a result, more important ideas are confused with lesser ideas.

c. Some students who mark books routinely while reading are lulled into a false sense of security by this habit and feel that they are studying when they are not.

d. Marking a book prevents students from putting the ideas into their own words and using the important process of recall. (Book marking involves no organization of material.)

e. An overmarked page is difficult to reread.

6. Although there are a number of problems with book marking, some students prefer this method to notetaking. If you are one of these students, here are some suggestions on how to make book marking more profitable for you:

a. Correlate your book marking with the SQ3R technique.

b. Survey the part you have chosen to study and mentally note the topic(s) only of the paragraph(s) or section.

c. Read the paragraph(s) or section. *Do not do any marking at this time.*

d. Using recall, state in your own words the main idea of the paragraph. Write it in the margin. Underline the topic and the most significant point made about the topic (often the conclusion) in the paragraph. Mark important supporting details. (Do not overmark. Be discriminating.) To avoid overmarking try to fix on key nouns, verbs, clauses, or phrases, rather than on sentences. In the margins put down "buzz words" to trigger your memory later on when you review.

Special Notes

1. It's probably a good idea to use the same color of pencil or felt marker pen throughout the book. However, you might want to use two pencils of different colors: one for main points and another for supporting details. Another helpful method in underlining material, is to use two lines for main points and one line for supporting details.

2. If the material is new to you, it's probably better to work with one paragraph at a time than with several.

Here is an example of marked paragraphs:

From *Physical Geography Today: A Portrait of A Planet* by Robert A. Muller and Theodore M. Oberlander, Random House, 1978.

Energy Transformations

Energy takes many different forms because it cannot be destroyed

You feel warm when you stand in the sunlight because <u>radiant energy from the sun</u> is being <u>converted to heat energy in your skin.</u> When <u>you run, you use stored chemical energy to produce energy of motion.</u> When you <u>go down a hill</u> on a <u>bicycle without pedaling,</u> you gain speed as your altitude decreases because your <u>gravitational energy is</u> being converted to energy of motion. The <u>principal reason that energy takes so many different forms is that it cannot be destroyed; it can only be converted from one form to another.</u>

Examples of energy conversion

Amount of energy in universe remains constant

Just as <u>energy</u> cannot be destroyed, <u>neither can it be created.</u> No matter how many energy transformations take place, the <u>total amount of energy in the universe remains constant.</u> The <u>electrical energy generated by a coal-burning power plant, for example, is gained</u> only at the <u>expense of the chemical energy in the expended fuel.</u> No way has ever been found to do useful work except by utilizing some form of energy, but the gain of one kind of energy is always accompanied by the loss of another kind.

Example

Energy degrades

Although <u>energy</u> is never created or destroyed, it is <u>frequently degraded into forms that cannot be used efficiently.</u> Imagine throwing a snowball at a wall. Your muscular energy gives the snowball energy of motion, but when the snowball hits the wall, it comes to a stop and loses this energy. Where does the energy go? Before the snowball strikes the wall, each of its atoms has the same average speed as that of the snowball. After it hits the wall, the atoms are jostled about. Their motion is transformed into a random, vibrating motion,

Examples

with each atom moving in a different direction. This random motion of atoms represents heat energy, and it has been gained at the expense of the snowball's energy of motion.

Practice A.

Use the combined notetaking-SQ3R method to study these two selections. Then, without looking back, answer questions on each selection.

1. From *We the People* by James I. Clark and Robert V. Remini, Glencoe Press, 1975, p. 46.

If Not a Noble, at Least an Esquire

In America hard work and thrift were surely necessary to clear a farm in the wilderness, to learn to make a pair of shoes while working as an apprentice, or to start a business. But given the virginity of the continent and the vast resources at hand, it is difficult to see how anyone could miss if he attended to those virtues. Despite possibilities for material gain, however, colonial society was hardly egalitarian. Those who came to America had, in their homelands, experienced some form of class system. This system, with certain exceptions, was transferred to the New World, and most colonials of the time approved of it. The class system was characterized by differences in wealth, of course, but also in dress, manners, occupations, and forms of address. Dirt farmers were generally referred to as yeomen or husbandmen, just as in England. They, as well as members of the lower class in villages and cities, were usually addressed as goodman, or goodwoman or goodwife. A man addressed as mister generally ranked on the next rung of the ladder, frequently in the artisan class. A person designated a gentleman was a man of means; a man with Esq. placed after his name occupied an even higher rank.

One difference between the American and the European systems was that no noble class developed in the English colonies. Another was that the American system was based not on birth, as in Europe, but on wealth. The system was, therefore, more fluid: in America a man could achieve a higher status than his father had enjoyed.

Among the early settlers of Virginia were a few sons of the nobility and members of the English classes. George Percy, for example, was the son of the Earl of Northumberland. Christopher Davidson, secretary of the colony during its early years, was the son of William Davidson, member of Parliament, Privy Councilor (adviser to the crown), and Queen Elizabeth's secretary. John Martin was the offspring of Richard Martin, who served twice as Lord Mayor of London. John Pory, ranked only as gentleman, was a Cambridge Master of Arts, a member of Parliament, and a geographer and historian.

Few middle- or highborn Englishmen remained in Virginia though. The aristocracy that developed there, and elsewhere in the South, was, for the most part, homegrown.

a. Notes:

Go on to answer questions before checking sample notes.

b. Answer these true/false questions. Put a T for *true* or an F for *false* in the blank.

_____ 1. Equality existed in colonial America.

_____ 2. In America, people generally had a chance to better themselves.

_____ 3. The English class system was condemned in America.

_____ 4. Birth was an important factor in the American system.

_____ 5. A gentleman in America was a man of means.

_____ 6. Esq. after a man's name was a title of high rank.

_____ 7. A few highborn Englishmen settled in Virginia.

_____ 8. Americans had experienced a class system in their homelands.

STOP. Check answers for parts (a) and (b) at the end of Lesson 13.

2. From *Physical Science* by Verne H. Booth and Mortimer L. Bloom, 3rd ed., Macmillan Publishing Co., Inc., 1972, pp. 75–76.

Vocabulary:

enigma—something hard to understand, a mystery

> Science without mathematics is impossible, for mathematics is the language of science. Mathematics expresses in a few symbols ideas, concepts, or laws that often require one or more paragraphs to state in words. This simplified representation and economy of thought, combined with the logic inherent in mathematics, is necessary for the comprehension of many natural phenomena. Physical science, first physics and astronomy, and later, chemistry, have long been mathematical, and geology is following in their footsteps, some branches far more rapidly than others. Biology, and even the social sciences, have also learned that some areas in their fields are better investigated by the use of mathematical tools.
>
> Mathematics, however, should not be thought of solely as a tool for the scientist. Hogben, in his book *Mathematics for the*

Millions, states that mathematics should be thought of as a language of size, in contrast to ordinary language of sort or kind. At the same time you should not allow the mention of mathematics as a tool of science to convince you that science must remain an enigma to you. In an elementary course the use of mathematics need not go beyond the use of simple arithmetic and the most elementary concepts of algebra and plane geometry, with perhaps some trigonometry. A clear understanding of ratios and proportions, and the use of the powers of 10 to express very small or very large numbers is absolutely necessary. It is assumed that you learned how to add, subtract, multiply, divide, and use decimals in elementary school. In fact, none of the mathematical techniques used in this text are above those taught in elementary school and the first two years of high school.

a. Notes:

Go on to answer questions before checking sample notes.

b. Answer these true/false questions. Put a T for *true* or an F for *false* in the blank.

_____ 1. Science is possible without mathematics.

_____ 2. Mathematics is useful only for the scientist.

_____ 3. Social sciences really can't use mathematics.

_____ 4. Mathematics tends to make things more complex.

_____ 5. Physical sciences were the first to use mathematics.

_____ 6. Mathematics is a language.

_____ 7. Mathematics is not necessary in order to understand natural occurrences.

_____ 8. Mathematics can be thought of as a language of size.

_____ 9. Mathematics is a tool.

_____ 10. Mathematics should not remain puzzling to the layman.

STOP. Check answers for parts (a) and (b) at the end of Lesson 13.

Practice B.

Read this selection and study it using a textbook-marking procedure. Without looking back at the selection, answer the questions.

1. From *Families: Developing Relationships* by Mollie Smart and Laura S. Smart, Macmillan Publishing Co., Inc., 1976, pp. 12–13.

     Polygamous. When one person has plural spouses at the same time, the marriage is polygamous. The most common form of polygamy is *polygyny*, in which a man has more than one wife. *Polyandry*, wherein a woman has more than one husband, is practiced by only a few societies. Polygamy, of course, makes for a family larger than the monogamous, conjugal nuclear family.

Common in Africa and the Middle East, polygyny most often occurs in places where the Islamic religion and culture dominate. The Bible records some polygynous families, such as Jacob's. Polygyny was practiced in pre-Communist China and by Hindus in India before 1957. In the United States, the Mormons used to be polygynous. There are still some polygynous families in North America. Even so, many North Americans have little understanding of polygyny; perhaps its being illegal makes it seem immoral. Probably the most common concept of a polygynous family is based on a visual image of an oasis, a harem, a handsome sheik, and a large number of beautiful young women in filmy, full trousers and floating veils. We ourselves admit to surprise and disappointment on first entering the harem (women's quarters) of a Muslim family in India. Secluded from the entrance and the rest of the house, it was an ordinary courtyard with ordinary rooms opening off it. The women's clothes were no different from those of women on the street, just everyday cotton saris. Rather than dancing and playing instruments, the women in the harem were preparing the next meal and taking care of the young children.

In polygynous families, wives are friends, sometimes sisters, often with close, affectionate feelings toward each other. The first wife is likely to have status and authority. Although there are sure to be some disagreements, clashes, or even jealousies when people live together, in the polygynous family there is nothing like the intense jealousy or sense of failure that many a North American wife feels when her husband takes a mistress. In a society where there is a great deal of housework to be done by women and where pregnancies are frequent, it may be much easier to share the wife's role with sisters and friends than for one woman to do it alone. There is also the matter of companionship. In polygynous and extended families, women enjoy talking while they work and knowing that a loved one is always there.

Among the polyandrous tribal people in the Himalayas, the ideal type of family consists of one woman with several husbands. Often the husbands are brothers. This custom occurs also in South India and among some Eskimo tribes. Where life is very hard and earning a living takes a great deal of effort, it may work out best to have several men supporting one woman and her children. Thus, the population is controlled, since one woman can bear only a certain number of children, no matter how many husbands she has. Female infanticide is often built into the poly-androus family system since the sex ratio will be upset if some women have plural husbands.

Go on to answer questions before checking sample marked page.

2. Answer these true/false questions. Put a T for *true* or an F for *false* in the blank.

_____ a. Polygamy is a form of marriage in which one person has many spouses in succession.

_____ b. Polygyny is a form of marriage in which one man has many wives at the same time.

_____ c. Polyandry is a form of marriage in which one woman has two or more husbands at the same time.

_____ d. Monogamy is practiced in the United States.

_____ e. Polygyny is practiced in Africa and the Middle East.

_____ f. The Mormons were polygamous in the United States.

_____ g. North Americans seem to understand polygamy.

_____ h. A harem is usually a very exotic-looking place.

_____ i. The women who share one husband do not have to do household chores.

_____ j. Women who share one husband do not usually resent one another.

_____ k. Polyandry is practiced in the Himalayas.

_____ l. Some Eskimo tribes practice polyandry.

_____ m. Polygynous marriages keep population numbers under control.

_____ n. Polyandry is practiced in places where life is difficult.

_____ o. The killing of some female infants may take place where polyandry is practiced.

STOP. Check answers for parts (1) and (2) at the end of Lesson 13.

LEARNING SKILLS: TEST-TAKING

The term *tests* seems to make most students shudder. However, tests are necessary to help you to learn about your weaknesses so that you can improve; they give you a steady and encouraging measure of your growth; and they are helpful for review.

As a student you have probably taken many tests. You know that the best way to do well on a test is to be *well prepared*. There are no shortcuts to studying. However, research has shown that people do better on tests if they know certain test-taking techniques and if they are familiar with the various types of tests.

Special Note

The lessons on tests and test-taking have been left for the last unit because all the material in the book up to this point is necessary for you to do well on tests.

General Test-taking Principles:

1. *Plan* to do well. Be prepared. Have a *positive* attitude. (See lessons on studying.)

2. Be *well rested*. (Don't stay up the whole night before a test.) Research has shown that sleep after studying, even a few hours, will help you to retain the information better.

Special Note

Cramming is not a good practice. It does not help you to retain information. It is justified only as a last, desperate resort. (See lessons on studying.)

3. Be prepared. The better prepared you are, the less nervous and anxious you are. (A small amount of tension is usually necessary to activate you to do your best.)

4. Look on tests as a learning experience. Plan to learn from them.

5. Look over the whole test before you begin. Notice the types of questions asked and the points allotted for each question. (Do not spend a long time on a one- to five-point question that you know a lot about. Answer it and go on.)

6. Know how much time is allotted for the test. Allot your time wisely. Remember to check the time.

7. Concentrate! (See Lesson 4.)

8. Read instructions *very* carefully. Do not read anything into them that is not there. If a question asks for a description and *examples*, do not forget to give the examples. If you do not understand something or if something does not make sense, ask the instructor about it. There may be an error on the test. Do not dwell on the point of confusion before you ask the instructor.

9. Begin with the questions you are sure of. This will give you a feeling of confidence and success. However, as already advised, do not dwell on these at length.

10. If you do not know an answer, make an intelligent guess. As long as you are not being penalized for wrong answers, i.e., as long as points are not being taken off for wrong answers, it pays to take a calculated guess. (Of course, if your guess is wrong, you do not get any points for it.)

11. After you answer the questions you are sure of, work on those that count the most, i.e., that are worth the greatest number of points.

12. Allow time to go over the test. Check that you have answered all the questions. Be leery about changing a response unless you have found a particular reason to while going over the test. For example, you may have misread the question, you may have misinterpreted the question, or you may not have realized that it was a "tricky" question. If the question is a straightforward one, it's probably better to leave your first response.

13. After the test has been graded and returned, go over it to learn from the results. Unless you find out why an answer is wrong and what the correct answer is, you may continue to make the same mistake on other tests.

14. Study the test after you learn the results to discover what your instructor emphasizes on tests. This will help you on subsequent tests.

VOCABULARY: COMBINING FORMS I

Combining forms are usually defined as "roots borrowed from another language that join together or that join with a prefix, a suffix, or both a prefix and a suffix to form a word in English." Combining forms in our language are often derived from Greek and Latin roots. Because the emphasis in this unit is on building vocabulary meanings—rather than on naming word parts—prefixes, suffixes, English roots, and combining forms from other languages will *all* be referred to as combining forms. *Combining form in this unit is defined as any word part that can join with another word or word part to form a word or a new word.*

Knowledge of the most common combining forms is valuable in helping you to learn the meaning of an unfamiliar word. For example, knowing that *a* means "without," *theo* means "god," and *ist* means "one who" helps you to unlock *atheist*, which means "one who does not believe in the existence of God."

As an indication of the power of knowing a few combining forms, it has been estimated that with the knowledge of thirty combining forms a person can unlock the meanings of as many as 14,000 words. Obviously, familiarity with a mere thirty forms is the quickest way to learning a large number of words. It's also a method that once learned helps you to unlock new words all through your life.*

Step I. Combining Forms

A. Directions:

Here is a list of combining forms with their meanings. Look at the combining forms and their meanings, and concentrate on learning each. Cover the meanings, read the combining forms, and state the meanings to yourself. Check to see if you are correct. Now cover the combining forms, read the meanings, and state the combining forms to yourself. Check to see if you are correct.

Combining Forms	*Meanings*
1. aut, auto	self
2. de	away, from, off, completely

*For more on combining forms, see Dorothy Rubin, *Gaining Word Power* (New York: Macmillan Publishing Co., Inc., 1978).

3. pro   before, forward

4. il, im, in, ir   not

5. mob, mot, mov   move

B. Directions:

Cover the preceding meanings. Write the meanings of the combining forms in the blanks.

Combining Forms	*Meanings*
1. aut, auto	_____
2. de	_____
3. pro	_____
4. il, im, in, ir	_____
5. mob, mot, mov	_____

Step II. Words Derived* from Combining Forms

1. *move v.* To change the place or position of; to persuade; to arouse or stir; in commerce, to dispose of goods by selling; to make progress; to advance. *n.* The act of moving; a change of residence; a step taken toward obtaining something. *John made a good move when he went back to school to finish his law degree because he now is a famous lawyer.*

2. *mobile adj.* Movable; not firm or stationary; easily influenced; changeable; in military usage, capable of being moved or transported; migratory. *n.* A piece of mobile sculpture. *People who live in mobile homes are probably those who like to move from one area of the country to another.*

3. *immobile adj.* Not movable; motionless. *During the holdup at the bank, everyone except the robbers was immobile.*

4. *motion n.* The act of moving; a gesture; a proposal; a suggestion; in law, an application to a court for a ruling, order, and so forth. *v.* To make movements or gestures with the hand, head, or any other part of the body; to give directions with the hand, head, and so forth. *At the meeting a motion was made to adjourn because there were not enough people present to transact any valid business.*

*Derived means "made up from."

5. *motor n.* An engine; anything that imparts motion; a source of mechanical power; automobile; a rotating machine that transforms electrical energy into mechanical energy. *adj.* Causing or imparting motion; of relating to or involving muscular movement; equipped with or driven by a motor. *v.* To travel by car. *When the mechanic told us that our car wouldn't run because we needed a new motor, we decided to get a new car.*

6. *automobile n.* A usually four-wheeled automotive vehicle designed for passenger transportation on streets and roadways; car. *v.* To ride in or drive an automobile. *An automobile is a necessity rather than a luxury in an area that does not have good public transportation.*

7. *automotive adj.* Self-propelling; relating to or concerned with vehicles or machines that propel themselves such as automobiles, trucks, airplanes, and motorboats. *No automotive vehicles such as cars and motorbikes are allowed on this resort island because the islanders want to prevent air and noise pollution.*

8. *emotion n.* A physical or social disturbance; turmoil in feeling; feeling; an expression of feeling. *When the doctors told him his mother was out of danger, his emotion was so great that he could only shake their hands in silence.*

9. *motive n.* Something within a person such as a need, an idea, or an emotion that stimulates him or her to an action; the consideration influencing a choice; cause; reason why. *The police said that the man had the opportunity and the means for the crime, but he did not seem to have a motive for it.*

10. *motivate v.* To stimulate; to move; to stimulate the active interest of a study through appeal to certain interests or by special devices; to make something interesting and appealing to students. *A number of bright students do not do well in school because they are not motivated to learn.*

11. *promotion n.* The act of being raised in position or rank; the act of setting up or furthering a business enterprise. *Some products are advertised by promotion designed to deceive rather than inform.*

12. *demotion n.* The act of reducing to a lower grade or rank. *Unless Mr. Brown accepted a demotion in his job, he would be asked to resign.*

13. *mobilize v.* To put into movement or circulation; to assemble and put into a state of readiness for active service in war. *The Mayor mobilized the standby riot police squads, even though the demonstration was peaceful.*

Special Note

Certain abbreviations are used to show what kind of word is being defined: *v.* for verb, *n.* for noun, *adj.* for adjective, *adv.* for adverb, and *prep.* for preposition.

Step III. Practice

Practice A.

Define the underlined word in each sentence.

1. Social promotion is advancing a student to the next grade based on age rather than on achievement.

   _____

2. Instructors can help to motivate students by making classes more interesting and by taking the needs and interests of students into account.

   _____

3. In the science fiction film the monster's deadly glance turned men into immobile statues.

   _____

4. Next semester I will move my belongings out of the dormitory and into an off-campus apartment.

   _____

5. Since I prefer to remain in one place rather than be mobile, I decided to turn down the traveling salesman job.

   _____

6. He works for the Ford Motor Company as an automotive engineer.

   _____

7. The doctor said that it's the motion of the ship that causes my seasickness.

   _____

8. When the crowd heard that their beloved leader had been assassinated, their emotion was so strong that they became hysterical with weeping.

   _____

9. Fred stupidly put leaded gas into the new lawnmower, and now the motor won't start.

_____

10. At rush hour thousands of drivers edge their automobiles onto one small piece of freeway and sit immobile until the jam clears.

_____

11. No one could understand her motive for leaving school because she seemed to be doing so well.

_____

12. After his demotion he became depressed and eventually he quit.

_____

13. Mobilize all reserve units for special duty.

_____

STOP. Check answers at the end of Lesson 13.

Practice B.

Match the meaning from column B with the word in column A.

	Column A	*Column B*
_____	1. mobile	a. act of being raised in rank
_____	2. move	b. concerned with self-propelled vehicles
_____	3. demotion	c. motionless
_____	4. promotion	d. act of moving
_____	5. motivate	e. assemble for active duty
_____	6. immobile	f. four-wheeled automotive vehicle
_____	7. motive	g. change the place of
_____	8. automotive	h. consideration influencing a choice
_____	9. automobile	i. act of reducing to a lower rank
_____	10. motion	j. feeling
_____	11. motor	k. movable
_____	12. emotion	l. stimulate
_____	13. mobilize	m. engine

STOP. Check answers at the end of Lesson 13.

Practice C.

Here are a number of sentences with missing words. Choose a word from the word list that *best* fits the sentence. Put the word in the blank.

Word List:

mobile, emotion, demotion, promotion, motivate, motive, automotive, automobile, motor, immobile, motion, move, mobilize.

1. Once the new styles come in, stores have a lot of difficulty trying to _____ their less fashionable merchandise.

2. The mass murderer had no_____for killing any of his victims.

3. After the plane crash, the survivors said that they had difficulty controlling their _____.

4. Most vehicles today are _____ ones.

5. I prefer a small_____because it gets better gas mileage.

6. At the meeting a student made a(n)_____that freshmen be allowed to keep cars on campus.

7. My sister and her husband could not find a house they liked, so they invested in a(n)_____ home on an attractive trailer site.

8. At the motel the television set was made _____ so that it could not be stolen.

9. An electric_____ powerful enough to move a car is a very simple piece of machinery; it's the weight of the batteries that makes an electric car impractical.

10. I bet you get a(n) _____ if you beat the Chairman of the Board at golf; he doesn't like to lose.

11. You'll find that it's not always the hardest worker who gets a(n) _____in this company.

12. I don't know what_____s her to behave the way that she does.

13. It was difficult to _____the troops in time for the major offensive.

STOP. Check answers at the end of Lesson 13.

READING: ANALOGIES I

Analogies have to do with relationships. They are relationships between words or ideas. In order to make the best use of analogies or to supply the missing term in an analogy proportion, you must know not only the *meanings* of the words but also the relationship of the words or ideas to one another. For example, "*doctor* is to *hospital* as *minister* is to_____." Yes, the answer is *church*. The relationship has to do with specialized persons and the places with which they are associated. Let's try another one: "*beautiful* is to *pretty* as_____is to *decimate*." Although you know the meanings of *beautiful* and *pretty* and you can figure out that beautiful is more than pretty, you will not be able to arrive at the correct word to complete the analogy if you do not know the meaning of *decimate*. *Decimate* means "to reduce by one tenth" or "to destroy a considerable part of." Because the word that completes the analogy must express the relationship of more or greater than, the answer could be *eradicate* or *annihilate*, because these words mean " to destroy completely."

Some of the relationships that words may have to one another are similar meanings, opposite meanings, classification, going from particular to general, going from general to particular, degree of intensity, specialized labels, characteristics, cause-effect, effect-cause, function, whole-part, ratio, and many more. The preceding relationships do not have to be memorized. You will gain clues to these from the pairs making up the analogies; that is, the words express the relationship. For example: "*pretty* is to *beautiful*"—the relationship is degree of intensity; "*hot* is to *cold*"—the relationship is one of opposites; "*car* is to *vehicle*"—the relationship is classification.

Practice A.

Find the word from the word list that *best* completes each analogy. There are more words in this list than you need. The symbol : means "is to" and the symbol : : means "as."

Example:

Happy is to sad as mobile is to immobile.

Happy : sad : : mobile : immobile.

Word List:

demotion, move, automobile, frigid, cool, hot, dense, solid, accessory, excellent, sew, seam, transport, adequate, warn, cryptic, swallow, mouth, blizzard, blow, bell, bite, impotent, diligent, powerful, help, slavery, automotive, motive, eat.

1. Juice : liquid :: meat : _____
2. Warm : hot :: cold : _____
3. Step : stroll :: stitch : _____
4. Spike : nail :: superior : _____
5. Ax : chop :: siren : _____
6. Rain : downpour :: snow : _____
7. Shovel : dig :: teeth : _____
8. Costume : disguise :: truck : _____
9. Fruit : apple :: vehicle : _____
10. Equivalent : equal :: potent : _____
11. Microscope : instrument :: scarf : _____
12. Content : satisfied :: bondage : _____
13. Thin : fat :: sparse : _____
14. Mobile : immobile :: promotion : _____
15. Toxic : poisonous :: secretive : _____

STOP. Check answers at the end of Lesson 13.

Practice B.

Find the word from the word list that *best* completes each analogy. There are more words in this list than you need.

Word List:

unyielding, knowledgeable, friendly, prune, verbose, brief, ocean, wily, competent, ball, ship, fruit, circle, nest, den, immobile, tennis, officer, navy, dome, point, ocean, concerned, paradox, movable, stationary, motivate, walnut, fish, delicate.

1. Bat : baseball :: racket : _____
2. Earth : mole :: water : _____

3. General : army :: admiral : _____

4. Pointed : pyramid :: rounded : _____

5. Grape : raisin :: plum : _____

6. Fidelity : faithfulness :: cunning : _____

7. Antonym : synonym :: mobile : _____

8. Prohibited : inhibited :: contradiction : _____

9. Rind : orange :: shell : _____

10. Abridged : expanded :: indifferent : _____

11. Affront : insult :: adamant : _____

12. Conceited : modest :: unqualified : _____

13. Sturdy : weak :: coarse : _____

14. Pessimist : optimist :: succinct : _____

15. Intricate : complex :: immobile : _____

STOP. Check answers at the end of Lesson 13.

Practice C.

Find the word from the word list that *best* completes each analogy. There are more words in this list than you need.

Word List:

goose, discord, barren, root, flower, bush, drake, imaginary, farm, sire, abhor, propelling, ewe, diligent, calm, story, tornado, syllable, blend, diphthong, discourse, argument, duckling, part, clutch, gear, immense, frog, love.

1. Chicken : rooster :: duck : _____

2. Caterpillar : butterfly :: tadpole : _____

3. Trunk : tree :: stem : _____

4. Wary : careful :: hate : _____

5. Fact : fiction :: lush : _____

6. Compact : sprawling :: harmony : _____

7. Whisper : shout :: garden : _____

8. Feign : pretend :: serene : _____

9. Persistence : perseverance :: mythical : _____

10. Pat : strike :: wind : _____

11. *Ea* : digraph :: *oi* : _____

12. Range : oven :: conversation : _____

13. Clutch : holding :: motor : _____

14. Fat : obese :: large : _____

15. Deny : admit :: lazy : _____

STOP. Check answers at the end of Lesson 13.

ANSWERS: Lesson 13 (pp. 362-388)

Learning Skills: Notetaking for Studying (pp. 362-373)

Practice A

1. a. (sample notes)

   I. The class system in colonial America

      A. Unequal class system existed
         1. Brought over from homeland with some exceptions
         2. Characterized by money, dress, manners, work, and forms of address

      B. Compared to European system
         1. No noble class in America
         2. In America—based on wealth, not birth
         3. Chance to improve self in America

      C. A few English noblemen settled early in Virginia
         1. Few noblemen however, remained in Virginia
         2. Virginia and elsewhere in the South developed their own aristocracy

   b. 1. F 2. T 3. F 4. F 5. T 6. T 7. T 8. T

2. a. (sample notes)

   I. Mathematics

      A. Mathematics is the language of science
         1. Simplifies expressing ideas
         2. Necessary to understand natural occurrences
         3. Physical sciences and chemistry have long been mathematical
         4. Some areas of biological and social sciences are using mathematics

      B. Mathematics is also a useful tool for simpler purposes
         1. It's a language of size (Hogben—*Mathematics for Millions*)
         2. Not something strange or puzzling
         3. Only simple mathematical concepts needed in an elementary science course

   b. 1. F 2. F 3. F 4. F 5. T 6. T 7. F 8. T 9. T 10. T

Practice B

1. (sample)

        Polygamous. <u>When one person has plural spouses at the same time, the marriage is polygamous.</u> The most common form of polygamy is *polygyny*, in which a man has <u>more than one wife</u>. *Polyandry*, wherein a <u>woman has more than one husband</u>, is practiced by only a few societies. Polygamy, of course, makes for a <u>family larger</u> than the monogamous, conjugal nuclear family.

        Common in <u>Africa</u> and the <u>Middle East</u>, <u>polygyny</u> most often occurs in places where the Islamic religion and culture dominate. The Bible records some polygynous families, such as Jacob's. Polygyny was practiced in <u>pre-Communist China</u> and by <u>Hindus in India</u> before 1957. In the United States, the <u>Mormons</u> used to be <u>polygynous</u>. There are still some polygynous families in North America. Even so, many North Americans have little understanding of polygyny; perhaps its being <u>illegal</u> makes it seem immoral. Probably the most common concept of a polygynous family is based on a visual image of an oasis, a harem, a handsome sheik, and a large number of beautiful young women in filmy, full trousers and floating veils. We ourselves admit to surprise and disappointment on first entering the harem (women's quarters) of a Muslim family in India. Secluded from the entrance and the rest of the house, it was an ordinary courtyard with ordinary rooms opening off it. The women's clothes were no different from those of women on the street, just everyday cotton saris. Rather than dancing and playing instruments, the <u>women in the harem</u> were <u>preparing the next meal</u> and <u>taking care of the young children.</u>

        In <u>polygynous families</u>, <u>wives are friends</u>, sometimes sisters, often with close, affectionate feelings toward each other. The first wife is likely to have status and authority. Although there are sure to be some disagreements, clashes, or even jealousies when people live together, in the polygynous family there is nothing like the intense jealousy or sense of failure that many a North American wife feels when her husband takes a mistress. In a society where there is a great deal of housework to be done by women and where pregnancies are frequent, it may be much easier to share the wife's role with sisters and friends than for one woman to do it alone. There is also the matter of companionship. In polygynous and extended families, women enjoy talking while they work and knowing that a loved one is always there.

        Among the <u>polyandrous</u> tribal people in the <u>Himalayas</u>, the ideal type of family consists of <u>one woman with several husbands</u>. Often the <u>husbands are brothers</u>. This custom occurs also in

South India and among some Eskimo tribes. Where life is very hard and earning a living takes a great deal of effort, it may work out best to have several men supporting one woman and her children. Thus, the population is controlled, since one woman can bear only a certain number of children, no matter how many husbands she has. Female infanticide is often built into the polyandrous family system since the sex ratio will be upset if some women have plural husbands.

2. a. F b. T c. T d. T e. T f. T g. F h. F i. F j. T k. T l. T m. F n. T o. T

Vocabulary: Combining Forms I (pp. 376–381)

Practice A

1. act of being raised in rank 2. stimulate 3. motionless 4. change the place of 5. migratory, moving from one place to another 6. concerned with self-propelled vehicles 7. act of moving 8. feeling 9. engine 10. four-wheeled automotive vehicles 11. consideration influencing a choice 12. act of reducing to a lower rank 13. assemble for active duty

Practice B

1. k 2. g 3. i 4. a 5. l 6. c 7. h 8. b 9. f 10. d 11. m 12. j 13. e

Practice C

1. move 2. motive 3. emotion 4. automotive 5. automobile 6. motion 7. mobile 8. immobile 9. motor 10. demotion 11. promotion 12. motivate 13. mobilize

Reading: Analogies I (pp. 382–385)

Practice A

1. solid 2. frigid 3. seam 4. adequate 5. warn 6. blizzard 7. bite 8. transport 9. automobile 10. powerful 11. accessory 12. slavery 13. dense 14. demotion 15. cryptic

Practice B

1. tennis 2. fish 3. navy 4. dome 5. prune 6. wily 7. immobile 8. paradox 9. walnut 10. concerned 11. unyielding 12. competent 13. delicate 14. verbose 15. stationary

Practice C

1. drake 2. frog 3. flower 4. abhor 5. barren 6. discord 7. farm 8. calm 9. imaginary 10. tornado 11. diphthong 12. discourse 13. propelling 14. immense 15. diligent

LESSON 14

Learning Skills: Notetaking (Lectures)
Learning Skills: Objective Tests
Vocabulary: Combining Forms II
Reading: Analogies II
Answers

LEARNING SKILLS: NOTETAKING (Lectures)

1. Notetaking while listening to a lecture is an important skill to master. The difference between just passing and doing well on an exam may be the lecture notes that you took. Many professors present material in their lectures that simplifies, clarifies, and otherwise highlights the key points of the information presented in textbooks. Obviously, it is helpful to have well-organized notes on these lectures. Even if a professor's lectures do not appear to be organized or related to the material in the textbook, the fact that something is presented in a lecture means that the professor thinks it is noteworthy. The professor may include some question(s) on the lecture material in an exam. (See lessons on test-taking.)

2. Taking notes while listening to someone talk is certainly more difficult than taking notes while reading a textbook. While reading you can go back and reread something if you need to; during a lecture you can't go back. Because of this, some students tape lectures. This is actually faulty economy of time and effort. If you tape the lecture, you still have to listen to it and then take notes on it. Also, if you take notes during the lecture, you are more actively involved because you have to concentrate. Learning to take good notes is better than taping the lecture.

3. Although no single lecture-notetaking technique is best for every student, a number of basic principles apply to everyone:

a. Come to a lecture prepared to learn something, that is, come with a positive attitude.

b. Come to a lecture well rested and well fed.

c. Sit in a seat where you can *see* as well as *hear* the lecturer. The speaker's facial gestures and body movements help give meaning to what he or she is saying. Try to sit as close to the front as possible. Make sure that you can see the chalkboard. Try not to sit near students who distract you. Avoid sitting near a door or window.

d. Come prepared with notepaper and pencils or pens.

   (1) A looseleaf notebook is better than a notepad because the pages are usually larger. You can easily take notes out and reorder them or insert other materials. (When you take a page out of a notepad, the whole business may fall apart.) However, the notepad is more convenient for taking notes in a large lecture hall where the seats have small armrests. It is also easier to carry. Therefore, whether you use a looseleaf notebook or a notepad is a matter of personal preference.

   (2) An inexpensive mechanical pencil is superior to a regular wooden pencil, if you use a pencil, because it always has a sharpened point.

4. The lecturer will usually give you a number of helpful clues. Here are some things to listen or look for during a lecture:

a. Emphasis announced with the words "This is a key point," "This is very important," "This is vital information," and so on. Write these points down and underline them.

b. Emphasis implied by time spent on a subject. Obviously the speaker feels something is important if he dwells on it. Underline or box your notes on the topic explained at length.

c. Announcements that you need *not* take notes. Perhaps the topic is a digression, a sideline of discussion; perhaps the lecturer knows that the matter is covered thoroughly in your text. Don't tire yourself with needless recording of a lecture.

d. Outlines of the lecture written up on the chalkboard. Copy them and leave room to insert additional points that arise in the lecture.

e. Guides in the form of main ideas listed on the chalkboard. (Sometimes only the main topic of the lecture is given.)

f. Handouts containing points to be covered in the lecture. (Be sure to insert these in your notebook. They aren't supplied for you to doodle on.)

5. The professor's quizzes give you vital information, especially the first quiz. You should use the quiz as a learning experience. From it you can find out what the professor feels is important. After a quiz you should go

over your lecture and text notes to compare them with what was on the quiz. (See lessons on test-taking.)

6. Ask questions. This is essential in helping you to understand something better. Don't hesitate to ask a question if you haven't understood a point. Asking a question slows down the professor, gives you a chance to catch up, and gives the professor some clue as to whether he is getting his material across to the students. (See lesson 12 for more on questioning as a learning technique.)

7. Before a lecture, *review* your notes from the previous lecture to set up continuity between the old and new material. In reviewing your notes, look at the "buzz" words (see item 8) and try to *recall* the key ideas presented in the last lecture.

8. The notes that you take during a lecture must make sense to you when you read them later, and they should be organized. You do not have to use a formal outline, nor do you have to write in sentences.

Here are some suggestions on the technique of taking notes during a lecture:

a. Do not attempt to write every word the instructor says. Use "buzz" words and "telegraphic writing" instead. "Buzz" words (words that sound a buzzer in the mind) are any words that take on particular importance in the discussion of a topic. Often they are technical terms or words used in a special way to explain or define a professional or academic subject. The great virtue of buzz words is that they are reminders of a wide range of facts, associations, and concepts in very small packages. Advertisers find them invaluable for getting ideas across in a few words. Think how the word *dentifrice* conjures up thoughts of clinical thoroughness, degrees in dentistry, professionalism, scientific exactitude. The common equivalent *toothpaste* just sounds like the last thing you'd want to put in your mouth. But all buzz words are not phony inflations of the commonplace. *Skinnerian* is the word for a particular psychological learning theory. It derives from the name *Skinner*, the man who pioneered in a certain kind of research on conditioning the mind and behavior, and who helped to develop programmed learning. *Skinnerian*, therefore, is a useful buzz word that recalls a sizable library of specialized knowledge. Listen for the buzz words in the subject at hand. You can usually spot them because they are unfamiliar and crop up often. Be sure you note them and learn what they stand for. "Telegraphic writing" involves the use of one or two words to recall a complete message. The words that are used are content words, that is, words that contain significant information. Economy of writing is important in taking lecture notes, but the notes should not be so bareboned that you have difficulty remembering what you "meant" to say. (Example of this paragraph reduced to telegraphic writing: Use buzz words; use telegraphic writing; Buzz words— words used in special way—recall sizable amount of knowledge; Telegraphic writing—one or two significant words—recall lecture.)

b. Concentrate on making generalizations (statements or conclusions based on an accumulation of specific data); to do this, you must be actively thinking. Indent important details under your generalizations. Leave some lines blank under each idea in case the speaker returns to an idea to emphasize or embellish it. Good notetakers space out notes so that they can add material if necessary.

c. It's sometimes a good practice to divide your page in half. Put your generalizations and supporting details on the right-hand (or left-hand) side; put the buzz words, comments, dates, questions (to ask when you can), and names on the other—as closely parallel as you can with the generalizations they refer to. If the professor provides an outline of the lecture on the chalkboard, do not immediately copy the whole outline and then try to "squeeze" in the lecture. It's better to write the professor's main topics and subtopics one at a time as the professor comes to them and then fill in the details. You can still divide your paper with your outline on one side and your buzz words, comments, dates, and so on, on the other. Remember to use the professor's clues in your notes. These help you know what to emphasize when studying for a test.

9. After a lecture, go over your notes to see if they make sense to you. If anything is confusing to you, don't hesitate to ask the professor to clarify a point for you.

Special Note

It's a good idea to date your notes. If you go over them and find that something is confusing, it is helpful to have a reference point for the notes. That way it's easier for another student or the professor to help you.

Here is an example of lecture notes:

Jan. 15

Few absolutes in mythology, if any
    What the word "Myth" means: (Greeks have other meanings)

Many diff. meanings of myth:

Mythology—body of myths or collection of all myths of God; mythology of God; collection;(no complete def., cuz very pervasive)

Mythology—"other people's religion" myths—used to mean a lie, untruths, but not simply untruths, fables, stories, etc. myths aren't really true or untrue for people who tell them

Myths used to structure reality:

Myths can be valid or invalid, in sense that interpret experience — genuine myths are narratives which tend to provide structure or order; every man's order is not the same, but each has some system of order

Myths—explain how world came into being, provide structure

If can't provide something, categorize it as "myth" examples: 1. botany/zoology structure of classifying plants and animals; 2. the idea that you can look at world objectively—myth cause can't prove

10. You should not expect to find someone else's notes helpful if you did not attend the lecture. The sample lecture notes are composed mostly of generalizations. When you read them, if you attended the lecture, they should bring forth a great amount of other information.

Practice A.

For this practice, you will need a partner. 1. Have your partner read the following excerpt of a lecture aloud to you. While your partner is reading, take notes on it. After you have taken notes on the lecture, read the lecture aloud to your partner and have him or her take notes on it. 2. Both of you should then turn the text of the lecture down, review your own notes and take the true/false test at the end of the excerpt. (Note that the person reading the lecture aloud first has a special advantage because he or she is exposed to the lecture twice.)

Lecture on "Bibliotherapy: Reading Toward Better Mental Health" by Dorothy Rubin.

Bibliotherapy is the use of books to help individuals to cope better with their problems and emotions. In its most extreme form it has been used with mentally ill patients for therapeutic purposes. Although there hasn't been much experimental research on the effects of bibliotherapy with the mentally ill, Menninger in 1937 wrote:

The whole matter of bibliotherapy, of the relief of suffering by the psychological processes induced by reading, is a field in which we have little scientific knowledge. But our intuition and our experience tell us that books may indeed minister to a mind diseased and come to the aid of the doctor and even precede him.

In its less extreme form, bibliotherapy is used to help individuals overcome or adjust to some specific problem. In this lecture, we are concerned with the aspects of bibliotherapy in its less extreme form in the elementary classroom.

Since in this lecture *bibliotherapy* is defined as the use of books to help individuals to cope better with their problems and emotions, the term *cope* should be defined. Coping is dealing with problems by acknowledging reality, it is, therefore, behaving in a positive manner.

The terms *catharsis, identification*, and *insight* have been used by psychoanalysts and psychologists to explain the process of bibliotherapy. Catharsis, which refers to "an emotional cleansing experience," is too clinical a process for the regular classroom teacher to handle. Therefore, in this lecture the notion of *empathy*, which is a coping mechanism, and one with which the classroom teacher can deal, is being substituted for *catharsis*. Empathy refers to an individual's being able to project himself into the personality or skin of another and know how that person feels. Unless the individual has experienced what someone else feels, either first hand, or vicariously (through books) he or she cannot empathize with that person.

In the process of bibliotherapy, the important first step is to *identify* with a character in a story. The next step is to *empathize* or to get inside the character's "skin." Then, how, the storybook character deals with his/her problems and handles his/her emotions can help the reader to gain insights into how to adjust or deal with his/her own real-life problems.

Bibliotherapy can be used in both preventive and ameliorative ways. That is, some individuals, through reading specific books may learn how to handle certain situations before they have taken place. Other persons may be helped through books to overcome some common developmental problem they are experiencing at the time. For whatever purpose bibliotherapy is used, it will only be of value if teachers are knowledgeable of how to use bibliotherapy in their classrooms.

In order to use bibliotherapy effectively in the classroom, teachers should know about children's needs, their interests, their readiness levels and their developmental stages. In the area of needs, teachers should recognize that all children have such needs as the need to belong, the need for affection, the need to achieve, the need to be relatively free from guilt, the need to be free from fear, and so on. Teachers should know about their students' varied interests and ability levels. Teachers should be aware that children throughout the grades have different developmental characteristics. For example, on the average, early elementary grade level children have a shorter attention span than middle elementary grade level children. Early elementary children seek approval from adults, whereas for middle elementary level children, peer group acceptance is becoming increasingly important. Also, differences in interests of boys and girls are not as evident in early elementary children as in middle elementary children. We need to remember these differences.

The kinds of problems that lend themselves to bibliotherapy are varied. For example, being the smallest boy in the class can be devastating to a child. Being an only child may cause difficulty for some children. A new baby may bring adjustment problems for some and going to the hospital may be a frightening event for others. Moving to a new neighborhood or the simple dislike of a name can cause problems for a number of children. Divorce of parents causes great anxieties on the part of children and just growing up can be confusing. These are just a few of the problems suitable for bibliotherapy.

By reading books that deal with themes such as those stated, children can be helped to cope better with their emotions and problems. Perceptive teachers sensitive to their children's needs can help them by providing the books that deal with the same problems that their children have. However, since teachers are not clinicians, children who are having serious adjustment problems should be referred for help to the guidance counselor or school psychologist. Also, teachers must be careful not to give a child who is anxious about a situation a book that would increase his/her anxiety. A teacher should also not single out a child in front of the class and give him/her a book which very obviously points out that child's defects. It would probably embarrass the child and upset him/her more.

1. Notes on lecture:

2. Answer these true/false questions. Put a T for *true* or an F for *false* in the blank.

_____ a. Bibliotherapy can be used only to help the mentally ill.

_____ b. "Empathy" is a coping mechanism.

_____ c. Bibliotherapy helps a child to deal better with other people's problems.

_____ d. Bibliotherapy is not useful if a problem does not already exist.

_____ e. The use of bibliotherapy does not require much knowledge by the teacher.

_____ f. Children usually have different developmental characteristics at different ages.

_____ g. For bibliotherapy, children's differences are not very important.

_____ h. A teacher should refer a seriously maladjusted child for help.

_____ i. Some books may make children more anxious.

_____ j. The use of bibliotherapy in the classroom requires perceptive teachers.

STOP. Check answers at the end of Lesson 14.

Practice B.

Reread the lecture "Bibliotherapy: Reading Toward Better Mental Health" and then write a short summary of it.

Summary:

STOP. Check sample summary at the end of Lesson 14.

LEARNING SKILLS: OBJECTIVE TESTS

An objective test is any test involving short answers, usually one or two words. Among the variety of objective test questions are true/false, multiple choice, matching items, completion or fill-in, and short answers. As there is only one correct answer for a given question, objective tests are, on the whole, easier to take and easier to grade. They can cover a good deal of subject knowledge but not in the depth a subjective test permits. One system of study preparation is appropriate for objective tests and another for subjective tests.

Because an objective test is comprehensive and aimed at discovering powers of *recognition* and *recall*, you must prepare for it by concentrating on details. Review important definitions, principles, concepts, formulas, names, dates, and terms that relate to the material to be covered on the test. *As you go over the details, be sure to review their relation to the whole.* Unless you know your facts and how they relate to the general content of the subject, you will find any examination difficult, if not bewildering.

1. Studying for objective tests.

a. True/false, multiple choice, and matching tests call for *recognition.* Fill-in or completion tests call for *recall*. Recall tests are usually more difficult than recognition tests because you have to produce the answer from memory. Recognition tests are usually easier because you have answers from which to choose. However, research has shown that students who do best on recognition tests also do best on recall tests. Presumably, those who know how to distinguish between items in a list also know the material thoroughly enough by memory to recall the right choices.

b. Although objective tests deal with recognition and recall, test questions can be devised to look for such things as your ability to think critically, to solve new problems, to apply principles, and to select relevant facts. You need a *fund of knowledge* and *reasoning ability*. If you have the reasoning ability but no fund of knowledge, you either have not studied the material or have not approached your studying from the right angle; you will probably not do well.

c. Research has shown that you *remember* generalizations longer than material memorized by rote with no attempt to make associations.

d. Research has indicated that people forget information mainly because in learning new information they put the old mentally to one side. If you *overlearn* the old material, learn the new material *and its relation to the old*, and continue to use the old as you work with the new, you are less likely to confuse the old with the new or forget the old altogether.

e. Overlearning (continuing of practice after you feel you know the material) the basic information in a field is essential. For example, in some subjects certain definitions, formulas, axioms, or concepts that are often used are worth overlearning.

f. Studying for generalizations does not mean that you should not memorize certain definitions, formulas, principles, and so on. The key thing is to understand how to use the material you memorize and to see its relationship to the whole.

g. The following steps are helpful in memorizing material:

(1) Read through the whole passage you wish to memorize. It's important to see the relationship of the parts to the whole and to make associations.

(2) If it's a long selection, break it up into manageable parts and memorize each part, but always remember to relate the part to its whole.

(3) As you learn a new part, go back over the old part and relate it to the new.

(4) Go over the whole selection a number of times. Remember, to *overlearn* something means that you practice it beyond the point of feeling you know it. Remember also, distribute your practice over a period of time. (See lessons on studying.)

(5) Use mnemonic devices. A mnemonic device is a memory association trick that helps you to recall material. For example: *HOMES* is a mnemonic device to help you to remember the five Great Lakes. Each letter of *HOMES* is the first letter of one of the Great Lakes— Huron, Ontario, Michigan, Erie, and Superior. But don't use a mnemonic device that's more complicated than the fact to be remembered. "Thirty days hath September, April, June, and November" is adequate. Who knows all of this?

> Thirty days hath September,
> April, June, and November;
> All the rest have thirty-one,
> Excepting February alone,
> and that has twenty-eight days clear
> and twenty-nine in each leap year

And who needs it? (Remember, the best way to commit information to memory is to learn generalizations and to look for relationships within the material you are studying.)

2. True/false tests.

a. Do not leave a true/false question unanswered. You have a 50 per cent chance of getting the answer correct just by guessing. (You are penalized for wrong answers on some standardized tests. See Lesson 13.)

b. *Always* read carefully any true/false question that says *always, never, all, none, impossible, nothing,* and so on. These are usually giveaways that the answer is false. Almost every rule has exceptions. Of course, there are times when inclusive categories such as *all, no, always* or *never* are accurate. Examples: All men are animals. (T); No man is without vertebra. (T); Children always learn to speak. (F); All people who study do well on exams. (F); All true/false tests are objective. (T); All children need ten hours of sleep. (F). Notice that when the answer is true for such categories as *all, no. always* or *never* the statement is usually a definition or a rule.

c. Rather than use giveaways such as *always* or *never,* professors usually make true/false questions more difficult by stating only part of a definition or by inserting something incorrect in a definition; that is, part of an accurate definition is given but the other part is left out or misstated. Obviously, you should be *well prepared* on details such as definitions for true/false tests. You should be very alert. Examples: (1) Language is defined as a shared, learned system used for all communication. (True or *False*) (Although what is said is correct, the statement is not *complete* enough to be marked true. The complete definition is *Language is a learned, shared, and patterned, arbitrary system of vocal sound symbols with which people in a given culture can communicate with one another.* (2) An amoeba is a single-celled plant. (True or *False*) (An amoeba is single-celled, but it is an animal not a plant.)

d. Statements that use words such as *sometimes, often, usually, many, generally, frequently, as a rule, some,* and so on are usually true. Examples: Usually children learn to speak. (*True* or False) As a rule, small children need ten hours of sleep. (*True* or False)

Special Note

Make your T's and F's very clear. It may be a good idea to write out *true* or *false* so that there is no question of misinterpretation. If the T or F is not clear, the instructor may mark it wrong.

3. Matching items tests.

a. In a matching items test you must usually match the items in one column with the items in another. Professors commonly use this kind of test to match the following elements: words with their meanings; dates with historical events; persons with their achievements; authors with their books; rules with their examples; and so on. Throughout this book in the Vocabulary sections you have had examples of matching items.

b. If the professor uses a variety of material on the same matching test, you have a better chance of doing well. For example, if authors are matched with titles of books, wars or major events with dates, terms with definitions, and rules with examples on the same matching test, your choices are more limited.

c. It is often useful to use the process of elimination to help you solve difficult matches. That is, once you have completed all matches you are certain of, you will have a much smaller list to choose from.

4. Multiple choice tests.

a. Multiple choice tests are not as easy to guess on as true/false tests are. But even on a multiple choice test if you have only four answers from which to choose for each question, you have a 25 per cent chance of being correct by guessing. Therefore, attempt to answer each question.

b. When taking a multiple choice test, read the statement or question and then before reading the choices think for a moment about what you feel the answer should be. Read the choices carefully to determine if one matches.

c. Read the complete or incomplete question or statement to be answered very carefully. If a negative is contained in the question or statements, note it. It may help to mentally check off each item in the positive. Example: Which of the following is *not* an example of a vowel digraph?

(1) ea   (2) ie   (3) oa   <u>(4)</u> oy

In your mind you could very quickly say the following: *ea* is a digraph; *ie* is a digraph; *oa* is a digraph; therefore, *oy* has to be the answer. Here are examples of syllabicated nonsense words. Choose the one that is *correctly* syllabicated:

(1) bloa/me/te   (2) cr/oy   <u>(3)</u> rein/tle   (4) plom/ant

In this example three are incorrect and only one is correct. Although you feel that you know your syllabication rules, and you come to the correctly syllabicated word quickly, take a moment to look at the others to make sure that you do indeed have the correct answer.

d. Look for professor's clues in multiple choice tests. Here are some give-aways: (1) a choice that is much longer and more detailed than the others is usually the correct answer; (2) a word in a choice that also appears in the statement or question usually implies that that choice is the correct answer; (3) ridiculous choices among the items allow you to arrive at the answer by elimination (usually, you can easily eliminate two items, but then you are left with a choice between the two remaining items); (4) a special part of speech required in the answer will identify the correct choice. Example: The definition of *optimist* is: (a) cheerful (b) looking at the bright side (c) one who looks at the bright side of things (d) being cheerful. The answer must be (c) because *optimist* is a noun.

5. Fill-in or completion tests.

a. The fill-in or completion test is one in which you receive a statement that omits a key word or phrase. You must produce from memory the missing item. Example: The sixteenth President was _____.

b. The fill-in or completion test is one in which you must *recall* the correct answer. Recall items, like recognition items, can test either for simple facts or for more complex understandings. For such a test, you should concentrate on details, but you should understand how the details are organized, that is, how they are related to what you are studying. Memorizing isolated details will not help you to retain the information or help you to understand it.

c. Sometimes the professor intentionally or unintentionally gives you grammatical clues. Be on the lookout for these. Examples: A person of high birth is called *an* _____ . A man who has many wives is called *a*_____ . (Here the indefinite article *an* is a clue that the answer begins with a vowel and the indefinite article *a* is a clue that the answer begins with a consonant.) Example: The authors of the paper describing the first transistor were _____. (Here the plural noun and verb tell you that the answer must be in the plural; that is, there is more than one author involved.)

6. Short answer tests.

The short answer test is very similar to the completion or fill-in test. It is similarly based on recall, and the correct answer is usually a word or phrase. However, in the short answer test a question or a simple statement is used rather than a statement with a blank for a missing word or phrase. Examples: Name the sixteenth President of the United States. What is the capital of California.

Special Notes

1. If you feel that a recall or recognition test item can be answered by more than one answer, bring this to the attention of your professor. It may be that the test question was incorrectly written. If the professor tells you that the question *is* correctly written, try to choose the best answer. However, you might write a note in the margin of your paper (if there is time) explaining why you think it could be the other answer, also. Then when you go over the test in class, bring this question up, or discuss this point after the exam with the professor.

2. Although an objective test question is usually supposed to have only one answer, it's possible that there may be more.

3. Completion and short answer tests lend themselves to more subjectivity than the other types of objective tests because students' recall responses may be worded in many different ways. The professor must interpret whether the response is the desired one or not. Wherever there is interpretation there is usually some subjectivity.

Practice A.

Here are a number of objective test questions. Almost all of them have a clue to help you figure out the answer. For each item, state the clue if there is one, state what the clue tells you, and give the answer for the item if applicable.

1. True/false

_____ a. All students who do well on recognition-type tests do well on recall-type tests.

_____

_____ b. Generally students who do well on recognition type tests do well on recall type tests.

_____

_____ c. No objective test is easier than a subjective test.

_____

_____ d. Many objective tests are easier than essay tests.

_____

_____ e. Some essay tests are easier than objective tests.

_____

2. Fill-in or completion

a. Man is a _____ because he walks on two legs.

b. _____ were the discoverers of radium.

c. The snake is an _____ animal.

d. A true/false test is an example of an _____ test.

3. Short answer

a. Which objective tests require recognition?

_____

b. Which objective test gives you the highest chance to get a correct response?

_____

4. Multiple choice

a. The capital of New York is

    (a) Washington, D.C.

    (b) New Jersey

    (c) Albany

    (d) San Francisco

b. The word *apprehensive* means

    (a) to tire

    (b) fearful

    (c) anticipate

    (d) fear

c. The main idea of a paragraph

    (a) is a complete statement

    (b) is general

    (c) is the topic

    (d) is the general concept that is the basis of the paragraph's content

d. The central idea of a story is

    (a) the main idea

    (b) the topic sentence

    (c) the details

    (d) the main sentence

5. Matching

Column A	*Column B*
_____ a. wily	1. *ea*
_____ b. digraph	2. cunning
_____ c. diphthong	3. *bl*
_____ d. *The Waste Land*	4. *oy*
	5. T. S. Eliot
	6. *tr*
	7. Shakespeare

STOP. Check answers at the end of Lesson 14.

VOCABULARY: COMBINING FORMS II

Step I. Combining Forms

A. Directions:

Here is a list of combining forms with their meanings. Look at the combining forms and their meanings, and concentrate on learning each. Cover the meanings, read the combining forms, and state the meanings to yourself. Check to see if you are correct. Now cover the combining forms, read the meanings, and state the combining forms to yourself. Check to see if you are correct.

Combining Forms	*Meanings*
1. oper, opus	work
2. co	with
3. biblio	book
4. graph	something written, machine
5. bio	life

B. Directions:

Cover the preceding meanings. Write the meanings of the combining forms in the blanks.

Combining Forms	*Meanings*
1. oper, opus	_____
2. co	_____
3. biblio	_____
4. graph	_____
5. bio	_____

Step II. Words Derived from Combining Forms

1. *operate v.* To perform a work or labor; to manage; to run; to perform an operation; to perform surgery; to carry on a military action or mission; to act as a dealer or broker in the stock market; to follow a course of conduct that is irregular or antisocial. *The gambling casino was operated by people who had had a number of run-ins with the law.*

2. *operator n.* A worker who operates a machine or device as his regular trade; a maker of quack medicines or fraudulent (intentionally misleading or deceptive) articles; a shrewd and skillful person who knows how to get around and evade controls or restrictions; a dealer in stocks; someone who manages or runs a business. *In the movie "The Sting" Paul Newman and Robert Redford played the roles of shrewd operators.*

3. *opera n.* A drama in which music is the essential factor and which consists of songs accompanied by an orchestra. *adj.* Suitable for use at an opera, such as opera chairs or opera glasses. *"Carmen" is my favorite opera, but my boyfriend prefers "Rigoletto."*

4. *operation n.* The work; the deed; the procedure carried out on a living body for the purpose of correcting some abnormal state; surgery; the state of being functional; an exertion of power or influence; a process in which one quantity or expression is derived from another; a business transaction especially if it is speculative (risky). *pl.* The staff agency as in a United States air headquarters. *When the surgeons completed the heart transplant operation, they were exhausted.*

5. *opus n.* A literary work or composition; usually referring to a musical composition or set of compositions generally numbered in the order of its issue. *A composer's first opus is usually too immature to gain permanent recognition.*

6. *cooperate v.* To act or work with another toward a common end; to operate jointly; to act together; to associate with another for mutual benefit; to unite. *All nations must cooperate in order for world peace to prevail.*

7. *bibliography n.* A listing of books on a subject by an author (the description includes author's name, title, publisher, date of publication, and so on). *Our instructor asked us to include a selected bibliography with our paper; that is, she told us to list only a certain number of important books on the topic.*

8. *biography n.* Person's life story. *Almost every famous person has had a biography written about him or her.*

9. *autobiography n.* Life story written by oneself. *Not all famous people feel the urge to write an autobiography.*

10. *autograph n.* Signature. *adj.* Written by a person's own hand: an autograph letter; containing autographs; an autograph album. *v.* To write one's name on or in. *When she entered the hotel, the movie star was besieged by fans who wanted her autograph.*

Special Note

You met the combining forms *or*, meaning "one who," and *tion*, meaning "the act of," in Lesson 9.

Step III. Practice

Practice A.

Define the underlined word(s) in each sentence.

1. Although I am not an autograph collector, I enjoy looking at a famous person's autograph to see if he or she has a special way of signing his or her name.

   _____

2. This biography of Stalin says that he probably caused even more deaths than Hitler.

   _____

3. Unless you know how to operate a business, don't invest all your money in one.

   _____

4. Although the plant has been open for a number of weeks, it will be a few months before we can make any profits from its operation.

   _____

5. If the student council wants to have any influence on campus this semester, we will all have to cooperate.

   _____

6. In *I'll Cry Tomorrow*, her autobiography, Lillian Roth records her painful battle with alcoholism.

   _____

7. The opera *Faust* by Charles Gounod is based on Goethe's tragedy.

   _____

8. Beethoven's Ninth Symphony is a symphonic <u>opus</u> that uses a chorus.

   _____

9. The <u>operator</u> of the crane was obviously skilled at his job.

   _____

10. Although our instructor gave us a certain form to follow for our <u>bibliog-raphy</u>, a number of students wrote their book lists incorrectly.

   _____

STOP. Check answers at the end of Lesson 14.

Practice B.

Match the meaning from column B with the word in column A.

Column A	Column B
_____ 1. operate	a. worker
_____ 2. operator	b. work together
_____ 3. operation	c. work or composition, usually mus-ical
_____ 4. opera	
_____ 5. opus	d. life story written by another
_____ 6. cooperate	e. list of books
_____ 7. biography	f. manage or run
_____ 8. autobiography	g. state of being functional
_____ 9. bibliography	h. signature
_____ 10. autograph	i. musical drama
	j. life story written by oneself

STOP. Check answers at the end of Lesson 14.

Practice C.

Here are a number of sentences with missing words. Choose a word from the word list that *best* fits the sentence. Put the word in the blank.

Word List:

opera, opus, operate, operator, operation, bibliography, biography, autobiography, autograph, cooperate.

1. Brahm's First Symphony, _____ number sixty-eight, was written late in his musical career.

2. The _____ was such a sophisticated one and the _____ s were so slick that no one knew that he or she had been swindled until a year later.

3. I forgot to give the publication dates in my _____ .

4. I had a lot of sympathy for the writer when he described his early struggle with poverty in his _____ .

5. I couldn't imagine why several people at the airport asked me for my _____ until I discovered that the cast of *A Chorus Line* was traveling on the same plane.

6. Unless the two rival gangs decide to _____ the police will have to take some drastic measures.

7. After Watergate it seemed as though every writer was working on a(n) _____ of Nixon.

8. Please help me to _____ this copying machine.

9. The _____ *La Traviata* is the story of a tragic romance.

STOP. Check answers at the end of Lesson 14.

READING: ANALOGIES II

This section presents three more sets of analogies based on a number of the words you have met in this book. Remember, the symbol : means "is to" and the symbol :: means "as."

Practice A.

Find the word from the word list that *best* completes each analogy. There are more words in this list than you need.

Word List:

bibliography, dual, signature, ten, son, emotion, isolated, work, operate, co-operate, opus, book, run, unite, go, obvious, endurance, walk, sister, daughter, tall, cure, inhabited, sibling, grave, immense, self.

1. Bio : life :: biblio : _____
2. Biography : other :: autobiography : _____
3. Candid : frank :: operate : _____
4. Perilous : dangerous :: stamina : _____
5. Nutritious : nourishing :: combine : _____
6. Father : parent :: brother : _____
7. Fragile : delicate :: autograph : _____
8. Assemble : adjourn :: desolate : _____
9. One : single :: two : _____
10. Frown : expression :: worry : _____
11. Cooperate : help :: serious : _____
12. Tired: exhausted :: large : _____
13. Potent : impotent :: subtle : _____
14. Operator : worker :: opus : _____
15. Automobile : transport :: remedy : _____

STOP. Check answers at the end of Lesson 14.

Practice B.

Find the word from the word list that *best* completes each analogy. There are more words in the list than you need.

Word List:

notice, dogmatic, spouses, thin, concept, obese, retreat, equitably, preceding, inclination, exclusion, thrived, boundless, specialist, burn, cook, inhibited, legal, sparse, expanded, food, marriage, women.

1. Peer : equal :: ostracism : _____
2. Modest : conceited :: limited : _____
3. Yield : surrender :: opinionated : _____
4. Content : dissatisfied :: contracted : _____
5. Groomed : disheveled :: generalist : _____
6. Wretched : miserable :: disposition : _____
7. Monogamy : spouse :: polygamy : _____
8. Chill : freeze :: fat : _____
9. Unwilling : reluctant :: restrained : _____
10. Suggest : command :: singe : _____
11. Objective : subjective :: advance : _____
12. Strange : peculiar :: fairly : _____
13. Infidelity : faithfulness :: succeeding : _____
14. Site : place :: idea : _____
15. Single : solitary :: flourished : _____

STOP. Check answers at the end of Lesson 14.

Practice C.

Find the word from the word list that *best* completes each analogy. There are more words in the list than you need.

Word List:

heir, water, affront, sire, lamb, arrest, drake, mean, scrutinize, sound, noise, hear, look, fins, ewe, doe, rigorous, implicit, interrogate, conversation, continues, dispute, increases, abates, homonym, synonym, brilliant, virtuoso, vacuum, wind.

1. Birds : wings :: fish : _____
2. Pardon : excuse :: discourse : _____
3. Horse : mare :: sheep : _____
4. Safe : secure :: severe : _____
5. Pagan : heathen :: expert : _____
6. Sheer : opaque :: antonym : _____

7. Bear : bare :: air :_____

8. Work : labor :: controversy :_____

9. Provoke : excite :: lessens :_____

10. Breeze : tornado :: skim : _____

11. Direct : explicit :: indirect :_____

12. Visible : see :: audible : _____

13. Specific : general :: compliment : _____

14. Female : male :: dam : _____

15. Saw : cut :: brake : _____

STOP. Check answers at the end of Lesson 14.

ANSWERS: Lesson 14 (pp. 389-416)

Learning Skills: Notetaking (Lectures) (pp. 389-397)

Practice A

1. (sample notes)

"Bibliotherapy: Reading Toward Better Mental Health"

Menninger--it helps-- intuitive feeling

Def. biblio—Books help people cope with probs. Extreme form—used with mentally ill

Less extreme form—used to help persons overcome or adjust to a problem

Lecture concerned with use of biblio. in regular classroom

Def. coping—dealing with prob. by working in reality—behaving in a positive manner

Process of biblio.—empathy, ident., & insight

"Catharsis" replaced by empathy

Empathy—an indiv. projects himself into skin of another & knows how he feels; Must have same experience to empathize

1st step—identif.; 2nd—empathy; 3rd—insight

Biblio. both preventive and ameliorative

Teachers need to know a number of things to use biblio.: needs, interests, readiness levels, devel. stages, & special char.

Probs. for biblio.—many and varied—exs.: smallest in class, new baby, going to the hospital, divorce of parents, etc.

Teachers—provide books that deal with probs. of studs.

Children with serious prob. referred for help

Teachers must be *careful* how to share book with indiv. child

2. a. F b. T c. F (Bibliotherapy helps one to deal better with his or her *own* problems.) d. F e. F f. T g. F h. T i. T j. T

Practice B (sample summary)

Bibliotherapy is the use of books to help people deal better with their problems and emotions. Bibliotherapy can be a useful tool to teachers if used properly. To use bibliotherapy effectively in the classroom, teachers must have an understanding of the process of bibliotherapy, of children's developmental stages and needs, and of the themes that lend themselves to use in the classroom. Also, the teacher must know how to introduce bibliotherapy for a problem in a careful and constructive manner.

Learning Skills: Objective Tests (pp. 398–405)

Practice A

1. a. F. the clue is *all*. The clue usually tells you that the answer is false because most things have exceptions. b. T. The clue is *generally*. This clue usually tells you that the answer is true. c. F. The clue is *no*. The clue usually tells you that the answer is false. d. T. The clue is *many*. The clue usually tells you that the answer is true. e. T. The clue is *some*. The clue usually tells you that the answer is true. 2. a. biped. The clue is *a*. It tells you that the answer begins with a consonant. b. Marie and Pierre Curie. The clue is *were*. It tells you that the answer is plural. c. apodal. The clue is *an*. It tells you that the answer begins with a vowel. d. objective. The clue is *an*. It tells you that the answer begins with a vowel. 3. a. true/false, multiple choice, matching. The clues are *tests* and *require*. They tell you that there are more than one that require recognition. b. true/false. The clues are *test* and *gives*. They tell you that there is only one. 4. a. The answer is (c). No special clue except that the other answers are ridiculous. b. The answer is (b). The clue is that *apprehensive* is an adjective. The only adjective in the choices is *fearful*. c. The answer is (d). The clue is the length of one of the choices. It tells you that (d) is probably the answer. d. The answer is (a). The clue is *idea*. The same word is used in the incomplete statement as in one of the choices. 5. a. (2); b. (1); c. (4); d. (5). The clue is that different kinds of items are being matched. This limits the choices.

Vocabulary: Combining Forms II (pp. 406–410)

Practice A

1. signature 2. life story written by another 3. manage or run 4. state of being functional 5. work together 6. life story written by oneself 7. musical drama 8. work or composition, usually musical 9. worker 10. list of books

Practice B

1. f 2. a 3. g 4. i 5. c 6. b 7. d 8. j 9. e 10. h

Practice C

1. opus 2. operation; operator 3. bibliography 4. autobiography 5. autograph 6. cooperate 7. biography 8. operate 9. opera

Reading: Analogies II (pp. 410–413)

Practice A

1. book 2. self 3. run 4. endurance 5. unite 6. sibling 7. signature 8. inhabited 9. dual 10. emotion 11. grave 12. immense 13. obvious 14. work 15. cure

Practice B

1. exclusion 2. boundless 3. dogmatic 4. expanded 5. specialist 6. inclination 7. spouses 8. obese 9. inhibited 10. burn 11. retreat 12. equitably 13. preceding 14. concept 15. thrived

Practice C

1. fins 2. conversation 3. ewe 4. rigorous 5. virtuoso 6. synonym 7. heir 8. dispute 9. abates 10. scrutinize 11. implicit 12. hear 13. affront 14. sire 15. arrest

LESSON 15

Learning Skills: Notetaking for Writing a Paper
Learning Skills: Subjective Tests (Essays)
Vocabulary: Combining Forms III
Reading: Analogies III
Answers
Crossword Puzzle
Homograph Riddles
True/False Test

LEARNING SKILLS: NOTETAKING FOR WRITING A PAPER

Notetaking is very helpful in writing research papers. Good notes can save you time and effort. Begin your notetaking when you begin to do your reading for the paper.

1. The *notecard* is an essential aid in recording notes for papers. The size of the card you choose should be based on your individual style of writing. If you write large and intend to use some long quotes, a larger size (5 X 7 inch cards) is better than smaller sizes (3 X 5 or 4 X 6 inch cards). Whichever size card you choose to use, be consistent; that is, use cards of only one size. Use one card for each note. Do not record two different ideas on the same card. Notecards are better than slips of paper because they are easier to handle. They are superior to regular notepaper because they are not only easier to handle but also more convenient to organize, store, and edit.

2. To save having problems when you come to write the paper, you should acquire some good habits. Make sure that every notecard contains this information:

a. The topic you are writing on or that topic and the subtopic to which the particular note applies. (If you don't know all this information for certain when you begin taking notes, leave room to fill it in later.)

b. The exact source of your information recorded at the bottom or the top of the card.

c. The information the card is to record. The information may be a summary in your own words (See Unit III), figures or statistics, a definition, a direct quotation, or some other bit of relevant knowledge.

Example of a Notecard and the Page from Which It Was Taken:

Topic

Main idea

Important
details

> *Concept Development*
>
> Children's concept development continues to grow as they acquire more language arts skills. They learn such concepts as homographs, synonyms, antonyms, relational concepts, and figures of speech.
>
> Dorothy Rubin, Teaching Elementary Language Arts, Holt, Rinehart and Winston, 1980, p. 25.

(Notecard contains a summary
of the paragraph.)

As children grow in their use of listening, speaking, and reading skills, their concept development continues. They learn that some words designate different levels of things and feelings. They put on their *coats*. They put *coats* of paint on the toy. These two uses illustrate a homograph. Children learn about different kinds of elevators, forms, cities. They develop the relational concepts of afraid, brave, proud, faraway, and so on. They learn the meaning of figures of speech, such as: "The trees trembled in the night" or "The wind roared its disapproval." Students should also learn the concepts of *synonyms* (words that mean the same or nearly the same) and *antonyms* (words that mean the opposite) in isolation and in context.

Special Notes

1. Your instructor will probably give you information on the bibliographical form he or she wishes you to use. If you have all the information recorded on your cards, you will have no difficulty writing your bibliography according to any given style.

2. If you have used a source before, you only have to record the author's last name and the page from which the information was obtained. Obviously, if you have two authors with the same last names, include the authors' first names, also.

3. Each note that you take should be so clearly written that you have no difficulty understanding it or why you wrote it.

a. If you are quoting an author's exact words, make sure you put them in quotation marks.

b. Try to summarize what you have read but be careful that you are stating facts, not opinions. (See Lessons 7, 8, and 9 on summaries.)

c. If you are giving your or someone else's opinion, make sure you record this on your card so that you will not confuse the opinion with fact.

d. Do not take notes on matters of common knowledge.

e. Do not take notes on the same information twice. If two or more sources give the same facts or ideas, note the idea only once. This rule should *not* be followed, however, if you are collecting evidence to prove or disprove something. The more evidence you can uncover that points to a single conclusion, the better you will be able to defend your position on the question.

Practice A.

Here are three sample notecards without topic headings. 1. Read each card and determine the writer's topic. 2. Write "yes" or "no" to show whether a source has been used before.

a.

> Animals· occur in all but the most hostile environments of the earth. A few sites that are too hot--some hot springs, for example--too dry, or chemically intolerable, as highly saline waters, lack animal life, but they are rare.
>
> Gordon et al., p. 28

b.

> Sparta was essentially a military and aristocratic city and not very interested in intellectual pursuits. As a matter of fact, it made it a point of honor to remain semi-illiterate.
>
> Marrou, p. 35

c.

> There was always some woman in every neighborhood who, for a small amount of money, was willing to take charge of the children and teach them. These schools were called dame schools.
>
> Clifton Johnson, Old-Time Schools and School-books, New York: Dover Publications, Inc., 1963, p. 25

1. a. _____

   b. _____

   c. _____

2. a. _____

   b. _____

   c. _____

STOP. Check sample answers at the end of Lesson 15.

Practice B.

For each of these sample notecards without topic headings, state the idea or ideas recorded. Write "faulty" on each card that contains more than one idea.

1.

> *Americans, especially on the frontiers and the cities, were prodigious consumers of beer, hard cider, and whiskey. A barrel of hard cider per family was no uncommon weekly ration, and in many homes, whiskey flowed equally at breakfast, dinner, and supper. Reformers waged war on drink. In 1826 the American Society for Promotion of Temperance was founded.*
>
> *Clark and Remini, p. 265*

2.

> *By modern standards the Civil War was still unmechanized. It was fought with rifles, bayonets, and sabers by men on horseback and on foot. Artillery was more used than in previous wars but was still a minor consumer of iron and steel.*
>
> *Parrish (ed.), p. 90*

3.

> *Research generally agrees that fathers are more interested and active than mothers in differentiating between boys and girls and in seeing that each sex behaves appropriately. After the young child has established a firm gender identity, there is still much to do in sex-role development.*
>
> *Smart and Smart, p. 87*

Card 1 _____

Card 2 _____

Card 3 _____

STOP. Check answers at the end of Lesson 15.

LEARNING SKILLS: SUBJECTIVE TESTS (Essays)

Essay tests are usually given when a professor wants to see that you know the material thoroughly enough to organize it and use it to draw conclusions, which is something more than merely knowing material well enough to recognize it. Subjective tests are more difficult to take and to grade than are objective tests. Their answers are not merely right or wrong but are demonstrations of reasoning, thought, and perception. In general, the closer you come to seeing the answer as your instructor sees it, the better your grade will be. The further your opinion is from your professor's, the better reasoned your answer must be.

1. Comparison of essay tests to objective tests.

a. On an essay test you spend most of your time thinking and writing, whereas on an objective test you spend most of your time reading and thinking.

b. You are more free to express your ideas and be creative on an essay test than on an objective test.

c. Objective tests allow you to guess at an answer; essay tests may encourage bluffing.

d. Both essay and objective tests can measure simple and complex concepts and knowledge.

2. Studying for an essay test.

Essay tests require you to recall material and to be able to express your ideas logically. Here are some study suggestions:

a. Look for broad, general concepts (ideas) and for relations between concepts. Study for main ideas and generalizations. Note the organization of details that develop the main ideas.

b. Distribute your studying time. (See lessons on studying.)

c. Study in particular the material your professor emphasized or spent much time on in class.

d. Try to anticipate some of the essay questions. It may be a good idea to work up one or two essays answering questions that you think your instructor is likely to ask. (See Special Notes.) Also, your text may contain "questions for discussion" at the end of each chapter. These questions are usually subjective questions. Go over them because they may appear on the test as they are or thinly disguised. If they are not given on the test, your study of them will at least have prepared you for the *kind* of question given.

Special Notes

1. Although it may be a good idea to try to anticipate essay questions and prepare one or two in advance, be careful! Do not spend a great amount of time doing this. It's better to spend more time on studying generalizations and relations between concepts.

2. If the essay you prepared in advance is not related to the question that is asked, *do not* give your prepared essay answer as the answer on the test. Answer the question. Perhaps you can use a small part of your prepared essay. (After the test, study the essay questions asked on the test and compare these with your text and lecture notes to try to determine why your instructor asked these questions. This will help you anticipate questions better next time.)

424/Reading and Learning Power

3. Taking an essay test.

a. Read the question. Make sure you understand it. Do not read into it what is *not* there. Check to see if examples or illustrations are asked for. Check to see if your opinion is asked for. If you are asked to list, name, or identify, do exactly that. Do not give more information than is asked for. If you are asked to summarize, give an overview. If you are asked to analyze, you must break down the question into its parts. The most general type of question is one that asks you to discuss or explain. In a comparison/contrast question, you must give similarities, differences, or both. If you are asked to evaluate, you must make a value judgment. This type question is the most difficult to answer because it requires that you know a great amount of information on the topic to determine what is best or correct.

b. Put down on a scrap sheet of paper any special formulas, principles, concepts, or buzz words that you have memorized and that you think will be relevant to the question. Do this immediately so that you will not forget to include the important details that you have memorized.

c. *Think* about the question.

d. Plan your answer. (Again, make sure that you are answering the question.)

e. Prepare an outline for your answer. (See Appendix II.)

f. Write out your answer. Use lists where applicable.

g. Check the time available to you.

h. Do not spend all your time on a single essay if there is more than one question.

i. Reread your essay to make sure that your ideas are clearly and logically stated. Make sure that you have used complete sentences and that each of your paragraphs expresses one main idea.

Special Note

Although it's usually permissible to list items in an essay test, some professors frown on your writing your complete essay in outline form. Be sure to check with your professor whether you can answer by outline *before* you proceed to do so. (See Lesson 12 on questions.) However, if you are pressed for time, and you have no choice, it's a good idea to present your essay in outline form.

4. Examples of some of the different ways essay questions can be worded.

a. Give the reasons for . . .

b. Explain how or why . . .

c. Present arguments for and arguments against . . .

d. Compare the poem＿＿＿＿to the poem＿＿＿＿in terms of the author's ability to portray fatalism.

e. Analyze the male character in ＿＿＿＿＿＿ .

f. Give the events that led to the ＿＿＿＿＿＿ War.

Special Note

Many tests are composed of both objective and subjective test items. On such tests you must plan your time especially wisely. Here are some suggestions:

a. Read the whole test through.

b. Notice how many points each part of the test is worth.

c. Put down any special formulas, principles, ideas, or other details you have memorized that you think may be relevant to your essay question.

d. Do the objective part first. It may give you clues for your essay question. The objective part of the test usually takes less time than the essay part. If you do it first you will be more at ease, more accustomed to the test, when you begin work on the essay questions. You will also be relieved to know part of the test is behind you.

Here is an example of an essay question and answer:

Question: Explain the major differences between objective and subjective tests. (15 pts.)

Begin with a general statement that directly begins to answer the question.

Give differences.

Answer: There are a number of major differences between objective and subjective tests. Objective tests allow for a more comprehensive coverage of an area while subjective tests cover subject matter in greater depth. Objective tests depend on both recognition and recall; subjective tests depend entirely on recall. Although objective tests can measure a student's ability to think critically, solve problems, and apply principles,

Stick to the
question.

they are usually aimed more at testing the student's grasp of detail than subjective tests are. Subjective tests are usually more concerned with generalizations and the logical organization of material.

Objective tests usually have only one correct answer, whereas subjective tests can sometimes have many different answers, whose "correctness" depends on an individual's interpretation of the question and subject. Objective tests are consequently easier to grade than subjective tests.

Practice A.

Write a short essay comparing the taking of essay tests with the taking of objective tests. (15 pts.)

STOP. Check sample answer at the end of Lesson 15.

VOCABULARY: COMBINING FORMS III

Step I. Combining Forms

A. Directions:

Here is a list of combining forms with their meanings. Look at the combining forms and their meanings, and concentrate on learning each. Cover the meanings, read the combining forms, and state the meanings to yourself. Check to see if you are correct. Now cover the combining forms, read the meanings, and state the combining forms to yourself. Check to see if you are correct.

Combining Forms	*Meanings*
1. deca	ten
2. deci	tenth part
3. cent, centi	hundred, hundredth part
4. milli	thousand, thousandth part
5. meter	measure

B. Directions:

Cover the preceding meanings. Write the meanings of the combining forms in the blanks.

Combining Forms	*Meanings*
1. deca	_____
2. deci	_____
3. cent, centi	_____
4. milli	_____
5. meter	_____

Step II. Words Derived from Combining Forms

1. *decade n.* Period of 10 years. *At my twentieth birthday, I will have been alive for two decades.*

2. *century n.* (pl. *ies*) Period of 100 years. *My great grandfather, who is 95 years old, has lived for almost a whole century.*

3. *centennial adj.* Pertaining to a period of 100 years; lasting 100 years. *n.* A one-hundredth anniversary. *The museum had a centennial exhibition that displayed many items from the year 1876.*

4. *million n.* One thousand thousands (1,000,000); a very large or indefinitely large number. *adj.* Being one million in number; very many; one thousand thousands. *When we went camping last summer our tent was invaded by what seemed to be a million mosquitoes.*

5. *millennium n.* (pl. *niums, nia*) Period of 1,000 years; a one-thousandth anniversary; a period of great happiness (the millennium). *In the millennium there will be no imperfections on earth, there will be perfect government, and there will be happiness for all.*

6. *decimal adj.* Numbered by 10; based on 10; pertaining to tenths or the number 10. *n.* A decimal fraction. *The number .90 is a decimal fraction.*

7. *decameter n.* In the metric system, a measure of length containing 10 meters, equal to 393.70 inches or 32.81 feet. *A decameter is equal to 10 meters.*

8. *decimeter n.* In the metric system, a unit of length equal to 1/10 meter. *It's easy to remember that decimeter is equal to 1/10 meter because "deci" means a tenth part.*

9. *meter n.* In the metric system, a unit of length equal to approximately 39.37 inches; an instrument for measuring the amount of something (as water, gas, electricity); an instrument for measuring distance, time, weight, speed, and so forth; a measure of verse. *Every month a man from the power company comes to our house to read the meter.*

10. *centimeter n.* In the metric system, a unit of measure equal to 1/100 meter (0.3937 inch). *When we change to the metric system, the common ruler will be in centimeters rather than in inches.*

11. *millimeter n.* In the metric system, a unit of length equal to 1/1000 meter (0.03937 inch). *The thickness of eyeglass lenses is measured in millimeters.*

12. *decimate v.* To take or destroy a tenth part of, to destroy but not completely, to destroy a great number or proportion of. *Inflation decimates our buying power.*

Special Note

The combining form *kilo* means "thousand." In the metric system, a *kilometer* is equal to 1,000 meters.

Step III. Practice

Practice A.

Define the underlined word(s) in each sentence.

1. In the metric system one uses <u>centimeters</u> and <u>millimeters</u> to measure length rather than inches. _____ ;

   _____

2. The plague <u>decimated</u> the population and left the survivors nearly help-less.

   _____

3. The <u>decimal</u> .25 is one fourth of one hundred.

   _____

4. Some people feel that rather than wait for the <u>millennium</u> we should work toward making life better on earth now.

   _____

5. One of the students at our college won the <u>million</u> dollar lottery and be-came a millionaire overnight.

   _____

6. The <u>centennial</u> celebration of the United States took place in 1876.

   _____

7. The <u>meter</u> in poetry tells you how the stress of words is arranged in rhythmic lines or verses.

   _____

8. You will not confuse <u>decameter</u> with <u>decimeter</u> if you note the spelling of the combining forms and remember that <u>deca</u> means "ten" and deci means "tenth part." _____ ;

   _____

9. After having lived for six <u>decades</u>, my grandmother says that she is not amazed at anything that she sees anymore.

   _____

10. In the twenty-first <u>century</u> we will probably still be coping with many of the same problems we have now.

    _____

STOP. Check answers at the end of Lesson 15.

Practice B.

Match the meaning from column B with the word in column A.

Column A	Column B
_____ 1. decade	a. one thousand thousands
_____ 2. century	b. 1/1000 meter
_____ 3. centennial	c. fraction based on 10
_____ 4. million	d. period of 10 years
_____ 5. millennium	e. unit of length equal to approxi-
_____ 6. decimal	mately 39.37 inches
_____ 7. decameter	f. 1/100 meter
_____ 8. decimeter	g. destroy but not completely
_____ 9. meter	h. one-hundredth anniversary
_____ 10. centimeter	i. 10 meters
_____ 11. millimeter	j. period of 100 years
_____ 12. decimate	k. 1/10 meter
	l. ·period of great happiness

STOP. Check answers at the end of Lesson 15.

Practice C.

Here are a number of sentences with missing words. Choose a word from the word list that *best* fits the sentence. Put the word in the blank.

Word List:

decade, century, centennial, million, millennium, decimal, decameter, meter, centimeter, millimeter, decimated, decimeter.

1. In the metric system, 1/10 meter equals a(n) _____ .
2. In the metric system, 1/100 meter equals a(n) _____
3. In the metric system, 10 meters equals a(n) _____ .
4. In the metric system, 1/1000 meter equals a(n) _____ .
5. In the _____ system, .50 equals one-half of 1.00.
6. A(n) _____ is a period of 1,000 years.
7. The _____ anniversary of the end of the Civil War was in 1965.
8. The troops were _____ and had to retreat.
9. I wonder what the world will be like in the twenty-fifth _____ .
10. Ten times one hundred thousand equals one _____ .
11. A(n) _____ is equal to approximately 3.3 feet.
12. In a(n) _____ I will be out of my twenties, out of college, and, I hope, pursuing a worthwhile career.

STOP. Check answers at the end of Lesson 15.

READING: ANALOGIES III

This section presents theee more sets of analogies based on a number of the words you have met in this book. Remember, the symbol : means "is to" and the symbol :: means "as."

Practice A.

Find the word from the word list that *best* completes each analogy. There are more words in this list than you need.

Word List:

decimate, meter, centimeter, decimeter, decameter, million, millennium, century, deceitful, millimeter, skim, apprehensive, vain, bough, grape, automobile, valid, brief, verbose, modest, intricate, sparse, friendly, kind, prune, body, competent.

1. One : ten :: decade : _____
2. Millimeter : centimeter :: meter : _____
3. Centi :: milli :: centimeter : _____
4. Centimeter : millimeter :: meter : _____
5. One : thousand :: thousand : _____
6. Opus : work :: fearful : _____
7. Immobile : stationary :: humble : _____
8. Twig : tree :: finger : _____
9. Excellent : good :: eradicate : _____
10. Optimist : pessimist :: simple : _____
11. Prudent : wise :: sound : _____
12. Saturated : drenched :: qualified : _____
13. Cider : apple :: wine : _____
14. Least : most :: succinct : _____
15. Polished : dull :: sincere : _____

STOP. Check answers at the end of Lesson 15.

Practice B.

Find the word from the word list that *best* completes each analogy. There are more words in this list than you need.

Word List:

discontented, scarlet, hate, play, inward, feeling, temperate, temper, sad, ornament, hue, green, external, absorb, millimeter, coarse, stop, abridge, red, ribbon, jollity, century, discourse, million, abyss, love, hire, millennium.

1. Tangible : intangible :: delicate : _____
2. Check : curb :: shorten : _____

3. Blue : azure :: red : _____

4. Average : excellent :: pit : _____

5. Gown : clothing :: necklace : _____

6. Alone : solitary :: color : _____

7. Easy : rigorous :: internal : _____

8. Cover : hide :: abhor : _____

9. Counsel : advice :: moderate : _____

10. Ten : decade :: hundred : _____

11. Hundredth : centimeter :: thousandth : _____

12. More : less :: satisfied : _____

13. Object : goal :: mirth : _____

14. Alarm : warn :: towel : _____

15. Prey : quarry :: conversation : _____

STOP. Check answers at the end of Lesson 15.

Practice C.

Find the word from the word list that *best* completes each analogy. There are more words in this list than you need.

Word List:

reason, hold, control, heat, less, expand, wily, dumb, new, never, now, ancient, abundant, lose, operator, confection, mean, oblivious, prosper, scrutinize, overemphasize, caring, humanity, bias, sympathetic, sparse, present, dirt, fence, crutch.

1. Courage : cowardice :: absent : _____

2. Thick : dense :: plenty : _____

3. Crack : split :: sly : _____

4. Fidelity : trust :: thrive : _____

5. Crew : band :: schemer : _____

6. Employ : use :: mankind : _____

7. Recent : current :: old : _____

8. Doze : sleep :: observe : _____

9. Expert : virtuouso :: heedless : _____

10. Fat : obese :: stress : _____

11. Pepper : spice :: lollipop: _____

12. Produce : yield :: motive : _____

13. Vault : store :: thermostat : _____

14. Promise : guarantee :: spread : _____

15. Scorn : disdain :: leaning : _____

STOP. Check answers at the end of Lesson 15.

ANSWERS: Lesson 15 (pp. 417-443)

Learning Skills: Notetaking for Writing a Paper (pp. 417–422)

Practice A (sample answers)

1. a. Distribution of Animals b. Spartan Education c. Formation of the Dame School 2. a. yes b. yes c. no

Practice B

1. Faulty. Two ideas—one concerns America's consumption of whiskey and the other concerns the temperance movement. 2. The Civil War was un-mechanized. 3. Faulty. Two ideas—father influences appropriate sex behavior; child's establishment of firm gender identity.

Learning Skills: Subjective Tests (Essays) (pp. 422–426)

Practice A (sample essay)

There are a number of similarities and differences in taking essay and objective tests. The major difference concerns how you spend most of your time. In taking objective tests you spend most of your time reading and thinking; whereas, in taking essay tests you spend most of your time thinking and writing.

For both types of tests you should look over the whole test before doing anything so that you have an idea of what you are required to do and how many points the items are worth. For both tests you should read questions carefully to make sure you understand what you are required to do, you should not spend all your time on one or two questions, and you should ration your time properly.

For objective tests you should look for professor's clues and read all the choices that are given in multiple choice tests. You must be careful not to omit any answers.

For essay tests you should jot down some key ideas on a scrap piece of paper, spend time thinking about the question, put down a brief outline, and then write the answer following your outline. You should reread your answer to make sure that it is clearly and logically written.

Vocabulary: Combining Forms III (pp. 427–431)

Practice A

1. unit of length equal to 1/100 meter; unit of length equal to 1/1000 meter
2. destroyed but not completely 3. fraction based on tenths 4. period of great happiness 5. one thousand thousands 6. one hundredth anniversary
7. measure of verse 8. 10 meters; 1/10 meter 9. period of 10 years 10. period of 100 years

Practice B

1. d 2. j 3. h 4. a 5. l 6. c 7. i 8. k 9. e 10. f 11. b 12. g

Practice C

1. decimeter 2. centimeter 3. decameter 4. millimeter 5. decimal 6. millennium 7. centennial 8. decimated 9. century 10. million 11. meter 12. decade

Reading: Analogies III (pp. 431–434)

Practice A

1. century 2. decameter 3. millimeter 4. decimeter 5. million 6. apprehensive 7. modest 8. body 9. decimate 10. intricate 11. valid 12. competent 13. grape 14. verbose 15. deceitful

Practice B

1. coarse 2. abridge 3. scarlet 4. abyss 5. ornament 6. hue 7. external 8. hate 9. temperate 10. century 11. millimeter 12. discontented 13. jollity 14. absorb 15. discourse

Practice C

1. present 2. abundant 3. wily 4. prosper 5. operator 6. humanity
7. ancient 8. scrutinize 9. oblivious 10. overemphasize 11. confection 12. reason 13. control 14. expand 15. bias

CROSSWORD PUZZLE

Directions:

The meanings of a number of the words and combining forms and of some of the ideas from Lessons 13–15 follow. Your knowledge of these will help you to solve this crossword puzzle. (Note that *combining form* is abbreviated Comb. f.)

Across

1. Informal discourses
6. Antonym of *liabilities*
9. Comb. f. for *again*
10. Modest
13. Homonym of *eye*
14. Same as #3 Down
15. Writing system used by the blind
16. Abbreviation of *and so on*
18. Same as #15 Down
19. Roman numeral four
20. Same as #14 Across
21. Least : most :: less : ___
23. Abbreviation of *Vermont*
25. To change the place of
27. Homonym of *two*
28. The humorous use of a word
29. A vowel digraph
30. Abbreviation of *District Attorney*
31. To eat supper
32. Comb. f. for *not*
33. Same as #27 Across
35. Antonym of *sparsest*
37. Homonym of *won*
38. A true/false test is a(n) ___ test
40. Abbreviation of *General Practitioner*
41. Mobile : movable :: field : ___

Down

1. A seafood; to complain
2. Antonym of *she*
3. Indefinite article
4. Prosper
5. An operator is usually this
6. When this begins a true/false statement, the answer is usually false
7. Appear
8. Used to show that the incorrect word was quoted exactly
11. Musical syllable
12. Offensively loud or obvious
15. Second letter of the alphabet
16. Break out
17. A decade equals this
22. Musical works
23. Egotistical
24. Exhausted
25. Engine
26. Exclamation
30. Destroyed but not completely
31. Snow White and the ___ Dwarfs
34. Very fat
35. Comb. f. for *away, from*
36. Threatening evil
37. Worked
39. Hand : grasp :: ___ bite
40. Famous physicist who won a Nobel Prize

Across	*Down*

Across

42. Same as #13 Across

43. Concept : idea :: snuggles : ___

46. Abbreviation of *southwest*

47. Finding the ___ idea of a paragraph helps you understand what you are reading

49. Antonym of *late*

51. Color

53. Slang for *girls*

54. You find this on a subjective test

55. Bone

56. A small child

57. Let it stand (used by editors and printers)

58. Same as #26 Down

59. Scarlet

61. Measure of verse

63. One of the R's in the SQ3R technique

65. Prunes and raisons are ___ fruit

67. Mature

68. Sheep : ewe :: deer : ___

Down

41. Hate

44. This helps you to find out your strengths and weaknesses

45. Cunning

48. If you have boundless land, you have ___ ___ of land

50. Comb. f. for *having, full of*

52. Antonym of *new*

53. Seventh letter of the alphabet

54. Plural ending of words ending in *sh* and *ch*

58. A poem

60. Abbreviation of *doctor*

61. A pronoun

62. Abbreviation of *Rhode Island*

64. Abbreviation of *account of*

STOP. Check answers on the next page.

Crossword Puzzle Answers

¹C	²H	³A	⁴T	⁵S	■	⁶A	⁷S	S	E	T	⁸S
⁹R	E	■	¹⁰H	U	¹¹M	¹²B	L	E	■	■	¹³I
¹⁴A	■	¹⁵B	R	A	I	L	L	E	■	¹⁶E	¹⁷T C
¹⁸B		¹⁹I	V	²⁰A		²¹M	²²O R	E		²³V	²⁴T
	²⁵M	²⁶O	V	E	²⁷T	O		²⁸P	U N	²⁹A	I
	O	■	E	³⁰D	A	³¹S	U	P		³²I	R
	³³T	³⁴O	³⁵D	E	N	³⁶S	E	S	T	³⁷O	N E
	³⁸O	³⁹B	J	E	C	T	I	V	E	⁴⁰G	P — D
⁴¹A	R	E	A		⁴²I		⁴³N	E	⁴⁴S	T L E	⁴⁵S
B	⁴⁶S	W		⁴⁷M	⁴⁸A	I	N		⁴⁹E	A R L	⁵⁰Y
⁵¹H	⁵²U	E		⁵³G	A	L	S		⁵⁴E	S S A	Y
⁵⁵O	S			⁵⁶T	O	T		⁵⁷S	T E	T	⁵⁸O
⁵⁹R	⁶⁰E D	■	⁶¹M	E	T	E	⁶²R		⁶³R E	⁶⁴A	D
	⁶⁵D	R	⁶⁶I	E	D		⁶⁷R	I	P E		⁶⁸D O E

HOMOGRAPH RIDDLES

Directions:

Here are several ways to use a single word. Find the right word for each group. Example: I'm a female domestic animal; I'm also a barrier preventing the flow of water, and I mean to block. (dam)

1. I can refer to someone's condition; I'm what people do when they declare something; and I'm also a nation.

2. I'm something you can do to your teeth; I'm a noisemaking device for a toy pistol; I'm used to seal a bottle; and I can be worn on your head.

3. I'm a series of words that can be printed, written, or recited; I'm a long, thin mark that divides things; I'm something you can hang clothing on to dry; and I can be a defensive position or front.

4. I'm a place where you can go on your vacation if you like water and rocket launchings, and I'm something that you can wear that has no sleeves.

5. I mean to charge head on or to strive for something; I'm a male deer or antelope; and I'm a dollar in slang.

6. I'm what your heart does; I'm a machine; I mean to question in slang; and I'm a shoe.

STOP. Check answers at the bottom of the page.

TRUE/FALSE TEST

Directions:

This is a true/false test on Lessons 13–15 in Unit V. Read each sentence carefully. Decide whether it is true or false. Put a T for *true* or an F for *false* in the blank.

_____ 1. Students should avoid asking their instructors questions.

_____ 2. Unless you know the relationship between the words in the given pair of an analogy, you can't finish the analogy.

1. state 2. cap 3. line 4. cape 5. buck 6. pump

_____ 3. It's important to use a formal outline while taking notes.

_____ 4. Generalizations help you to retain information.

_____ 5. Matching tests require recognition.

_____ 6. All objective tests require recall.

_____ 7. Tests are useful for diagnosis but not for review purposes.

_____ 8. Notetaking is a study tool.

_____ 9. *Demotion* and *promotion* are antonyms.

_____ 10. An automotive machine is usually not self-propelling.

_____ 11. Decimate : obliterate :: damage : destroy.

_____ 12. Centimeter : decimeter :: millimeter : centimeter.

_____ 13. A meter is greater than a decimeter.

_____ 14. Some tension is usually necessary if you are to do your best on a test.

_____ 15. To "overlearn" something you should discontinue practice after you feel that you know the material.

_____ 16. A test item may give a grammatical clue to its answer.

_____ 17. Practice without knowledge of results is useful.

_____ 18. A decameter is greater than a meter.

_____ 19. On essay tests it's important to begin writing immediately.

_____ 20. You should never guess on an objective test.

_____ 21. A speaker's facial gestures help give meaning to what is being said.

_____ 22. Questions help slow a professor down in a lecture.

_____ 23. It's unnecessary to review notes before a lecture.

_____ 24. In telegraphic writing you write the whole sentence.

_____ 25. You should avoid overmarking in your textbook.

_____ 26. Notecards are usually used for short papers.

_____ 27. Notecards should always contain the complete reference.

_____ 28. Each notecard should contain at least two ideas.

STOP. Check answers on the next page.

Answers to True/False Test

1. F 2. T 3. F 4. T 5. T 6. F 7. F 8. T 9. T 10. F 11. T
12. T 13. T 14. T 15. F 16. T 17. F 18. T 19. F 20. F 21. T
22. T 23. F 24. F 25. T 26. F 27. F 28. F

Appendix I
SELECTED REFERENCE SOURCES

Biography (indexes)
    Biography Index
    New York Times Index
    Reader's Guide to Periodical Literature

Book reviews (indexes)
    Book Review Digest
    Book Review Index
    Education Index
    Humanities Index
    New York Times Index
    Social Science Index

Encyclopedias
    Afro-American Encyclopedia
    Encyclopedia of American Facts and Dates
    Encyclopedia of Education
    Encyclopedia of Psychology
    Encyclopedia of Science and Technology
    Encyclopedia of World History
    The New Encyclopaedia Britannica

USING THE CARD CATALOGUE*

In most card catalogues, books are listed by author, title, and subject.

If you know the author's name, you can find all his or her books that the library has by looking under his or her last name.

If you know the exact title of a book, you can check in the catalogue under the first word of the title, omitting *a, an*, and *the*.

Most often you will be looking for books on a specific subject.

*Trenton State College Library, Trenton State College, New Jersey.

Subject entries are filed in the card catalogue *after the author entries and before the title entries*.

For example, these entries are filed in the following order:

Author entry	Irish, Richard K.
Title of the book	Go hire yourself an employer.
Subject entry	IRISH–CARICATURES AND CARTOONS.
Title entry	The Irish.

When using the subject approach, choose the most specific word to describe the subject you wish to find.

Please remember that subject terms used in the card catalogue are standardized terms, so-called *subject headings*. The subject headings used by the library are the headings established by the Library of Congress, the national library. These headings are published in the Library of Congress Subject Headings and its supplements.

You should use the accepted subject headings to find quickly whether the library has any books on this subject.

Generally, you should use common sense to look up the word that corresponds to your subject. For example, if you want books on abortion, you should look in the card catalogue under ABORTION to see what books the library owns that deal with abortion.

However, in many cases subject headings do not conform to the way *you* use the language because (1) word uses change faster than the catalogue can, (2) a more specific way of referring to the subject has been agreed upon, and (3) your word may not be accurate. If libraries assigned headings without using an approved list of subject headings, books on the European War could be found under a variety of subject headings, such as World War I, War in Europe, First World War, etc., and there would be a possibility that you might miss some important title. By using an approved list of headings, all the books in the library on this subject can be found under European War, 1914–1918.

For example:

Not: World War I	but, EUROPEAN WAR, 1914–1918.
Not: Movies	but, MOVING-PICTURES.
Not: Indians	but, INDIANS OF NORTH AMERICA: INDIANS OF SOUTH AMERICA, etc.

Information on a Catalogue Card*

(1) Call Number   (7) Number of Pages, Height

(2) Author   (8) Series Note

(3) Title   (9) Bibliography

(4) Place of Publication (10) Subject Heading

(5) Publisher   (11) Technical Notes for Librarian

(6) Date of Publication

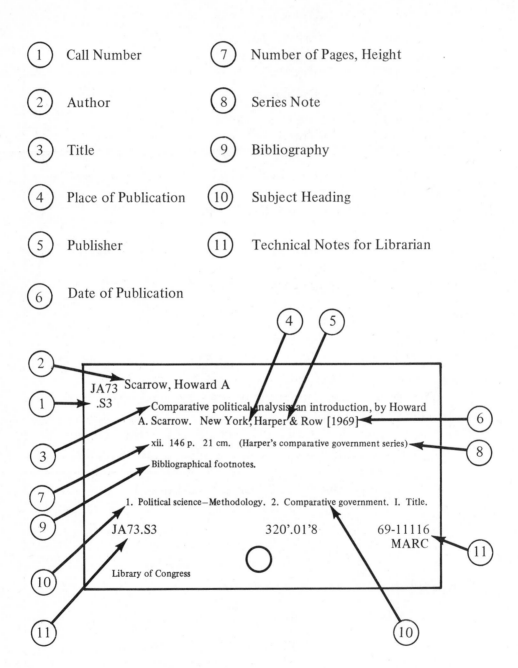

TITLE CARD

Comparative political analysis; an introduction.

JA73
.S3

Scarrow, Howard A
    Comparative political analysis; an introduction, by Howard A.
Scarrow. New York, Harper & Row [1969]

    xii. 146p. 21 cm. (Harper's comparative government series)

    Bibliographical footnotes.

    1. Political science–Methodology. 2. Comparative government. I. Title.

JA73.S3   320'.01'8   60-11116

                                                        MARC

Library of Congress

SUBJECT CARD

POLITICAL SCIENCE – METHODOLOGY

JA73
.S3

Scarrow, Howard A
    Comparative political analysis; an introduction, by Howard A.
Scarrow. New York, Harper & Row [1969]

    xii. 146 p. 21 cm. (Harper's comparative government series)

    Bibliographical footnotes.

    1. Political science–Methodology. 2. Comparative government. I. Title.

JA73.S3   320'.01'8   69-11116

Library of Congress   MARC

SUBJECT CARD
(older cards have
subject words
typed in red)

COMPARATIVE GOVERNMENT

JA73
.S3

Scarrow, Howard A
    Comparative political analysis; an introduction, by Howard A.
Scarrow. New York, Harper & Row [1969]

    xii. 146 p. 21 cm. (Harper's comparative government series)

    Bibliographical footnotes.

    1. Political science–Methodology. 2. Comparative government. I. Title.

JA73.S3   320'.01'8   69-11116

Library of Congress   MARC

Appendix II
OUTLINING

I. Main topic
    A. Prime importance
        1. Joins everything under it
        2. Signaled by a Roman numeral (I, II, III, and so on)
        3. Begins with a capital letter
    B. Example: I. The main topic in an outline

II. Subtopics
    A. Grouped under main topics
    B. Related to main topics
        1. Indented under main topic
        2. Signaled by a capital letter (A, B, C, D, and so on)
        3. Begin with a capital letter
    C. Example: I. The relationship of subtopics to main topics
                    A. How related
                    B. How written

III. Specific details
    A. Grouped under appropriate subtopics
    B. Represented by Arabic numerals (1, 2, 3, 4, and so on)
    C. Example: I. The dictionary
                    A. An important reference tool
                    B. Uses of dictionary
                        1. Information concerning a word
                        2. Other useful information

IV. More specific details
    A. Grouped under appropriate Arabic numerals
    B. Represented by lowercase (small) letters (a, b, c, d, and so on)
    C. Example: I. The dictionary
                    A. An important reference tool
                    B. Uses of the dictionary

      1. Information concerning a word
        a. Spelling
        b. Definitions
        c. Correct usage
        d. Syllabication, and so on
      2. Other useful information
        a. Biographical entries
        b. Signs and symbols
        c. Forms of address, and so on

V. Types of outlines
  A. Topic outline
    1. Consists of phrases
    2. Useful in preparing either short or long papers
  B. Sentence outline
    1. Consists of complete sentences
    2. Used primarily in planning long papers

Appendix III
APPLICATION FORMS

1. Here is an employment application form. This form is similar to others that you may have to fill out. See how well you do in following directions.

In filling out the form, note the last question. Why is this question a very important one? How should you answer this question? (Answers are given at the end of completed form.)

After you fill out the application form, check yours with the sample completed form on pp. 453–455.

— An Equal Opportunity Employer —

APPLICATION FOR EMPLOYMENT

PERSONAL DATA

Last Name	First Name	Middle Initial	Specify any other name under which you have been employed.

| Home Address

Street

City & State | Have you ever been employed by ___ or any of our subsidiaries? ☐ Yes ☐ No

If yes, when?

What was your position? |
|---|---|

| Home Phone

(   ) | Any other phone number at which we could reach you?

(   ) | Are you willing to travel?

☐ Yes ☐ No |
|---|---|---|

Position Applied For	List names of relatives employed at ___ or subsidiary, or write "none."

| Are you available to work overtime?

☐ Yes ☐ No   Comments: | How were you referred to us?
(Name newspaper, agency, employee, or other) |
|---|---|

| Are you at least 18 years of age, but less than 65 years?

☐ Yes ☐ No	Date available to start work

Have you ever been convicted of any crime? ☐ Yes ☐ No

If yes, give dates and details.

| Technical or Professional Societies | For Clerical Positions Only, estimate your speeds:

Typing_____ wpm   Steno_____ wpm

Speedwriting_____ wpm |
|---|---|

450

EMPLOYMENT AND BUSINESS EXPERIENCE

To be completed by all persons with full-time work experience. A resume may be substituted to the extent that the required information is contained in it. *Include all full-time positions,* excluding Military Service. Be exact as to dates. *List most recent position first.*

Name of Company	Co. Phone Number ( )	Title of Position	Salary
Street	Actual Duties		
City and State			
Immediate Supervisor			
Date Employed From _____ 19 ___ to _____ 19 ___	Specific reason for leaving or desiring change		

Name of Company	Co. Phone Number ( )	Title of Position	Salary
Street	Actual Duties		
City and State			
Immediate Supervisor			
Date-Employed From _____ 19 ___ to _____ 19 ___	Specific reason for leaving		

Name of Company	Co. Phone Number ( )	Title of Position	Salary
Street	Actual Duties		
City and State			
Immediate Supervisor			
Date Employed From _____ 19 ___ to _____ 19 ___	Specific reason for leaving		

Other Periods: State what you did in other periods not already covered. Include periods of unemployment, self-employment, part-time or temporary work.

From	To	Employer and Job Title
_____ 19 ___	_____ 19 ___	_____
_____ 19 ___	_____ 19 ___	_____
_____ 19 ___	_____ 19 ___	_____
_____ 19 ___	_____ 19 ___	_____

If now employed have you informed your present employer of your intention to leave?

☐ Yes ☐ No Comments: _____

If now employed, may we refer to your present employer?

☐ Yes ☐ No Comments: _____

EDUCATION

School	Name and Location	Yrs. Completed	Degree or Diploma	Major Courses
High				
College				
Business or Tech.				
Other				

Special training or skills (include any foreign languages you can speak, understand, or write):

U.S. MILITARY SERVICE

Branch	Highest Rank Attained	Any Service Connected Disability? ☐ Yes ☐ No

If yes, specify percent and nature of disability.

Describe your duties and responsibilities.

List any military training schools attended (include military-sponsored training). Also specify number of weeks for each.

What specific education, experience, and/or personal characteristics do you have which qualify you for the position for which you are applying?

IMPORTANT – PLEASE READ CAREFULLY AND SIGN

The information contained in this application is accurate and correct to the best of my knowledge. I understand all information contained herein is subject to check and verification by _____ Inc., and its subsidiaries, and any incorrect or misleading information may render this application void and/or be cause for immediate dismissal in the event of my employment. I hereby give_____ Inc., and its subsidiaries, permission to contact any or all the persons or companies named on this application except, as may be noted, in the case of my present employer. I further understand that I am required to successfully pass a physical examination as a condition of permanent employment, unless it is waived by the Company.

_____ and its subsidiaries are equal opportunity employers, and having developed the policy shall take definite affirmative action to provide equal employment and promotional opportunities for all persons without regard to race, color, religion, sex or national origin.

DATE _____   SIGNED _____

COMPLETED SAMPLE APPLICATION FORM

– An Equal Opportunity Employer –

APPLICATION FOR EMPLOYMENT

PERSONAL DATA

Last Name	First Name	Middle Initial	Specify any other name under which you have been employed.
Taylor,	Ralph	J.	None

Home Address
2321 Ocean Ave.
Street
Matawan, N.J.
City & State

Have you ever been employed by ___ or any of our subsidiaries? ☐ Yes ☑ No
If yes, when?
What was your position?

Home Phone (201) 947-2759	Any other phone number at which we could reach you? ( )	Are you willing to travel? ☐ Yes ☐ No *(Maybe)*

Position Applied For
Clerk

List names of relatives employed at ___ or subsidiary, or write "none."
None

Are you available to work overtime? ☑ Yes ☐ No Comments: *No Tuesdays or Thursdays*

How were you referred to us? (Name newspaper, agency, employee, or other)
Saw ad in newspaper (Asbury Park Times)

Are you at least 18 years of age, but less than 65 years? ☑ Yes ☐ No

Date available to start work
Immediately

Have you ever been convicted of any crime? ☐ Yes ☑ No
If yes, give dates and details.

Technical or Professional Societies
None

For Clerical Positions Only, estimate your speeds:
Typing 0 wpm   Steno 0 wpm
Speedwriting 0 wpm

EMPLOYMENT AND BUSINESS EXPERIENCE

To be completed by all persons with full-time work experience. A resume may be substituted to the extent that the required information is contained in it. *Include all full-time positions,* excluding Military Service. Be exact as to dates. *List most recent position first.*

Name of Company MAX'S LUNCHEONette	Co. Phone Number (201) 612-4177	Title of Position Busboy	Salary $85/wk
Street 43 Boardwalk Ave.	Actual Duties Clean Tables. Wash floors.		
City and State Long Branch. N.J.	General Counter duties		
Immediate Supervisor Max Krisky			
Date Employed From May 15 19 78 to Sept 15 19 78	Specific reason for leaving or desiring change Returned to school		
Name of Company Camp So-Jor-nay	Co. Phone Number (617) 884-9317	Title of Position Camp Counselor	Salary $200/summ.
Street	Actual Duties Supervise one cabin of 9 year old		
City and State White Pines, New Hampshire	boys at sleep-in camp. had complete charge		
Immediate Supervisor Tom Elliot	10 boys, including cleanliness of cabin, safety of boys in		
Date Employed From July 1 19 77 to Aug 30 19 77	Specific reason for leaving activities take care of minor scrapes, End of Summer discipline, etc.		
Name of Company	Co. Phone Number ( )	Title of Position	Salary
Street	Actual Duties		
City and State			
Immediate Supervisor			
Date Employed From 19 to 19	Specific reason for leaving		

Other Periods: State what you did in other periods not already covered. Include periods of unemployment, self-employment, part-time or temporary work.

From	To	Employer and Job Title
Spring 19 69	Spring 19 72	Self-employed - Newspaper delivery route.
19	19	
19	19	
19	19	

If now employed have you informed your present employer of your intention to leave? *N.A.*

☐ Yes ☐ No Comments:

If now employed, may we refer to your present employer? *N.A.*

☐ Yes ☐ No Comments:

EDUCATION

School	Name and Location	Yrs. Completed	Degree or Diploma	Major Courses
High	*Monmouth Regional High*	*4*	*General*	*History, English, Math, French*
College	*Brookdale Community College*	*1*		*English, Sociology*
Business or Tech.				
Other				

Special training or skills (include any foreign languages you can speak, understand, or write): *Read and write some French*

U.S. MILITARY SERVICE   *None*

Branch	Highest Rank Attained	Any Service Connected Disability? ☐ Yes ☐ No If yes, specify percent and nature of disability.
Describe your duties and responsibilities.		

List any military training schools attended (include military-sponsored training). Also specify number of weeks for each.

What specific education, experience, and/or personal characteristics do you have which qualify you for the position for which you are applying?

I have always completed the jobs I have had to the full satisfaction of my employers. I never missed a day on my paper route, except when I was sick, and then I always called so that a replacement could fill in for me. I was always on time with my boys at camp for Reveille, General Assembly, Special Events, etc. I am a hard worker and like to do a full days work every day, no matter what the work.

IMPORTANT – PLEASE READ CAREFULLY AND SIGN

The information contained in this application is accurate and correct to the best of my knowledge. I understand all information contained herein is subject to check and verification by _____ Inc., and its subsidiaries, and any incorrect or misleading information may render this application void and/or be cause for immediate dismissal in the event of my employment. I hereby give _____ Inc., and its subsidiaries, permission to contact any or all the persons or companies named on this application except, as may be noted, in the case of my present employer. I further understand that I am required to successfully pass a physical examination as a condition of permanent employment, unless it is waived by the Company.

_____ and its subsidiaries are equal opportunity employers, and having developed the policy shall take definite affirmative action to provide equal employment and promotional opportunities for all persons without regard to race, color, religion, sex or national origin.

DATE   *5/5/79*   SIGNED   *Ralph Taylor*

Answers

The last question is *less specific* than the others. It gives the employer an opportunity to learn something about your attitudes and the way you think. In filling out this question, you should try to state all your positive traits and characteristics. Although you may have considered a past job to be trivial, the fact that you kept the job and "stuck to it" shows perseverance (persistence) and character. That's what employers want to see.

2. Here is an application form for a charge card. This form is similar to others you may have to fill out. See how well you do in following directions.

After you fill out the application form, check yours with the sample completed form on p. 457.

REQUEST FOR _____ **MASTER CHARGE CARD**

FIRST, MIDDLE INITIAL, LAST NAME				DATE OF BIRTH
HOME ADDRESS–NO. & STREET		APT. NO.	HOME TELEPHONE NO.	NO. OF DEPENDENTS
CITY, TOWN, POST OFFICE	STATE	ZIP CODE	YEARS THERE	SOCIAL SECURITY NO.
PREVIOUS HOME ADDRESS			YEARS THERE	SEND MAIL TO ☐ HOME ☐ BUSINESS
FIRM NAME OR EMPLOYER		TELEPHONE NO.	DEPARTMENT	POSITION
BUSINESS ADDRESS			ANNUAL SALARY $	YEARS THERE
NAME AND ADDRESS OF PREVIOUS EMPLOYER (IF ABOVE IS LESS THAN 2 YEARS)				YEARS THERE
REAL ESTATE OWNED ☐ HOME ☐ OTHER	NAME OF LANDLORD OR MORTGAGE COMPANY		ADDRESS	RENT/MTGE. PAYMENT $
CHECKING ACCOUNT, BRANCH ADDRESS		ACCOUNT NUMBER	SAVINGS ACCOUNT, BANK & ADDRESS	ACCOUNT NUMBER
NAME AND ADDRESS OF NEAREST RELATIVE (NOT LIVING WITH YOU)				

EQUAL CREDIT OPPORTUNITY ACT NOTICE — IF INCOME FROM ALIMONY, CHILD SUPPORT OR MAINTENANCE IS NOT RELIED ON FOR CREDIT YOU DO NOT HAVE TO DISCLOSE SUCH INCOME

OTHER INCOME ☐ SUPPORT ☐ DISABILITY ☐ ALIMONY ☐ OTHER AMOUNT WK ☐ MO. ☐ PLEASE STATE SOURCE

IF YOUR SPOUSE OR OTHER PERSON WILL HAVE USE OF THIS ACCOUNT OR WILL BE CONTRACTUALLY LIABLE FOR PAYMENT OF THIS ACCOUNT, PLEASE COMPLETE THE FOLLOWING:

NAME	EMPLOYER	ADDRESS	ANNUAL SALARY $

LIST ALL DEBTS OWING (INDIVIDUAL OR JOINT) IN ANY NAME USED BY PERSONS SIGNING THIS APPLICATION.

NAME AND ADDRESS	ACCOUNT NUMBER	UNPAID BALANCE	MONTHLY PAYMENT

I (WE) REPRESENT AND AFFIRM THAT ALL THE STATEMENTS MADE BY ME (US) IN THIS APPLICATION ARE TRUE AND CORRECT AND HAVE BEEN MADE IN ORDER TO INDUCE YOU TO GRANT CREDIT TO ME (US). I (WE) AUTHORIZE _____ TO EXCHANGE CREDIT INFORMATION WITH OTHERS IN CONNECTION WITH THIS APPLICATION. I (WE) FULLY UNDERSTAND THAT THE USE OF THE CREDIT CARD IS SUBJECT TO THE TERMS AND CONDITIONS OF THE MASTER CHARGE CARD HOLDERS AGREEMENT. I (WE) AGREE THAT THIS APPLICATION SHALL BE AND REMAIN YOUR PROPERTY WHETHER OR NOT THIS APPLICATION IS APPROVED.

SIGNATURE	DATE	SIGNATURE	DATE

FOR BANK USE ONLY	CARD NO.	CREDIT LINE		DATE
	NO. CARDS REQUESTED	EXPIRATION DATE	APPROVED BY	

COMPLETED SAMPLE MASTER CHARGE FORM

REQUEST FOR _____ **MASTER CHARGE CARD**

FIRST, MIDDLE INITIAL, LAST NAME			DATE OF BIRTH
James I. Jones			2/12/52

HOME ADDRESS–NO. & STREET	APT. NO.	HOME TELEPHONE NO.	NO. OF DEPENDENTS
921 Pleasant Ave.	3D	448-4000	1

CITY, TOWN, POST OFFICE	STATE	ZIP CODE	YEARS THERE	SOCIAL SECURITY NO.
New Jersey		08540	3	193 46 5721

PREVIOUS HOME ADDRESS	YEARS THERE	SEND MAIL TO
241 Detmar Dr. Winter Pk., Fla. 32789	2	☑ HOME ☐ BUSINESS

FIRM NAME OR EMPLOYER	TELEPHONE NO.	DEPARTMENT	POSITION
Bucks Construction Firm	882-9100	—	Carpenter

BUSINESS ADDRESS	ANNUAL SALARY	YEARS THERE
1520 North Lane Trenton, N.J. 08628	$15,000	3

NAME AND ADDRESS OF PREVIOUS EMPLOYER (IF ABOVE IS LESS THAN 2 YEARS) | YEARS THERE

REAL ESTATE OWNED ☐ HOME ☐ OTHER	NAME OF LANDLORD OR MORTGAGE COMPANY / ADDRESS	RENT/MTGE. PAYMENT
	Resa Realty Co. 771 Main St. Hightstown	$400/mo.

CHECKING ACCOUNT, BRANCH ADDRESS	ACCOUNT NUMBER	SAVINGS ACCOUNT, BANK & ADDRESS	ACCOUNT NUMBER
New Jersey Central	J1093	Jersey Savings & Loan	7659

NAME AND ADDRESS OF NEAREST RELATIVE (NOT LIVING WITH YOU)
Jack Jones 110 E. 190th. St. N.Y.

EQUAL CREDIT OPPORTUNITY ACT NOTICE — IF INCOME FROM ALIMONY, CHILD SUPPORT OR MAINTENANCE IS NOT RELIED ON FOR CREDIT YOU DO NOT HAVE TO DISCLOSE SUCH INCOME

OTHER INCOME ☐ SUPPORT ☐ DISABILITY ☐ ALIMONY ☐ OTHER	AMOUNT WK ☐ MO ☐	PLEASE STATE SOURCE

IF YOUR SPOUSE OR OTHER PERSON WILL HAVE USE OF THIS ACCOUNT OR WILL BE CONTRACTUALLY LIABLE FOR PAYMENT OF THIS ACCOUNT, PLEASE COMPLETE THE FOLLOWING:

NAME	EMPLOYER	ADDRESS	ANNUAL SALARY
Vivian	Brown and Brown	71 Nassau Street	$10,000

LIST ALL DEBTS OWING (INDIVIDUAL OR JOINT) IN ANY NAME USED BY PERSONS SIGNING THIS APPLICATION.

NAME AND ADDRESS	ACCOUNT NUMBER	UNPAID BALANCE	MONTHLY PAYMENT
Central Bank of N.J.	2749	$2500	$100

I (WE) REPRESENT AND AFFIRM THAT ALL THE STATEMENTS MADE BY ME (US) IN THIS APPLICATION ARE TRUE AND CORRECT AND HAVE BEEN MADE IN ORDER TO INDUCE YOU TO GRANT CREDIT TO ME (US). I (WE) AUTHORIZE _____ TO EXCHANGE CREDIT INFORMATION WITH OTHERS IN CONNECTION WITH THIS APPLICATION. I (WE) FULLY UNDERSTAND THAT THE USE OF THE CREDIT CARD IS SUBJECT TO THE TERMS AND CONDITIONS OF THE MASTER CHARGE CARD HOLDERS AGREEMENT. I (WE) AGREE THAT THIS APPLICATION SHALL BE AND REMAIN YOUR PROPERTY WHETHER OR NOT THIS APPLICATION IS APPROVED.

SIGNATURE James L. Jones	DATE 4/19/79	SIGNATURE Vivian Jones	DATE 4/19/79

FOR BANK USE ONLY	CARD NO.		CREDIT LINE		DATE
	NO. CARDS REQUESTED	EXPIRATION DATE	APPROVED BY		

Glossary A
SPECIAL TERMS PRESENTED IN
READING AND LEARNING POWER

Accent.   A mark (′) used to show which syllable in a word is stressed, that is, spoken with greatest intensity or loudness. This mark usually comes right after and slightly above the accented syllable. (In some dictionaries the accent mark is placed right before the accented syllable.)

Accent Rules.   In two-syllable words the first syllable is usually stressed, except when the second syllable contains two vowels. Examples: pi′lot, ap′ple, pro′gram, pro ceed′, pa rade′. In three-syllable words it is usually the first or second syllable that is stressed. Example: cap′ i tal. If a three- or four-syllable word ends in *tion* or *ic*, the primary accent is usually on the syllable before *ic* or *tion*. Examples: he ro′ic, con sti tu′tion.

Analogy.   Word set based on relationships. In order to supply the missing term in a proportion, you must know how the meanings of the words relate to each other. Example: Prince : princess :: wizard :_____ (witch).

Antonym.   A word that is opposite in meaning to another. Examples: tall–short, fat–thin.

Appendix.   A section of a book that contains extra information that does not quite fit into the book but that the author feels is important enough to be presented separately.

Bias.   A mental leaning, a partiality, a prejudice, or a slanting of something.

Book Marking.   A technique in which passages are underlined or marked directly in the textbook.

Breve.   The short vowel mark (˘).

Buzz Words.   Words that "sound a buzzer" in the mind. They are any words that take on particular importance in the discussion of a topic. They are reminders of a wide range of facts, associations, and concepts.

Central Idea.   (See Main Idea.)

Closed Syllable.   (See Syllable.)

Combining Forms.   Roots, often borrowed from another language, that join together or that join with a prefix, a suffix, or both a prefix and a suffix to form a word. In this book a combining form is defined as any word part that can join with another word or word part to form a word or a new word. Examples: *bio*—life, *cardio*—heart.

Comparison. A demonstration of the similarities between persons, ideas, things, and so on. (See Supporting Details.)

Completion Tests. (See Objective Tests.)

Compound Word. Separate words that combine to form a new word. Examples: dishwasher, cowgirl, grandfather, grandmother, head-on.

Concentration. Sustained attention. It is essential not only for studying but also for listening to lectures.

Connotative Meaning. Emotional associations of a word. The connotative meaning of a word goes beyond its direct, specific meaning.

Consonants. The consonants are represented by all the letters of the alphabet that are not vowels.

Consonant Blends. Two or more consonant sounds blended together so that the identity of each sound is retained. Examples: bl, cr.

Context. The words surrounding a particular word that can throw light on its meaning.

Contrast. A demonstration of the differences between persons, ideas, things, and so on. (See Supporting Details.)

Denotative Meaning. The direct, specific meaning of a word.

Diacritical Marks. The marks that show how to pronounce a word. (See Breve, Macron, and Accent.)

Dictionary. A very important reference tool that supplies word meanings, pronunciations, and a great amount of other useful information.

Digraphs. 1. Consonant digraphs: Usually two consonants that represent one speech sound. Examples: *ch* (chair), *sh* (shame), *th* (thumb), *ph* (phase), *ng* (sung), *gh* (tough). 2. Vowel digraphs: Two vowels adjacent (next) to one another in a word or syllable and standing for a single vowel sound. Examples: *oa* (boat), *ei* (receive), *eo* (yeoman), *ea* (beagle), *ie* (believe), *ai* (rain).

Diphthongs. Blends of vowel sounds beginning with the first and gliding to the second. The vowel blends are represented by two adjacent vowels. Examples: *oi* (boil), *oy* (boy), *ow* (cow), *ou* (bough).

Editorial. An expression of opinion on a specific topic, usually in a newspaper or magazine.

Essay. (See Subjective Tests.)

Fact. Something that exists; a true statement. Example: Albany is the capital of New York.

Figures of Speech. Word usages that give color, decoration, and life to language. 1. Hyperbole—The use of gross exaggeration for effect. Example: I walked a million miles today. 2. Oxymoron—The combining of opposites to convey a particular image or to produce a striking effect. Example: A loud silence. 3. Metaphor—A comparison between two unlike objects without the use of *like* or *as*. Example: He is a jellyfish. 4. Personification—The giving of human characteristics and capabilities to nonhuman things such as nonliving objects, abstract ideas, or animals. Example: Winter's icy breath. 5. Simile—A comparison between two unlike objects using *like* or *as*. Example: Her disposition is like glass; it breaks easily, and when it breaks, it cuts.

Fill-in Tests. (See Objective Tests.)

Foreword. (See Preface.)

Glossary. A listing of the meanings of specialized words or phrases.

Homographs. Words that are spelled the same but have different meanings. Examples: I *saw* him yesterday. Be careful when you use the *saw*. Some homographs are spelled the same but do not sound the same. Examples: I *object* to that question. What is that *object*?

Homonyms or Homophones. Words that sound alike but have different spellings and meanings. Examples: two, too, to; pare, pear; bare, bear.

Hyperbole. (See Figures of Speech.)

Index. A listing of topics discussed in a book and page numbers where discussed.

Inference. Understanding derived from an indirect suggestion in what is stated. (See Jokes and Proverbs.)

Jokes. Words or actions that are funny. To understand and enjoy jokes you must be able to see double meanings and read between the lines. Often the most important part of the joke is not what is written, but what has been left to the imagination.

Macron. The long vowel mark (⁻).

Main idea. The central thought of a paragraph, section, chapter, or article. All the sentences in a paragraph or all the paragraphs in a section, chapter, or article develop the main idea.

Matching Items Test. (See Objective Tests.)

Metaphor. (See Figures of Speech.)

Mnemonic Device. A memory association trick that helps in recalling material.

Multiple Choice Tests. (See Objective Tests.)

Notecard. An essential aid for recording notes for papers.

Notetaking. A useful study and paper-writing tool.

Objective Tests. Tests involving short answers, usually one or two words.

There is usually only one correct answer for each question on an objective test. Examples of objective tests: True/false, multiple choice, completion or fill-in forms, short answer, matching.

Open Syllable. (See Syllable.)

Opinion. An attitude or feeling. Opinions vary from person to person; they cannot be proved conclusively right or wrong. Example: Bob Hope is a good actor.

Overlearning. A technique for retaining information. Overlearning occurs when learners continue practice even though they feel that they have already learned the material.

Oxymoron. (See Figures of Speech.)

Paragraph. The smallest developmental unit in writing. Paragraphs are set off from each other usually by indenting the first line.

Personification. (See Figures of Speech.)

Phonics. The study of the relationships between the written symbols of a language and the sounds that they represent.

Preface or Foreword. A short introduction to a book presented at the beginning.

Prefix. A letter or a group of letters added to the beginning of a root (base) word to form a new, related word. Examples: *ex*—out; *re*—again, back.

Propaganda. Any systematic, widespread, deliberate indoctrination or plan for indoctrination. People who use propaganda are trying to influence others by using deceptive methods. Examples of propaganda techniques: Name Calling, Bandwagon, Card Stacking, Transfer, Plain Folks.

Proverbs. Short sayings in common use that aptly express some obvious truth or familiar experience. To understand proverbs you must be able to read between the lines.

Questions. A good way for students to gain a better insight into a subject that also gives the instructor feedback and slows the instructor down if he or she is going too fast.

Recall. The process of finding the answer to a question in your memory without rereading the text or notes. (See SQ3R.)

Root. The smallest word unit that can exist and retain its basic meaning. Examples: run, rope, do.

Scanning. Rapid reading.

Schwa. The sound often found in the unstressed (unaccented) syllables of words with more than one syllable. The schwa sound is represented by an upside down *e* (ə) in the phonetic (speech) alphabet. A syllable ending in *le* preceded by a consonant is usually the final syllable in a word and contains the schwa sound.

Short Answer Test. (See Objective Tests.)

Silent Consonants. Two adjacent consonants one of which is silent. Examples: *kn* (know), *pn* (pneumonia), *gn* (gnat).

Silent *e* Rule. In a word or syllable containing two vowels separated by one consonant, and having an *e* as the final vowel, the first vowel is usually long and the final *e* is usually silent. Examples: nōt¢, tāk¢.

Simile. (See Figures of Speech.)

Skimming. Rapid reading to locate information.

Special Letters. 1. The *y*—When *y* is at the beginning of a word or syllable it is a consonant. Examples: yes, yet, yellow, young. When *y* acts as a vowel it represents the short *i* sound, the long *i* sound, or the long *e* sound. Examples: baby, my, gym. 2. Some words beginning with *c* or *g* can cause problems. The letters *c* and *g* stand for both a hard and a soft sound. Examples of soft *g* sound: gym, George. Examples of hard *g* sound: get, go. Examples of soft *c* sound: cent, cite. Examples of hard *c* sound: came, course. 3. The *q* is always followed by the letter *u*. It represents either one speech sound or a blend of two sounds. At the beginning of a word *qu* almost always represents a blend of two sounds (*kw*). Examples: quick, queen. When *qu* appears at the end of a word in a *que* combination it represents one sound (*k*). Examples: antique, clique. 4. A vowel followed by *r* is controlled by the *r*. As a result, the vowel is neither long nor short. Example: bar.

SQ3R. A widely used study technique that involves five steps: Survey, Question, Read, Recite or Recall, and Review.

Subjective Tests. Essay tests. Essay tests are given when an instructor wants to see whether students know the material thoroughly enough to organize it and use it to draw conclusions.

Suffix. A letter or a group of letters added to the end of a root (base) word to form a new, related word. Examples: *tion*—act of, state of, result of; *y*—having, full of, tending to, like.

Summary. A brief statement of the essential information in a longer piece. The main idea of an article and the important events should be stated in a summary, although not necessarily in the sequence presented in the article. The sequence *should* be followed if it is essential to understanding the article. A summary does *not* include the summarizer's opinions of the article.

Supporting Details. Additional information that supports, explains, or illustrates the main idea. Some of the ways that supporting details may be arranged are as cause and effect, examples, sequence-of-events situations, descriptions, definitions, comparisons, or contrasts.

Study, How to. 1. Build good habits. 2. Devise a system that works for you. 3. Keep at it. 4. Maintain a certain degree of tension. 5. Concentrate.

Syllabication. The division of multisyllabic words into single syllables.

Syllabication Rules. 1. Vowel Consonant/Consonant Vowel Rule—If a vowel is followed by two consonants and a vowel, the word is divided between the two consonants. Examples: clat/ter, bat/ter, fif/ty. 2. Vowel/Consonant Vowel Rule—If a vowel is followed by one consonant and a vowel, the consonant usually goes with the second syllable. Examples: ti/ger, cra/zy, la/dy. 3. Special Consonant *le* Rule—If a consonant comes before *le* in a word of more than one syllable, the consonant goes with *le* to form the last syllable. Examples: mum/ble, han/dle.

Syllable. A vowel or a group of letters with one vowel sound. Examples: a, o, be, mle, mon, pre. 1. Open syllable—A syllable that contains only *one* vowel, the vowel comes at the end of the syllable, and the vowel sound is usually long. Examples: gō, wē. 2. Closed syllable—A syllable that contains only *one* vowel, the syllable ends in a consonant and the vowel sound is usually short. Examples: cŭt, păt.

Synonym. A word similar in meaning to another. Examples: small—little; fat—corpulent.

Table of Contents. A listing of chapter titles, major headings, and page numbers at the beginning of a book.

Telegraphic Writing. The use of one or two words to stand for a complete message. The words used are content words that contain significant information.

Topic Sentence. A statement of what a paragraph is about by naming the topic.

True/False Tests. (See Objective Tests.)

Vowels. The vowels are represented by the letters *a, e, i, o, u*, and sometimes *y* and *w* in such words as *say, cry, hymn, saw, how*, and *draw*.

Glossary B
VOCABULARY WORDS PRESENTED IN
READING AND LEARNING POWER *

(The number after the meaning refers to the lesson in which the word is presented.)

Abate. Decreases; lessens; diminishes. 8

Abhor. To hate extremely; detest; loathe. 2

Abundance. Plentiful quantity or supply. 9

Abyss. A bottomless pit (hole). 9

Adamant. Stubborn; unyielding. 5

Affluent. Wealthy. 5

Affront. Insult. 5

Aggregate. Things gathered into a mass or total; a collection of things. 8

Ancient. Old; relating to a remote period, to a time early in history. 6

Annual. Yearly. 4

Apprehension. Anxiety; fear. 5

Ascetic. Self-denying; characteristic of a very severe existence; characteristic of self-denial. 9

Autobiography. Life story written by oneself. 14

Autograph. Signature; written by a person's own hand: an autograph letter; containing autographs; an autograph album; to write one's name on or in. 14

Automobile. A usually four-wheeled automotive vehicle designed for passenger transportation on streets or roadways; car. 13

Automotive. Self-propelling; relating to or concerned with vehicles or machines that propel themselves such as automobiles, trucks, airplanes, and motorboats. 13

Bass.* Edible (able to be eaten) fishes of the perch family. 3

Bass. The lowest male singing voice. 3

Bibliography. A listing of books on a subject by an author (the description includes author's name, title, publisher, date of publication, and so on). 14

Bill. A name; a statement of money owed; a piece of paper money. 3

Biography. Person's life story. 14

Bondage. Slavery. 7

*Although a word may have a number of meanings, only those meanings used in this book will be presented.

Boundless. Unlimited. 7

Capital. Money. 4

Centennial. Pertaining to a period of 100 years; lasting 100 years; a one—hundredth anniversary. 15

Centimeter. In the metric system, a unit of measure equal to 1/100 meter (0.3937 inch). 15

Century. Period of 100 years. 15

Chaotic. Completely confused or disordered. 2

Clad. Dressed. 1

Coarse. Vulgar; lacking taste; common. 6

Coarsest. Roughest; Most lacking in fineness or delicacy of texture. 9

Column. A regular article or feature; a long narrow formation of troops in which the troops are one behind the other; a slender, upright support that is generally ornamental. 3

Combine. A machine for threshing grain. 3

Combine. To unite or join together. 3

Competent. Qualified. 6

Complementary. Completing or making perfect; helping to fill out. 2

Compulsory. Required, obligatory. 1

Concept. Idea. 8

Conduct. To direct. 3

Conduct. Personal behavior. 3

Conscientious. Careful; thorough. 1

Content. Satisfied. 3

Content. All that is contained in something. 3

Controversy. A discussion of a question in which opposing opinions clash; a dispute; a quarrel. 8

Cooperate. To act or work with another toward a common end; to operate jointly; to act together; to associate with another for mutual benefit; to unite. 14

Corpulent. Fat. 4

Count. A nobleman in some European countries; rely on; to inventory or check by numbering off. 3

Cumulative. Increasing or growing by successive additions. 8

Decade. Period of 10 years. 15

Decameter. In the metric system, a measure of length containing 10 meters, equal to 393.70 inches or 32.81 feet. 15

Deceitful. Given to trickery; cheating. 6

---

*Words that are spelled the same but pronounced differently will be presented separately.

Decimal. Numbered by 10; based on 10; pertaining to tenths or the number 10; a decimal fraction. 15

Decimate. To take or destroy a tenth part of; to destroy but not completely; to destroy a great number or proportion of. 15

Decimeter. In the metric system, a unit of length equal to 1/10 meter. 15

Demotion. The act of reducing to a lower grade or rank. 13

Derogatory. Belittling. 10

Desolate. Uninhabited; isolated; deserted. 2

Diligent. Constantly trying to accomplish something; industrious. 2

Diminished. Made less. 7

Discord. Disagreement; lack of harmony; difference; conflict. 2

Discourse. A communication of ideas; a communication. 8

Disposition. Leaning; inclination. 7

Dogmatic. Stating opinions as if they were facts; excessively positive in stating opinions; opinionated. 7

Dual. Double. 1

Egotistical. Vain. 4

Eminent. Distinguished. 6

Emotion. A physical or social disturbance; turmoil in feeling; feeling; an expression of feeling. 13

Equitably. Fairly; evenly. 7

Equivalent. Equal. 4

Excerpts. Passages taken out of a book, document, film, and so on; extracts. 2

Exerting. Putting forth, as power. 8

Exhausted. Tired. 4

Expanded. Spread out; enlarged. 7

Extent. Limit or degree. 1

External. Outward. 9

Feigned. Pretended; made believe. 2

Fidelity. Faithfulness. 7

Fiscal. Financial. 8

Foul. Vile; unfair; stinking; loathsome; in baseball, a batted ball that falls outside the foul lines of the infield; indecent; obscene. 3

Fragile. Easily broken or damaged; delicate; frail. 2

Gossip. Idle talk or rumors. 9

Grave. Serious. 4

Harmony. Agreement; accord; a consistent, orderly, or pleasing arrangement of parts. 2

Hue. Color. 9

Humanity.   Mankind; the human race. 7

Immature.   Childish. 4

Immense.   Huge. 4

Immobile.   Not movable; motionless. 13

Implication.   A logical relationship between two propositions in which if the first is true, the second is true; that from which an inference can be drawn; something not directly stated; a hint or suggestion. 8

Impressive.   Imposing; awesome (an overwhelming feeling of admiration, fear, reverence, and so on, produced by that which is grand, extremely powerful, or the like). 9

Indifferent.   Apathetic; uninterested. 6

Infamous.   Notorious. 4

Inflation.   An increase in the amount of paper money in circulation that decreases its value and causes a large rise in prices. 8

Inhibited.   Held back; restrained. 7

Innumerable.   Very many; countless. 6

Intangible.   Unsubstantial; unable to be touched; vague. 9

Interrogates.   Questions. 5

Intimidate.   Frighten. 4

Intricate.   Complex, complicated. 2

Jeopardy.   Danger. 4

Kilometer.   1,000 meters. 15

Lucid.   Clear. 6

Malady.   Illness. 5

Mean.   Average; selfish; unaccommodating; offensive; have in mind, purpose; intend; shabby; poor. (pl.) Money; riches. 3

Meter.   In the metric system, a unit of length equal to approximately 39.37 inches; an instrument for measuring the amount of something (as water, gas, electricity); an instrument for measuring distance, time, weight, speed, and so forth; a measure of verse. 15

Millennium.   Period of 1,000 years; a one-thousandth anniversary; a period of great happiness (the millennium). 15

Millimeter.   In the metric system, a unit of length equal to 1/1000 meter (0.03937 inch). 15

Million.   One thousand thousands (1,000,000); a very large or indefinitely large number; being one million in number, very many. 15

Mirth.   Amusement; jollity. 9

Mobile.   Movable; not firm or stationary; easily influenced; changeable; in military usage, capable of being moved or transported; migratory; a piece of mobile sculpture. 13

Mobilize. To put into movement or circulation; to assemble and put into a state of readiness for active service in war. 13

Modest. Humble. 5

Motion. The act of moving; a gesture; a proposal; a suggestion; in law, an application to a court for a ruling, order, and so forth; to make movements or gestures with the hand, head, or any other part of the body; to give directions with the hand, head, and so forth. 13

Motivate. To stimulate; to move; to stimulate the active interest of a study through appeal to certain interests or by special devices; to make something interesting and appealing to students. 13

Motive. Something within a person, such as need, an idea, or an emotion, that stimulates him or her to an action; the consideration influencing a choice; cause; reason why. 13

Motor. An engine; anything that imparts motion; a source of mechanical power; automobile; a rotating machine that transforms electrical energy into mechanical energy; causing or imparting motion; to travel by car. 13

Move. To change the place or position of; to persuade; to arouse or stir; in commerce, to dispose of goods by selling; to make progress; to advance; the act of moving; a change of residence; a step taken toward obtaining something. 13

Mythical. Imaginary; fictional; from mythology. 2

Naive. Childlike; unsophisticated. 6

Nutritious. Nourishing. 2

Obese. Very fat. 7

Oblivious. Unmindful. 7

Obsolete. No longer in general use; no longer in fashion; out of date; archaic. 2

Opera. A drama in which music is the essential factor and which consists of songs accompanied by an orchestra; suitable for use at an opera, such as opera chairs or opera glasses. 14

Operate. To perform a work or labor; to manage; to run; to perform an operation; to perform surgery; to carry on a military action or mission; to act as a dealer or broker in the stock market; to follow a course of conduct that is irregular or antisocial. 14

Operation. The work; the deed; the procedure carried out on a living body for the purpose of correcting some abnormal state; surgery; the state of being functional; an exertion of power or influence; a process in which one quantity or expression is derived from another; a business transaction especially if it's risky. (pl.) The staff agency as in a United States air headquarters. 14

Operator. A worker who operates a machine or device as his regular trade; a maker of quack medicines or fraudulent articles; a shrewd and skillful person who knows how to get around and evade controls or restrictions; a dealer in stocks; someone who manages or runs a business. 14

Opus. A literary work or composition; usually referring to a musical composition or set of compositions generally numbered in the order of its issue. 14

Ornament. Decoration. 9

Ostracism. Exclusion; banishment. 7

Overemphasized. Too greatly stressed. 7

Paradox. Self-contradiction. 7

Peers. Persons who are equal in rank. 7

Perceived. Saw; thought of. 1

Perilous. Risky. 4

Perseverance. Persistence; steadfastness; the act of continuing in a task once it's undertaken. 2

Pertinent. Relevant; being to the point; relating to or bearing on the matter at hand. 6

Pessimist. One who looks on the dark side of things. 6

Phenomenon. A circumstance that is apparent and can be described. 7

Pilfer. To steal in small quantities. 1

Polygamous. Having more than one husband or wife at the same time. 7

Potent. Powerful. 5

Precedes. Comes before. 1

Present. A gift. 3

Present. To give or bestow formally. 3

Principal. Head; chief or highest in importance; the amount owed or an investment minus the interest or on which interest is computed. 3

Prior. Earlier in time; preceding. 7

Promotion. The act of being raised in position or rank; the act of setting up or furthering a business enterprise. 13

Prudent. Wise; sensible. 5

Range. An area equipped with targets for shooting weapons; roam; to pass from one point to another; to vary within stated limits; a cooking stove; a chain of mountains. 3

Raze. To demolish. 4

React. To respond. 7

Recipient. Receiver. 1

Reiterate. To say again. 2

Reluctant. Unwilling. 5

Remedy. Cure. 4

Residential.   Suitable for homes. 2

Revoke.   To withdraw. 1

Rigorous.   Exact; precise; severe. 8

Robust.   Strong. 6

Run.   To operate; to flow as a liquid; a series of sudden and urgent demands on it for payment; cost; to meet or find accidently [run across]; in the end [long run]; to exhaust a quantity or supply of [run dry]; to strike or to drive a vehicle into someone [run down]. 3

Sags.   Declines; sinks. 8

Sarcastic.   Cutting; sneering; describing by opposite quality; drawing attention to failings by referring to their opposites insincerely. 1

Saturated.   Filled to capacity. 7

Scarlet.   A bright red color. 9

Scorn.   Contempt. 1

Scrutinize.   To observe very carefully. 8

Serene.   Calm; peaceful; tranquil; undisturbed. 2

Siblings.   Brothers or sisters. 1

Significant.   Important. 1

Somber.   Gloomily dark. 9

Sparse.   Thinly scattered. 7

Specialist.   A person who devotes himself or herself to a particular branch of a profession. 7

Spirits.   Strong alcoholic beverages obtained by distillation; frame of mind; mood; supernatural beings such as ghosts. 3

Spouse.   Husband or wife. 7

Stamina.   Resistance to fatigue. 1

Subsistence.   Means of support; the minimum necessary to exist. 9

Subtle.   Delicate; elusive (hard to identify); indirect. 6

Succeeding.   Following; coming after. 8

Succinct.   Brief. 5

Tempered.   Moderated. 9

Texture.   The characteristic physical structure given to a material by its size, shape, and so on. (The term *texture* is usually used in relation to a woven fabric or textile.) 2

Thrifty.   Economical. 6

Thrived.   Prospered; flourished. 8

Tumult.   Disturbance; commotion. 5

Valiant.   Courageous; brave. 5

Valid. Sound. 5
Verbose. Wordy. 5
Vindictive. Vengeful; inclined to revenge. 6
Virtuoso. Expert. 4
Void. Empty. 4
Wary. Cautious; careful. 2
Wily. Cunning; sly. 7

Glossary C
COMBINING FORMS PRESENTED IN
READING AND LEARNING POWER

(The number after the meaning refers to the lesson in which the combining form is presented.)

Aut.   Self 13
Auto.   Self 13
Biblio.   Book 14
Bio.   Life 14
Cent.   Hundred; hundredth part 15
Centi.   Hundred; hundredth part 15
Co.   With 14
De.   Away; from; off; completely 13
Deca.   Ten 15
Deci.   Tenth part 15
Graph.   Something written; machine 14
Il.   Not 13
Im.   Not 13
In.   Not 13
Ir.   Not 13
Kilo.   Thousand 15
Meter.   Measure 15
Milli.   Thousand; thousandth part 15
Mob.   Move 13
Mot.   Move 13
Mov.   Move 13
Oper.   Work 14
Opus.   Work 14
Pro.   Before; forward 13

Index

Abbreviations. *See* Dictionary
Accent
  and pronunciation, 243
  and schwa sound, 243
  and syllabication, 243
  mark, 243
  rules, 243
  See also Pronunciation
Alphabetizing. *See* Dictionary
Analogies. *See* Reading
Antonyms
  and contrast, 26, 143
  definition of, 143
  See also Context clues

Base word. *See* Root word
Bias
  definition of, 339
  See also Propaganda
Book marking. *See* Notetaking
Buzz words
  examples of, 391
  explanation of, 391-392

Central idea
  of a group of paragraphs, 78-79
  example of, 79-83
  of an article, 102
  of a story, 134
  See also Main idea; Inference; Textbook
Closed syllable, 58, 189, 191

Combining forms
  and vocabulary expansion, 376, 406, 427
  definition of, 281, 376
  See also Vocabulary
Compound word
  definition of, 281
  syllabication of, 148
Concentration, 71-72, 96, 125
  and following directions, 311
  and test-taking, 375
  test of, 128-131
  See also Lecture
Connotative meaning
  definition of, 299
  examples of, 300
Consonant
  blend, 91
  description of, 17
  digraph, 91
  silent, 91
Consonant blend. *See* Consonant
Consonant digraph. *See* Consonant
Context. *See* Vocabulary
Context clues
  and homographs, 53-54
  and textbooks, 185, 240
  examples of, 25, 26
  See also Antonyms; Synonyms; Vocabulary

Denotative meaning
  definition of, 299

and quizzes, 390-391
  example of, 393
  hints about, 390
  how to take, 391-392
example of, 364
explanation of, 362-363
for writing a paper, 417
notecards, 417-419
  example of, 418
  kinds of, 417
  pointers on, 419
See also Buzz words; Telegraphic writing

Objective tests. *See* Test-taking
Open Syllable, 58, 59, 190, 191
Overlearning, 21, 398, 399

Phonics
  definition of, 30
  process of, 30-34
   a simulation of, 31-34
Prefixes
  and combining forms, 281, 376
  definition of, 280
  examples of, 148, 280
  syllabication of, 148
Pronunciation, 118, 189
  and diacritical marks, 59
  See also Accent; Schwa; Syllabication;
   Vowel rules; Vowel sounds
Propaganda. *See* Reading
Proverbs. *See* Inference

Questions, 334
  and examinations, 335-336
  and grading, 336-337
  and learning, 334
  how to ask, 337
  kind to ask, 335
  See also Lecture; Test-taking

Reading
  analogies, 410, 431
   examples of 382
   explanation of, 382

distinguishing fact from opinion, 315
knowing your source, 296
propaganda
  and bias, 339
  definition of, 338-339
  techniques of, 339
questioning what you read, 296-297
See also Central idea; Context clues;
  Inference; Main idea
"Reading between the lines." *See* Inference
Root (base) word, 280, 281, 375

Schwa, 118, 189, 243
Silent consonant. *See* Consonant
Skimming
  and SQ3R, 37, 169
  and studying, 38, 168
  definition of, 168
  examples of, 169-171
  uses of, 168-169, 170
Special letters and sounds, 59, 117-119
  See also Schwa
SQ3R
  example of, 38-39
  steps in, 37-38
  See also Notetaking; Skimming;
   Studying
Studying
  and concentration, 71, 125
  and generalizations, 398, 399
  and main idea, 2, 48
  and memory techniques, 399
  and notetaking, 363
  and SQ3R, 37-39
  building good habits in, 20-21
  introduction to, 1
  procedures for, 1
  See also Overlearning; Skimming; Test-
   taking; Textbook
Subjective tests. *See* Test-taking
Suffixes
  and combining forms, 281, 376
  definition of, 280
  examples of, 148, 280
  syllabication of, 148, 189-190